THE
CRUISING
GUIDE
TO
CUBA

2nd Edition

- HAVANA • CABO SAN ANTONIO
- ISLA DE JUVENTUD • CAYO LARGO
- CASILDA • TRINIDAD • MANZANILLO
- CABO CRUZ • GUANTANAMO
- SANTIAGO DE CUBA • BARACOA
- PUNTA MAISA • VARADERO
- THE CAYS

A Note of Thanks From the Author:

Many people have assisted, directly or indirectly with the compiling of this edition. Some, in letters to my publishers, have sent information gathered from their own experiences traveling in Cuba; nostalgia tinged letters, without which this book would be far, far poorer. Some have given me of their time in Cuba itself, in cramped cockpits, surrounded by crumpled charts and salt-stained notes. And some have pointed me along the way, assisting when it was within their power to hinder. In this last group must be placed those dedicated, patriotic Cubans who have seen my work as in some small way beneficial to their country's best interests.

To all the above, I express my heartfelt thanks. Your contributions have made the path smoother for those who follow in our wakes.

Especial thanks are due to Kathy Thompson, Alain Foucard, Señor Armando Polo, Russel Haetrl, "Piré", Don Law, Ken Clark, Mads Nielsen, Colin and Ingrid on *Sababa*, Don Brantingham, Brian Mindel, and Jürgen of *Contentessa*, gone from this world but standing his ground above.

Finally, I would like to thank Simon Gandolfi for making bearable the lost months.

About The Photography

Most photos in this guide were taken by Simon Charles during his many visits to Cuba. There are a number of other photos in the color sections (including the front cover) which were taken by a talented photographer Mark Burrell. These photos are indicated by credit lines. Mark Burrell and his company, *Zapotech*, provide images and research related to Cuban culture for publications worldwide. For further information about his photography, he can be reached at *Zapotech*, P.O. Box 396, Winter Park, FL 32790-0396.

Cruising Guide Publications, Inc. is a special interest publisher of sailing guides to cruising in various areas around the world and other publications of nautical interest. CGP endeavors to provide comprehensive and invaluable materials to both inveterate sailors and less experienced seafarers seeking vital vacationing tips and navigational information relative to the journey to and the enjoyment of their destinations.

The publisher makes no warranty, express or implied, for any errors or omissions in this publication. Skippers should use this guide only in conjunction with governmental navigational charts and/or other navigational aids and not place undue credence in the accuracy of this guide. *The Cruising Guide to Cuba* is not intended for use for navigational purposes.

Published by

Cruising Guide Publications, Inc.
P.O. Box 1017
Dunedin, Florida 34697-1017
PHONE: (800) 330-9542 • (813) 733-5322 • FAX: (813) 734-8179
E-Mail: cgp@earthlink.net

Editors
NANCY SCOTT • TOM HENSCHEL
BARBARA LIEBLING

Art Director

TOM HENSCHEL

Photography & Cartography
SIMON CHARLES

Marketing Director
MAUREEN LARROUX

Administration
JANET JOYCE

ISBN 0-944428-36-3

TABLE OF CONTENTS

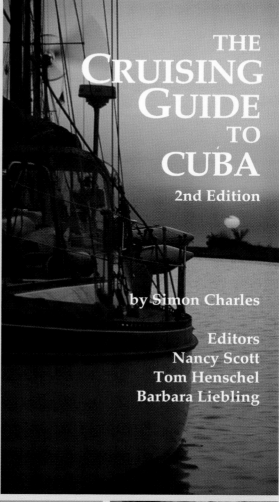

THE
CRUISING
GUIDE
TO
CUBA

2nd Edition

by Simon Charles

Editors
Nancy Scott
Tom Henschel
Barbara Liebling

I went to Cuba because I was curious; because no one agrees on its strengths; because I'd read so much about it; because it is forbidden; because it's heartbreakingly lovely; because so many people have championed it while so many others have abandoned it; because Cubans make great music and aromatic cigars; because they've thumbed their nose at their former patron for more than three decades; because I'd grown weary of writing about Latin American "democracies" where forlorn illiterate campensinas sit on city street corners selling combs, nail clippers and undervalued handicrafts while their malnourished barefoot youngsters turn their palms up and say "gimme" instead of learning how to hold a pencil or read a sentence; because of its rich literary tradition; because my favorite players on the Washington Senators in the 1950's were Cuban; because I'm an incurable romantic; because we still have a navy base there; because Cuban women are astute and alluring; because in the last five hundred years of travel writing few cities in the world have been so effusively praised as Havana; because

Teddy Roosevelt led the charge up San Juan Hill; because I liked "Our Man In Havana" and "The Old Man and the Sea"; because I got a kick out of Dezi Arnaz; because I was distrustful of Cuba's bashers and its cheerleaders; because I liked the twinkle in Fidel's eyes; because I'd never been to a Communist country; because I wanted to learn to rumba; because Columbus landed there; because it has hundreds of miles of unspoiled beaches; because of its mystique.

INTRODUCTION

This, the second edition of the *Cruising Guide to Cuba* has been made necessary, not only by the passage of time, but also by the sweeping changes coursing through Cuba. Changes not solely confined to the yachting and cruising community, but rather changes which have affected the island as a whole.

In the intervening years, new philosophies have been implemented by the country's leaders. Gone is the idea that somehow Cuba can stand alone, an eternal reproach to its closest neighbors — Cuba is tentatively reaching out to the world again.

Almost gone too, is the idea that only by rigid dogma-based control can a just society be achieved. This last may have been perhaps only grudgingly accepted, and even more slowly implemented, but nevertheless the changes inexorably wrought can only auger well for the future of this wonderful country. Hopefully, these changes will come through the wishes of the Cuban people, rather than maneuvering of outside interests.

Simon Charles at the helm.

Regarding the yachting community, there has been a tremendous explosion of interest in cruising the Cuban coastline. Prior to the first edition of this guide, where once I encountered less than twenty foreign boats in the whole country, this past year I found some seventy yachts in Havana's Marina Hemingway alone. Nevertheless, given the tremendous size of the cruising grounds, this is still but a drop in the bucket, and it will be years before the sight of a nearby yacht at anchor is commonplace.

Ending this short introduction, I should once again like to dedicate this book to Fiona, without whom it could not have been done, and to the people of Cuba, without whom it would not have been worth doing.

"Hobbes" at anchor in South Cuba.

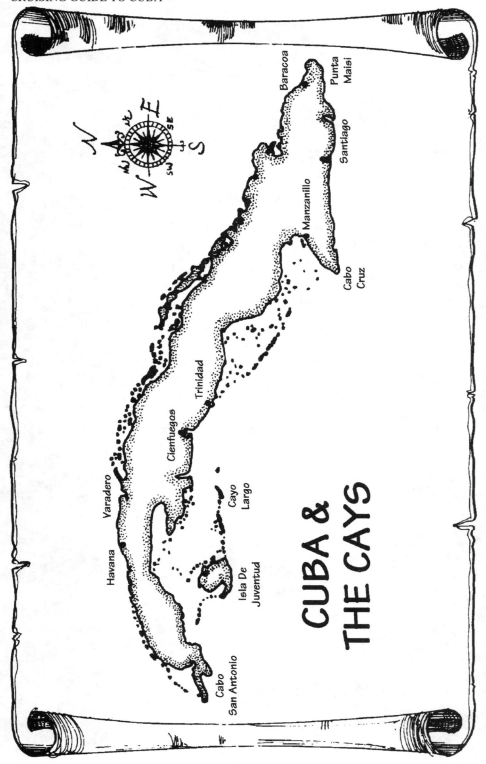

CUBA &
THE CAYS

CUBA AND THE YACHTSMAN

uba, the land of a thousand sepia myths; the land of rhythm and rum; of sugar and smoke; of cigars and crooners, croupiers and cashiers. Of pistols fit for a lady's purse, blood debts and knife-play. A land of glittering night-clubs, waving canefields and dusty green tobacco; where heroes mingle on fading, curling photographs; and a sultry Nat King Cole can glance, casually, across to the young guerilla on the opposite page of our long discarded magazine memory. The silk, the rags, the microphone, the eyes, the beard, and the rifle — Cuba, the land of revolution and rumba.

But, this is a cruising guide, a guide striving to remain neutral. Hopefully unswayed by extremes of opinion, slogans bandied about, and the political pressures of 'our side', and 'their side'. No, the following chapters are for those who use the seas to travel where they will. For those who prefer to see for themselves, rather than accept the word of the paid hack or the political commentator; and for those who desire the finest cruising in the hemisphere.

No tiny atoll, this; jammed with pale packaged tourists stumbling to the latest Caribbean dance, and trying on funny hats in the market. This island is an experience.

You come here not for laundromats, happy hour, hot water, and a glut of full service marinas; but rather, for untold miles of empty beach, crystal blue water, stunning cliffs, secluded bays, and deserted cays. No boat-boys here, with their panhandling little threat, "Hey, mon... Watch your boat?". Your boat is alone, surrounded by all this.

We come for the cities too. Ancient cities, crumbling cities; cities much as they were before the chrome-neon rape of the

A yacht enters Santiago harbor.

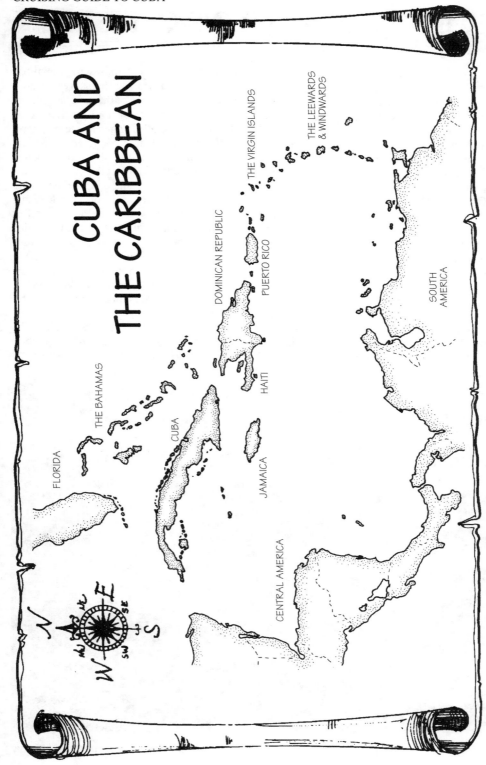

modern west. Undeveloped perhaps, economically isolated perhaps, but charming cities still, where pedestrians still rule and families sit late in the streets, gossiping.

Balconies, monuments, facades, washing, children, screams, Packards, bicycles, noise, smoke, dust, and smiles.

But we come for the people most of all, a people who have bounced back from a thousand blows. From within, a nation under guard, whose every movement is regulated, and watched — a nation, mistrusted by its very leaders.

From without, a nation under siege, whose every stumbling step towards an uncertain future is threatened and sabotaged; and until it bends the knee, a nation mistrusted by its very closest neighbor.

And a people who, despite those thousand blows, still love their fellow man.

In Cuba, overcrowded, rattling buses may belch diesel, but they'll always stop for just one more passenger; and hitchhiking is a way of life (just how it used to be), not an invitation to violence.

It's where a stranger's approach is greeted with a smile, not doubt; and conversations, so easy to start yet so difficult to stop, revolve around literature, politics, religion, the latest fads in your country; and what are you doing later on?

Those very conversations, sometimes abruptly dropping to conspiratorial whisper and theatrical sideways-glances. After all, perhaps, those walls might indeed have ears.

Your cruise is about these things and more. Bays, so narrowly guarded by ruined fortresses perched among the creeping vines, and yet so wide, so sheltered, and so hospitable inside.

The cays too; still pristine, isolated and echoing to the cry of bird and beast rather than bulldozer and boom-box. Ashore, that path you made through the trees will likely be the only sign of human presence for years to come; and there's only one boat at anchor in the emerald bay — your boat.

The beaches along those cays too, with sand white enough to melt a snowbird's heart; and while there are plenty of those along the northeast coast, they're absolutely deserted elsewhere.

No, none of those stylish coconut-branch beach-bars, so artfully contrived to look sort of "local", and selling beer that costs five dollars a shot to the Jimmy Buffet wanabees.

Instead, it's where the last yacht you anchored alongside was Thierry's (you *always* know their names), 400 miles back on the south coast near Casilda.

Yes, Cuba is for serious cruisers.

INTERNATIONAL PASSAGES

For a North American based cruiser planning a journey further afield towards the West Indies or Mexico, the island of Cuba just cannot be ignored.

As the largest land mass in the Caribbean, Cuba stands along the direct route from South Florida down through the chain of islands which stretch as far as South America; and only a few miles off the direct route to Mexico. A glance at an overall chart of the Caribbean will confirm its strategic position.

For example, Havana is approximately 90 miles south of Key West in the U.S.

The eastern tip of Cuba is about 170 miles from the Dominican Republic; while were you to have braved the traumas of Haiti, the city of Santiago would be even closer along the route.

Jamaican cruisers (longtime visitors, albeit in small numbers), find Santiago only 120 miles to the north of Kingston, and there are other Cuban ports not 90 miles from Montego Bay.

The closest international port in Cuba is about 180 miles from the Isla de Mujeres in Mexico, or approximately halfway the direct distance to Key West. For a Central American cruise, this makes for an easy run across to Havana, then westwards along the coast, and on to Mexico.

Were you to plan a trip north from the Cayman Islands, then the distance between Cayo Largo and Georgetown is around 140 miles. Departure could be even more easily accomplished from Cayman Brac, making that another alternative were you traveling northwest from Jamaica.

And, of course, the Cuban coast runs parallel to the Bahamas, whose shoal waters might dissuade many.

CUBA: A BASIC OVERVIEW -- AS MUDDLED AS THE COUNTRY ITSELF

Over 750 miles long and covering some 44,200 square miles, Cuba is the largest island in the Caribbean, comprising over half of the total land-area of the West Indies!

Its median width is about 60 miles, ranging from only five miles in the extreme west to over 120 miles in the east.

Lying along the Tropic of Cancer at the entrance to the Gulf of Mexico, it is positioned only 90 miles from the Florida Keys at the northwest end of the Caribbean chain of islands. It is made up of one large and numerous smaller islands, islets, and cays.

Cuba is as large as England.

The terrain is varied, 60 percent of which is lowland plains, basins and foothills. There are three major mountain systems.

1. Oriental: The Sierra Maestra in the eastern part of the country, containing such notable peaks as Turquino (over 6,000 feet).

2. Central: A number of lower hills and ranges, such as the Escambray Mountains.

3. Occidental: Along the western quarter of the country, the Cordillera de Guaniguanico and the Sierras de los Organos; a most spectacular formation of Karst topography where the limestone mountains have been severely affected by underwater erosion.

The river Cauto (160 miles) in the south-east is the largest in the island and is the island's principal inland waterway.

The climate is semitropical, officially averaging 79°F.

Seasonal temperatures range from 77°F in January to 87°F in August, but do not trust these figures too much. I have recorded over 100°F during the daytime inside my vessel (with all windows open), dropping only as far as 87°F at night in the summer.

Water temperatures average out less, but vary considerably depending on where you are, being hotter by some 4-5°F on the southern side of the island.

There are two seasons, the "wet" (May-October) and the "dry" (November-April), with most of the rain falling in the form of tropical rainstorms and averaging 54 inches per year.

The hurricane season runs June through November, but in spite of popular mythology they are rare.

Apart from the mountains in the east, the island is covered by lush vegetation encouraged by the balmy climate and the abundant rainfall. There are tropical pine and mahogany forests, and a profusion of other trees such as kapok and the stately royal palm (the national tree).

Physical culture and sport for all -- Cienfuegos.

Statue of Antonio Macéo, hero of Wars of Independence -- Havana.

Fruit also features prominently, consisting mainly of lime, lemon, papaya, and most significantly, grapefruit and orange. The agriculture is based on the cultivation of sugarcane, coffee and rice.

There are only modest mineral resources in Cuba, with a little oil being extracted around the Cardenas Bay in the north, but there are substantial deposits of nickel further east.

The original Indians having been rendered nearly extinct, the population (estimated at 11 million) is composed of three main racial groups; mulattos, blacks and whites.

During the last century there was a majority of mulattos and blacks, the descendants of some 750,000 slaves imported in the 18th and 19th centuries, but now it is estimated that about two-thirds of the population is of white descent.

Traditionally power has been mainly vested in the white population, but strenuous efforts have been made during the last thirty years to broaden the base of political and social influence, and as a result racial conflict is rare. Although there is still undeniably an economic underclass, it is refreshing to be able to walk freely without feeling threatened by one race or another.

Marxist-Leninist ideology is the dominant force in secular life; all other political parties being proscribed. There is however, a growing disenchantment with the status quo.

Irrelevant aside, number one: Do not believe a word of it when you are told, "It's for your own security, Señor".

It isn't.

In spite of official disavowal of religion in the 1960's and 1970's there has been a certain accommodation recently so that now some 40 percent of the population consider themselves to be vaguely Roman Catholic or similarly Christian. There is too, a small practicing Jewish community.

Fidel Castro is a product of a Catholic, Jesuit education.

Increasing efforts by nondenominational humanitarian organizations, like the group

7

"El Capitolio", the old seat of parliament in Havana.

Pastors For Peace, have also obtained some (if presently limited) successes in local involvement.

All over Havana and other cities, houses of worship still stand unoccupied while awaiting the future, and even though there is continuing tension between state and church those buildings have remained largely unmolested. Whatever that signifies.

It would appear likely that in spite of official statements, the traditional religions will be gradually reasserting their influence over the next few years.

There is also a certain influence derived from traditional Afro/Spanish religions, such as *Santeria*. This makes itself felt in the various festivals, and also in the growing use of Santeria as part of the tourist trade.

Following the revolution in the 1960's, there was heavy migration from the rural areas, but since the 1970's this has been ended by the government. Nevertheless, some 70 percent of the population is now urban, concentrated in the city and province of Havana.

Education and health have received much attention over the last thirty years (fully 25 percent of the government budget goes on this) and within the limits of available funds could be said to be the envy of most countries.

Social security programs offer a wide range of benefits, including sickness benefits, old-age pensions, maternity leave and benefits, workers injury compensation, disability and survivors' pensions.

In spite of the chronic shortages affecting the country, the population's health is generally good, and in spite of what I read elsewhere I would venture to say that I have never seen any other nation looking so fit (See Brendan's comment later, under *Manzanillo*).

Hospitals are open to all, and in spite of the economic difficulties are modern and certainly well-staffed, especially when compared with the abysmal facilities only grudgingly offered in the rest of Latin America and the Caribbean. The main problems being faced by the health system are economic rather than ethical.

Life expectancy is 74 years, infant mortality is the lowest in Latin America, and all sections of society have easy access to medical facilities in the workplace, schools and in the neighborhood.

There are more doctors per capita in Cuba than any other country, and while they may not have access to the most sophisticated drugs available elsewhere, there is no doubt that the system makes efficient use of what it does have. Nevertheless, under deliberate pressure from outside, the system is under severe stress.

Having abolished private and religious institutions, the government is in charge of all education, which is free at all levels up to and including degree courses. Based on Marxist-Leninist principles, it combines study with manual labor, but unfortunately political considerations still affect entry into the universities. Nevertheless, in addition to the University of Havana, there are 40 other institutes of advanced training.

You see a lot of people reading.

The media is rigidly controlled by the state, which issues its edicts and disseminates blatant propaganda through the radio, television, and the newspapers, of these the newspaper *Granma* is the main culprit. Although there is much reporting of North American, European, and other foreign news, nothing unfavorable to the government gets through.

Personally, the radio stinks.

Strangely, the cinema offers some respite, being an odd mix of art and trash. On the one hand you can see Russian versions of "The Invisible Man", and on the other, you can join astonishing queues to see Sylvester Stallone deal death and destruction.

Artistic endeavor is to a large extent controlled by the state, with political criteria being a major factor. The official view must be expressed if one wishes to succeed, and in addition there are many other more subtle forms of censorship. Many Cuban artists have left under this burden and more will continue to do so for the foreseeable future.

Musical traditions in Cuba have been formed by combining African rhythms and instruments, such as conga drums, maracas and claves with the Spanish guitar; leading in the 1920's to the development of Son, its more formal neighbor Danzon, and the Rumba.

Perhaps due to the former influence of Eastern Bloc countries, classical music and ballet still strongly survives amidst the other more traditional forms of entertainment.

Irrelant aside number two: Even if the public facility you most need is suspended just when you need it, do not believe a word of it when you are told "It's under repair, Señor."

It isn't.

Cuba is a one-party state, and the Communist Party of Cuba (PCC), with a membership of some 475,000, rigidly controls all formal government institutions. The party's Political Bureau is the highest policy making body on the island.

The constitution of 1976 confirmed the Communist Party's supremacy in law and government, and established the electoral systems in use today.

The People's Supreme Court exercises the functions of the judiciary. Legislative power is vested in the National Assembly of People's Power whose members are elected by the municipalities, but the party still oversees its work.

The powers-that-be favor grandiose titles.

The economy is centrally-planned, and until the collapse of the former Communist Bloc was heavily subsidized by the U.S.S.R. There are frequent and growing shortages of consumer goods, despite gross national product (GNP) estimates placing Cuba among the leading nations of Latin America.

The continuing economic embargo placed by the U.S. government has led to increasing problems in the economy as traditional trading partners have been pressured to abandon further commerce with Cuba. Even foreign firms are threatened now by U.S. economic sanctions designed to force economic and social collapse.

Within Cuba this action is called the "Blockade".

Irrelevant aside number three, do not believe a word of it when you are told "It's for Cuba's own good, Buddy."

It isn't.

The agricultural economy (one-seventh of the GNP) of the island is in a shambles, and not solely due to the embargo. Just one example of what passes for careful forward planning is that the main agricultural exports are based on sugar and tobacco!

Sugar may be the principal source of foreign exchange (presently 80-90 percent) but it can hardly be said to have a secure future in the light of current health concerns.

And what can one say about tobacco.

Citrus fruit, such as grapefruit, is an increasing source of export earnings, but presently the official production of staples such as rice and beans does not meet the demand.

Private agricultural holdings are apparently limited to 160 acres.

There is a growing private economy within Cuba, with open markets in most cities.

Most agricultural products are on sale here during the harvest seasons, as farmers are permitted to sell their "surplus" crops freely. Prices are regulated however, to avoid the worst excesses of the free-market system.

Nickel is the principal ore extracted, with Cuba holding the fourth largest deposits of the mineral in the world. There are also smaller quantities of iron, copper, and chrome being mined.

Despite the above, manufacturing is still limited, being confined to light industry, foodstuff processing and textiles.

Ghastly fashion-shows are seen as an integral part of entertaining tourists. Tourism is increasingly seen as a means of earning foreign exchange but it is unlikely that this can stem the tide of a huge balance of payments deficit.

The government is actively seeking to expand trade with all interested parties (Canada, Mexico and Europe), but sometimes it seems that regarding commerce, the penny just hasn't dropped. Perhaps it is due to the historic stigma surrouinding actual *earning* a living, but all businessmen I have spoken to report ceaseless and sensless difficulties by an inert beaurocracy.

Most of Cuba's foreign trade is now carried on with Canada, Mexico, and Europe.

Cuba is the "Land of the Committee".

Oil wells at Varadero behind the marina.

A roadside attraction on the road into Havana.

MODERN HISTORY

Modern Cuban history could be said to have started when Christopher Columbus discovered the island on his first trip to the New World on Oct. 27, 1492. Prior to that the island was inhabited by several small Indian groups, the Ciboney, the Guanahatabey, and later the Arawaks from other Caribbean islands.

The Spanish quickly took control, conquering the Indians, and in 1511 Diego Velasquez established the first permanent settlement at Baracoa. The island was soon divided into seven Villas (or Garrisons) to defend it against pirates and later it became a base for expeditions further afield. One such expedition was that of Hernan Cortés, who left from the city of Santiago on his way to conquer Mexico in 1519.

Unbelievably, the British (who used to just love this sort of thing) captured and held Cuba from 1762-1763, then swapped it with Spain (again) for Florida!

During the 18th-19th centuries the island's economy prospered, and owing to the rapid expansion of the sugar trade some 750,000 African slaves were imported until the practice was halted in 1865, and legally abolished in 1886. By the mid-19th century, the sugar industry was the most highly mechanized in the world, and produced one third of its sugar.

Towards the middle of the 19th century various nationalist movements tried without success to cede from the Spanish colonial empire, and there were occasional bloody rebellions, notably the Ten Years War between 1868-1878.

Prominent figures in the liberation struggles were Maximo Gomez and Antonio Macéo, along with the poet philosopher, José Martí. Their names are still invoked today, by both sides.

By the late 19th century, the U.S. had become the largest trading partner, and the delay in Spain's granting political autonomy to Cuba was seen as a pretext for the Spanish-American war in 1898, which eventually led to U.S. occupation of the island.

In 1901, the U.S. granted for itself the right to oversee Cuban internal and foreign affairs, reserving the right to intervene militarily in domestic matters, and turning the island into a protectorate after independence. By its own decree, the U.S. also obtained Guantanamo Bay, *in perpetuity* for an annual rent of less than $5,000.

Various presidents came and went but unrest continued, leading to further military occupation in 1906, 1912 and 1917, while North American capital invested heavily in sugar, tourism, and gambling. U.S. companies, in fact owned some 40 percent of the sugar industry and 90 percent of all public utility companies by the end of the fifties.

In 1958, the nationalist popular revolution of Fidel Castro finally triumphed over the dictator Fulgencio Batista, but rapidly

11

Street musicians and an audience in Cienfuegos.

converted to communism in the face of increasing U.S. hostility in the early 1960's. This led to the state appropriation of industry and agriculture.

The low point in U.S. Cuban relations came in 1961 with the abortive Bay of Pigs invasion, which was actively supported by the CIA, and the Missile Crisis in 1962.

In return for the withdrawal of U.S.S.R. missiles, the U.S. pledged that it would not seek to overthrow the government of Fidel Castro. Unfortunately, it is a matter of public record in the U.S. that several attempts have since been made by CIA agents on the life of the Cuban president. When CIA chief, William Colby, was asked about the figure of 20 attempts, he expressed surprise, remarking that he was only aware of five.

Understandably, over the following 20-30 years, Cuba allied itself more and more closely with the Soviet Bloc. This led to a complete suspension of all economic and cultural ties by the U.S. government, and degenerating into a total economic embargo designed to force the existing regime from power.

It is said that President Kennedy only signed the embargo into law the day after amassing over a thousand Cuban cigars in his private stock. He had estimated that this would suffice.

After 30 years of support, the collapse of the Soviet Union in the late 1980's placed additional strain on the island's economy and infrastructure. Cuba has to some extent finally managed to rise above the drastic effects of the loss of trade from this quarter, but despite the help of Canada and Europe, it is likely that some sort of accommodation will have to be made with the U.S. over the next few years.

VERY MODERN HISTORY

As you read this, Cuba's history is still being written.

We are all involved.

12

THE LAW AND THE YACHTSMAN

Vague talk of visas and other nearly impossible-to-satisfy criteria is just that; merely talk. For the yachtsman to enter Cuba he will need a boat, its papers, a passport and nothing else, apart from funds. And unlike many another country, no one in Cuba has ever asked me if we had sufficient funds for our projected stay.

The emphasis being presently placed on tourism by the Cuban government has led to a considerable opening-up over the last few years, but not long ago popular opinion amongst foreign boaters was that you only had to stray close to the 12-mile limit to be strafed by jets or boarded by gunboats.

This view is slowly losing ground, but nevertheless still does command a considerable following, and in idle conversation we are routinely commented upon as being somehow blessed not to have been detained by the Cuban authorities.

West Indian Customs and Immigration officers always remark, "So they let you out, eh?", when we clear our papers, and usually seem a bit skeptical when we say, quite truthfully, that we have never had the slightest hint of trouble in our dealings with the Cuban authorities, nor have we ever had a single request denied unnecessarily.

On our travels we have met many nationalities in a variety of boats, and not one of them has shown any reluctance to return. In fact, I would say that the average yachtsman encountered in Cuba, is on his second, third, or fourth visit.

It cannot be denied that the continuing confrontational relationship between the U.S. government and Cuba has restrained many U.S. yachtsmen

from venturing over to their closest and certainly most fascinating neighbor. In spite of this, what is clear is that the existing tension between the governments is confined *solely* to that level, and every American I have met who took the plunge has remarked that they have encountered absolutely no hostility from anyone at all. Indeed, it is probable that nowhere else in the world will a U.S. citizen receive a greater welcome. If you don't believe me, ask any Cuban, anywhere. Or ask anyone who's been.

Unfortunately, there are mechanisms in place to prevent free travel between the two

Outer marker at Marina Hemingway.

countries, and one of these mechanisms is the existing trade and economic embargo, whose provisions as yet are imperfectly understood and just as imperfectly applied.

Note: As recently as 1996 two light airplanes piloted by members of a Cuban exile group were shot down while attempting to drop leaflets on the city of Havana. In an immediate response, the U.S. government passed the Helms-Burton bill, which seeks to penalize foreign firms doing business with Cuba. The bill has been vociferously condemned by almost every other country in the world, and only time will tell what the final outcome will be, but as far as concerns the yachtsman, it is of note that:

1. The provisions of this bill are meant to punish *international* trade with Cuba, and have no effect on the present laws which make it perfectly legal for a U.S. citizen to travel by his private boat to Cuba.

2. The U.S. government has issued both warnings and an Emergency Cease and Desist order to any U.S. registered aircraft which violate Cuban territorial airspace, authorizing action *against* them — See Consular Information Sheets, Aug. 8, 1995 (released before the incident), and May 22, 1996 (on the adjoining page).

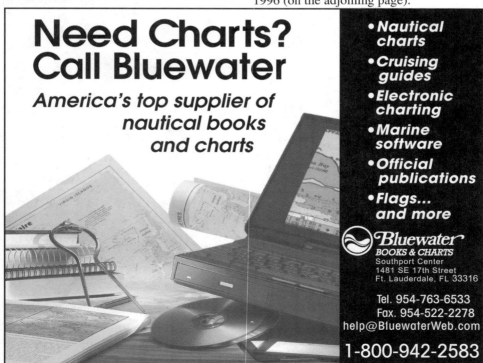

THE OFFICIAL U.S. POSITION:

Taken From: Cuba - Consular Information Sheet May 22, 1996
Country Description:
Cuba is a developing country under the communist rule of Fidel Castro. The United States has no direct diplomatic relations with Cuba.

Entry Requirements/Travel Transaction Limitations: The Cuban Assets Control Regulations of the U.S. Treasury Department require that persons subject to U.S. jurisdiction be licensed to engage in any transactions related to travel to, from and within Cuba. Transactions related to tourist and business travel are not licensable. This restriction includes tourist or business travel from or through a third country such as Mexico or Canada.

Transactions are authorized by general license for U.S. and foreign government officials traveling on official business, including representatives of international organizations of which the United States is a member; journalists regularly employed by a news reporting organization; and family visitors traveling once a year due to extreme humanitarian needs. The Treasury Department will consider specific licenses on a case-by-case basis for other humanitarian travel including cases of extreme hardship relating to close relatives residing in Cuba, for telecommunications activities, and for travel in connection with professional research and similar activities.

Additional Information may be obtained by contacting the Licensing Division, Office of Foreign Assets Control at the U.S. Department of the Treasury: tel: (202-622-2480). Failure to comply with these regulations could result in civil penalties and criminal prosecution upon return to the United States.

Should a traveler receive a license, a passport and visa are required for entry to Cuba. For current information on Cuban entry and customs requirements, travelers may contact the Cuban Interests Section, and Office of the Cuban Government, located at 2630 16th St. NW, Washington, D.C.20009, tel. (202) 797-8518.

Entry and exit from Cuba is strictly controlled by Cuban authorities. Attempts to enter or exit Cuba illegally or to aid the illegal exit of Cuban nationals are punishable by jail terms of up to 5 years. Entering Cuban territory, territorial waters or airspace without prior authorization from the Cuban government may result in arrest or other enforcement action by Cuban authorities for violation of Cuban law. Any vessel or aircraft that enters the 12-mile limit off Cuba would be inside Cuban territorial waters or airspace and thus subject to the jurisdiction of the Cuban government. If persons enter Cuban territorial waters or airspace without prior permission, they may place themselves and others at serious personal risk.

On February 24 1996, the Cuban military shot down two U.S. registered civil aircraft in international airspace in violation of international aviation law. As a result of this action, the President declared a national emergency, invoking emergency authority relating to the regulation of the anchorage and movement of vessels, and the Federal Aviation Administration (FAA) issued an "Emergency Cease and Desist Order and Statement of Policy" that allows for vigorous enforcement action against U.S.-registered aircraft that violate Cuban territorial airspace. Additional information is available through the FAA and the U.S. Coast Guard.

Currency Regulations (Cuban): Since the Cuban government legalized the use of dollars in July 1993, U.S. dollars are accepted for all transactions.

Currency Regulations (U.S.): Only official government travelers traveling on

Continued On Next Page

official business, including representatives of international organizations of which the United States is a member, journalists, and family visitors traveling once a year due to extreme humanitarian need may spend money on travel to Cuba without obtaining special permission from the Treasury Department; such expenditures may only be for travel-related expenses at a rate not exceeding $100 per day. U.S. Treasury Department regulations now prohibit remittances, including family remittances, without a specific license from the Office of foreign Assets Control. The only exception is the transfer of up to $1000 to pay travel expenses for a Cuban national who has been granted a migration document by the U.S. Interests Section in Havana. For further information, travelers may contact the Office of Foreign Assets Control.

Dual Nationality: The government of Cuba considers all Cuban-born U.S. citizens to be solely Cuban citizens. The Cuban government does not recognize the right or obligation of the U.S. government to protect dual U.S./Cuban citizens and has consistently denied U.S. consular officers the right to visit incarcerated dual U.S./Cuban nationals to ascertain their welfare and proper treatment under Cuban law. Dual U.S./Cuban nationals are required by Cuban law to enter and depart Cuba using Cuban passports. Using a Cuban passport for this purpose does not jeopardize one's U.S. citizenship; however, such persons must use their U.S. passports to enter and depart the U.S. and to transit any countries en route. Dual U.S./Cuban nationals may be subject to a range of restrictions and obligations, including military service, in Cuba.

U.S. Representation/Registration: The United States does not maintain an Embassy in Cuba. U.S. citizens who travel to Cuba may contact and register with the U.S. Interests Section of the Swiss Embassy, located in Havana at Calzada between L & M, Vedado; telephone 33-3550 through 33-3559. There is no access to the U.S. Naval Base at Guantanamo from within Cuba. U.S. citizens who register at the U.S. Interests Section in Havana may obtain updated information on travel and security within the country.
No. 96-098

This replaces the Consular Information Sheet dated November 13, 1995, to update Entry Requirements and to include information concerning the shooting down of U.S.-registered aircraft.

U.S. Government Publication: Consular Information Sheet: May 22, 1996.

Note: Please note that apart from slight changes in wording and the inclusion of the items dealing with the downing of aircraft, the above statement has not been significantly altered over the last few years.

There are three points to be made here:

1. Although it *is* against the law to engage in Travel Transactions such as commercial airline or maritime travel, you will note that nowhere does the statement declare that it is actually against the law to merely *go* to Cuba. Rather, it is against Treasury Department regulations to *spend* money there.

2. Remember too, that you should only have *crew* aboard, not passengers. Failing this may place you in breach of the law.

3. It is important to be aware that while no U.S. agency is spying on you in Cuba, U.S. Customs can occasionally look for evidence of non-compliance in the form of Cuban receipts among a returning boat's papers. And it goes without saying too, that there should be no Cuban goods aboard either.

Despite the mention of arrests and the like, unless you have been an extremely silly boy, no fuss is made over your journey. Apart from U.S. citizens, there are no restrictions on the travel of other nationalities to Cuba, but although the bulk of cruisers used to come from Europe and Canada, one is now encountering a majority of U.S. flagged vessels.

Incidentally, the vast majority of foreign boats cruising Cuban waters have transited from Florida, and many still winter there yearly.

For full details of U.S./Cuban entry and exit procedures, please see "Marina Hemingway" in chapter five.

PLANNING YOUR CRUISE
WHAT YOU NEED TO KNOW ABOUT, OR TAKE

Of course, we all have different comfort levels and budgets. This mega-yacht was berthed at Marina Hemingway, Havana.

Okay, so you're beginning to think about it, and you're wondering... Well, I've just pottered about in the old girl for the last few years. Do I have the right gear? Is the boat going to be okay? And, am I going to be okay?

Of course you are. Just read the following chapter carefully. There's a lot in it that you already have, can beg, can borrow, or can do without.

And there's a lot you could usefully know before arriving in Cuba.

Do you have a modicum of common sense?

Yeah, you'll be okay.

THE IDEAL BOAT

This one's easy. A trip of this nature is not going to be the sort of thing that requires transatlantic capability, so, just as long as it's not a patently unsuitable boat and it fulfills a few basic criteria, the choice will be wide indeed. Just remember, it has to arrive safely, you've got to live on it for as long as your projected cruise, and it's got to stay on the right side of the surface.

To start off, you'll need to have a serious look at your boat.

Is it safe enough? Is it large enough?

I've seen people arrive in Havana using outboard-powered open fishing boats, which looked more suitable for a swift midnight run out to some matt black freighter. And I've seen the sort of craft that had three masts, 900 h.p. below decks and a paid crew in white duck trousers and enough braid to rewind an alternator.

Somewhere between these two extremes will be where most of us fall.

SIZE
First, your vessel at minimum must be capable of crossing open water where winds

17

and waves can rise without warning. If coming in from the USA, the Gulf Stream is a fast-running current which can increase your navigational problems, as well as your approximately 90-mile planned distance. Nevertheless, having said that, this journey is actually shorter than the distance between Miami and Key West, and less than half that of a trip from St.Petersburg in Florida to Key West.

Were you to be coming in from say, the Dominican Republic, you'd be facing a journey of perhaps, 120 miles, with only the uncertain welcome of Haiti as a refuge. But if you're in the Dominican Republic, then you've already sailed many times this distance safely.

Regarding size, I'm a great believer in having room to go and sulk in, so if it's going to be a long cruise we'll need couples in one cabin, and the kids or your friends in another. Very good friends may only use one bed, but that still makes for a complete cabin for them. One thing you'll not really want, unless it's going to be a very short cruise, is to have snoring bodies sprawled all over the main salon. For our part, we have a rule on board that no one dozes-off there either. That way there's at least one neutral room. And if you keep it clear of personal items like clothes, that will make it even more habitable for all aboard.

Of course, there will be exceptions too, so don't become too much of a dictator over this.

RANGE

We'd like our boat to be as autonomous as possible too, so if you're planning a longer cruise you'll want a sailboat, or as economical a motor boat as possible. In spite of what you hear elsewhere, it *is* possible to purchase diesel or gasoline fuel in all of the major ports, but as of 1996 the diesel price was ranging between 60 and 90 cents a liter in places, which translates as anything up to $3.42 a gallon. Additionally, although fuel is usually available most places, it may not be available just where you happen to be at the time. It's important to note that Cuba has more than 1,500 miles of navigable coastline, so if you want to go all the way around, the cruising range of your craft is a necessary consideration.

DRAFT

Draft can be a small factor too if you are going to be exploring the cays. In general, if you're pulling six feet or less you will be okay for most places, but I am increasingly meeting yachts which draw anything up to nine feet. While this does rule out a few of the shallower cays, most of them still get by fine.

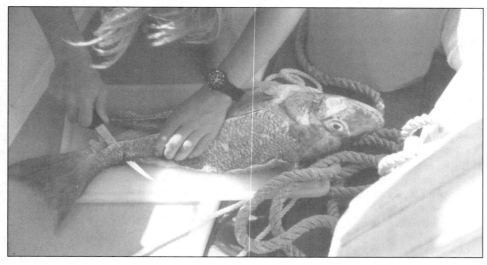

Filleting a snapper.

18

Although they are still relatively rare, larger numbers of cruising catamarans are showing up now, and would appear to be the best all-round cruising boat. Unlike conventional marinas, there are not many docks in Cuba which place limits on boat width; and a multihull's shallow draft can make even the most tricky passage a piece of cake.

Mind you, a swing-keel monohull would be really neat too.

In the end, what you really want is a boat you are comfortable with, and a boat that is also going to be comfortable with you. Far better you do your cruising in a boat you can operate by yourself in a pinch, than something that offers more features, but is less handy coming in through a tricky entrance or going alongside a couple of rafted tug-boats in a current.

Maybe a few words about what we use wouldn't go amiss here.

Our boat is a 21 year old 34-foot trawler with a single engine of 120 h.p. In spite of its relatively small size, it has an aft cabin, a main salon and a forward vee-berth; so when we cruise with guests aboard it's not too much like a madhouse. What is important is we're comfortable with it, and it has good sea-keeping qualities along with a handy draft of just 3 feet 9 inches.

I'd love to have twin screws with an extra couple of feet all round, but at the end of the day you go with what you can afford, and it's more important to go than to sit around dreaming.

But then, life's like that in so many ways.

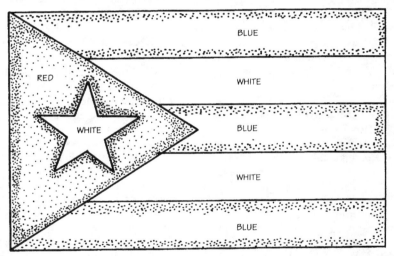

Measure and use dimensions if making your own.

FLAGS

Simple really; it's yours, theirs and a quarantine flag.

You'll need a Cuban courtesy flag, which you fly upon entering Cuban national waters. Surprisingly, these are readily available in the U.S. Pick one up in any of the chandlers or marine shops along the coast in Florida. They are more difficult to come by in the islands, but never mind, the Cuban authorities won't get too upset if you don't have one upon arrival. They fly a lot of them from balconies, so you can pick one up there.

Incidentally, if there's a chance of continuing on down through the islands or going someplace after Cuba, then buy those flags too in advance.

You'll need a yellow quarantine flag for entering foreign waters, and a nice touch would be to take a few pennants along. These might be those of your yacht club association or any nautical design, and make nice gifts.

DOCUMENTS

PASSPORTS AND PERSONAL

To enter any country, you need your personal travel documents. I've heard claims that a U.S. citizen can enter on a driver's license or voter's registration card for up to 72 hours, but on a boat I wouldn't try it. I already know of someone who's been tossed out for this impertinence, so take your passport or be prepared to be really, really persuasive (mind, it actually *can* be done by the exceptionally silver-tongued).

And, if you're a U.S. or E.E.C. citizen, you won't need a visa when entering by yacht. In spite of what you'll often read elsewhere, you don't need to inform anyone in advance — just show up.

For US $20.00, you will be issued with a 30-day temporary visa at the port of entry, and may renew it twice (sometimes more) for $25.00 each time.

By the way, Cuban immigration officers *never* stamp your passports, they give you a pink slip.

YOUR VESSEL'S TRAVEL DOCUMENTS

Reacting to what I've heard about other places, I've taken along all my ownership papers, title, old bills of sale and so on, but no one's ever shown the slightest interest in those. The only thing we ever get asked for is the Registration Document. But nevertheless, just in case, it may on occasion be helpful if you have photocopies of all your vessel's documents on board. And in all cases you should leave copies at home with friends or relatives who may have to act for you in any unfortunate and unforeseeable instance.

If you're borrowing or hiring someone else's boat, then you may need to show proof in the form of a signed and notarized document giving permission. Make it out in Spanish too.

CREW LIST

We have found that it is handy to have already prepared a couple of dozen copies of the crew list with passport details that is headed by the boat's name and registration number. Something similar will be required by officials all round the coast, so you might as well have it ready.

If you have clearance out of the country you've just left, it should list Cuba as your destination. This document is called a *"zarpe"* in Spanish, and they will want to see it upon entry. On the other hand, if you're coming from the USA, you don't need outwards clearance, so don't bother about it.

A few passport sized photos might come in handy too. Even though I've never needed them here, you can't tell when you might need some extra document. I always carry some, no matter what part of the world I'm in.

YOUR FOLDER IS YOUR TRUMP CARD

All of these documents and all the passports will need to be accessed frequently while you are there, so keep them safe in *one* place. Some sort of a cheap vinyl folder with a zipper is the most convenient thing for this purpose. As soon as your papers have been dealt with, put them all back in it along with all the extra bits you've just been issued, and sling the whole caboodle onto the bookshelf in one lot. The vinyl will also keep them dry when you dinghy ashore to some out of the way outpost.

Note that, along with courtesy, having these documents ready and easily accessible will be the single most important part of dealing with officials who might otherwise become somewhat tetchy. So do it right!

In addition, you may want to carry a few sheets of carbon paper, some paper-clips, a pen and maybe a small paper stapler. These can also go into the folder ready for instant use.

You can throw your wallet with credit cards, drivers license and the like into the back of a drawer for when you need them. And don't forget your address book. Your friends in Seattle or Utah will be tickled pink to get a card from you.

OFFICIAL DETAILS — YOUR VESSEL AND PASSENGERS

This document will save time and energy

Copy and insert your own details once only — Afterwards (but before arrival), photocopy as many as you need

Los detallles del embarcación "Jennifer"

Nombre:	Jennifer	(Boat's name)
Bandera:	Estados Unidos	(Flag – US)
Maticula:	Florida: No. Reg. FL12345	(Registration)
Tipo:	Motor Yate / Yate de Velas	(Choose one: In order, Motor yacht / Sailboat)
Casca:	Fibra / Hierro / Madera	(Hull Material: In order, Fiberglass / Steel /Wood)
Eslora:	10.3 mtrs.	(Convert LOA to metres)
Manga:	3.1 mtrs.	(Convert Beam to metres)
Calado:	1.5 mtrs.	(Convert Draft to metres)
Tonnelada:	8 tonnes	(Weight)
Color:	Blanco / Azul / Rojo / Verde	(In order, White / Blue / Red / Green))
Motor:	Ford, 6 cylindros	(Engine: Manufacturer / cyls.)
HP:	120 Caballos	(Horsepower)

Tripulación

Nombre:	Paul James Smith (Capitán)	(Name and position -- Cap't.)
Nacionalidad:	Estadounidense	(Nationality -- US)
Pasaporte:	1234567	(Passport number)
Nacido:	28/4/48 -- Estados Unidos	(Date and Place of birth -- USA)
Nombre:	Mary Jane Jones (Tripulante)	(Crewmember)
Nacionalidad:	Canadiense / Británica	(Canadian / British)
Pasaporte:	ABC 7654321	
Nacido:	18/12/52 Canada / Inglatera	(Canada / England)

21

Yeah, isn't it a bitch.

You need U.S. dollars here; period.

Theoretically you might be able to pay in hard currencies like British pounds, Swiss francs, and the like. That's fine if you want to pay in theories, if not, just use dollars.

Perhaps you've used Bhats in Thailand, Quetzales in Guatemala, and Cruzeiros in Brazil, handling the black-market like a champ. But here, until the regulation of the so-called parallel economy is liberalized, it's going to be different. Certainly within Havana and the major the tourist areas (except for the produce markets) it is presently difficult for a foreigner to spend Cuban pesos.

Further away, things are more relaxed, and meals can be bought in local restaurants using pesos. But generally, all official services, fuel and the like, will still have to be paid for in dollars.

Now I know there are those who will say they've managed to do the opposite, but by and large, at dockside you're going to be limited to spending only hard currency.

I won't go on except to say that it's just the way it is.

A startling fact surrounding the economy, is that on the street, the peso has actually *appreciated* against the dollar over the last three years... Weird.

CASH

First and foremost, the easiest form of payment will be cold hard cash, which will not cause the same alarm it increasingly causes in the U.S. (which is the *only* place in the world that views cash with such paranoia). Just make sure you take it in small denomination bills.

There is, in common with most Latin countries, a problem with making change. So, aside from major purchases of fuel and such stuff you might have a problem breaking anything larger than a twenty.

On this note (hah), you may be surprised to receive what looks rather like play-money in your change, namely cheaply printed bills or aluminium coins.

Don't worry, these are merely issued in lieu of American dollars by the Cuban government to make up for the shortage of change in circulation. At first you may be somewhat reluctant to receive them but never fear, you can use them quite freely in place of genuine dollar bills and may also exchange them upon departure if you haven't spent them already.

Finally regarding cash, certain hotels issue little interlocking plastic beads to their guests for use in place of currency! This phenomenon occurs mainly in package-tour hotels along the northern cays and supposedly allows half-naked guests to string their cash around their necks. Not a totally unpleasing effect if you're into red, yellow, or blue beaded necklaces and little else apart from a tan. Incidentally, these are usually given names like *"coquitos"*, or something similar in an attempt at cuteness.

PLASTIC... CHECKS?

You might have problems using plastic in some of the smaller towns, but in the major tourist areas you may use credit cards as long as they are not American Express. If using others, just be sure the cards aren't actually issued in the U.S. In your outrage please remember that it's not their fault, and that Cuban businesses have in the past accepted U.S. cards in good faith, only to have payment denied later on in the U.S.A.

Travelers checks are also acceptable, however there can be similar problems there too.

On occasion, I've had to travel great distances along the coast before finding a hotel where I could exchange them for cash, and you may need to use them sooner than this. In Havana even, I once had to go all the way to the Central Bank downtown to cash some. The Russian airline *Aeroflot* wouldn't accept them for a flight to Dublin.

Please note that even if you've arrived from some West Indian island, and have a pocket full of Barclays or somesuch European bank's checks, the drawing bank might well be their New York branch. So, be careful to scrutinize the face of your checks for this aspect.

NECESSARY PRECAUTIONS

You may have to make a stash somewhere down in the bowels of your vessel to safeguard all this, but fortunately there's not a whole lot of crime against boats and you'd have to take far more precautions in Miami.

FOOD, WATER & THAT SORT OF THING

You've already heard of the chronic shortages affecting the Cuban economy, so it won't come as any great surprise when I say stock the boat well. Nevertheless, in contrast to a few years ago when the embargo was biting deeply, and the only options were (generally dreadful) official restaurants or foreign-currency shops, things have changed somewhat.

There are now privately owned restaurants offering much better service, and markets where fresh vegetables will not have to be purchased with your soul.

MARKETS

Over the last few years, there has been a relaxation in the laws governing the sale of agricultural products, and growers are now allowed to sell their surplus crops for cash. Consequently there has been an enormous growth in local produce markets.

The range of goods being sold is usually limited to what is locally in season, but they are well worth the effort to find, and the prices are excellent. You may use pesos when shopping here, and there is always someone hanging around outside who will discreetly change your dollars into pesos.

As in all markets anywhere in Latin America, it pays to get there early, and not to be put off by conditions surrounding the storage and display of fresh meats. Check your supermarket standards at the gate.

PRIVATE RESTAURANTS

There has also been a sudden upsurge in the Cuban restaurant trade. Called *"paladares"* (after a cafe belonging to the heroine of a popular soap opera), private restaurants are springing up all over the major towns.

Around Havana, only dollars are accepted (the owner has to pay government tax in dollars), but they are still both cheaper than the official restaurants, and offer much better service. They are also limited by law to only 12 chairs, so there is a pleasing atmosphere of home cooking. Indeed, in many of the smaller towns, you will in fact be eating in the dining room of an ordinary Cuban household. Please do not be loth to attend these paladars, as they represent one of the

A private "paladar" restaurant, Havana.

most significant improvements that I have encountered in the last few years. Not only do *you* bring significant income into the ordinary citizens' lives, but *they* bring a welcome glimpse of Cuban life to you.

SHOPS

In major metropolitan areas and hotel lobbies, we find the uneasy (and socially divisive) phenomenon of so-called *"diplo-tiendas"* or hard-currency shops. Imported items such as tinned or packaged foods, and even some hard-to-get Cuban products, can be had here, but solely on a foreign currency basis. This has led to a two-tier economy, as that proportion of the population which has no access to foreign currency is restricted to dealing on the black market for consumer goods — or awaiting the favor of some faceless committee which doles out such things to favored sons or daughters.

Until the liberalization of the currency laws of 1993, these shops were only for foreigners. Cubans, even holding their own U.S. dollars, could not enter. Now, providing they have foreign currency, *anyone* can buy produce there which has led to a lessening in the embarrassment factor. Considered a necessary evil by the government, these shops are nevertheless one of the most troubling aspects of shopping in Cuba.

In Havana there are a couple of these shops which are rather like general stores cum supermarkets. Pretty well anything you need will be available, but there will be few bargains, and don't necessarily expect to get your favorite brand. Expect to pay two or three times what you might in the U.S., and maybe twice as much as in any of the islands.

The selection of foodstuffs will probably surprise you if you are only accustomed to U.S. style supermarkets. There will be a much higher percentage of Argentinean, Italian, or French foodstuffs, for example, and the other products may indeed be different too. There will usually be complete ranges missing, e.g. no tinned tuna and such for a week or two, and you may find there are three complete shelves taken up with the likes of olives or salted peanuts, all of which depends on the latest trade deal or the arrival of the latest ship in port.

Especially expensive, or sometimes hard to find will be the old sailors' staples like corned-beef or ham, while you may expect to part with an arm and a leg for cheese of any acceptable flavor.

Do not buy the rip-off stuff like vastly over-priced lobster. Instead bargain for it in the cays later on down the way.

Potatoes, rice and greens can usually be found, but at no time can this be guaranteed. The only thing you can count on is that the item you so desperately need will not have been seen that week. When shopping, buy what you can expect to use, even if not that week, and look for substitutes.

Oh, buy bread whenever you see it. It will not be there when you return.

In the larger diplotiendas and such stores, you will also find general products like brake-pads for Russian automobiles, strange faucets, Chinese bicycles and ghastly lampshades. You will not find batteries to fit your particular radio, but you will find batteries for everyone else's. And if I were you, I'd be taking along all the sanitary and paper products you may have become used to elsewhere.

SHIPS CHANDLERS

Another handy thing to know about is the existence of *"provedores"* which are establishments set up specially to deal with ships in any of the more major ports. The dockmaster will advise you about them, and if he doesn't, just ask.

Operated by *Sumarpo*, these chandlers will usually consist of a sort of discount bulk store, dimly lit, with piles of dusty tins, bags, sacks, rope and assorted items.

You may be taken around from pile to heap, followed by a solicitous clerk with a price list and an order form. Your purchases will be recorded, packed and delivered to your boat.

A small token of appreciation may or may not be donated to the clerk, who will have sat in spectral gloom to record everything in longhand and in triplicate, without the aid of carbon paper.

Sometimes this service is provided by boats directly alongside, and sometimes there might be a visit from a mini-van which departs with many promises of delivery and little hope of the same.

LIQUOR

By and large *all* spirits (and there will be lots of imported brands) are going to be cheaper than you remember — so take lots of aspirin.

Cuban rum is always available, and according to my not inexperienced palate is right up there among the best in the world. This at least is usually a great bargain, so shop around the diplotiendas for the brand that suits you best. Rum can also be bought on the street, far more cheaply, by asking around in the barrios. Someone always has a few bottles for sale at about a third of the official price. Even if it isn't Havana Club, it's still good enough to drink straight-up all night, and I have to confess to more or less confining my consumption to this selection now.

Cuban beers are not great deals compared to the wide range of foreign beers available, but in any case *all* beer costs too much here.

A state-run retail shop where the concept of customer-friendly marketing has not yet sunk in. Notice the murals above the shelves.

YOUR OWN STORES

You may, depending on the humor of the agricultural officer who boards you upon entry, be permitted to enter with fresh meats and the like in the 'fridge. Then again, you may not, so don't depend on it. The sandwiches you packed for the journey across, but didn't eat, will probably be okay though, and similarly those vacuum packed things you're going to do without later on.

That same agricultural officer will probably scratch his head somewhat over your fruit and those hanging nets of onions, but if there isn't any evidence of weevils, you'll probably be able to keep them.

On board our boat, we have as much food as possible, stashed in drawers and under the bunks; paying as much attention as possible to those items that can be kept indefinitely, like tinned or dried meats, pastas, rice and dried beans. Protected from vermin and moisture of course.

And, La Fiona the kitchen goddess, who's mad keen on paper towels and that sort of thing, keeps a dozen rolls or more miraculously hidden too.

We've also started to carry more of our own flour, yeast and baking powder, as a reaction against the shortage of such products. Incidentally, you can stock up with those tinned or otherwise packaged doughs which turn into buns, muffins and the like at the drop of an oven door. You'll love them in some misty deserted cove at 6 a.m. in the morning with a steaming cup of black Cuban coffee. And doesn't your boat smell nice too.

Here's an item the average shoreside household should never be without in any case; a pressure-cooker. This conveniently sized and sturdy pot will cook enough for the crew without the need for another container. Properly used, it will do so efficiently on less than a quarter of the gas you might otherwise burn, and will do so in less than quarter

A roadside butcher set up opposite the Comittee for the Defence of the Revolution offices in Santa Fé.

the time.

Buy one, read the instructions, and use it ashore for a few days. You'll never be without one again, and it will eliminate at least one other pot from your cupboard.

Filled early with a tasty stew, or soup, your pressure cooker will fit handily in the sink where it will stay safely through wave and wind with the top fastened on, ready for a quick warm-up later on when the need is greatest. The graveyard shift will thank you again and again.

A CIGAR SMOKER'S HEAVEN

And speaking of graveyards. If you're a smoker, and especially if you smoke cigars, you're going to be in hog-heaven.

Even though Fidel Castro gave them up after a valiant struggle, the Cuban cigar is still recognized as the ultimate smoking experience. The mere sight of them in those air-conditioned cabinets is going to have you in the grip of an uncontrollable desire. There is a great temptation to buy from the hundreds of touts who approach you on the side of the road, but beware. No matter what they claim, they are *not* selling genuine Cojibas or Monte Cristos, which even in Cuba, go for high prices.

Nevertheless, the ordinary cigars are certainly much better than the run-of-the-mill cigars normally available in the U.S.A., and at a few cents each, will do wonders for your image. They are not allowed back into the U.S.A., so *do not have any on board upon your return* or they will certainly be confiscated.

American brands of cigarettes are cheaper in Cuba than in the U.S., but on occasion you might not be able to get your favorite brand. Be prepared to sometimes smoke Winston instead of Marlboro, but buy by the 10-pack carton in Cuba and don't bother to stock up for the trip.

Cuban cigarettes are readily available, but they

26

are for hardened addicts only. Cubans love to offer you one just to laugh at your face when you first inhale. Send some to your ex-boss.

WATER

Water and it's conservation should be thought about too.

When washing dishes and pots, use only a couple of drops of detergent, fill the bowl a few inches deep and wash the plates, cutlery, and pots therein. We've never rinsed them prior to draining nor have we ever suffered for not so doing. You may pre-clean in a bucket of sea water, or even do all your washing in salt-water if you like. We use only fresh, 'cause we've got it.

A swim at dusk is one of the real pleasures of Cuban cruising, when you know you're the only human being for miles around, and having saltwater dry on your body is not at all disagreeable once you've gotten used to it. If you do find it so, then use a dedicated towel for drying off the sea water so the other towels will stay clean, and you won't notice any salt crystals irritating your skin. Hey, we used to be fish, they say.

If you must use fresh water to shower after a swim, then turn the taps off while soaping down and you'll not use much. In any case, rinse off from the top down.

We do our best to ensure our water doesn't

Street water pump.

get contaminated or stale by putting in a tablespoon of any household bleach (like Clorox) with every full tank. We've never tasted the bleach, but if you'd prefer, there are also proprietary products which do the same for more money.

You will of course, also need to take a longish hose which you can keep down in the lazarette for use when filling the water tanks. It may help if it's one of those flat rolled jobs, but we've never used one. They just look neat. Take along an adapter to fit the end of strange taps which you run into even at places where foreign yachts are commonplace. And perhaps, one of those dohickies to repair the hose when it gets cut, as it inevitably will one day.

There will perhaps be the occasion (perhaps indeed through adventure), when you need to dinghy water out to your yacht, or just lug it down some awful wharf. Use those plastic emergency five-gallon containers which you keep on the aft deck ready to deploy in a hurry. This is as good an emergency as any, and they are as useful for carrying your supplies out as they are for looking pretty.

As an aside here, when storing that same emergency water supply, leave a little air-gap inside the containers so they'll float if chucked over the side in haste.

FUEL: QUALITY AND AVAILABILITY

While on the subject of liquids, we might as well get on to fuel.

Although the overseas press generally reports that no fuel is available, this is simply not true, and fuel can be bought both ashore in roadside stations and at dockside. There are also wild tales about the quality, but we have purchased fuel all over the island and have never had a single problem.

Nevertheless, while fuel *is* available in all of the major ports, it is expensive compared to the prices you have been paying prior to arriving, and availability may well change from day-to-day given the chang-

ing conditions existing at time of going to press.

This should not be taken to mean that you won't be able to obtain supplies, but it does mean you should be prepared for the odd occasion when you may have to continue on to the next stop.

It goes without saying, also, that you won't find anything in an 80-mile stretch of cays where you're the only person around.

Fuel prices will continue to be in flux, but in late 1996, the price of diesel fuel ranged from 55-90 cents (U.S.) per liter, depending on where you got it and how firm you were with your position over the cost. Low octane petrol (gasoline) was more expensive still, and don't ask me about the high octane stuff.

If, in spite of the above, you are still worried about the quality, a few precautions like visual inspection, funnel filters and a regular (if not increased) schedule of filter changes will keep you going.

We have always carried a large funnel for decanting fuel, and it has it's own gauze strainer in the bottom. I respect the warnings I've received over the years, but this setup has proved adequate when combined with a couple of extra wall-mounted fuel filters on the engine supply lines.

The only time we've had a problem with fuel was when it was decanted directly from a dubious tank into buckets and then carried down to our vessel. This in fact is where a large funnel shows it's worth. That time, the fuel was gray, with only God knows what mixed in, but it still got us to Havana and the wall filters intercepted the muck. However, I do intend to carry a more sophisticated filter in our funnel in the future as I'd prefer to intercept sand, and small beetles (yes, I found both of those items in the filters) before they get into my tanks.

There are products available to treat your diesel's fuel, but on a cruise such as this you'll be using it at a rate that doesn't allow microbes to grow in the tanks. However, if you do leave your boat sitting around for a long while, or if you have a sailboat and only use the motor occasionally, then you should treat your fuel to prevent it becoming black and slimy.

ECONOMY

Our vessel, as mentioned before, is a 34-foot trawler, and as such we are absolutely dependent on our engine, so perhaps our approach to the question of fuel may be of some help.

The engine, which incidentally is over twenty years old (and with an uncertain history), pumps out 120 h.p. at 2,200 rpm, at which eyeball-buzzing speed the vessel scrapes 8.5 knots. A quick call to the boat's original manufacturers revealed that the theoretical hull speed could be attained on only 90 h.p., and according to one of the design team, wild claims from some owners about speeds of 10 knots couldn't be attained even if it went down Niagara Falls.

So we run our boat at a gentle 1,600 rpm, at which speed it attains seven knots. A reduction in speed of 1.5 knots for a reduction in fuel consumption of 40 percent. And incidentally, a glance at the power curve shown in the engine's manual shows that the motor is giving 80 h.p. at these revolutions, and is right on the torque curve peak, which is the point at which it is most efficient.

The engine appreciates it, my pocket appreciates it, and our cruising range is greatly increased.

You could quite easily do similar calculations for your own boat, and perhaps gain a similar increase in economy and range.

THOUGHTS ON CARRYING EXTRA FUEL

When we first traveled to Cuba, we were merely en route to the Cayman Islands, and uncertain about the availability of fuel, we

Manzanillo market.

28

Like small boys anywhere: Cuban youngsters returning from the "hunt".

investigated the idea of carrying a bag-tank somewhere aboard with an extra few gallons to get us there. A little shopping around showed this to be out of the range of our pockets, but five-gallon plastic jerry cans proved to be a lot cheaper and were much easier to store. That trip, I remember we carried 105 gallons stashed in the forward cabin and under our bunks in the rear. This gave us a conservatively calculated total range of about 900 miles. It wasn't so difficult to find places to put them once we really thought about it, and we probably could have carried 20 gallons more without any difficulty.

The thing is, we found fuel available both in Havana and along the way.

Nevertheless, we still carry at least 50-60 gallons under the bunks just in case.

STOVE GAS

The vapor you burn in your stove is also a fuel, so we'll mention it here.

A full 20-pound bottle should last you a month or so, and if you are going to bake a lot then it's not hard to find somewhere on deck (always on deck, never below decks) to store another. It's handy to have the bottles with fitted contents-gauges so you know what's going on.

It is not out of the question to obtain extra gas in Cuba, as we have done on more than one occasion in various out of the way places. If you do get a bit low, ask around wherever you're moored. You'll be surprised to find out what can be arranged.

EMERGENCY AND SAFETY EQUIPMENT

Everyone has their own comfort level here, but you will face a recently imposed safety inspection in Havana if you go there. This is part of a new cruising permit and will cover things like lifejackets, extin-

guishers and so on. I'd better allow a few words on the topic.

ON THE SUBJECT OF LIFERAFTS

I'd love one if I could afford one, and I

An infrequent sight: patrol boat on duty in the cays.

lust after those I see on better appointed yachts. They automatically inflate in the water, have all the right stuff packed inside, and have saved many an otherwise hopeless crew. They should be stored where the lashings can be freed without endangering the person doing it, and not covered by all kinds of gear limiting its use to a slow laborious release. Remember that cargo ships which run you over don't wait for a convenient time to do the dirty. They do it at night when you're asleep.

Having said all that, we just don't have the funds, and mindful of my remarks about going with what you can afford rather than sitting about dreaming about it, we've just had to make do with what we've got.

Firstly, we keep our dinghy inflated and positioned sideways-up on the stern transom, where a quick slash with the cockpit-knife frees it in seconds to fall upright into the water. Then next to it we have a couple of containers with emergency drinking-water. We used to use large Gatorade bottles, but have moved up to sturdier stuff now with two purpose-built five-gallon containers which are lashed together and have enough extra line attached. Fiona always checks the emergency bag we keep packed nearby, and makes sure it has knives, fishing line, garbage bags, inflator pump, tins of emergency rations, something to protect us from the elements, thin rope and lots more. The important thing about what we carry, is that anything in there can be improvised into useful tools or survival aids, and

at the end of the day the bag's still not more than the size of a single 5-gallon container.

We always carry our most up-to-date flares in it too.

Please, no matter how bad it seems at the time, do not abandon ship unless it is actually sinking under you or drifting helplessly onto a pounding shore. No matter if it's half full of water it is still better that you stay and fight, remembering that even water-logged most boats can still float unless a large hole exists in the hull. This especially goes for the unlikely event of a storm. You're better off on board rather than in a raft, and many an abandoned vessel has later been found floating while the crew has long since gone.

FIRE EXTINGUISHERS AND FLARES

They'll want to see your extinguishers (with the expiration dates) in Havana, and you should in any case have one in each cabin. And then there are the flares you keep aboard, which should likewise be in date. But you knew that, didn't you?

No one's ever complained about our big flaregun, so I don't think it'll be classed as a firearm, even though at short range.

OH, DEAR... FIREARMS

In Cuba, firearms are of little use and they will be removed from the vessel by customs officials in Havana and the larger ports. They will be returned to your possession while you're cruising the coasts, but will merely constitute useless baggage and unwanted bureaucratic hassles in port. On balance, there is no real reason to have any aboard, as quite frankly they're more likely to get you into rather than out of trouble.

BOOKS ON SAFETY

I would recommend to anyone to have on board, and to read, any of the excellent books on safety at sea. There are too many to list, but a selection can be found on any marine bookshelf. Particularly useful too might be one of those which deal with emergency repairs afloat.

Perhaps the best safety feature you can possibly have is an awareness of what you can do, what you shouldn't do, how to fix what you've done wrong, and an awareness of what's going on about the boat at all times. Extend this philosophy to other aspects of your daily life, and you'll be well off for it too.

When all is said and done, if you keep a good watch on passage, with an eye on the weather, an eye on your boat, and an eye on where you are, a genuine life threatening emergency should never arise.

SPARE PARTS

After the first edition of this book, two separate cruisers berated me for my emphasis on spares and preparation. Both of these ended up using replacements from my stocks.

Were your boat to suffer damage or an engine failure in the Bahamas or the Florida Keys, you might well expect to find spare parts or other materials available off the shelf, or perhaps through a dealer who might even arrange special delivery within a day or two. That same dealer might have a well-equipped workshop where the repairs could be carried out, or at least he might be able to recommend somewhere else. Here you are going to face a different set of circumstances which can create many difficulties; and especially if you wish to obtain spares for a motor not commonly used locally (i.e., Volvo or Iveco). Don't think you're going to speedily acquire some exotic part, as it might have to come in from Mexico, and let's not contemplate right now what that might entail. If you're lucky, and there *is* something available in Havana, we still won't want to contemplate the level of bureaucracy or deviance involved in its ownership passing to you.

So, within the boundaries set by your pocket and space, take what you might

A nesting osprey.

need, and do all your maintenance in advance.

Obviously, without going broke, you are limited in what you can take, but at least carry a few simple routine engine spares like fuel lift-pump diaphragms, impellers, and filters. This way you can carry out simple tasks if needed, and make sure a major breakdown doesn't occur. We take parts for both the engine and the boat itself, making sure that we've set out with it in as good a condition as we possibly can, and we carry enough tools to cause a discernible list to starboard.

The engine requirements depend on the length of the cruise too, and if you are going to circumnavigate the island by motor you'd better be prepared to do at least one oil and filter change halfway round, as well as replacing the anodes on your hull.

Aboard, we keep enough oil for one and a half complete changes having also changed everything before departure. You can get oil in the major ports without much problems, but (call me old-fashioned) I prefer to use the same brand I've always used. In any case I've still run out of oil and twice had to use locally purchased oil for changes. We carry lots of oil filters too.

To change the oil in a boat you need a pump. That way you suck it out of the sump through the dipstick and into an old oil container or two, which you can then discard properly. They're available in both hand operation and electrical modes.

Remember you need to change oil in the transmission too, and that may well be different. Your special brand will probably be harder to obtain than regular engine oil.

We have a very sophisticated fuel filter setup, but still change them more frequently than usually recommended, and have enough for at least four changes. Dirty fuel might cause unscheduled replacements, so provide for that.

I once flew out of Havana, but made sure I brought back more filters to replace those I'd used already.

There are impellers for the raw water pump, and a whole spare engine water pump with a thermostat too. And while I think about it, the cooling system sometimes requires a zinc anode too. Change it frequently until you get a feel for its schedule.

We have on board four or five extra engine water pump belts, and I check daily the condition of the one in use. (See, maintenance)

Remember that the engine has what seems like a dozen hoses. Take the more obvious ones, but you can sometimes use flexible corrugated hose which can be cut to length and bent. This makes it truly multi-use, and you might be able to eliminate a couple of similar diameter hoses with one spare length of this.

We once had trouble with the charging system, and I replaced the whole setup with a more manly alternator and wiring system. I had the old one repaired, and it remains aboard always ready for re-use.

There's the odd fuel injection line, and because I was a bit short of funds at the time, the innards of an injector nozzle rather than a whole new one.

A head gasket was contemplated, but I reckon that if the head needed lifting there would be more that needed fixing inside it, so I held off. I do, however, carry a rocker-cover gasket.

For the boat's systems you'd like a couple of toilet (head) repair kits, simple to fit and the thought of not being able to fix a head is too, too horrible to contemplate. Bucket and chuckit.

There's the main pressure pump in the fresh water supply to the faucets and shower which need spare diaphragms. And having fixed that leaking tap, did you get an extra washer too?

All those bulbs which the family leaves on need spares and while getting them, pick up a couple for the navigation lights, which always seem to live half-submerged in salt water.

A sailboat needs other spares in addition to those above; shackles, trunions, stainless steel cable, and all manner of cleats. Just look at your boat and ask what might disable you in some unlikely event, or even ask yourself what bits you've always been a bit skeptical about.

Epoxy resin and cloth may well be needed, and don't be caught out without a bit of that epoxy putty, which you knead together and it sets rock hard even under water. We once sprang a leak in one of our water tanks while in the southern cays near Cienfuegos and repaired it in 10 minutes flat! To this day it's still holding fine. Paint, varnish, and that sort of thing might only be needed on more extended cruises, but we carry it all and have used it all.

You never know what might suddenly let go, or what you might discover, so try to be flexible in the way you look at spares, tools, and bits and pieces.

We always make a point of keeping odd bits of steel, wood, pipe, and even plexiglass scrap, tucked away in the gaps under drawers where it's out of the way and they've come in more than useful in emergencies.

In that vein, there is no handier product in a wider range of repairs than an old fashioned wire coat hanger. We carry loads, both to hang clothes on, and to fix whatever needs fixing. Below decks, I suspect most of the boat is held together with the stuff.

CHECK POTENTIAL PROBLEMS BEFORE SETTING OUT

On our first visit to Havana, when we were headed down to the Cayman Islands, we discovered by chance that a concealed portion of the anchor post had completely rotted through below decks in the soaking lazarette, where all manner of evil lurked unseen under the anchor rope. I won't go into why we'd not discovered this before, but for now the anchor post was only loosely attached to the boat by the friction of that portion which passed through the deck. We temporarily repaired the damaged foot of the post using old scrap steel strips of what used to serve as rubrail edging. Drilling through the straps and cutting them into one-foot lengths allowed me to screw a lattice of them around the rotten portion and down to a more solid piece still further below. The repair held through many a night at anchor until months later when we replaced the whole post. But, I should have discovered the problem before setting out in the first place.

YOUR TOOLS AND SKILLS

For all of this you'll need tools and testers. Depending on your skill with them, you may opt for a full range of mechanics tools, or at the other extreme, a tupperware box with a couple of adjustable wrenches and a screwdriver. I used to be a professional auto mechanic and may be somewhat biased, but these are what's going to get you out of trouble if anything really does let fly, so I lean towards the extreme of every type and size. Whatever, you definitely need more than the average car carries in the back. I won't go on about it, 'cos you know it makes sense.

You'll need at least an electrical test light tool which, even if you don't know much about electric circuits, will tell you how far the current reached before it got interrupted.

Throw in a couple of rolls of good strong tape, some wire, a couple of connectors, a

An example of Cuban ingenuity. This bicycle has an engine from a fumigator.

positive attitude and you'll muddle through.

Where all this fits may seem daunting at first, but in fact, it all disappears pretty soon if you look for storage. Remember the oil, filters, hoses, and assorted engine spares may well fit quite conveniently down below in the engine compartment, just don't block routine access.

Keep your tools up in the dry, and where you can get them without necessarily having to go into the engine compartment.

Finally, keep all the manuals for all the equipment you have on board, and purchase a couple of those books which deal with maintenance and repair of marine systems.

It goes without saying that you should read the materials whenever you're bored.

If all else fails and you can't fix a problem on your own, remember that years of making do have raised that skill to an elevated level among the multitude of Cuban mechanics who throng the ports. Even if it really is some exotic machine, it's unlikely that anything you can bring in hasn't been seen before, so don't worry, someone will be able to get you going again.

MEDICINE

You should, as a responsible adult and as a good skipper, know a certain amount about first aid and CPR. In addition to this, your first aid kit should be as comprehensive as you can afford and simple enough for you to use. If you look after yourself properly then there's no good reason it should ever come out of its drawer, except for the patent hangover cure and the insect bite stuff.

The Cuban medical system is one of their proudest achievements of the past few years, but aboard a yacht, miles away from help, you're on your own. There is an excellent book I would wholeheartedly recommend you have aboard called *Where There Is No Doctor* (ISBN # 0-942364-15-5). While it is primarily written for third-world villagers, you're one of those when you're out there by yourself in the cays. It's published by the Hesperian Foundation, P.O.box 1692 Palo Alto California, 94302 and is available on bookshelves in places like Bluewater Books and Charts in Ft.Lauderdale, Florida. There are also other books dedicated

solely to boating accidents too, and whichever you get, you should read it before you really need to.

If however, you do have a problem in Cuba, there are more doctors and hospitals than you could ever have imagined. There are medical posts in all the hotels, and there certainly will be medical help available anywhere ashore at a moments notice, usually only a few hundred yards away from wherever you're moored.

The service will usually be free for most minor ailments or accidents, although you might have to pay for medication, which you acquire from the nearby pharmacies. I've had only good experiences with it, and I know where I'd prefer to have emergency treatment without insurance.

Remember the shortages have also affected the supply of drugs, so take what you might regularly need, and remember that any of the clinics near your dock will be overjoyed to receive any extra medicines you may have brought — anything at all.

CHARTS

I have encountered occasional yachts making their way with nothing more than a single large scale chart covering the entire island, and on one notable occasion, merely the first edition of this guide. But for serious cruising with peace of mind you need a bit more than this.

Nevertheless, if you do not manage to get hold of all you require, then a couple of

"El Navigante" chart shop, Havana.

sheets of tracing paper and a friendly yacht with the requisite charts will see you further along your way. I once gave tracings to a French yacht in Casilda on the south coast, and encountered them safely again in Havana some three months later.

CUBAN

No doubt about it, your best bet will be the excellent charts published by the *Instituto Cubano de Hydrografia* (ICH).

These charts, to a scale of 1:150,000 cover the coastline and cays in sufficient detail for all practical purposes, and include the most up-to-date information available about buoys and marks. Originally published in 1975, they receive yearly updates at the ICH offices in Havana, and I would use them in preference to all others.

Note: These charts use the NAD 27 datum if you're going to adjust your GPS to suit. *But it's not that important.*

To get a rough idea of the coverage offered, 26 charts would take you safely around the island, but you could easily stock even more detailed charts if you wanted more information.

A cruise from Havana to the western tip of the island would require four, and the trip from Havana to the eastern tip would require ten. Similar quantities cover the southern side of the island.

For serious cruising in the cays they are unsurpassed, and allow you to search out the most unlikely holes to rest up at night. The color versions are only available in Havana through the following:

• *Centro de Produccion de Cartas y Publication Nauticas (CPCPN)*
Carretera de Berroa Km 2.5 Havana del Este
Ciudad de Havana, Cuba
Tel: 65-0324

Or more conveniently in Old Havana at:

• La tienda *"El Navigante"*
Mercaderes 115, entre Obispo y Obrapia
Havana Colonial, Cuba:
Tel: 61-3625

They are available too at the new nautical club at the Marina Hemingway in Havana, but you may have to wait a day or two for delivery, and you cannot browse.

At any of the above they cost around $16 each in 1997, but supplies are limited, and you may find it advisable to obtain these same charts in the U.S. before leaving.

Conveniently, in Florida, black and white Xerox copies are available through Bluewater Books and Charts of Ft.Lauderdale, (1-800-942-2583) at a price of $15 each, and I have also used these with total confidence all over the country.

Finally, the ICH is now producing a small series of local chart kits dealing with certain areas such as the Marina Hemingway, and some of the cays. These are available only in Havana.

U.S. CHARTS

The U.S. government has long had available a larger scale series of charts to a scale of 1:300,000, which, in spite of being twice the ICH scale and containing some notable inaccuracies surrounding reef positions, I have also used cautiously without prob

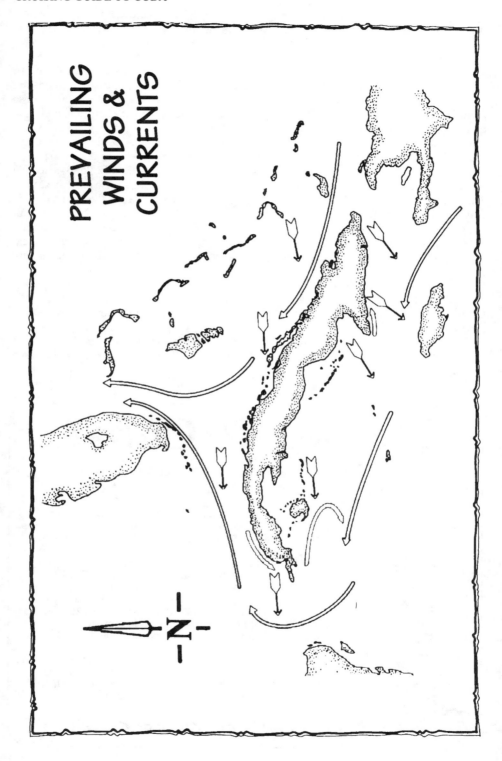

lems. The latest ones use a WGS-84 standard.

Rumor has it that they have recently released some previously restricted charts covering the coastline in greater detail too, so it may well be wise to investigate which are available in your area if time is limited.

British Admiralty charts are also sold widely, and while they may be somewhat old, they do contain quite sufficient information.

GENERAL CHARTWORK

It's nice to have a large scale chart of the West Indies too, as you can use it to plan your route further along, or back via a different route.

There is a wonderful book of charts put out by the DMA called Pilot Charts. These show the climatic conditions for every area of the Caribbean for each month of the year. They are used to plan your journey by giving you a statistical probability of wind directions, strength, and currents for each month and are published in a set of 12 monthly charts.

These charts used to be available in a Caribbean only version up to 1993, but

have now been amalgamated into a larger collection of 37 pages, which contain North Atlantic information. The price has gone up commensurately to about $25, but it's still good value and may well help you avoid traveling in certain areas when the winds aren't going to be favorable. It's great for avoiding the hurricane season too, or for showing the statistically normal path they take during the season.

I am not aware of any electronic charts out there, but I'm sure they exist somewhere on some databank, perhaps held by the U.S. government, so we may expect them to become available in the future as and when relations thaw.

Of course, in addition to all this, you will require plotting instruments for laying off your course. These are many and varied, but in the end, like so many things, it boils down to what you're comfortable with. You can make do with surprisingly few, and we only use a divider, with a cheap plastic course plotter. That way, when they get lost, or warp like pretzels after an hour or two in the sun, we don't weep. Incidentally, our dividers are over a hundred years old and still work fine!

WIND, CURRENTS AND TIDES

Once again, for passage making, the pilot chart will be of use for currents over the whole area of the West Indies, but locally in any case, here's a sketch which shows the major influences you're going to encounter around the coast. You may use the countercurrents to your advantage at certain times so have a good look at it.

Wind and current can dominate you, or can help you along your way. As you can see, the major influences are going to be the Gulf Stream along the northwest; the Old Bahamas Current along the northeast; the Yucatan Current at the western tip; and the westerly current between Haiti and the southeast coast. There are a few easterly

counter currents along the southern cays depending on the time of the year and the current is negligible inside the reef there. Windwise, the prevailing breezes are easterly and northeasterly, but you'll certainly be receiving a lot more shelter from these while you meander about the cays on the southern side of Cuba. All of which seems to indicate that the logical route round the island should be counterclockwise.

If you have other reasons for going clockwise, then you're just going to have to search out the dead areas inside the drop off along the reef, trying not to tack out too far while beating against the prevailing east winds. At least this will have the effect of giving some shelter from the swells, but be prepared to slug it out. I've met yachts in Varadero some 60 miles east of Havana that didn't, and had to take detours using the Gulf Stream northeast over towards the Bahamas to obtain favorable wind direction later.

TIDES

As regards to tides, there isn't a lot to worry about along most of the coast. The only places I've encountered any tides which called for much notice are around the northeastern coast, and even there we're only talking about a foot or two.

NAVIGATION EQUIPMENT

The most important instrument aboard is without doubt, the ship's compass. For centuries, vessels of all kinds have navigated their way about the world with only rudimentary charts and hearsay to guide or point them along that way. It goes without saying that you should have it where you can see it. Move it if you can't tell exactly where you're headed from your normal and most comfortable position at the wheel. It isn't difficult, and in any case you've probably fitted a few items to the boat since you last had it swung.

Huh, swung?

All compasses are calibrated upon leaving the factory, but they don't know what old iron you've got next to it in your boat. When I got my present boat the compass was at least 15 degrees out, and it wasn't just a case of twisting it in its mounts. It's a black art involving sun sights, peloruses, compensating magnets, and grizzled old men who mutter. Have it done whether you decide to cruise further afield of Maine or not. That new depth sounder you fitted last year's probably put it out a couple of degrees in any case.

By the way, does it's bulb work?

Speaking of depth sounders, this is probably the next most important instrument you've got aboard.

We've got three fitted, and have been grateful for each and every one.

Down below, there's the old flasher unit which still hums away above the wheel where anyone can see it, and up on the flybridge we have two more. Firstly there is a bright orange digital LED unit, which due to accidents of history, is now only good at less than 50 feet, but is absolutely inch-accurate when we're in shallow waters. We also have alongside it a LCD fishfinder affair, which shows the bottom contours on a small screen. We acquired this mainly for use searching out proper dive sites where we might want ravines and narrow gorges, but it also gives an indication about the bottom composition. In fact, a major drawback to this unit, which was not evident at the time of purchase, was the fact that the LCD display which thrives on sunlight, is all but unreadable if you're wearing polarized sunglasses! Nevertheless it has its uses along the wall and reef.

If I had to pick one and stick with it, it would be the little digital LED unit with its glowing figures and squealing alarm.

Incidentally, we know to within an inch the exact depth we draw, and this figure is written large alongside the instruments. With our sounders we are accustomed to trickling about with only a couple of inches below the keel while feeling out anchorages or passages.

GPS

The argument rages as to what constitutes a good sailor. Well, I've had my share of harassment from the traditionalists who ask rhetorically what I'd do without my

A Havana bus called a "camel."

Cuban fishermen in the northeast cays.

electronic aids. My reply is, I'd go right back to using dead reckoning like I used to.

But seeing as I've got those aids, by gum I'm going to use them. As far as I'm concerned, the prudent skipper carries two! That really get's the old salts going.

Along the reef, I like to know where l am, even if I haven't been paying attention over the last hour or so; and with my GPS receiver it takes only 30 seconds for me to have a neat cross on my chart, instead of laborious calculation while a frightened boat lies dead in the water.

GPS has given us faithful service and accuracy down to 50 feet all over the Caribbean, and the old salts aren't going to make me give it up for traditions sake.

All the coordinates given in this book are from GPS, and you should set your instrument to reflect the chart datum corresponding to your chart publisher (NAD 27 for Cuban charts).

With regards to the traditionalists, I also have a marvelous alloy Zeiss sextant aboard, with all the books. In total, it's cost me as much as my GPS did, and now you can buy a GPS like mine for a quarter of what I paid! And of course, a sextant is accurate only to about five miles on average, and twice a day at unsociable hours.

Best get a GPS unit that can be wired into your boat's power and has an external antenna for better reception, or at least one that can be slipped into an adapter, which does that for the GPS unit.

Whatever, even though you have a GPS receiver and good charts aboard, you should still be careful as the charts can often contain errors as to the lesser used reef entrances. Go slow, and keep your eyes open.

LORAN

A couple of years ago, most U.S. boats carried Loran C receivers and this still is a cheap and accurate instrument. It's perfectly good for the U.S. and even the northern Bahamas. You may absolutely rely on it if you're only planning to cruise the north coast of Cuba, but its accuracy does begin to go off as you get out of range. Believe it or not, ours was *usually* spot on as far as the Cayman Islands, but there were times when it did give false readings of up to 15 miles. At that point, it needed turning off then firing up again, and the trick was to make sure it was right before leaving harbor, at which point it was generally okay all day, so don't give up on them. We still carry ours in a drawer as a spare.

Approaching a charted entrance and using GPS, you'll be fairly certain of your position, but if you're using your Loran receiver, then it would be wise to have corrected the readings against some known point in advance so that your own coordinates are exact. Take a reading when you are at some location whose position is charted *precisely*.

Your instrument will probably show a slight error due to signal deviation, range and other factors, so using the instrument's manual, fill in the correcting data. This should be done every time you move far out of your normal cruising area. And especially if you've changed between transmitting beacons.

OTHER EQUIPMENT

We'll need a hand-bearing compass too, for taking bearings along tricky courses and getting other fixes on exits which you might need to record for later use. I would recommend one which you can see in the dark, or at least in the dusk, as that always seems to be the time.

Then there are binoculars, the lighter the better. Not much to say here, except that there are some really pricey ones on the market, gyro-stabilized and all that. But simple and cheap is good. I use the pocket ones which are really a bit low-powered, but they do the business and fit in my pocket when I'm ashore. Mine have crossed the Andes, and climbed the Himalayas with me.

Lights are essential too. Aboard we have aboard a large Q-beam, which connected via the cigar lighter is operated by the boat's batteries. It is powerful enough to give you a good tan, and can be operated for a couple of hours at a time. But here too, we've found more day-to-day (night-to-night) convenience in a large, eight-battery, pistol-type divers light. As a matter of fact we carry a couple of dive lights. Handy for the dinghy when you might well be occasionally soaked, handy for the engine room, handy for the boat, and handy for diving.

The big Q-beam hardly gets used now.

Strictly speaking, the next item shouldn't be classed a navigation aid, but I will. It consists of a set of passage notes, perhaps jotted into some sort of a spiral bound notebook, and prepared in advance so they can be consulted at a moments notice. The items recorded could include plans for the day's passage, with projected courses, alternate harbors, and so on. The whole lot could be recorded while poring over the charts at the beginning of the run, or while waiting for the morning's coffee to cool. It's much handier than screaming at your mate because you've forgotten what the next leg should be.

BOAT PREPARATION & MAINTENANCE

As mentioned in the previous sections, facilities for repair are few and far between, while the supply of spares is uncertain. So it only makes sense to spend a day or two going over the boat making right those little items you've been meaning to sort out for the last year or so. And this makes just as much sense, if not more, when the engine has only been recently serviced.

ELECTRICS

Were you to find yourself unable to start

your engine when necessary, somewhere in the Virgin Islands, you might be no more inconvenienced than the time it took for some Good Samaritan passing by to answer your VHF and arrive waving a set of jumper cables and a blank visa pad. This same problem might be considerably more serious were it to occur out in the southern cays; so let's make sure the batteries can start your engine, even though the lights have long since dimmed and the refrigerator is leaking. When I rationalized the electronics on our boat following our experience along those lines, I knew there wasn't room below for a generator nor funds available for same. We were able, however, to set up a system which allocated two batteries for the circuit covering the lights, fridge and electronics, and also a separate battery dedicated solely to starting the main engine.

This has enabled us to start our main engine no matter the state of our other electrics. The individual batteries are always isolated when the main engine is off, so there can be no mistake. We also took the opportunity to upgrade our alternator from a wimpy 55 amps to a more manly 125-amp unit. This is perhaps the bottom limit, but in fact we've never had any more problems and the set up is now able to run all the main electric systems for three days before we need to run the main engine.

We are, to be honest, apart from running a refrigerator at all times, frugal in our uses of power, turning off all lights when not needed. There are larger vessels which, running diesel generators, can utilize much more power quite freely at the expense of only a couple of gallons a week. And there are simpler craft than ours, who happily use much less power than we do. But, we've even come across yachts which utilize none at all, keeping strips of "*boucan*" or dried meats in the rigging, and using kerosene lanterns and stoves. They have as much fun as us, while eating and drinking at least as well. Well, red wine after all doesn't need chilling.

Mind you, the cost of solar panels is coming down too, and seems to be the ideal for a sailboat.

Get a good book on marine electrics, and check out your requirements properly, or go by what your experience tells you.

Of course, there is shore power available for hook up at the marinas in Havana, Santiago, Cienfuegos and other major ports.

CHECK FLUIDS, BILGES, AND BELTS DAILY

Daily before each run, when checking the engine oil and water, inspect the water pump belt. Do not overtighten, or you run the risk of ruining the bearings in the alternator.

On some engines, including our own, one needs to remove a water hose to get the belt around the pulley. We temporarily removed the hose in port, fitted three or four spare belts in place behind it and fastened them up and away from the pulley with plastic ties. A belt which breaks in service can now be easily replaced in two minutes, instead of

Engine rebuilds aboard are not comfortable.

having to struggle to fit a new one, while pressurized boiling water sprays from a disconnected hose and the boat drifts towards the reef. Believe me this strategy is a savior at those times when the engine's temperature alarm (which you've previously checked) sounds.

Have a look at the hoses, squeezing them and replacing those which show signs of cracking or otherwise giving cause for concern, then to round off the cooling system, change the impeller on the raw water pump and the zinc (if fitted) in the cooling system.

When changing your oil and filters, remember that there may be an oil change required for the injector pump too. Forget this one at your peril.

Once again, if you aren't up to doing all the engine work yourself, you should have a service done by a competent mechanic, but make sure you personally check out the items afterwards.

The bilge pumps can be run a few times, and maybe the wires looked at. There are some excellent waterproofing compounds or sprays which can seal off the connections on those old repairs done to the wiring by who knows whom. If they can't stand a good tug, they can't be trusted.

ROT

The sails may be inspected both before your cruise and at regular intervals while on the water. It would hardly do for a sail to blow out just when you're beating into a fresh northeaster with daylight fading. Of course the runners and other rigging come in for the same treatment too, and the shrouds may have corroded during the lay-up. Sort them out in advance.

Remembering my tale of the rotted anchor post, slimy things lurk down in damp lazarettes, if left unchecked. Inspect yours thoroughly.

The auto-pilot, while largely maintenance-free, might benefit from a check on both its mountings and its connection into the steering system. If it is hydraulically operated, then the hoses and connections need inspection with a dry rag and a bright light, while if it's chain connected, you'll not want slack links riding up on the sprocket

Santiago castle walls with view of the coastal approaches.

in a heavy following sea when the servo motor is whizzing around from port to starboard and back like a demented thing.

SCOOPS

Air scoops for cabins need a bit of thought. It's going to be hot if you travel in the summer months between March and September. You may be able to purchase a designer scoop, or with a little skill you could improvise some canvas into the same shape which may be tied into place facing into the wind. Remember that you also need to get the heated air out too, so try to maintain a complete through-flow along the length of the vessel and out the back.

ICE AND COLD STORAGE

We're lucky in that we have a refrigerator aboard, but give due thought to the capacity of your freezer if you're thinking of pre-preparing meals. Given the actual capacity and power of most 12 v. fridges fitted to the average yacht, you may in fact find there's not a lot of advantage to this. Especially if, like us, you do not have a generator aboard. We prefer to keep the little freezer compartment as full of ice as possible for those rum and cokes at the end of the day, restricting the opening of the flap to when necessary, and refilling the trays just before we go to bed at night when there isn't going to be any more loss of cold air.

Of course this leaves room for the dainty little treats you'll pick up along the way, like fresh snapper, shrimp and lobster.

If you're among the sailors who don't have a refrigerator, but rather an ice-box, then you'll be able to pick up ice in the ports along the way, provided the ice-plants are working that day. Just don't always count on it.

A better bet, is to stop at any of the many *"acopios"* or free-standing fishing docks which dot the cays. There is usually a cold store on the dock, and ice will be freely given if you only ask.

On the other hand, you can salt your fish or meats, and hang it in the rigging to dry in the sun during the day.

Bring it in, away from the dew at night. It really does work, and adds that touch of authenticity to the craft and crew. The Cuban fishermen will love you for it.

Mind you, if you have a generator aboard to power a 110 v. refrigerator/freezer, all bets are off.

SOME THOUGHTS ON REFRIGERATION

Refrigeration may benefit from a word here for the neophyte cruiser. There are several types of units now available. The first is a plain, simple ice box into which you put blocks of ice and rely on the insulation to preserve the ice for as long as possible, depending on how much food you put in, and how often you open it to take that food out.

And there are the electric refrigerators which run off your batteries, a separate generator unit, or even an engine linked compressor. They are generally either water or air cooled, and even though it is beyond this book to describe all these in detail, if your choice hasn't already been made by the boat's manufacturers, then the most efficient units are water cooled. Your

choice should be governed by space considerations, but if you can in fact fit a water-cooled 'fridge, then it will use anything up to 50 percent less power (with consequently less wear) than an air-cooled job.

Having said that, if you are forced to use one of the more readily available, economical (at least as far as initial purchase price goes), and smaller overall air cooled units, then increase the through flow of cooling air from outside. On our vessel we have had to cut four cooling vents behind the compressor to allow in twice as much air as recommended by the manufacturers. The unit still runs acceptably, in spite of temperatures far in excess of those it might normally experience in the U.S. where it was purchased.

A note of caution, we once took so much green water over the bows that it squirted in through the side vents, shorting out the powerpack. We've now fitted baffles to prevent this occurring again and have had no further problems in spite of equal seas. (See sketch.)

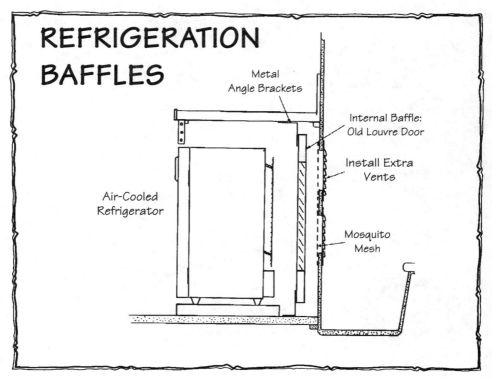

REFRIGERATION BAFFLES

Metal Angle Brackets

Internal Baffle: Old Louvre Door

Install Extra Vents

Air-Cooled Refrigerator

Mosquito Mesh

ANCHORS & ANCHORING

There are in the main, four types of bottom which will be encountered in Cuba — grass, mud, sand, and coral. Of these, inside the reef, where the majority of us will spend our nights, *the most likely is turtle grass* or some similar vegetation.

This is not to say that one will not spend long periods of time anchoring in sand or coral. But at first glance it might appear that in an ideal world your primary anchor should be the most suitable for turtle grass or the like; heavy at the tip, and perhaps with a

sharp point, suitable for penetrating through the mat of vegetation, and into the sand below. Almost all anchor manufacturers produce figures which show the theoretical holding power of their anchors in various ground conditions, but I note that they are universally reticent on the subject of penetration into turtle-grass.

The best type for this is the old fashioned kedge anchor such as you see tattooed onto sailors forearms, but unfortunately, it is little used nowadays as it can be bulky and

"Hobbes'" anchor wench in operation.

ANCHOR
SELECTION CHART

Boat Length in Feet	16	18	20	22	24	26	28	30	32	34	36	38	40	42	44	46	48	50	52	54	56	58	60
West Marine Performance	PERF-5						PERF-12					PERF-20				PERF-35				PERF-70			
West Marine Traditional	TRAD-4		TRAD-8			TRAD-13				TRAD-22			TRAD-40										
Danforth Deepset II	T-II-1200						T-II-1800			T-II-2500		T-II-3000											
Nav-X Fortress	FX-7						FX-11			FX-16			FX-23			FX-37			FX-55				FX-85>
Nav-X Guardian	G-5	G-7			G-11		G-16																
Bruce	Bruce 11			Bruce 16.5		Bruce 22			Bruce 33			Bruce 44				Bruce 66							Bruce 110
Simpson Lawrence CQR	CQR 25							CQR 35								CQR45							60, 75
Simpson Lawrence Delta	Delta 14						Delta 22					Delta 35				D44				D55			
Paul Luke 3-Piece Yachtsman	Luke 40 (20' LWL)					Luke 50 (25' LWL)					Luke 70 (35' LWL)												
Anchor Line dia x length	3/8" x 200' (28)					7/16" x 200' (28)			1/2" x 200' (28)			5/8" x 250' (36)				3/4" x 300' (43)				7/8" x 300 (40)			
Proof Coil Chain, size x length	3/16"PC						1/4"PC					5/16" PC or BBB				3/8" PC or BBB				7/16"PC			
Hi Test Chain, size x length	1/4"HT												5/16"HT							3/8"HT			

- Chart based on a sand bottom: call for mud anchor suggestions.
- Suggested sizes are for boats of average windage and proportions.
- Anchor sizes for other than Bruce anchors based on wind speeds up to 30 knots.
- Bruce anchor suggestions based on wind speeds of 42 knots by request by Peter Bruce.
- Delta suggestions based on light displacement craft; heavier types would be from 10-20 percent shorter re: to Simpson Larwence.
- For storm conditions, use one or two sizes larger.
- Recommended scope: 7:1 for rope/chain and all-chain in shallow water, 4:1 for all-chain in deep water (over 30').
- Chart based primarily on anchor manufacturer's suggestions.
- Numbers in ( ) parentheses are maximum water depths for anchor line shown at 7:1 scope.
- We suggest between one-third and one boat length of chain.
- High test chain recommendations revised downward due to lack of high-strength shackles to attach them.

The above chart has been reproduced with the kind permission of *West Marine*, a large retailer and mail order supplier of anchors and other marine products, with branches across the USA. As with other similar businesses in the industry they produce a massive Master Catalogue which, as well as showcasing their products, includes many pages dealing with numerous aspects of the art of sailing and cruising. The large section dealing with anchors, rodes, and anchoring techniques (some seven pages of good advice on this subject alone) is especially well-written and I would advise any cruiser to have aboard one or other of these types of catalog, not just for the information they supply, but additionally in case you need to order up a much-needed item.

difficult to store.

However, all is not lost, as the multitude of boats which safely anchor over this sort of terrain daily attest, and they all seem to use different anchors!

In any case, we would not really wish our main anchor to be too dedicated as it were to one type of bottom, given that we will almost certainly anchor over a different type the day after tomorrow. In fact, it might well be argued that when anchoring in turtle grass, we are already in some sort of shelter, and more often than not are in a position of leisure, whereas sand and coral bottoms might be found closer to dangers. Be that as it may, we do need multi-bottom capabilities in our anchors, with ultimate strength a high priority for emergency conditions.

I won't enter into the conflict between the various manufacturers over which anchor is better all round, except to say that whichever you choose it should be matched by your anchor rode, and that anchoring technique will be more important than the arguable superiority of one type over another.

Were I setting out on a long cruise, I might well be tempted to renew my anchor rode, saving the old one whole for use in cases of hurricane or storm mooring.

Many of the boats happily pottering about U.S. waters are equipped with minimal anchors. I remember when my own vessel was purchased, it came with an anchor which looked increasingly piddly with every degree further south we traveled. I *have* survived with underweight anchors, but it's extremely unwise. In fact, I've even brought an anchor back to the U.S. as hand luggage on a commercial airline to part exchange for a heavier one when I had the chance.

There is some controversy about whether or not an all chain rode is superior to a three-strand nylon rope, but what is not in doubt is that some sort of chain is required at the business end to prevent the actual rode chafing through on sharp bits of coral. It also has the function of both providing the required weight to cause the angle of the anchor to as closely approach horizontal as possible, and providing enough weight to act as a shock-absorber. Thus, preventing the rise and fall of the bows in a turbulent sea from working the anchor loose. Although you *can* just about get away with about 15-20 feet of chain, we use more than 70 feet.

Indeed, if you do go to an all-chain rode you are likely to be faced with a considerable weight requiring a sturdy windlass to raise the anchor rather than mere muscle-power. Failing this you may be faced with acquiring a sturdier anchor wench!

On our boat we have often experimented with La Fiona handling the helm and controls, while I do the raising and lowering,

Marina Hemingway: Visiting sportfishermen and marlin catch.

but this has invariably led to arguments. You need to do better than us in this aspect. (Heh, heh.)

DIVE YOUR ANCHOR

Diving the anchor is better than any other method for acquiring peace of mind and a secure fastening of boat to ground. Snorkeling above and watching an anchor tear loose while the crew backs the motor will give an unforgettable image of just what goes on below the surface.

Remember that in among otherwise impenetrable turtle grass, there are usually gullies every so often. The diver can swim down and physically shift the anchor over into one of these where it will dig into the walls rather than slide over the surface.

COMMUNICATIONS AND FORECASTS

For those of you leaving from North America, why not remove your VHF unit and take the opportunity to have it looked at by a competent technician in any one of the dozens of radio retailers who offer service facilities. You may find that it has drifted off frequency in the years since you've installed it, and you might be surprised at the increase in performance acquired for only a small sum.

The popularity of hand held units has made them an alternative, but their range is less than a properly wired in permanent set; and of course they cannot be left on all the time, which limits their use somewhat. In spite of only rarely having heard a radio conversation between boats in Cuba, and even more rarely been called-up, we always leave our sets on 16 all day while on passage. Remember to set the switch on your radio to the "International" setting for channel adjusting.

We've also replaced the old antennae on both our units. A 9 dB antenna gives the best range as it puts out a flatter signal beam, but this can limit its use on yachts which are heeled over. Far better is the theoretically shorter-range 6 dB unit mounted atop the mast. Compared to the 9 dB antenna on the spare radio, we have still obtained better all round performance from this set up on our main unit because we've been able to get it up higher.

Along the northwest coast of Cuba, between Varadero and the western tip, you may use your VHF to pick up the U.S. weather stations on the Wx frequencies, but further afield you may need to go to short wave for your reports. There are the normal Cuban AM radio stations on the medium wave, however, if like mine, your Spanish is less than perfect, you might prefer to receive your forecasts in your native language on shortwave.

If you feel the need to communicate over long distances independently of the telephone system, then you will have to go to shortwave transmitters requiring complex antennae and licenses. But this is by no means necessary if you merely need to receive the long range weather reports. These can be perfectly well picked up on any good portable *single sideband* shortwave receiver. This unit will also pick up all the local AM/FM radio stations for your daily dose of local news and music, while you lounge on some beach.

El Moro: Ancient castle and signal station at Havana entrance.

SHORTWAVE FORECASTS

You will want to listen for the Offshore North Atlantic and Caribbean forecasts which are broadcast on a regular schedule from various North American shortwave stations on the upper sideband. Below and on the adjoining page you will find a list of the times and a map of the sea areas to which they refer.

Regarding the stations, there has been some considerable change since 1995. I would put my faith in NMN from Norfolk, Virginia, and the Florida Station WOM, both of whom are still broadcasting. But New Jersey's WOO is somewhat quirky, and following the unfortunate withdrawal of free NOAA support, the Mobile, Alabama station WLO has discontinued its service.

In spite of what I have heard elsewhere, I have never received station WAH out of St. Thomas.

If listening to NMN from Virginia, you'll have to wait for them to wade through 10-15 minutes of forecasts for the northern U.S. coastline before getting down to what concerns you. But stick with it, and don't worry if you tune in late, as they probably haven't reached your area yet.

On the other hand, WOM out of Ft.Lauderdale starts off with a bang, and the announcer doesn't hang about, so be ready with pencil poised, at the hour appointed.

It will be well too, if you have a sheet of paper already laid out with the sea areas already written in, so all you have to do is note the figures and directions as they spew forth. Believe me, you won't have time for much more, and you can then analyze what's going on at your leisure.

We keep a small dedicated notebook for the purpose, so we can look back over the last day or two to see how systems may be developing. Listen daily, to get a feel for the language used before you need it for real.

Finally, all the stations will begin and end their broadcasts with any hurricane-warnings, so if fright has frozen your pencil finger, you'll get a second chance. In the event of this sort of thing, note the position, direction and speed of movement, then plot the system onto your large scale chart of the West Indies to see if you're in the danger zone, and you can make arrangements well in advance for your safety.

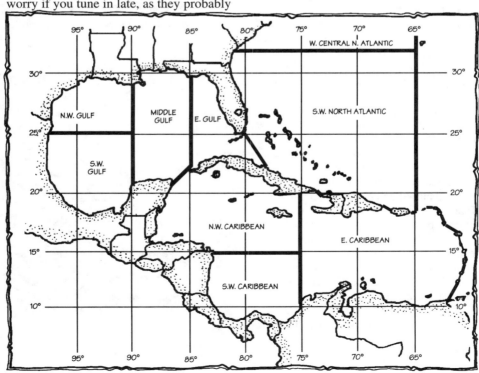

SHORT WAVE WEATHER FORECAST SCHEDULE

GMT (kHz)	EDT	EST	Station	Location	Broadcast Frequency		
1000	6am	5am	NMN	Virginia	4426	6501	8764
1200	8am	7am	WOO	New Jersey	4387	8749	
1300	9am	8am	WOM	Florida	4363	8722	13092
					17242	22738	
1600	Noon	11am	NMN	Virginia	6501	8764	13089
2200	6pm	5pm	WOO	New Jersey	4387	8749	
			NMN	Virginia	6501	8764	13089
2300	7pm	6pm	WOM	Florida	4363	8722	13092
					17242	22738	
0400	Midnight	11pm	NMN	Virginia	4426	6501	8764

Note: 1. **Your radio must be capable of Upper Side Band reception**.
2. Experiment with higher frequencies during the day and lower frequencies at night.
3. Sometimes stations will delay broadcasts if busy with tele
phone relay traffic.

INTERNATIONAL PHONETIC ALPHABET
(At least know your own boat's name)

A - Alpha
B - Bravo
C - Charlie
D - Delta
E - Echo
F - Foxtrot
G - Golf
H - Hotel
I - India
J - Juliet
K - Kilo
L - Lima
M - Mike

N - November
O - Oscar
P - Papa
Q - Quebec
R - Romeo
S - Sierra
T - Tango
U - Uniform
V - Victor
W - Whisky
X - X-Ray
Y - Yankee
Z - Zulu

WEATHER

Cruising the Cuban coast may present the occasional drawbacks for the inexperienced, but one of the advantages you will find here is that all journeys are short, and shelter is near.

Use common sense, and you are unlikely to find yourself caught out in a major blow, unless it is one of those that springs up from nowhere. Only a sixth sense developed from years of observation and experience will warn you of those.

Once again, there are many books dealing with how you can predict the weather over the next couple of days. This particular book does not pretend to teach you how you may do much more than normal daily passage planning, and for more than that I would urge you to read one of those books while avoiding becoming too bogged down.

I have even come across formulae which predict storm velocities and paths from the length and frequencies of the waves, but none of these have I ever remembered to use, and consequently master. My methods are considerably simpler, and while they may not make me an expert, they have worked adequately for me wherever I have sailed, and they should certainly work on a

Street services in Manzanillo on the south coast.

cruise around Cuba, remembering that you'll never be lost on the high seas for weeks on end.

A few clues:

Pay attention to the radio.

Be aware of the Kabatic effect around the coastline.

Look out of the window in the morning.

Finally, remember what it was like yesterday.

Cold fronts will sweep in from the Gulf and Florida, and the radio reports will tell you what's setting up over there towards Africa, or the Lesser Antilles, when major trouble starts brewing. By and large, you will have a few days warning if you're listening to the shortwave stations, and as you plot the storm system's approach, you must at this point make arrangements for fight or flight.

If it's a hurricane, then there is no question. It is flight.

HURRICANES AND STORMS

There are those who will not cruise in the Hurricane season between June and November. The theory being that their boats are safer in the Florida Keys. Well, there's no shelter anywhere in Florida comparable to what is commonly available in Cuba.

Nevertheless, anyone who has been in a hurricane will confirm that the fury of the winds are beyond anything one can imagine. The hurricane that wiped out a portion of Miami in 1992 should have shown many prospective cruisers just what is entailed in survival ashore, and they at any rate can imagine what it would be like aboard a boat. There aren't many boats, large or small, which are going to survive a *direct hit* from a hurricane out at sea, and precious few which will survive one inshore at anchor either, no matter what the shelter or what you have arranged in the line of tethers. The only thing you can do is get the boat as far inland as possible so that the force of the wind has to some extent been dissipated by the land by the time it strikes you. Then there's the storm surge to be considered, where the river may well rise by 20 feet or so! It would not be uncommon to find your boat up to a mile or more inland from the banks of your refuge upon your return. Your boat is going to be a low priority in the eyes of any rescue or rebuilding effort by the authorities who will be coping with far, far greater problems. This goes for all parts of the world which might be affected and not just Cuba.

To lessen your chance of that direct hit, you need to get out fast from the projected path. If that is not possible, then move the vessel to whatever shelter is available, tether it as best you can, and remove yourself to a place of safety. You can get another boat, after all.

Having said that, there are hurricane-holes, flats, and the like, which will provide shelter in the more likely event of a glancing blow or just a strong gale, so use your head, and make your own value judgment as to which refuge you seek. A complete discourse on boat survival is beyond the premise of this book, but there is an abun-dance of literature on the subject, and all competent skippers should be familiar with their options.

Remember all that line you saved when you changed the anchor rode? Well store it where it can be reached easily, as too often vital equipment is kept where its access is so difficult as to actually *discourage* its use.

You will also have to remember that in any sort of a blow you need to double or triple the length of the anchor line played out, and that all chocks should be fitted with anti-chafe protection.

ON A MORE REGULAR NOTE: THE KABATIC EFFECT

This is the name of the phenomena which causes the wind to blow towards the land during the day, the wind to blow away from it at night, and the lull we experience at dawn and dusk.

If you think of a land mass as something which might heat up during the day under the influence of the sun, then you can un-

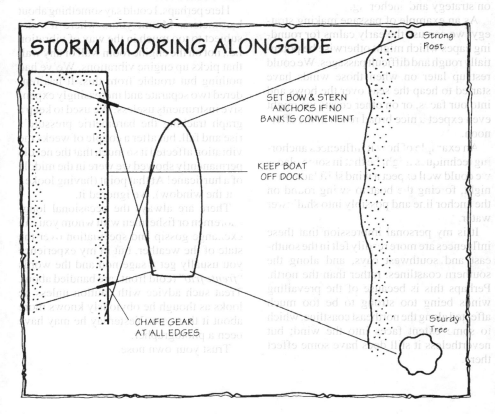

STORM MOORING ALONGSIDE

SET BOW & STERN ANCHORS IF NO BANK IS CONVENIENT

KEEP BOAT OFF DOCK

CHAFE GEAR AT ALL EDGES

Strong Post

Sturdy Tree

derstand that the air directly above it might be also heated in turn by the land. That air has a tendency to rise as it expands. Consequently cooler unheated air rushes in from the sea to fill the void left under that warm air which having risen to its maximum height will spread out away from the land, cool down, and sink. Again, this incoming cooler air will also be heated, and the whole process thus continues in a loop until sundown. Then the land will chill, and the air above it becomes cooler than the air over the sea. Now, the air above the land will contract and become denser, causing it to fall towards the land, at which point it will spread out away from the land and over the water.

We find a trend that during the day, the incoming air will come from the sea towards the land, and at night the breezes will take the opposite path; with calmer periods at daybreak and nightfall when the two features are equally balanced.

This effect thus has a distinct influence on strategy and anchoring.

As an example of passage making strategy, we can use the early calms for rounding capes which might otherwise be potentially rough and difficult passages. We could rest up later on when those winds have started to heap the seas over the bows and into our faces, or on other coasts we might even expect a nice broad reach in the afternoon.

An example of how it influences anchoring techniques might be that in some places we could well expect a wind shift later on at night, forcing the boat to swing round on the anchor line and possibly into shallower water.

It is my personal impression that these influences are more readily felt in the southeast and southwest cays, and along the southern coastlines, rather than the north. Perhaps this is because of the prevailing winds being too strong to be too much affected along the northeast coastline, which to some extent faces into the wind; but nevertheless it still does have some effect there.

USE YOUR OWN SENSES TO JUDGE WEATHER

Look out the window in the morning; does it look gray and stormy? Has the boat acquired a coating of spray rather than the usual dew? Or does the light just look a bit odd?

Why bother to leave just then? Assuming your radio has not given any indication of stormy weather or gales (and to be honest, in spite of everything they are still not *that* common), then make a leisurely cup of tea and wait. If the weather has been steady for the last couple of days, and unless conditions have markedly changed, it may only be a minor cold front passing through. Your barometer will give some indication of just what you can expect later on. Is it falling rapidly? Uh, oh, better get out the foul weather gear and look to your ground tackle.

If however, it's holding steady, then you may well assume it's temporary, and a minor delay in your departure could be all that's called for.

Here perhaps, I could say something about barometers. Mount yours where it's not subject to too much in the way of vibration i.e., not on the engine room wall or any wall that picks up engine vibrations. We've had nothing but trouble from this. It has rendered two separate and increasingly expensive instruments useless. We used to keep a graph tracking the barometric pressure's rise and fall, but after a couple of weeks the vibration affected it so much that the needle permanently showed we were in the middle of a hurricane! At that point (having looked out the window), we ignored it.

There are always the occasional longshoremen or fishermen with whom you can exchange gossip and speculation over the state of the weather, but in my experience you usually get a sage nod and the words "*frente frío*" (cold front) are bandied about. Treat such advice with caution unless he looks as though he obviously knows more about it than you. Yesterday he may have been a photographer.

Trust your own nose.

YOUR DINGHY

What can I say about them? There are so many prides and prejudices governing the choice, but in any case a word or two cannot go amiss.

It is indisputable that a rigid craft like a small skiff rows more easily but this may present storage problems when compared with a deflatable which is sold on its potential for storage. The ubiquitous inflatable, however, is not all that easily broken down and reinflated on a daily basis, and I've never come across anyone who routinely did this.

Nevertheless, this capacity just cannot be ignored unless you either have ample room on deck, or davits fitted which permanently store the auxiliary craft out of the water securely. So, in spite of the recent availability of strange folding boats, I shall confine my remarks in the main to the inflatable.

Your mind may well have been made up for you some time hence, but if considering a purchase you will wisely be governed by size and weight, as much as price.

Be guided by what you can comfortably lift into place aboard, rather than other considerations like total size or other factors. You may find that to heft a 10-foot inflatable is just too much if there are only two elderly crew aboard. Go to a smaller size and reduce your expectations of what it will carry. After all, you will have to lug it aboard every time you make a passage. A 10-foot inflatable will comfortably carry four persons through most of the seas you will be using it in, and if you need that sort of capacity you will likely have extra labor to bring it aboard or up into its cruising position. Of course, the size of your vessel will have its say governing the dinghy's size too, so think of where it will be stored when the boat is under way.

The same goes for the outboard engine if you are using one. There are those who see no point in the extra bulk and the other considerations surrounding an outboard, preferring to row; but you may find this somewhat limiting in the huge area of the Cuban cays, or when moving about bays and harbors which may be a mile or more wide.

There is a limit, generally set by the dinghy's manufacturer governing the amount of allowable horsepower you may fit to an inflatable. If you exceed this it may void any insurance or warranty claims, as well as causing an occasionally uncontrollable craft, but within these limits I would go for the maximum power which you can find in an easily liftable package.

It can be a bit uninspiring to spend an hour slogging along with wavelets sending spray over the bow when you could have planed over them a lot faster and more smoothly using say a 15 h.p. motor weighing exactly the same as your 10 h.p. engine, and costing only $100 more. The same might also go for the 5 to 8h.p. motors.

We have never regretted getting the more powerful engine fitted to our inflatable, especially as we use it so often.

The various engine manufacturers give the weights in their catalogues, so look at this factor closely before buying.

While on the subject of weight, you may be tempted to tow your dinghy rather than bring it into the cruising position. I would recommend against this practice, as on the rare occasion we have done so, we have invariably reversed onto it having forgotten its presence in the wake. If however, you opt to do this, then please take note of the time when crossing a bumpy Harwich Harbour in England, my uncle Mark looked back at the dinghy, and turning with a suddenly white face demanded, "Did *we* take the outboard off the dinghy?"

We hadn't ; the waves had.

Security: Before reading the following, please note that in all our years cruising the Cuban coasts, and traveling to every out of the way harbour and cove, we have never, ever, lost *anything* to theft.

If you're moored in some ports, you may well be asked to bring the dinghy aboard at night, or to chain it up. At first I thought this was mainly on account of a reluctance to allow free and unrestricted immigration, but later on another visit, I discovered it was not merely that.

A tale: Four years ago, I became friendly with a couple in a yacht who were able to tell me about their dinghy, which had been stolen while they were in supposedly secure docks in Havana the year before. Apparently someone had distracted the guards while their dinghy was stolen from right under their noses. Later, they received full compensation from the marina offices, who were understandably embarrassed over this incident. I could not bring myself to tell anyone, that a day or two before hearing the tale, I had been asked by some Cubans to repair a dinghy for them. I declined, because as visitors our position was tenuous, and in any case I had no means of knowing if in fact they were genuine. However, offering advice regarding using it for fishing purposes, I did get a glimpse of the craft. It had the name of the stolen dinghy all over its bows.

There is no need for undue alarm in most places, but occasionally it may be wise to retain your dinghy securely by means of a stainless steel cable, such as you may find in any ship's chandler. This may be fitted with eyelets swaged on at both ends, such that a lock may pass through and the whole rig fastened at one end to the outboard. The other end may be fastened to your vessel

having first passed the line through the towing ring at the bow. There are many locking devices which in turn fasten the outboard to the transom securely, making it impossible to steal the whole show.

If you have recently overhauled your yacht, you may well have a length of old stainless steel rigging, and in lengths of over 20 feet this is ideal. You will also find it second hand in many dealer's yards, and it's a lot lighter and friendlier than chain. We have only rarely felt the need to use this setup in Cuba, and I am sure that in any other country we would have lost the dinghy long ago.

Common sense may call for vigilance on your part, but always less so than in the rest of the West Indies.

Trinidad: A fishermen carries his catch home.

THE BICYCLE AND OTHER PERSONAL TRANSPORT

Bicycles: There are millions of bicycles on Cuban roads, and you'll be glad you had one aboard. Often it hardly merits discussion. We acquired an ancient rusty second hand model before our first trip, and it saw constant use. Even two-up, with Fiona perched crosswise on the centre-bar in the West Indian fashion, as opposed to the more unstable Cuban method of transporting passengers on the rear carrier-rack. The saddle was a sorry mess of protruding wire springs covered with a torn plastic bag, but we loved it and mourned its eventual loss (in another part of the world, I should add) to a casual thief. It lived on deck, and consumed huge quantities of WD#4O oil to hold the salt at bay. Even hardened officials, having a bad day, were softened by the sight.

The usual bike in Cuba is a sturdy old fashioned Chinese model the sort you'll see all over the world, and if you wish to blend in then this is the sort to have. No gears, an upright handle-bar, and a picturesque name ("Flying Pigeon"). However, this may be somewhat difficult to transport in a small inflatable, so you might be tempted along the lines of any of the folding bicycles available. You should in any case invest in a sturdy locking chain, much as you would anywhere else.

Personally, I do not think that a 10-speed racing bicycle would be strong enough for the sort of work it might be called upon to perform, but more and more cruisers are traveling with its cousin, the mountain bike. Nevertheless, it might be a bit flashy if that sort of thing matters to you.

You will need to take a patch-kit and a pump just in case, but the pump can also be used to inflate the boat's fenders and even to pump up the accumulator tank on the water system! Leave it in the engine room, and do not carry it around on the bike.

Motorcycles: Amazingly, in spite of the obvious problems, there has even been an increase in the amount of cruisers arriving with motorcycles or scooters strapped to the boat. While not terribly handy if one is going to be in the cays for any length of time, for those based in the major cities, they have made a huge difference. Even we, who have prided ourselves on being minimalist cruisers, have traveled with a 20-year old Honda 350, which we once based in Havana for almost seven months.

The beast will have to be both registered with the authorities, and listed on your vessel's manifesto upon arrival; all of which means you will have to leave with it. Sometimes you may be allowed to deposit it in the temporary care of the authorities for collection upon your return, and in this case a document will be prepared by the marina.

To register the motorcycle, go to the local customs officer and obtain a temporary permit to import a vehicle. This will give you enough time for you to go downtown to the vehicle offices and obtain a license plate (*chapa*). During the period between obtaining the temporary importation document and the plate, you may use the bike provided you carry all the relevant papers. Although you may be stopped frequently, it really is quite amusing to gad about Cuba on a motorcycle with Florida plates.

Recently, there was an indication that complete documentation facilities for motorcycles would soon become available in the customs post at the Marina Hemingway,

Our motorcycle on Hobbes' stern deck, strapped down for transit.

Private taxis waiting for hire in downtown Havana.

but only time will tell.

Gasoline was costing .90 cents a litre ($3.42/gallon) in 1996, and was available at roadside stations all over Havana and the major towns. In the countryside, the stations are rather more infrequent, and you will have to ask around; so if traveling far afield, set your mileage counter religiously, and fill up whenever you can.

Please give lifts to those pedestrians who stand near the crossroads with their thumbs out. After all, it is often the only way for an impoverished cruiser to get around sometimes, and many Cubans have done the same for me.

LOCAL TRANSPORT

First, buy yourself a good map before leaving home if possible. Order one from a specialist if you have to, as supplies in Cuba are not certain. Get one with the city maps included if you can, as even if you do obtain a city map from a car rental agency it will be close to useless. We have an old photocopy of a Freytag Berndt map.

When in port, it will not be uncommon for your dock to be situated some distance away from whatever attractions the city has to offer. Let's consider the options here.

You can obtain taxis merely by contacting the management of whichever dock you find yourself moored at, and at night the watchman will happily do the telephoning for you. Prices will be in U.S., and there will be a meter showing the charges. These are the official state taxis, and cost correspond-

ingly more than the private taxis plying for hire.

There are those too, who will act as your personal chauffeur in their own cars (yes they exist), and you can obtain their services for a whole day. You will need to ask around on the sly for this service, but *everyone* knows someone who operates a private car, and this costs much less than you would ordinarily pay for a taxi.

There are city buses (called *gua-guas*, or "*wah-wahs*"), which you board having first joined the wrong queue. They only stop at designated halts, so don't expect to hail one on the move as in the rest of Latin America. Having no name up front you would be hard pressed to know the destination if they did stop. You pay on entrance, or if boarding from the rear, just send your coin up to the driver via other passengers. Things change, so find out locally what the routes and standard fares are when you arrive in Cuba. Use local currency, which you can easily obtain.

You'll be stunned by the amount of gaily decorated horse-drawn carriages all over the countryside, especially in the south with passengers being picked up on an ad hoc basis. Good fun, and you can be assured of a long conversation with all and sundry aboard; and perhaps, even more fun afterwards as someone's guest. Called "*caballitos*", these can be hailed by sticking your hand out, and will drop you anywhere along the route. At about a peso per trip, I cannot recommend these wholeheartedly enough, and even if you are somewhat shy at first, you should lose your inhibitions. The passengers are friendly, and Cuban life is, after all, what you came for.

Intercity buses are available at the main terminals, but you will have to work hard to get a reservation. They will be full normally, so if the management of your marina has obtained a seat for you, show up early and be prepared for anything. Just outside the main terminals, there are usually long-distance cars plying for hire. Once they have obtained a full load (say four or five passengers sharing), they travel between the cities. Just hang around and you'll get the hang of it.

Trains can be also used to get about. As with long distance buses, the management of the docks can sort it out for you, but you may also go down to the station to obtain tickets in advance.

Aero-taxis will take you between major resorts, and I still remember my wonder at the quaint radial-engined Russian biplane bringing in tourists to the airstrip only a few hundred yards away from my dock in Cayo Largo. These, and other more conventional aircraft, may be your best bet if you want to leave your boat while you see a bit more of the country than your schedule might otherwise allow.

Wonderful large, Russian hydrofoil boats rise out of the water on winged struts, and can cheaply and easily transport you at

Air transport at Cayo Largo.

tremendous speeds between Batabano and the Isla de Juventud. You'll love them, but stay out of their way if sailing in the area!

Rental cars are theoretically available almost anywhere, although sometimes outside the larger towns, you may find that they're all mysteriously under repair or out on hire.

The phrase "rental car" is synonymous with "rip-off" in my mind, so be warned. You will find the prices absolutely exorbitant (expect over $50 per day for a cheapy, plus a whole bunch more for insurance), and you can expect to pay about .90 cents a litre of gasoline with limited refueling facilities. We have found that it is better to obtain the service of a driver with his own private car (see opposite).

And finally, there are both mopeds and bicycles available for rent at most of the tourist resorts near which you might be docked. Just ask around at the dock.

Thumbing a lift in downtown Havana.

MOSQUITOES AND OTHER CRITTERS

At certain times you will swear that these little critters have it in solely for you. Never fear, they go for everyone. It's just that you probably haven't got whatever antibodies Cubans normally carry in their blood, to lessen the effects.

At the calm which occurs dawn and dusk, as you sit on deck listening to the BBC World Service on short-wave, watching fish jump and sipping your carefully crafted rum cocktail, you may feel a sharp nip. Look around, announce calmly that you are just going below for a short while, and get out of the way of the stampede to follow in less than 20 seconds. That's about how long it takes for the real onslaught to begin.

Take heart, this is the time you can use to prepare supper, and perhaps, get the forecast for the next day, because in an hour it will likely be all over as the wind picks up. This will send them back to shore, and you can come out again.

Before leaving home you will be wise to fit mesh screens to all including the tiniest openings. Velcro will suffice for some, but the main cabin door (okay, companionway) will really need a sturdy plastic zipper all the way round. Search out *each and every* *gap* and put mesh there (including refrigerator vents), because if you don't the mosquitoes will find them.

At the height of the assault, you will see them clustered on the window or doorway mesh waving their stings at you and drooling hungrily. Mosquito coils, which smoulder for up to eight hours seem to keep them at bay, or at least hiding in nooks. These are cheaply obtainable anywhere in the southern U.S. or the West Indies. They're not so accessible in Cuba, so plan to pack enough to burn an average of two per night. You might find that citronella candles, equally unavailable in Cuba, also have some effect, so by all means try them.

We have heard from more than one source that vitamin-B has a repellent effect as it is exuded from the skin, but personally I have no experience of this, so please let me know if it really works.

Pets come in all shapes and sizes. This one's a jutia.

No matter how careful you have been, there always seem to be a couple of mosquitos which get in during the day. Just one of them on the prowl will keep you awake all night with its whining threat, so before retiring we always carry out an organized slaughter. The Cuban variety seem faster than any I've come across, with reactions quicker than a wielded towel, so the ultimate answer is a purpose built fly swatter. Use a damp tissue to clean up what was originally *your* blood.

If in spite of repeated hunts there still remain a stubborn two survivors in the sleeping compartments, your only recourse if you wish a peaceful night may be to remember that their bite is infinitely easier to bear than their bark, and you can always wear earplugs.

There are also various preparations available over the counter, to both repel them and to lessen the sting after failing. One of the hardest things to do is to avoid incessant scratching at your bites, but this only serves to intensify the itching a minute later and leads to open wounds eventually, so no matter what, resist.

Then there are the "no-see-ums" already familiar to many. They seem to be especially prevalent in certain parts, and like the mosquitos are active at dawn and dusk. Plan for them too, with your own favorite chemical weapons. These little buggers get right through to your scalp so if you're spraying yourself spray your hair too.

READING MATERIALS

At last we're getting to the end of things you should take, ending with reading materials you might wish you had aboard at some time or another.

GUIDEBOOKS

A couple of years back, for whatever reason, North American bookshops exhibited a strange reluctance to stock politically neutral books, but thankfully, this is changing. Now, any of the major booksellers will order up your choice if they do not have it in stock on their shelves. There are the various guides to inland Cuba and its history, and you should have at least one aboard.

There are several books presently on the market, but at least three or four to my knowledge are more style than substance, being full of glossy photos and glossier articles. These offenders even share their contents, and merely change their name to suit a slightly different layout — Beware of them.

The two which I would recommend are:
Steven Fallon's *Guide to Cuba*, available from Globe Pequot Press (ISBN Nos.1564407004);
Cuba: The Travellers' Survival Kit, by Simon Calder and Emily Hatchwell from Vacation Work in Oxford, England (U.K ISBN No.1854580914). This last is available on the shelves at Bluewater Books and Charts in Ft.Lauderdale, or can be quickly obtained by any bookshop.

Both of these are down-and-dirty guidebooks which give you real information not glitter.

SHIPBOARD BOOKS

Absolutely essential, even if you are a skipper with lots of hard won experience of your own, are those reference books you might need for safety, literature which might be relied on in a medical emergency, and your engine or electrical manuals. A less experienced skipper might see fit to have aboard a couple of the multitude of "how-to" books with a nautical theme and books treating the skills of sailing e.g., Nigel Calder's excellent *Mechanical & Electrical Manual,* or *Chapman's Piloting.*

Ernest Hemingway wrote many of his books in Cuba where he is still idealized, and some have Cuban themes. One or two would not go amiss to while away some quiet hours, and I think that any of the increasing quantities of good Latin American authors should find space on your shelves. They really do have a distinct style and will serve to get you into a Latin frame of mind. You will now be, after all, in Latin America.

You might like to take a few books in Spanish too, with American or European authors. Although Cubans are well educated, with an education system (and lack of television saturation) which has made them highly literate compared to North Americans, supplies of foreign books are severely limited. This is not solely due to censorship, but more by the economic straits the country finds itself in, so any books will find enormous favor as gifts which will be read and passed on. If you can, then you too can read them, but by no means do you need to have this level of Spanish to get around comfortably.

SPANISH (YOU *CAN* GET BY WITHOUT IT)

Let's get this clear. You will enjoy yourself a lot more if you can do more than point hopefully at an object and rub your fingers together — how thick, or how much? Nevertheless, we have encountered many cruisers whose command of the language was limited to precisely that, and it didn't seem to have tremendously curtailed their travel, or their appreciation of the country.

In fact, although my Spanish was learned in the streets of Bogota at age 26, it is by no means great. What I do have is a desire to gabble on with all and sundry, which is much appreciated. Cubans are delighted to talk with anyone, even if your grammar isn't too hot.

Fiona, the "anchor-wench", speaks little or no Spanish, and I don't think she's too lonely when I'm not around. I usually come back to the boat to find someone or the other trying his English out against her limited vocabulary of Spanish words. She understands most of what's said because she's heard so much, and she's flattered too.

In the tourist areas, especially where the large hotels cater to Canadian tourists, you will find people who can assist you in English. And as those same tourist areas receive most of their clientele from Europe, there is also someone who speaks Italian, French, or German too. Indeed, you may find that they go so far out of their way as to be almost embarrassing to one not accustomed to it.

Nevertheless, in spite of the above, there will be times when you have no choice but to understand someone's Spanish, or to get your own idea across; so carry a dictionary.

Remember, that even though you may be dealing with some official in a little coastal village, one of his primary tasks is to assist you, and unlike those in supposedly more developed countries, he understands that! If the official who requires some document or the other cannot understand you, he will get someone who does speak English to translate. It will help if you can offer the translator a dictionary and perhaps a notepad.

Finally, there is at the back of this book a small section dealing with Cuban-Spanish nautical terms.

TELEPHONES AND THE LIKE

International calls: Telephones are available inside any of the hotels, so, if trying to place an overseas call, ask at the desk. There are also many dedicated telephone (and post) offices who will arrange calls for you, but remember that the cost is generally quite astronomical.

Without doubt however, the best method is using an international calling card, available in the post offices or at a hotel desk.

This will allow you to dial direct (good connections), and a digital display will even track the amount left on the card as you speak. Unfortunately, since the last little spat with the U.S. government, the states cannot be dialed direct on this service. You will have to use an ordinary phone, and go through an operator. In spite of this, calls to and from the U.S.A. are easily made and there is little if any delay.

If calling Cuba from stateside, you may dial direct using the country code 54.

Faxes and so on can be arranged through any of the larger hotels or telecom offices, but make sure you very obviously time the call yourself to avoid being told you needed four minutes for one page. This holds especially true for the service at the Marina Hemingway telephone center.

Local calls: Within the confines of any of the marinas, you will find the staff only too willing to contact any Cuban destination for you over the telephone. They'll even make calls searching out information for you, such as to embassies or airlines.

In town, if you need a taxi, you'll be welcome at any office building to ask them to call you one, but they'll probably draw the line at that.

In the streets, you need a few five centavo coins for use in the old telephones, and they only call locally. With the newer models you can use 20 centavo coins too, and these handle long distance as well. Put in more than you need, and get your change back on completion.

CUBAN HOSPITALITY

The Cuban government is presently making strenuous efforts to change the emphasis in language teaching from Russian and German to English. I'm not sure just how many Cuban students really did end up learning Russian fluently, but it seems that they're all learning English now.

Be that as it may, relatively few in fact, actually speak English fluently as yet; with those that do confined to industry and tourism. Those who are still at school will only be too delighted to practice with you, and it's hard sometimes to take a simple walk in certain cities without being engaged in some sort of conversation. Usually this takes the form of a request for the opportunity to practice English, but after a short while, the conversation invariably gets round to how things are outside Cuba. If your Spanish is better than their English, then be prepared to spend anything up to an hour, and in occasional cases, much more discussing the state of the economy, religion, external politics, cars, and a never failing subject... how much you earn in other countries.

And Cubans love to invite you back home. Visiting a Cuban household, you shouldn't think you have to shower gifts all round just because you are a rich foreigner. On occasion this might even cause embarrassment, so don't go overboard here. Your main attraction is merely being you. Don't spoil the effect.

Cubans are proud people, and you can easily understand how it would feel if a visitor to your house thought it was incumbent on him to pay for the hospitality you have extended to him. Try to be sensitive

Musicians on the northeast coast.

with any gift you might bring to a household. Reciprocal hospitality may sometimes cause a problem in certain places where there aren't many foreign boats. In harbor, the port captain will usually request that you not have visitors aboard without first notifying his office. This leads to an uneasy situation, because only rarely will the average Joe be allowed onto your vessel. Traditionally, the Cuban government has looked suspiciously on foreign influences, and unfortunately this paranoia still holds true in certain areas. On the one hand, there may be the suspicion that a shoreside visitor is on your boat with an ulterior motive; and on the other, there is the suspicion that he may become infected with foreign ideas and thus less malleable. This concept may be hard to handle, but unfortunately it is still there to a certain extent, and until things change, it's just one of those contradictions you just have to live with. In practice, your visitor is far more used to dealing with such permissions than you and accepts them as normal, ironically referring to the "control" which is everywhere. Comfort yourself in the knowledge that every Cuban who is turned away from visiting you, represents another nail in the coffin.

Fishermen and other sailors, however, are usually delighted to come aboard without reference to mere officials, sneering at such petty restrictions; and they will view your boat with professional curiosity and delight. You will have to show the cabins, bring out charts, discuss various routes, and accept advice for the next leg. Your navigation instruments will be lovingly inspected,

your engines will be compared, and lies about performance will be swapped; just like enthusiasts anywhere, except that here they are a bit *more* enthusiastic.

You will be invited back aboard their craft to treat it as your own too. Be careful, because when rum is produced and begins to flow back and forth, you'll be lucky to make that other appointment you had thoughtlessly made for later on. Yes, you will remember the first time you stagger back across from an unexpected session aboard a Cuban tugboat, for the rest of your life.

Your rum may be pressed into service here too.

SILENT SLANG AND A FEEL FOR THINGS

One of the things you will pick up on, as you become more familiar with Cuban conversation, is just what is actually unsaid. Life in rigidly controlled regimes evolves like any other, and like any other, it develops its own lines of casual disrespect. Even though you may find that President Fidel Castro is at one moment idealized and referred to as "El Commandante," later on in the same conversation, he may be referred to silently by a significant stroking of an imaginary beard. This usually signals caution on the part of the speaker at some sensitive point.

You might on another occasion be tapping gently into some stream of discontent and notice the lowered voice and conspiratorial whisper followed by theatrical glances around. Then a touching of invisible epaulettes with two fingers on the speaker's shoulder will indicate unmentioned authorities.

Never forget that this is still a police state, and those authorities can have extraordinary powers over the ordinary citizen. Always try to be prudent in both conversation and action, remembering that as happened in any former Eastern Block state, there

Domino players.

are still informers here who can befriend you. On occasion, I have known with absolute certainty that I was being examined by parties who were not what they purported to be, and it can happen to you.

AVOID UNWISE ACTIONS (READ THIS WELL)

If you do get drawn in to the undeniable political undercurrent, you must know that as a prudent skipper it is incumbent on you to ensure the safety of your vessel and crew above all other considerations. Part of that prudence requires that you observe local laws and customs, and my advice is to remember this at all times.

It would be a pity to end up in serious trouble over some quixotic notion which may have been cultivated in you quite unconsciously, somewhere else. I do not think, for example, that even if as a private individual you were a sympathizer of relaxed drug laws, you would wisely get your boat mixed up with traffickers off the Colombian coast. So treat Cuban politics with the same circumspection.

And now that we have touched delicately on that subject, it leads naturally on to those authorities with whom you will come into frequent contact, and through whom most of the other official contacts will flow.

Officials clearing "Hobbes" into port.

THE GUARDA FRONTERA

Literally the "Frontier Guard", this organization maintains posts at all ports and regulates the comings and goings of marine traffic in and around the Cuban coastline. As far as concerns the boater, this is the group which authorizes any transits along the coast, and to whom you report both when entering and leaving port.

You will recognize their sometimes rickety installations by their frankly, military look with gray barracks, radio masts, flag-poles, patrol boats moored alongside, and green-uniformed soldiers. They may be situated at the head of a river, downstream from an inland town, or perhaps even mixed up among a cluster of docks and surrounded by fishing boats who also report to them.

They will normally be meticulous in their behavior to you, with an impressive courtesy and an even more impressive love of paperwork. Perhaps this is an unfortunate oversimplification, but the fact is that they

American yacht clearing in at Marina Hemingway.

have been trained to be ever vigilant for any perceived threat to the integrity of the state. And historically they have been taught to expect an invasion or some sort of infiltration, ironically along the lines of that carried out by Fidel Castro himself all those years ago.

It does not help anyone's cause that the Bay of Pigs invasion was just the sort of example that I am talking about, so we just have to live with it.

ENTERING PORT: INTERNATIONAL ARRIVALS
(FINALLY, YOU'VE DONE IT)

You're crossing that invisible line beyond which you suspect anything can happen. This is the 12-mile limit.

Should you stop? And if not, will they send a gun-boat to blow you out of the water?

Should you call in on the VHF for permission? Will they even answer?

In my experience, the answer to all the above is... no.

If you don't stop, you won't be delayed waiting for an answer, which in all probability won't come, so just keep on going and call in as you get a bit closer.

First Contact: In many of the ports which you will be using, outside of Havana and perhaps Santiago on the south coast, you may find yourself communicating with officials using handheld radios, whose range is limited by both battery power and antenna height.

Rig your Cuban courtesy flag, and below it fly the yellow quarantine flag, which denotes that you are asking permission for clearance. Continue on in towards your destination, calling at comfortable intervals in a *clear distinct voice* for official permission to enter.

Please remember that if you're going to Havana, you don't need to be communicating with the harbor officials in the castle (call sign "Morro Havana" on 16). You need, in fact, to be calling the authorities at the Hemingway Marina (See page 105).

Note: In spite of the above, it is *quite usual to receive absolutely no reply* to your calls. In this case, just proceed all the way in, secure in the knowledge that only in Havana and maybe Santiago or Cienfuegos is it at all common to receive a reply to your transmissions. I repeat — do not worry unnecessarily, just keep your radio on, and proceed into port. Remember, that even in the very largest ports like Santiago and Havana, we just nose on in, trusting observation and instinct to guide us correctly, and thus far we've never gone seriously wrong. Your experiences shouldn't be much different.

There are several names which might elicit a reply, so try any of the following:

- **Marina XXXX** (the local marina, if there is one)
- **Seguridad Marítima** (Marine Security).
- **Portuaria** (Harbour Master's Office).
- **Capitanía** (Ditto).
- **Morro** (an old castle which once guarded the entrance but now houses the port officials).

Always append the name of that port towards which you are headed. Sooner or later you may (or may not) be favoured with a reply, requesting the name and flag of the vessel calling.

In all cases, you will be treated with courtesy, and you should respond equally correctly. Your Spanish or their English is likely to be heavily accented, so if you do have some Arkansas drawl, you should mute it into as neutral an accent as possible, and do not speak quickly. Especially emphasize your consonants, and the vowels will take care of themselves.

Entering: Sometimes the marina will ask you if you need a guide through the reef, and if you're being escorted into port, let matters take their own course. But if you're coming in on your own, then your next destination will be the Guarda Frontera post already discussed.

Entering strange ports where there is some doubt about the location of the post, just shout across at any sailor in the harbor as you pass his boat. If your Spanish is limited shout "Guarda Frontera, donde?" or "Gu-arda Fron-tera, don-de?", use your hands a lot, and look at his hands as he points.

Come alongside the indicated wharf carefully, having made sure your lines are all ready in advance, and do not get into dis-cussions about documents until your boat is secure. There are likely to be a few spectators or soldiers about who will handle your lines, but you should not disembark until it is obvious that senior officers have approached to begin the formalities. Shake hands and invite them aboard.

BOARDING

One thing a lot of proud skippers are somewhat picky about is having black army boots/shoes on their deck. Get real! You're not at home now, and their boots are certainly not dirty.

Formalities: At this point, if you've not done it before, it's likely to become somewhat hectic aboard. Take things as they come, and it will all sort itself out eventually.

Somewhere like Casilda on the south coast, you will probably be boarded en mass, and your cabin or cockpit might resemble a crowded subway carriage. But in larger ports things will be done in a more structured way, so I'll explain it in logical order.

First to board will be the medical officer who will not delay you more than a minute or two. He (or equally likely she) will be followed by immigration officers from the Ministry of the Interior, who will appreci-

One of the many weird vessels visiting Marina Hemingway, this strange vessel, a Trumpy, travels with art-deco statues as a look-out.

ate somewhere to place their caps, and as with all officers, you should indicate a comfortable seat at a table of some sort for their papers. Someone may possibly speak English, but if you can handle things in Spanish then it will be appreciated, and you might as well start learning the correct names for things.

You will be asked for your "*zarpe*," or clearance papers from your last port, the vessel's registration papers, and the passports for every member of the crew. If, as suggested before, you have all your documents together, then you can produce them logically as they are requested, rather than letting things end up in total confusion. This is likely to be a long process, with lots of questions, and all your documents being handed around the officials, while a collection of freshly filled forms finds its way into your hands. To ease things, this is when you can produce copies of your pre-prepared crew list.

You will be asked how long you wish to stay, and no matter if you intend to leave next week, you should ask for the maximum as: A) You *will* want to stay longer, and B) You will have to pay $25 for an extension or "*proroga*" when you do. The first time we entered, the immigration officer smiled at me and said, "Here, I give you maximum. You come me when you want more, eh?" We'd only really wanted 10 days, but we stayed late, as he knew would happen.

By the way; remember that if a crewmember leaves the country later on by another means, you should have him removed from the crew list. This signing-off process ("*desenrolo*") merely entails a $15 document from the customs officer of the port when you're leaving.

Next aboard will be the customs officials, who will probably want the same papers all over again. More forms requiring three copies or more will be filled in, and

you might as well start handing out that carbon paper you've got in your folder, and expect this process to take an equally long time.

Each of the above categories of official will have a senior officer who does most of the talking while a more junior officer handles the paperwork, so your cabin is likely to be rather hot after a while. As the perspiration begins to drip, why not offer a soda from your stock? Everyone will appreciate it, and eventually your consideration will be reciprocated.

After the bulk of their paperwork is over, the vessel will he inspected; but this usually involves no more than an opening of the various drawers, cupboards, compartments and so on, and requires no more than a few minutes. You will, however, be asked to surrender any arms which you will be carrying. Don't worry, they will be scrupulously returned to you upon departure from that particular port.

I would strongly advise against the carriage of illicit drugs.

All the above will be followed by the veterinary officer, or the agricultural inspector. They may take an interest in any fresh fruit to prevent infections entering, but if yours show no signs of infestation all will be well. Your fresh meats may be another matter, so don't count on them getting through.

A word of warning: Remember that all the above may board you at the same time, so whatever happens, relax and go with the flow. Ever tried to come in at Miami airport when it's busy?

In all this confusion keep track of your documents, replacing them in their dossier when they are not in use and doing the same with the documents you will be given. You will be surely asked for them later on down the line, and at times like these the dedicated paperwork-folder shows its worth.

All in all you might end up with any, some, or every single one of these documents:

- Immigration's pink slips (to be retained in your passports).
- Entrance clearance for the vessel (with space on the reverse for subsequent ports).
- Official crew list.
- Customs receipt (approximately $35) for processing vessel.
- Customs declaration (money, jewelry, cameras etc., brought in).
- Search party act, showing you've been searched.
- Firearms receipt.
- Ministry of Health's clearance.
- Ministry of Agriculture's clearance.

This whole process can take an hour, but is an amiable as well as formal process, and finally, you can take down your quarantine flag. You're in Cuba!

ALONG THE COAST

Entering any port, even after you have already cleared into the country, the vessel

And one day, the Russians just upped and left. Photographed "somewhere" in Cuba.

is equally likely to be boarded and inspected, and the endless forms which are called for may sooner or later begin to wear you down, but the Guarda is a military body, and they too have to file even more reports later, so be patient.

Patience, however, should in no way be confused with obsequiousness. As captain of your vessel you not only have duties but rights, and you may insist on being treated fairly in the most unlikely instance of a problem.

By and large all inspections are friendly affairs, and we usually take the opportunity to offer the Guarda Frontera a chilled soda. In turn, we receive useful information about the port, its services, and attractions. In a considerable departure from that which you might expect in any other country, they will usually also be only too happy to arrange these services for you, or even advise about further transport if you wish to travel inland.

BE PREPARED

The main differences between the above scenario and that of an international arrival, is not so much in the level of documentation as in the varying levels of officialdom with whom you deal.

As an example, while in the major ports, you might expect all the original entry documents to be re-examined by a full complement of officials, berthing at one of the smaller docks may only involve being boarded by a solitary representative of the Guarda Frontera. This gentleman might restrict his interest to the boat's travel permit (the "*despacho*" described in the section on Leaving Port) and perhaps your passports. Whatever, harking back to my emphasis on having all your documents ready and in one place, you can affect the time involved.

You should in all cases resist any requests for the removal of the ship's documents. If an official insists that he needs to retain your documents until the vessel leaves port, you should be equally firm that the only documents you will permit off the boat are the photocopies of the ship's papers, which you have conveniently prepared before arriving in Cuba.

GETTING ACCUSTOMED TO BOARDING

There will, in spite of the foregoing, be many occasions when you just dock and go about your business, while nevertheless, expecting a later visit from a perspiring soldier on a bicycle. Always show courtesy and remember that you are probably interrupting their routine as much as they are interfering with yours. Sometimes, when the same document is slowly examined and re-read by the same official who did it not three minutes before, and who now finds some other point to pause over, I find my own temper slipping too. But at these times, I can only consider that the document is the first one of its type that this official has seen. That's how it is when you're the only yacht that's entered the harbor in two years.

Many U.S. citizens might not know this, but one is subject to a similar, if much less intrusive, form of control if you're a foreigner operating a boat in U.S. waters. I have been threatened with "astronomical fines" (their words) for not knowing this on one occasion, when I moved my vessel (within Florida) from Key West to Miami without informing the Coast Guard.

The difference is that in the U.S. you are unlikely to be physically inspected at every port, and that you can report by telephone.

Although Cuba is not unlike the rest of Latin America in this respect, the endless cycle of documentation is without doubt, the single biggest complaint among cruisers. I do admit, that in spite of all my rationalization, it can grate on the nerves after a while. Especially when, not a day after arriving, and having been at anchor in view of the harbor officials, you are again inspected upon departure.

Thankfully, you will rarely be inconvenienced once already cleared into port, or when anchored out.

Tourist liason at Cayo Largo. "Pire": your go-to guy.

GENERAL ADVICE ON SMALL PORTS

In some of the harbors which line the Cuban coast, the Guarda Frontera post may not be quite so visible. It is not always necessary to actually hunt them down, as they may well come out to your boat if you anchor in the harbor, so in the event of your wishing to dock somewhere, it is as well to visit the post first. In these cases, as described before, we tend to approach as close as safety allows to whatever convenient dock has a manned fishing boat alongside. They will be only too happy to direct you further.

When wishing to merely anchor overnight in an inhabited bay which contains a port, you might see fit to anchor some distance away from the township. In this case, it is possible that sooner or later a small wooden dinghy will be rowed laboriously out to your boat with a perspiring fisherman and a Guarda Frontera. Usually, a quick glance at your papers are all that are required, especially if the remainder of the crew have gone below to rest.

Just to round off the confusion surrounding the question of establishing your presence, there will be occasions when you might find that you're merely expected to dock at a fishing depot (or perhaps a "*basé naval*" in Spanish), where a friendly Guarda Frontera is on duty. These are the best, as from then on you are more or less a full part of the brotherhood of sailors. Break out the liquor, and ready the aspirin. And clear the stove for action.

Finally, out in the cays, or in some almost uninhabited cove, you are unlikely to be troubled by anyone at all.

Not merely a reversal of the process you went through upon arrival, the way you make your initial arrangements here may well influence all subsequent arrivals. Get it right and you will breeze through your cruise. But on the other hand, a simple mistake can cause hours of frustration and delay down the line, so the time to get it right is the very first time you do it.

The key here is to understand that to leave all ports within Cuba you need an official clearance to depart for your subsequent planned stop. The tiny, but important document you will be issued with by all harbor authorities is called a *"despacho"* (or dispatch), and it will be inspected at the next stop, where it will he retained and a new one issued upon departure. It is issued only at the last moment, when actually leaving.

In addition to this, you will need either a *"guia de recalas"* or a *"permiso de salida"*; one of two similar documents showing your intended route; sometimes you get this one a bit earlier.

GETTING YOUR PAPERS

Taking Havana as our example of the correct way to arrange your onwards documentation, you should follow roughly this format:

First, vaguely determine just where you are going to be cruising and for how long, then request your clearance from the local officials at dockside as soon as possible.

In Cuba, as in all centrally planned and directed societies, there is a reluctance to accept that you may have no specific plan, and you will be asked for a complete itinerary with stops and schedules listed. The idea will then be to issue you with a permit to continue to the next stop, and for them to continue in the same vein. Unfortunately, this will complicate matters when you in fact, have only a general idea of your route, preferring to meander as and when you see fit.

From the outset, make it clear that you are voyaging with no set plan, except that you

may ultimately end up in such-and-such a place. Thus, the permiso de salida or the guia de recalas can be prepared with your ultimate destination listed, along with potential intermediate stops. You may even list a circuit of the island as your purpose, and a general list of the major stops along the line.

We always ensure that the document notes our aim to anchor out as much as possible, and we mention our desire to dive on scuba too. This request has never been turned down, or modified in any way by the Ministry of the Interior to whom it is submitted.

In any of the major ports, this document is usually available almost immediately, but it pays to start asking for it at least a day ahead of time if you've never gone through the process before.

You will, as well as this document, be issued with the usual despacho, which will list your first expected stop, but if you miss this stop, the permiso de salida will establish that your itinerary was vague in the first place.

Remember the despacho is issued by the last official to visit your vessel before you leave.

OH, JUST ONE MORE THING...

Recently, the Ministry of Transport has begun to insist on all foreign registered yachts receiving a cruising permit. This document is called a *"Direccion de Seguridad e Inspection Maritima"* and shows that your vessel has been inspected for safety. It is valid for six months, and can be arranged upon arrival. Be prepared to pay a sliding scale, ranging from $25 for a 10-meter yacht, to $100 for 30 meters.

It, too, goes into your document folder, along with the rest.

Luckily, as recently as mid-1997, this permit was not required, or even known about in the southern ports, but presumably it's implementation will spread to those areas soon. Don't ask, don't tell.

TIME AND MOTION

Entering: If this impressive list of documentation in your folder has daunted you, later on you'll find that in many places you will only have to present the last despacho, the list of ports received at the onset, and the passports to gain entry to harbors; so let judgment guide you as to which documents can be kept at the back.

As an illustration, on one of our visits to Varadero, 70 miles east of Havana, we immediately presented the boarding official with the documents experience had shown us he would most likely need, and no others. He departed in four minutes, saying that we were free to go about our business, but that if anything more was required someone would call round sometime. At dockside, a friendly Canadian couple who had assisted with our lines, were astounded when we promptly set off for town, claiming that the process conducted by the same official that morning had taken them nearly four hours involving further visits from immigration!

Leaving: It is up to you to emphasize in advance what time you plan to leave port, and that time should be of your choosing not anyone else's. It is you after all who is going to be the one affected by a subsequent late arrival at a strange port in the dark.

The actual process of leaving a major port like Havana can take up to an hour, or much more if you haven't arranged the time in advance, but subsequently you can be more relaxed about things. Especially as further along the coast there will probably be only one visitor who handles all functions.

Nine times out of ten in these cases, departure can be sorted out in the time it takes to write out your fresh despacho. Say 10 minutes or less, and you're on your way.

To end off the subject of documentation, there is one thing to be borne in mind... unlike the rest of Latin America, a bribe can really get you into trouble.

MARINAS

Visitors who usually like to confine their mooring to the plethora of full service marinas in the Caribbean and Florida are probably going to be disappointed here.

In spite of the emphasis on tourism, there

A Cayo Levisa walkway.

are only a couple of genuine marinas in Cuba, and they are considerably drabber than those you will have been accustomed to.

You can find them in Havana, Santiago de Cuba, Cienfuegos, Varadero, and perhaps three other tourist areas, so don't base your cruise around them.

They usually supply freshwater and 110 v electrical hook-ups, with an expensive 'phone line available in Havana. One thing to look out for is that the standard hose or power connection which you have aboard may not work with the different fittings used in Cuba, but generally there will be an adapter (or a bodge-up) available on request. You can usually purchase fuel and oil too, with access to servicing facilities not generally available. Try to schedule oil-changes and the like for these stops.

Some (a notable example being Havana's Marina Hemingway) may offer shops, discos, and even a sometimes usable laundry and bath-house, but in general they should be regarded as a civilized base for further cruising, rather than a mooring for your entire holiday, and you can expect to pay anything up to .55 cents/ft. overnight, with slightly less being the norm.

One major facility offered, however, should not be spurned and is a considerable help to novice cruisers and perhaps those with limited Spanish making their first visit, i.e. your documentation.

The management staff of all Cuban marinas are only too delighted to arrange all aspects of this, liaising between you and the various officials more efficiently than you would be able to. So if you've had any recent problems, then take advantage of this service to rectify matters.

A point to notice here is that they usually have a different frequency for VHF work, so be prepared to use Channels 72, 68, and 06, in addition to 16, if you're trying to make contact. Normally they are more conscientious about keeping a radio watch than other organizations, so you're more likely to receive a reply.

Varadero Marina

Seven miles west of Havana, the Marina Hemingway monitors channels 16 and 72, and will accept all calls for inward clearance arranging for an escort in and official reception. About 70 miles to the east, the Marina Acua in Varadero also listens in on channels 16 and 68, and handles the same functions. Two other marinas are based there, but for documentation purposes it is best to clear in at the Marina Acua.

Along the southeast coast, inside the immense and wonderful harbor at Santiago de Cuba, the marina at Punta Gorda can be contacted by the Morro (castle), whom you call on VHF 16 and converse with on VHF 10. Once again, all formalities will take place at the marina facilities upon docking.

Along the middle of the southern cays, the best marina to contact will be at Cayo Largo, southwest of the Bay of Pigs. Call Cayo Largo Marina on VHF 16 and 19 to spread your bets. They'll offer an escort through the reef.

Other marinas are to be found in Cienfuegos, and the Bahia de Naranjo, but neither is too worried if you show up unexpectedly.

ANCHORING OUT

If the preceding lists of documentation and officialdom have gotten to you, or if you merely anticipate it happening, then note that on our first trip round from Havana to Cayo Largo (almost 400 nautical miles) we were never once asked for a single document! On that occasion we anchored out all the way through the cays. And we slept in sheltered bays along the coastline, docking alongside fishing-boat wharves situated away from the mainland, where friendly fishermen kept us entertained for days.

Everyone's reasons for anchoring are different, but we receive an enormous amount of pleasure from gently lowering the hook in a deserted bay at the end of an easy run. It is here, surrounded only by trees, limpid water, and gulls, that we feel most at home with nature. Our drinks are sipped in silence broken only by the splash of a fish falling back from an attempt at his supper, and the shrill cry of a wild animal that has almost certainly never seen a man.

You can almost guarantee that your anchorage will not welcome another vessel tonight, and if you have arrived from more crowded parts of the world, you will be awed by the untouched beauty of the cays.

There is neither need nor reason for hurrying if you have the mindset for anchoring out, as it is perfectly feasible to arrive in Havana or one of the large ports, take your fill of historic buildings, street scenes, museums, wonderful inland journeys — and then leave them all behind for days or even weeks on end.

In the 175 miles between Havana and the western tip of Cuba, only the first 60 miles are unsuitable for anchoring out, with the remainder containing dozens of secluded cays and inlets where a boat might rest for however long the crew desired.

From the eastern tip of Cuba, as far west as Havana, there are about 250 miles of coastline where anchoring would be best confined to the large regularly spaced bays, and 250 miles of countless islands and cays where shelter can be found almost anywhere.

Cliffs line the extreme southeastern coast, but traveling further west there must he hundreds of anchorages among the cays making up the next 500 miles, and encompassing aptly named areas like "Twelve League Labyrinth" and the "Gardens of the Queen".

Nowhere between Canada and the Antarctic South Pole will you find any equivalent cruising ground, still unspoiled, and so conveniently located.

FISHING AND DIVING

Anchoring leads naturally into the question of fishing.

All I'll say here is that you'll have endless opportunities to fish, both at anchor and trolling along your route.

Take a medium weight spinning-rod for casting out at anchor, and if you prefer to fly fish over the flats where the cays get shallow and the bonefish feed, then this can be done from the dinghy with a fly rod.

En route, along the coast, you'll need to stay well outside the reef where the depth drops to thousands of feet, and where you can troll for larger fish with heavier gear. If you stray in over the shelf where the depth suddenly becomes less than 100 feet you'll certainly have a barracuda on the line every few minutes. In spite of rumor, these fish are good eating as long as you don't try the very large specimens. Ask any local fisherman.

Inside, amongst the cays, you may trail a

black and silver lure for mackerel and the like.

Overnight you can lower a baited hook, which more often than not will attract something of interest like a nice grouper, if you're in anything around 20 feet or more.

Apart from what you think you'll use, take plenty of hooks of all sizes, especially the large types as they make excellent gifts for fishermen who you meet along the way, and who will be endless sources of information. The same goes for line, as both these articles can be in short supply.

While diving the anchor to see if it's set, you may feel it wise to occasionally take along a speargun and snorkel and you'd be right. Practice going down vertically, using slow easy finning motions, and you'll be surprised how easy it gets after a while.

A word of caution here. Do not attempt to stay down beyond your limits.

The main danger here is that of "shallow water blackout", which is the phenomena of blacking out while actually on the way up due to the drop in partial pressure of oxygen in the lungs. You won't feel it coming on if you've overstayed your welcome at depth, and it is a real danger.

I have seen it come on quite suddenly in a couple of occasions, and only prompt rescue saved the swimmer.

A lobster spear can be made up in an emergency by using two 18" prongs hacksawed from some abandoned steel rod, and if the cut has been made at an angle, then the sharpening will be facilitated. The rods can be fastened to your unscrewed

Crew of the good ship "Hobbes".

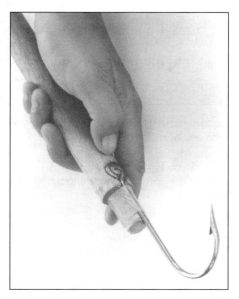

Lobster hook.

own tanks, and have them filled with air at any of a multitude of dive shops in hotels along the coast. The diving along the southern cays is equivalent or superior to anything in the Caribbean, and they're situated sufficiently far from the main island to be unaffected by silt washing out from rivers.

Dive the wall *anywhere* along a thousand miles and be assured you're the first.

AND FINALLY!

The next chapter, dealing with how to navigate safely through the cays and along the coastline, should be read thoroughly. There are hundreds of routes through thousands of cays and no book can hope to cover them all in full detail.

What we have to say about traveling safely and competently will ensure that when you deviate from any route shown here (as I know you will, endlessly), you can do so in safety, and as importantly, in confidence.

When we first traversed the coast, we had no guide and on occasion no good charts; so the thoughts contained in the next chapter are gleaned from those experiences. Used with prudence, they will ensure your safety as they ensured ours.

deck broom handle by means of two hose-clips, and this set up is the equivalent of anything a shop could sell.

Look for the antennae sticking out below ledges of coral in easy snorkeling depths, and only make your move when you are certain the lobster is at least six inches long over the back of the main shell (carapace). Aim for the center of the shell, and thrust quickly from not more than eight inches away, pinning the beast to the floor. Grasp firmly with a gloved hand, and keep him on the spear until back at the surface only removing him when certain he is "in the bag".

Another lobster gig can be made by *securely* fastening a large hook to the end of a pole or mop handle. The hook can be eased beneath the lobster and then twisted upright while being sharply withdrawn. With practice, you will hook the animal from below and he can be brought to the bag in the same way as before.

Marinate the butterflied lobster for half an hour in a little lime juice, a little sugar, olive oil and lots of garlic. Cook only until no longer translucent (three minutes maximum), and receive the accolades of your crew.

If you're a scuba diver then take your

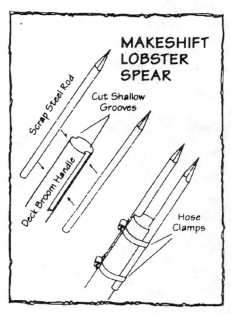

MAKESHIFT LOBSTER SPEAR

Scrap Steel Rod

Cut Shallow Grooves

Deck Broom Handle

Hose Clamps

NAVIGATING AND ANCHORING
IN THE CAYS AND ALONG THE COAST

I n a sense, this chapter is going to determine your enjoyment of any cruise you make around the coasts of Cuba. Given the sheer size of the potential cruising grounds, the numerous routes one can choose between countless points, and the changes taking place in Cuba, any attempt to prescribe rigid routes will be doomed to failure. At best, the following chapters can only be an effort to show a series of passages upon which you may base further cruising; and you would be unwise to think that any book can define your every route precisely. That's not how it should be.

In subsequent chapters, we'll be describing in detail a number of passages, anchorages, and ports; but for maximum enjoyment you should deviate anytime you see fit. Indeed you would be shortchanging yourself and your crew if you didn't. After all, that's how knowledge is acquired, and disseminated.

So, regard this particular chapter as our philosophy for cruising unknown waters, and use it to arrive safely into ports and harbors not covered by the passage guides in this volume. It illustrates how you may safely choose your own routes through strange reefs, along coastlines and into tiny anchorages. All in the knowledge that you were one of the first.

GENERAL LAYOUT OF THE COAST

In the previous chapter we touched only briefly on the makeup of the Cuban coastline, but you might remember that there were a lot of cays mentioned in relation to the prospects of anchoring out.

Well, here are some figures gleaned from a variety of sources.

There are two main islands (the big, long one, and the little one hanging underneath the western half).

The coastline contains over 200 bays and 289 beaches, being stretched out into an official figure of 5,746 kilometers (3,102 nautical miles). Note that this figure is measured with all the ins and outs taken into consideration, and is thus both hugely magnified, and hugely irrelevant.

Of more interest to the yachtsman is the 10-fathom line off the coast. There are approximately 1,500 nautical miles along that 10-fathom line — and within it 4,010 cays and islets.

Although this is a somewhat inflated figure too, they stretch out along some 50 percent of the coast. Cruise Cuba and there's still

A view of Samá Harbor.

going to be a lot of messing about in those cays.

The Cays: Unlike the Florida Keys where a large percentage of first time cruisers may have acquired most of their experience, there is no well marked Intra-Coastal Waterway; and apart from a few buoyed channels plied by merchant ships, the small vessel will find there are few defined routes.

The cays are more or less confined to four large areas:

1. Along the northwest coast between Havana and the western tip of Cuba.

2. Ringing the huge Gulf of Batabano on the southern side of the island, opposite Havana.

3. Between Trinidad midway along the southern side and eastwards to Cabo Cruz.

4. A large stretch on the northeast coast, between Havana and the eastern tip of Cuba.

The Cliffs: In addition, there are two notable areas of coast which are comprised of steep cliffs sweeping down to the waterside. These are contained both along the eastern portion of Cuba opposite Haiti, and along the south side of the peninsula at the western tip of the island.

The Bays: Near Havana and at the extreme northeast section of the island, the coasts are somewhat flatter with mountains to be seen inland, notable for deep bays and beaches at the water's edge.

MAGNETIC DEVIATION

As a final point, it should be noted that there is no magnetic deviation to be allowed for at the western end of the island, but by the time you have reached the eastern tip you'll be adding nearly six degrees! If you have purchased an overall chart of the West Indies, such as the DMA international chart No.400, for general passage planning around the Caribbean, then along with the major current flows it will also show the curving lines demarcating areas of magnetic variation increase or decrease.

WHY YOU'D WANT TO HANG OUT IN THE CAYS

'Cause you won't find another yacht within 50 miles.

And you won't be hassled by anyone else either.

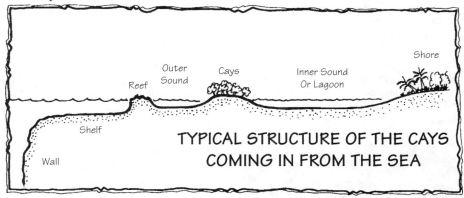

Outer Sound · Cays · Reef · Inner Sound Or Lagoon · Shore · Shelf · Wall

TYPICAL STRUCTURE OF THE CAYS COMING IN FROM THE SEA

STRUCTURE OF THE CAYS

Above, you can see a fairly typical cross-section showing the undersea features you're going to come across in the cays. An awareness of what you're likely to encounter and a method of predicting what lies below will be of tremendous benefit here, and could be said to be the key to safe cruising in uncharted waters. Combining this with good charts, there's no reason to

believe that a relative novice keeping his guard up should encounter any problems, *if he looks for the clues.*

CLOSE ENCOUNTERS OF THE WALL KIND

Taking our typical coastline above, we can see that as we come in from the dark blue waters outside, we first encounter the so called "wall". At this point, the depth can change from perhaps 5,000 to 30 feet in the time it takes to read this, so always keep an eye out for the color change, which accompanies the depth change. It will always be there.

Oh, scuba divers just *love* to dive the wall.

In from the wall, above the shelf, the depth change will bring a corresponding color change from indigo to a lighter blue, and depending on the actual depth of water there may be a corresponding change in wave motion. The large swells of the deep can sometimes become shorter and choppier, occasionally making this a welcome alternative to staying outside the wall when cruising the coast. A good lookout must always, however, be exercised when utilizing this technique.

At this point, still outside the reef, the bottom composition is nearly always coral. Do not damage it.

Were you to experience some form of emergency while running parallel and outside the wall, it might be wise to come in over the shelf to where the anchor could be lowered to settle properly on the floor, rather than hanging it down uselessly in the deep. The jagged top edge of the wall can saw through the line in minutes as you drift in.

Be mindful of the fact that even if there is no fringing reef between the shoreline and the wall, the waves can begin to surge as the bottom shoals close to shore. This can break

Maintaining "local danger" buoys for placement near Cayo Largo.

out the anchor, so get it down near the lip.

THE REEF... OR, THINGS THAT GO BUMP IN THE NIGHT.

The outer wall is not always the only change in bottom characteristics coming in, and attention should be paid to the possible existence of a "fringing reef" some way in from the wall itself. This will show itself, not only by a line of breakers or raised swells, but once again by a color change.

This reef can be near the wall, or perhaps a bit further in, but recognizing this hazard is one of the most vital functions of the helmsman at this point.

The color of the water will change depending on the bottom composition, but in general you will be looking out for dark patches or blotches in the water. You might see a dark brown or olive color for some corals, or it could even show as more orangey if there was a lot of elkhorn coral reaching up.

Whatever, if you are approaching something odd, *do not wait for confirmation* but put your helm over hard and skid to a halt as it were. For the moment, you'll want to take all the way off your boat as if it should indeed turn out to be elkhorn coral, which grows vertically up from the bottom and spreads out at the top, it will hole your boat just below the waterline.

Don't worry, one of the good things about this sort of coral is that it shows up well, and it isn't that difficult to spot if you're looking out for it.

THE SOUND

On the other side of this reef will be the "sound". This is a shallower area protected from the waves outside, and once again there will be a color change. If the bottom here is sand, then the sound will become a beautiful light or sky blue, mottled on the floor by the light refracting through the wavelets, becoming turquoise as it shallows to unnavigable depths. The bottom can almost always be clearly seen, and any isolated coral stands will also show up well as darker patches.

If on the other hand, there is turtle grass below, then the bottom will not be quite so distinct and the water will be greenish. Be conscious of the fact that if traversing a large area of turtle grass, your attention may well drift, and the terrain slopes gradually. Luckily, the bottom here is usually soft.

OUTER CAYS ALONG THE REEF

There may well be outer cays growing up out of the water here along the reef, with another sound between them and the shoreline. These cays

will usually be relatively low lying and thickly covered with vegetation. The edges are usually outlined with white sandy beaches or bordered by mangroves, whose roots eventually become the very land they once lined, and whose tops may reach above mast height.

And then, still further in, we come to the shoreline of the main island of Cuba, its beaches and its trees.

Cruising the cays can be a study in contrasts. For example, along the northwest coast, the inner sound can be as narrow as a few hundred yards, making for a snug refuge anywhere, while in the southeast it can be anything up to forty miles wide and deep enough to have large waves.

ENTERING THROUGH THE REEF FOR THE FIRST TIME

The pages of children's literature have been filled throughout the ages with imaginary tales of mighty galleons ripped asunder by pounding surf. The cries of survivors sounding weakly amongst the roar of the waves and similar imagery.

Well, all that make believe stuff was really true after all. Never forget that.

Having made countless entries through or over a reef towards the refuge of a sound, and sometimes in fading light, there's still a certain tension on the bridge as we come through.

Maybe that's good, 'cause it's certainly kept us on our toes; and afloat.

REEF? WHAT REEF?

But, hang on, is there in fact a reef?

The charts you have aboard should certainly tell you at least that much. And if you have the before mentioned Cuban government charts, they will even show coral heads far below the depths you'll be worrying about. The originals printed in color make everything obvious, but if you're using black and white copies, the reef may sometimes be lost among a mass of contour lines and figures. Be careful to check your charts closely, and be especially on the look out for the symbols for submerged rocks, which may be isolated from the main body of a reef.

If in fact, there is a reef, then don't push your luck unnecessarily. There will probably be a charted entrance not far away. Very few reefs off the coast are unbroken, and the entrances which exist are usually known and surveyed, so truck on towards one of those.

If the entrance is a major one, used by cargo vessels, then it is likely to be marked by buoys, pylons, stakes or whithies. If there is a preferred course in (to avoid some hazard), there may be range marks as well (you line them up one in front of the other and go in along that track). More often than not, if there are range marks they will be shown on the charts, but it is a different story with buoys. Storms, old age, and perhaps even collisions can take their toll, while there may also be new markers, where none were shown before.

The buoys and pylons will follow conventional IALA Region B colors as used in the U.S. ("Red Right Returning"), but sometimes a single, unpainted, wooden stake may be the only marker where the vessels are smaller, and this should be treated with caution. It will not usually be obvious which side you should keep to when confronted by a single stake (or even if it actually marks an entrance), so in any case you should keep a sharp eye out for signs of swells, breakers and the color changes denoting coral and reef below the surface.

Sometimes the stakes are not placed at the very end of the reef, and the actual entrance may be up to 50 feet away, so be circumspect.

BEING AWARE

And what if you don't have good charts, your instruments are on the blink, you don't know where you are; or you can't see any markers and you need to be inside? You'll need a heightened sense of awareness, but things will still be okay.

At this point, if you have a large motorboat then you are at a decided advantage, as you'll need a good look around and you have the flybridge to steer from. If you have a sailboat and the water's not too rough, then it might be handy to have someone up the mast, but if this is impractical a crew member should get as far forwards and take as high a vantage point as possible.

With a low sun in your face the reflections will blind you and you may have no choice but to remain at sea. If this isn't the case then polarized sunglasses will prove their worth here, as they screen out some of the surface reflections, and allow you to see below. Amber lenses offer the best visibility under these conditions showing the coral heads better than the gray ones, but even cheap polarized lenses will be better than the expensive non-polarized ones, so keep a pair around, and try to keep them clean of salt and scratches.

Coming in through an unfamiliar reef, it might be as well to do it under power, as you may have to ease up close and parallel the reef looking for a break. You definitely do not want to be swept in by waves which might even broach the boat, so keep in water which is deep enough to allow adequate maneuverability in all directions, and be patient while looking for a spot which fulfills all the criteria for safe water i.e.: no breakers, sudden swells, discolored patches or evil changes in water color.

Remember too, that the sound on the other side will have to be deep enough for your vessel, so look carefully for clues to that too. If it is very flat with hardly a ripple, then this may be a sign of shoal water, so look carefully at the surface with binoculars. This also goes for navigating between cays and searching out internal channels. Birds do not walk on water, so if they're standing up...

Be especially cautious, when swells are pushing in, and do not find yourself in a position from which you cannot escape if a hazard suddenly presents itself.

When all is said and done, if there is any doubt; stay away.

ENTERING / EXITING A FAMILIAR ENTRANCE IN HEAVY SEAS
(Or, When To Remain In Shelter, And How Not To Underestimate Conditions)

I used to have to do this almost daily when skippering a dive boat which had to keep to a schedule. We knew we could find calm waters to dive on the other side of the small island we were based in, but why *you* should wish to leave a snug harbor in heavy weather, I do not know.

It's almost certain to be still rougher outside, and if you don't really have to go out, then why not remain in comfort mode, and kick back with a day off? This really is one of those times when you can be seriously lazy in all good conscience. Break out that bottle of rum, and blame the conditions for your idle good-for-nothing attitude. If you feel energetic, then take the dinghy ashore.

Having said all that, there may be circumstances which make it imperative you leave, so let's look at the conditions, and see how best they might be coped with.

EXITING

Exiting safely with seas sweeping sideways along the reef is so difficult that you may have no choice but to remain in shelter, but if the waves are headed more or less directly into the exit, and aren't curling over to break with a crash, then with care, you may make it without mishap.

The major danger in leaving into a heavy swell lies in taking heavy seas over the bow. This can smash the forward windows and swamp a motor vessel, or it could lead to the boat submarining deep under the following wave, and driving deeper, stopping it altogether. To a lesser extent, the same can happen to a yacht, so our energies will be aimed at preventing this.

Remain near the entrance, balancing the boat against the waves with the engine, and wait awhile to observe the rhythm of the swells. There will likely be a visible lull every few waves (some say every seven), and this may be your opportunity. Increase speed to full, and get the vessel as far along its way as possible before the next large swell comes at it. As the boat rises to meet the wave, let its head come up until near the top of the swell where the power can be eased right back, and then let the wave pass beneath the hull. This will prevent the craft plunging down the other side and into the following wave, instead allowing it a controlled slide downwards to lift its bow again at start of the next cycle. As the bow lifts you may again increase the power to drive upwards, then as before decrease the power at the top. Hold the vessel always head on into the swells, and with luck you can find yourself right outside without taking a drop over the bows. Of course it also depends on your not having underestimated the conditions in the first place.

As with all reef maneuvers, don't allow yourself to end up somewhere from which there is no turning back because it will not be possible to turn around safely in a narrow entrance if there is any sort of a heavy swell.

ENTERING (FOLLOWING SEAS ARE ALWAYS TRICKIER)

Entering through a gap in the reef (a "cut") can be even more difficult, and boats were regularly lost doing this in the islands where I worked. The first thing to be sure of is that there is enough water there in the first place. In the trough between waves, the depth may well be considerably less than normal, so allow for this, and once again do not underestimate the conditions.

Try to visualize your reactions in advance, and have the crew well braced.

Apart from "pooping" (being filled from behind by a crested wave), the main danger here is that of being broached, or swung sideways, and hit broadside by a large wave. Even if the vessel rides it out you are likely to drive straight into the side of a narrow entrance, so devote all energies and maneuvers to keeping the vessel straight.

I have found it best in familiar waters to minimize the amount of time the boat is actually stern on to the waves, and to this end, I like to run parallel to the reef as closely as I dare, which can sometimes be as little as 50 feet, if there is adequate depth. With one eye open to the possibility of being pushed sideways onto the reef and anticipating the waves as they come, I cal-

The author navigating at sea.

Surfing into Marina Hemingway during bad weather. That's one of the inner channel markers!

culate my arrival to coincide with an observed lull in the swells. Here I like to make a sharp turn at the point of entry and get my speed up to outrun whatever I can. Remember that this procedure can be dangerous in unfamiliar waters, because you won't get a feel for the waves until it is too late to abort. So in this instance you may find it better to make your approach from further out.

Of course it will not be possible to outrun everything and in this case you must saw the wheel to keep the vessel straight as the swells lift the stern and pass under. Sometimes, as the waves pass forward under the hull leaving the boat in the trough, it will veer uncontrollably off line, requiring both a determined spin of the wheel to get it back on course. Here, an instant (and only temporary) drop in power will keep the vessel from driving itself at right angles onto the reef at the entrance.

Keep the power up when you can, drop it when you should, and don't think it's not going to be exciting. I always reckoned that was where we earned our corn.

As before, please remember that it's rarely the waves, but rather the coral which sinks a yacht, and stay out at sea if you have to. If necessary you can usually find a broad safe

entrance a little way on if you don't let impatience get to you.

THE INNER CAYS AND SOUNDS

Conditions inside the smaller sounds are in sharp contrast to those existing outside the reef. Gone will be the swells, and instead all will be calm. There may be a chop if the sound is large and deep, but even so, there are unlikely to be any waves worthy of the name unless there is a stiff wind.

Now is the time to write up the ship's log, perhaps putting in a sketch of the entrance and any bearings, or GPS locations of significance, buoys, ranges and other features, so do it while the details are fresh, and *before* the vessel is prepared for anchoring.

An often overlooked point is that you may find your notes useful if you have to leave through the same gap, and especially if you have to do it at night.

These notes will be invaluable still later on, as inevitably you will either wish to return to some of your favorite discoveries, or to merely reflect at ease one day upon your trips. A well-written log is the equivalent of all other travel writers' books combined; and with the salt and sweat stains, it comes in "Smell-O-Rama" too.

In the relative calm following entry, you may again consult your charts to compare them with what you can see, and perhaps set visual courses for promising anchorages. Remember the floor will probably now be visible, and you should begin to take note of the colors and associate them with bottom-composition and depth.

Auto pilots are useful inside the reefs too, as some of the gulfs are large enough for all land to be well out of sight, and the next marker may well be some 15 miles away. Any Cuban cruise will entail long passages on the inside, and with the auto pilot set you may go about other tasks, while always maintaining a lookout.

Hand-bearing compasses, while also useful for plotting marks and bearings on entry, will be useful if you wish to identify cays which show at a distance as you cruise past. You will find as you search for landfall among those cays that your eye-level above the water determines how soon you may expect to see them. Given the average height of the vegetation on the cays, we usually begin to pick them up from the bridge at about eight miles off, but your different height will determine your own distance. Make a few notes in the log, and you'll soon know exactly how far off you may expect to be before picking them up for yourself.

LOOK FOR CLUES FROM FISHERMEN

As you spend time pottering about in the cays looking for anchorages, or just feeling your way amongst coral heads and islands, you will begin to notice various clues that fishermen may have left to denote entrances and passages into the heart of the cays. The charts are incapable of showing all of the entrances to lagoons, or even the myriad passages through a closely packed group of cays, but local fishermen will have almost certainly explored the area at some time. They may well have left markers in the form of "whithies" (branches haphazardly

Typical "whithy":
Port or starboard?

stuck into the bottom), or perhaps a buoy made from a floating bottle of bleach. At first you may be somewhat skeptical about using some branch or even a large twig as a navigation mark, but they usually mean something significant, so take note, and regard them as privately maintained channel marks. As they are used by small shallow draft boats, sometimes powered by oars or simple sails, your trick is to determine if they show a deep enough channel for you and which side you should pass.

Often you will find that in one particular area all the marks should be passed on the left, but a little further on, the opposite convention applies. Use your observation, and feel your way if the water is shallow, always being ready to instantly back off in the event of approaching critical depth. As before, binoculars can be useful in scanning the surface further ahead for signs of absolutely flat water, mangrove tips sticking up, birds wading, or other warning signs. Depth alarms should be set on the echo sounder, and you should observe them, rather than developing a tolerance for their squealing.

Of course, if you're inside a large gulf like Batabanó, or even Guacanayabo in the south, then the main passages are likely to be well marked, showing deep channels through and into commercial harbors. These lights and buoys are usually well maintained, but as with all man-made aids to navigation you should not rely on them absolutely.

Incidentally, the larger structures (sentry box lights) can have small concrete storerooms atop the legs with equipment inside for servicing their lights. The whole affair is usually painted in a color denoting which side you pass on. In many cases, however, in spite of the best efforts of deterrent spikes, seabirds such as cormorants will perch on the platforms to dry their wings, and their droppings can totally obscure the original color. Indeed, due to this camouflage, some may even become almost invisible in the distance.

Inside the cays you are likely

to have much to distract you, what with cruising past deserted beaches on paradise islands and cups of tea being handed up from below. If like us, your attention wanders frequently while you scrabble about on the cockpit floor for that dropped biscuit, then it is as well to be prepared for the occasional grounding. The bottom can, in places, shelve so gently that the color does not noticeably differ from 10 minutes ago and besides... wasn't someone else looking?

RUNNING AGROUND

As mentioned before, we keep our depth sounder's alarm set. And amongst coral we like to give ourselves a goodly couple of feet of leeway, while keeping a rigid nomistake lookout, and steering clear of coral heads which could well puncture a hull. However, cruising above the turtle grass or sand of the inner sound, and feeling out an unfamiliar entrance to some lagoon with the alarm on the bare limit, we have occasionally come to a lurching stop. The key here to getting off is to get the power down as soon as possible, letting fly the sheets on a sailboat, or dropping the revs and putting the engine into neutral at once. If your speed was low in the first place, then it may be a simple task of backing off, but if this does not work then sterner measures may have to be taken.

A couple of strong crew members in the water may well provide enough force when pushing from the bows to assist the engine, while on occasion a rocking movement from side to side has also proved successful in dislodging our boat. Extreme care must

be taken here, and good communications between the helmsman and those in the water is essential, while needless to say, only a responsible adult should be in control of the motor to prevent what is only a minor event from becoming a life threatening disaster. It is as well to note that there isn't much in the way of tide inside the cays, so your vessel will not be left keeled over on its side, and unless the incident took place at dead high tide, there may still be enough to lift it off later. You may often find it best to just wait.

If none of these methods prove successful, then stop the engine to prevent it sucking in silt through the intakes and apply the kedging off technique, which essentially means that an anchor is taken out away from the boat by foot or in a dinghy and lowered to provide a point from which force may be applied, perhaps via one of the boat's winches.

Yachts may be heeled well over sideways, either by crew members hanging onto the boom swung far outboard, or by a rope attached at one end to the tip of the mast and at the other to a block on an anchor securely embedded in the bottom. Don't worry, the mast can take it. This may decrease the draft enough to allow the engine, or another anchor astern to drag the vessel off.

If these still fail, there is always the likelihood of decreasing the weight at the point where the vessel is most firmly grounded. A substantial amount of weight can always be found at one end of the boat or the other, and in relays this can be moved aft quite quickly and easily. Scuba tanks,

Better guess right about which side you pass a whithy! South Cuba.

anchors, rolls of spare line, bags of diving equipment, spare fuel, tools and other items can easily add up to a couple of hundred pounds, and not only will you have removed the weight from the affected area, but in transferring it to the other end you will still further lift the lightened area.

Having made sure you have already placed your anchor *off* the stern, that line should be under tension to prevent further grounding, and a crew member should pull it in quickly as the engine powers the boat backwards, and so prevent it from wrapping round the propeller shaft.

If all of this alarms you, then please remember that to compile this guide, we run aground almost as a matter of routine.

BEWARE OF FLOATING NETS

While on the subject of wrapping things about the shaft, we have come across a multitude of nets with floats strung along just below the surface. These seem to have no common denominator, being made from easily seen white polystyrene, or difficult to see cork, in equal quantities. There are fleets of fishing vessels which operate nets in the Gulf of Batabanó, or other similar large protected bodies of water; and the vessels range in size from large ferrocement or steel boats of over 60 feet down to smaller wooden craft around the 35-foot range, all with a couple of dinghies as tenders.

Cuban fisherman.

The mother-vessels play out their nets, while the dinghies arrange it neatly in the water and attend to lobster pots some distance away.

It must only be our imaginations, but it seems that they only begin their maneuvering to lay out the nets as we approach, causing much swerving and swearing under our breaths, so be aware of this little foible. It's worth noting that sometimes the nets are floating some four or five feet below the surface, and we have safely passed over them on occasion, but I'm sure it's only a matter of time.

Then there are the lobster pots, which in some areas are as thickly laid as in the Florida Keys. Not only will you see the floats bobbing on the surface, but there will be passages on which you may see what appear four-foot square objects on the bed below as you pass. A quick drop over the side with a snorkel will show them to be full of lobster awaiting collection. Under no circumstances should anyone ever molest fishermen's gear. If you do, you deserve all you get, and additionally may bad karma be upon you. God, after all, will see.

PLAYTIME AMONG THE NATURAL WONDERS

While cruising those same gulfs in the south, like us, you may be forced to dodge what appear to be large translucent lobster-pot floats just below the surface. Finally, losing patience after 20 or 30 occasions, you will slow down to discover that they're in fact jellyfish rhythmically pulsing along their way and were it not for having thoroughly irritated you already, they might appear quite beautiful.

And then there are those silver-gray torpedoes, which burst out of crystal waters to leap and skim across the wavelets, while dancing on their tails and turning sharply. They're the houndfish and their smaller cousins, the needlefish. Sometimes these aptly named needle-nosed beauties will put on their display twisting and turning for a hundred yards or more, while you look on fascinated, and wonder what would happen if they ran into your inflatable.

At rest over the sand in the cays, you may find an inquisitive stingray taking his pleasure below your vessel, much in the same way that the barracuda takes his in the deeper waters over the wall, but outside the reef. Don't be frightened as you'd have to be startlingly unlucky to ever be molested by either of these much maligned creatures.

Try feeding the seagulls from your hand as they sail in low overhead, cocking their heads sideways to check on you. With patience it can be done.

An interesting behavior can sometimes be observed outside the reef where occasionally a pair of gulls will take up station 50 feet or more above the bows. They're waiting for flying fish to be flushed out of the water into flight, and as they do this, the gulls swoop like fighter planes twisting and dodging in pursuit between the waves. Sometimes they win, and sometimes they merely splash down to rearrange their feathers with an embarrassed look.

ANCHORING AND ANCHORAGES

As noted elsewhere, shelter may be usefully sought near the reef if you don't wish to venture far inside to seek out a temporary anchorage. Even if there are breakers on the reef outside, it's fair to assume that the force of the waves will be dissipated before crossing it. We have found that overnight anchorages here are surprisingly comfortable, while in addition you maybe assured that there will be no mosquitoes. Lobster may well be found in the lee of the reef under coral ledges, so while diving the anchor why not go take a look?

One advantage of this anchorage is that speedy exits are possible if you need to make a long outside passage the next day, but in this case, good bearings and an easy exit channel are required if you're going to be leaving in the dark. If you've just come in, it may well be prudent in any case to take a bearing on the exit while it is fresh in your mind, as even in daylight uncertainty may have crept in, and you could waste time searching it out again.

SOMEWHERE TO DROP THE HOOK

Of course, you might prefer to anchor near any of a few thousand cays. Determine from the charts whether there is a handy lee in which to moor, or even whether there is a small inlet which might afford protection from all sides.

Often a closer look can show useful nooks where the charts are vague on the subject, so it pays to start browsing in advance. You don't want to be caught in fading light, and faced with a mutinous crew snarling back from the anchor while you say, "Hmmm, not here either. Maybe over there?".

Taking advantage of the lack of significant tides, we like to anchor with only a foot or two under the keel, and while bringing us into range of the local mosquitoes, it does allow us to get in close to the cays for both shelter and a certain peaceful communing with nature. But whatever, we always endeavor to be at rest before the light begins to go.

There have been occasions when due to our own greed, we pushed the day's journey to the limits and were faced with a low sun off the water, and into our eyes. At this point, no sunglasses will suffice and trusting to luck, while occasionally successful, cannot but result sooner or later in disaster. In fact, we have twice run aground in a perfectly familiar channel, due to a blinding low sun in our eyes.

Anchorage at sunset.

If you are into taking the dinghy ashore then you might as well be tucked in close so that later on a tired, and perhaps well-wined crew, do not have to do battle with anything more than their condition can handle. But be aware of potential wind shifts which can easily mean nightly 180-degree changes due to the kabatic effect. I well remember a memorable four-man barbecue one night on Cayo Blanco, where we each consumed two lobsters and three-quarters of a bottle of rum, then promptly fell asleep on the sand next to the smouldering embers. The four of us grudgingly awoke later to bury the ashes and mount a clammy dinghy out to the boat in ill-natured silence. Two hours later, I was forced awake by the banging of the rudder against its stops, as the wind shift swung the stern all the way round onto a bank near the shoreline! We were not happy campers that time; no, not at all.

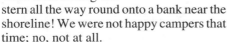

A fisherman manning the oars.

TRADES ARE PREDICTABLE

By and large, the trades will make for a fairly predictable breeze (and on the northeast coast will be hardly affected by the kabatic effect). In general, you can look to the western shores of a cay for shelter, but winds may rise sufficiently to negate your shelter, so be careful of bottom composition, which may have a bearing on the available holding.

We have touched upon the anchors you maybe carrying, but no amount of fancy anchors are going to make up for poor anchoring itself, so it's well to establish a good routine early on for this. Remember that an anchor which doesn't hold with the engine in reverse probably won't hold in a blow. Now it's obviously impractical to apply full revs if you're one of the overpowered brigade, but you must put enough force on it to know if it'll take strain, and to this end, we run our engine up to half speed, and if there is any doubt then take the engine a bit higher to see if there's movement. At the end of this exercise you should be able to get the rode tight enough to "thrum" under the strain.

DIVING YOUR ANCHOR

The subject of diving the anchor has been brought up before, but if you're going to be having a swim at eventide , then why not do it early enough to see where the anchor is, and how well it is dug in.

With a snorkel you can observe the anchor's behavior under stress, and if it repeatedly pulls out of turtle grass before your very eyes, then there's always the option of swimming down to it and either forcing it in by hand, or placing it right side up in a depression or a gully into whose sides it can dig. The anchor will weigh a lot less below water, so this is certainly not as difficult as it sounds.

You really want the flukes of your anchor to get right down below the surface, so as to pull the anchor further in. Anchors seem to dig in a lot better where the bottom is not covered with a mat of grass, so this process is probably going to be easier in sand or heavy mud, but there's not going to be a lot of mud on this trip.

In regards to coral, your anchor will get a good grip on something here, but you must be extremely careful about the rode being sawn through on something else if there isn't enough chain to keep the rope off the bottom, so be careful. At these times you're grateful for the extra chain you've fitted to the anchor rope, or that all-chain rode, but to be honest there will be few occasions when you need to anchor overnight on coral.

In fact, you should try to avoid anchoring in coral as it causes irreparable damage to live coral, so the extra weight of an all-chain rode may be an all around disadvantage. A combination chain/rope anchor rode would seem to be best, unless you have a good winch.

We'll want the angle of pull to be nearly horizontal on the anchor, so be sure to pay out enough so that the curve of the rode under tension lies as flat as possible along the bottom (weight is one of the functions of the chain at the business end). For normal purposes, you should have about seven times the distance from anchor roller to the bottom. If anchoring in six feet, with an additional four feet from the waterline to the roller, use around 70 feet of line. In dodgy bottoms, or cases of high winds and waves, then you should let out 10 or 12 times the distance so that the rise and fall of the bows will not wriggle the anchor loose.

Of course, if the wind is getting up you may need two anchors out, so here's where your spare comes in handy. Most serious cruising yachts keep twin rollers with two anchors in the bows, but if yours is not so equipped, then you should have at least 200 feet of rope/chain permanently bent (attached) to your spare, and the whole lot close at hand for emergency deployment. It will not do to have it in some inaccessible spot, so keep it clear of junk and the like. You deploy this one by lowering your primary anchor, and then under power moving some distance at right angles to the wind, to lower the second on. Allow the boat to drift back, and make fast when you have played out as much rode as possible, and hope for an angle of about 10-20 degrees between the two.

This is a good time to record GPS readings, or a series of bearings with a hand-compass to compare later on at night when a worried looking guest comes to shake you awake, and a note of the depth will also go a long way to reassure him. Of course, allowance should be made for the swing of the boat too.

All these precautions may seem excessive at first, but you will probably have need to remember them later on if you neglect your duties here.

One summer we anchored near the northeast corner of the Isla de Juventud (or "Pines" if you prefer) in a rising wind. We brought our boat to within about 150 feet of a nice, broad screen of unbroken cays with vegetation reaching at least 40 feet high for protection, then dropped anchor (a Bruce), set it somewhat casually and retired below to supper, a cup of tea, and the first three tapes of *The Hitchhiker's Guide to the Galaxy*.

Two hours later as the wind now sang in the in the darkness, I casually glanced at the depth sounder. It read 18 feet! And we'd recorded seven feet earlier on!

Still there was no thought of panic, until the restarted GPS showed a difference of over half a mile!

We battled back as close in as before, and hung out two anchors this time, with an extra 50 feet, but we still slid out again.

The second anchor (a Danforth) had seemed to be holding well by the look of the line, until I merely grasped the rope and pulled by hand. It came in so easily that I gasped, "The damn thing's come loose from the shackle!", and looked about for someone else to blame.

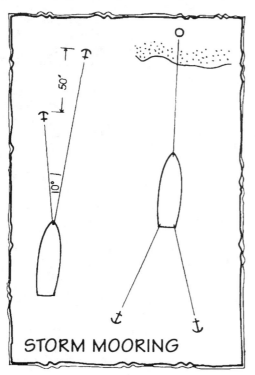

STORM MOORING

It was still there, however, firmly attached to the chain at the end, but planing and sailing smoothly over the thick mat of turtle grass below.

It took us a few tries, but we finally set the main anchor properly, and its rode hummed all night, but this time didn't drag.

That night in the dark we hadn't been able to see any shoreline, so we couldn't tell where we were apart from our earlier records, and we were lucky to have picked up the drift before it became serious, and luckier still that the wind hadn't swung round.

AT ANCHOR

A good routine should be established here so you won't forget anything, and while the boat is being put to bed, so to speak, the final entry in the log should be written up.

I know this point has been harped on, but it's such a simple thing to do, only taking a minute while the details are still fresh in your mind, and hey, do it while someone else is doing all the real work!

The boat having been settled, the crew can drop over the side for a swim (water temperature off the coast of Cuba will be around 82° Fahrenheit in the cays), and if there was any doubt about the anchor, it can be inspected by snorkel. It's unlikely you'll be in water much over 10 feet at anchor, so you'll have a good view, and if it's not well dug in you can have someone aboard run up the motor to rearrange it while you're in the water screaming instructions no one understands.

Turtle grass is host to a surprising amount of life if you take the time to hover motionless above and drift lazily. You'll probably notice conches, good to eat, raw in salads or stewed (ask a fisherman to show you how to get the meat out). Then there are anemones, sea urchins lurching slowly amongst the vegetation (a good reason not to jump in so deep that your feet get punctured), equally slow moving starfish and multicolored fishes who get friendlier with familiarity. There's a lot more too as you get in close to the shoreline into about two feet of water.

Look for the depressions and gullies, duck-dive down, and look under the ledges. As a coral reef diver, I was stunned by the life in an area I'd previously thought practically uninhabited.

If you're anchored in deeper water or over sand and coral, you'll find a practical use for the early evening swim if you keep a speargun aboard. Your spear is, after all, the only piece of scuba equipment you'll ever buy which actually pays its way!

Take only what you need, and remember fish are magnified 25 per cent by the water, so don't bring back something which is undersized.

There are plastic fish identifying cards and waterproof books which you may even take with you to consult under water, and these will add immensely to your pleasure as you'll remember a lot more if you can actually put a name to the fishes. We keep aboard a couple of books to consult in greater detail later, and they're the most popular references at anchor.

A TIME TO RELAX

Back on board, you can dry off with a towel solely dedicated to seawater use, or take a quick shower if you've got the water to spare, and then relax with a drink.

If you're into mixers, then actually keeping the sodas in the 'fridge will necessitate less ice, so keep it stocked up during the day when perhaps the engine's alternator or the solar panel is putting out lots and lots of volts, which can be usefully used for cooling. And of course, it will cause lots of aggravation if whoever used all the beers didn't replace them. However, don't do that now. At this time the 'fridge should only be opened for taking stuff out, and it should be closed immediately.

Don't stay below, even if the day has been hot and sunny, this is when it cools down, and the time spent on deck in the twilight hours with a cool drink in hand will be the abiding memory of your trip; long after you've forgotten that cobbled street with the old cathedral at the end.

If you feel like it, this is a good time too for fishing as the fish begin to feed, and with skill and luck you might find you've got a self sustaining boat.

Of course, speaking of fishes and fishing, there are always the occasional visits from friendly fishermen who may be in the area. Their boats stay out away from harbor for days on end, and like anyone else after a while they get bored. You can pass hours on end, if your command of Spanish is anything more than basic, and if you have a genuine liking for gossip.

The advice, information and just plain fun that can be had alongside a salt stained wooden fishing boat can't be recreated anywhere else, and as a further benefit you'll find almost unlimited opportunities for bargaining for seafood.

LISTEN TO WEATHER FORECAST

As darkness descends we still have the weather forecast on shortwave to attend to, and maybe you should try to fit it in while supper is being cooked. Remember, there's an irritating gap in the shortwave broadcasts between 8 p.m. and midnight, so don't get caught out if intending an early night and an early morning departure (see Pg. 49 for schedule).

On the shortwave, it's always best to listen to the forecast areas nearby, and to blend them into one if you're near the border between two sea areas.

More conveniently, on the northwest coast, you'll be able to pick up the Key West transmissions on VHF (Wx) at any time, but if listening to the VHF forecast, then you may have no choice but to extrapolate somewhat for the weather in your area.

Finally, as you prepare to shut down for the night, you can help with conserving both water and electric power by turning off the master switch to the water pump (leaking joints) then restocking the 'fridge with soft drinks and filling the ice trays. These

Courtyard in Trinidad, South Cuba.

will then have a chance to freeze overnight as the 'fridge won't be opened again.

GOING ASHORE BY DINGHY

Well, you've been lugging the dinghy all over the place, so why not get your money's worth?

Getting the inflatable into the water is the easy part, but the engine can be a bit more difficult, and many are the men who have dropped it in by mistake. If you took my advice about power to the extreme, you may well have an outboard at the limits of not just your stretch, but your strength!

It takes but a moment to fasten a line to the transom brackets, and this way if you do drop it in (you will one day), you can get it out a moment later. Don't worry, take the plug out to clear inside the cylinder, and sooner or later it'll run again, even though you may have to drain the carburetor floatbowl if it's in for any length of time. Pour bowls of fresh water over the motor and spray it down thoroughly with one of those magic water-dispersing sprays they sell.

Everyone has their own method of mounting the outboard, but in all cases you should tie the dinghy in close so it won't drift away as you handle the motor, and make sure you have a good footing before beginning the process.

Before going ashore for a picnic, you might rather fancy a couple of nice fat lobsters, and if everyone partakes in the hunt, then the whole crew will have even more fun later on.

You're going to be looking for areas of coral which have overhangs under which lobster like to shelter, so trickle the dinghy in a search pattern, looking down at intervals for the patches which seem to have potential. Someone can drop over the side with a mask, or just lie over the sides and look down. When you're in a really good area you'll maybe see their antennae waving out from below the ledges, but in any case, if there are likely overhangs, then drop a mushroom anchor, and someone should go down for a look. See the last chapter for descriptions of how to catch them, and the kids can stay aboard the dinghy to mind the goody bags if they aren't going to be involved.

Ashore you'll always be able to find some driftwood to build a fire, but don't go overboard and build a hazard to the environment. Make a low wall of rocks around the fire, leaving a gap through which air can enter to support combustion, and you can bury foil-wrapped fish or lobster in the hot embers for a few minutes to enjoy food cooked in its own juices. You may, of course, prefer to just impale your prepared catch and cook it above the flames, being careful not to scorch it.

These affairs are inevitably marked by someone or the other stepping on a hot ember in bare feet, so if a glowing coal spits out of the fire, don't just shove it into the sand with a stick and cover it with a sprin-

A French-Canadian catamaran at anchor in Manzanillo.

kling. Bash its life out with a big rock if you can't get it back into the fire, and bury it deeply.

Please remember that you are a visitor in someone else's country, and as such, are also responsible for the image of your own. So make sure you don't leave litter or do anything that might be construed as vandalism. Make sure the embers are all well covered with sand, and clean the area of any signs of your presence. Even if it doesn't affect *you*, your behavior will certainly affect those who come behind you.

On a more somber note, most boating accidents take place when not actually aboard your vessel, so always be careful in dinghies, and especially if you're somewhat judgment impaired after a good evening ashore.

Whether or not you take the dinghy aboard will be your own call based on your condition at the time, but remember that it can be a hindrance later on in the water.

MORNING PREPARATIONS

You might like to pick up the shortwave forecasts while breakfast is being prepared so you can discuss the weather later on like any civilized couple ashore, except that here it's more than just a polite interest . You'll need it to plan the day's sail.

Afterwards, with the table cleared, the charts can come out and the passage looked at in detail. Remember that while plotting your courses, it will be a good idea to make jottings in a passage notebook showing bearings, cays and anchorages along the way.

Even if the day's passage is not expected to be rough, the vessel should still be made as shipshape as if it were putting out to sea. Clear the decks of all those drying towels, or if they just have to be left out, then at least make sure they're fastened to the lines.

We make exactly the same checks every day on the engine, and this can be done by one person while the other sets about the other aspects of departure preparation.

The engine's oil and water must always be checked, as must the water-pump/alternator belt, and any topping up or tightening should be done as soon as needed. It's a good idea to make exactly the same log-entry detailing oil, water, fuel, and belt checks at the beginning of each passage so there is no danger of forgetting them. If the belt shows signs of wear, then it should be replaced before it breaks and subsequently causes a rise in engine temperature.

While this is going on, the cockpit can be arranged by someone else. Plotting instruments can be laid out, navigation instruments turned on, pencils sharpened, and binoculars, cushions, caps, sunglasses and other gear all need setting out as well.

Raising anchor can be a strain on the elderly or the just plain bad-backed, so if you don't have a winch, then go ahead slowly, and do pay attention to the bowman's directions. This can be an ill-tempered job, so try to look sympathetic too. It will help to allow the person up front to occasionally make a few turns around the post with the line, and rest for a minute or two before you slowly go ahead again.

When the chain hangs down vertically, you may sometimes need to power the boat right over it to break the anchor free, but if it still won't come loose, then you might just have to take a look with a mask on. If you habitually anchor near coral, then you should have a buoyed tripline fastened to the other end of the anchor. You can haul on it to reverse the angle of pull, and draw the anchor out backwards. If you have to abandon the anchor temporarily, the buoy will mark the spot too.

Don't allow the more discolored splashes of water brought up on the anchor rode to remain for long on the deck. Mixed with a little organic matter they can be the very devil to remove later, so brush it into the scuppers with a wet deck-broom.

In the relative calm that follows raising the anchor, and while the engine is still coming up to temperature, a final glance round the decks is in order to see that all has been put away.

The anchor should be pinned and the ropes coiled, while if a boathook or a broom is lying about on deck, it will go overboard as soon as the first wave hits.

AND FINALLY

In addition to the last couple of chapters, there will be further advice scattered throughout this book (sometimes not in any logical order), and information given in one chapter is also probably applicable to another where similar circumstances exist. Read all the chapters through, even if you only plan to cruise one particular area.

The following chapters will describe passages around the coastline and through the cays, but they will not give every route possible. For better enjoyment of your particular cruise you should use them as a guide only, deviating as and when the fancy takes you.

Please, in the instance of discovering new (hopefully better) passages and anchorages, update the author (I may always be contacted through the publishers). While if you also discover errors or glaring omissions, I would be grateful for prompt corrections, which may benefit future editions.

Many of the drawings shown later are subjective and made clandestinely or from memory, as there have been occasions when

Girls rowing in the morning mist at Cienfuegos.

I have not thought it wise to sit in full view of the Guarda Frontera making sketches of what might possibly be considered sensitive locations. Forgive the cruder aspects, they have all been done with the best of intentions, if not always under the best of circumstances.

Cuba is changing daily. New vistas are opening up as you read this, not only in the world of cruising, but more importantly in the social aspects of day to day and political life. All these have a bearing on the future of not only Cubans, but visitors as well. Please bear this in mind as you cruise, and take delight in the fact that you are indeed part of that change.

This man refills disposable lighters with hair spray... It works fine.

CHAPTER IV

PLANNING YOUR ROUTE

O n our first visit to Cuba a couple of years ago we didn't know a thing about the country. We just turned up, cruised the island, and took our chances. We didn't know what we would find, but what the heck, we had time to spare.

You on the other hand, having been graciously allowed two weeks paid vacation, might still be counting on returning to your job and finding it there. Perhaps it would be best if you managed your time better than us.

If it is just a stop off along a greater route, all well and good, but if your journey is a holiday cruise, then what you want from it will determine where you go on it.

So, just what are you expecting from your trip?

WHERE YOU WANT TO GO

Your own particular route is going to be determined by two major factors which we will discuss later; wind and current. But within those parameters...

A HOLIDAY CRUISE ON THE NORTHEAST COAST

For a holiday cruise with lots of snow-white beaches for the kids, hotels, entertainment, a marina berth and assorted tourist facilities, your best bets are along the north coast. This would start in Varadero, and looking east, along the cays where the the newer self-contained, hotel/resorts are being constructed. Varadero, in fact, has a convenient airport from which you can fly to any part of Cuba, as well as offering regular sheduled flights to Nassau, Bahamas. This is very convenient if you need to get to the U.S. quickly, as from Nassau there are countless daily flights to Ft. Lauderdale.

From Varadero you may visit Havana by road.

Much further east, after the cays, the coast is deeply indented with huge "pocket bays" evenly spaced about a day's sail apart.

HEADING WEST FROM HAVANA

Going the other way, west from Havana where the cays stretch out along the north coast of Pinar del Rio province, your vacation takes on a different aspect. The few resort areas that do exist here are smaller. Any cruise in this area might require a bit more self sufficiency, but the cays are far more accessible and the waters more easily

A Varadero beach scene.

navigable. This would be the best bet for a short trip over from the U.S. if you wish to combine cruising the cays with a few days spent in Havana.

THE MAGNIFICENT SOUTHEAST CLIFFS

At the other end of the island in the extreme southeast, the coast is unlike any-where else in Cuba. Sheer cliffs, rocky walls undercut by the pounding surf and enormous boulder strewn mountains sweep-ing right down to the sea. There is also the historic city of Santiago (the "Heroic City" in modern Cuban mythology), from where a rental car provides easy access inland to the prehistoric parklands and valleys. This coastline is without a doubt the most spec-tacular in the whole of Cuba, and has har-bors evenly spaced out along it.

THE INNER CURVE OF THE SOUTH COAST

Split into an eastern and western section,

the inner curve of the south coast is ringed with cays on both sides of the Island of Juventud (itself easily as large as most of the British West Indian islands). Along the coastline, far inside the two major gulfs, the historic city of Trinidad and other notable ports offer communication by road and rail to Havana and the rest of Cuba. Behind Trinidad, there is a beautiful range of tall mountains which can be visited by road. Cayo Largo is the only tourist resort out among the deserted keys, and communica-tion to the mainland from some of these can require a journey of a day or more.

Being so vast and due to its location, this area will require the most commitment from a cruiser but is also the most rewarding.

THEN THERE IS HAVANA

Havana itself is worth a separate visit if you've only got a week, or even if you've just got a long weekend.

WHAT DETERMINES YOUR ROUTE

WINDS

As you can see from the table on Page 97, the predominant winds around the coasts are from the east, with swings to the north-east (especially during periods of low pres-sure). The winds are regular and can be counted on about 70-80 percent of the time, and the days on which you might expect turbulence are concentrated in the summer months. There are five locations shown from which you can calculate what you might reasonably expect in any of the main cruising areas.

Note: The wind directions shown are median monthly directions, and *not* shown in the tables are the frequent swings to the southeast and northeast under the influence of low barometric pressure. Neither are the high winds from the north and northwest, when the cold fronts come sweeping through in winter.

There are also short local disturbances in May and November which affect the north and south coasts. The Gulf of Batabano is

especially affected by a west or southwest wind called "La Virazon" by local fisher-men. This wind can be accompanied by storms and small cyclones. It is considered a harbinger of further periods of bad weather. The Gulf of Ana Maria on the south coast is also subject to short periods of high winds during the mornings in springtime.

However, heavy storms (while not *rare*) are unusual. You should not be overly pre-occupied if you miss a forecast or two, as long as you do not make it a habit.

HURRICANE SEASON

One cannot discuss the weather in the Caribbean without mentioning hurricanes, so we had better get it over with. Apart from advising a certain caution over the question of traveling down to the West Indies in the season, there's not a lot that one can advise here.

The hurricane season begins in June and lasts until the end of November. In the unlikely event of a hurricane coming in, its normal path would be along a northwestern

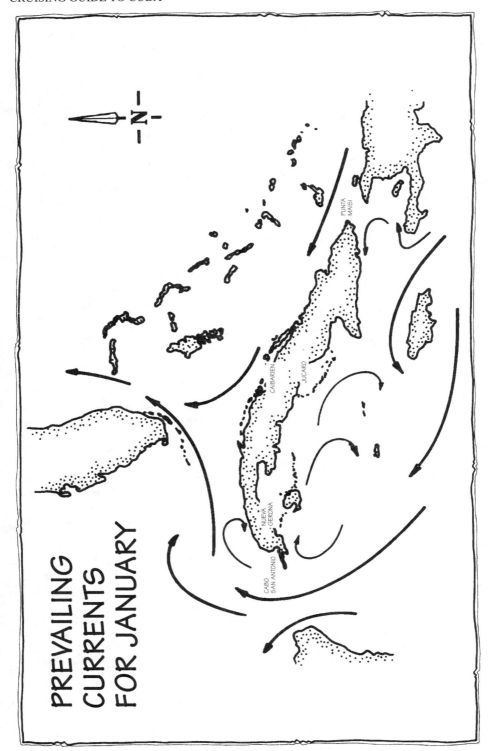

PREVAILING
CURRENTS
FOR JANUARY

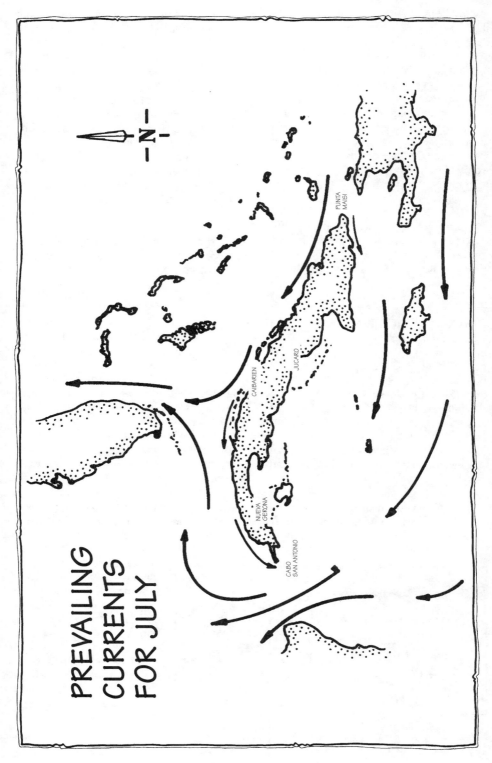

PREVAILING CURRENTS FOR JULY

PUNTA MAISI

CAIBARIEN

JUCARO

NUEVA GERONA

CABO SAN ANTONIO

N

track. The main shelters available are along the north coast, where there are several deep pocket bays with high steep walls.

You probably would not be heading down to the West Indies during that season, but it is comforting to know of the existence at these refuges.

Along the southeast coast there are a couple of really good refuges like Chivirico and Santiago, but as mentioned before there is not much that one can do in the event of a direct hit. Instead, apply all your energies to getting out of the way.

CURRENTS

A major influence while passaging along the coast is the current found on both coastlines.

As a general rule, the Bahamas Current comes in from the east and sweeps up alongside the northeastern coast. There it gets necked down and speeded up by the venturi between the Bahamas and Cuba.

A small quantity of this current is earlier diverted west along the extreme southeastern coast, seeking to join the current which flows up along the southern side of the island chain. However, here it meets a different current closer into the coastline. This small countercurrent, flowing eastwards along the Cuban coastline, diverts it down to the southwest before finally hitting Mexico. There it becomes the Yucatan Current and squirts northeast as the beginning of the Gulf Stream.

It is as well at this point to look at the drawings of the currents on the adjoining pages as this will make it clearer.

CONCLUSIONS

CIRCUMNAVIGATION

This guide is formatted to allow a logical progression with one cruising area leading naturally into an adjacent area. That way, the reader may guess relatively easily where the information he seeks is located. Thus, the guide will be approached as though the reader were actually conducting a circumnavigation of the island.

Taking the **anticlockwise** (or counter clockwise) route, we note that the south coast is largely made up of cays. Through these easily navigable waters the average yacht might wish to meander. Courses would therefore be off the wind for much of the time. The prevailing easterlies would be much modified by the shelter of the island. The current too, which might otherwise sweep northwest, is negated and even pushed back by the countercurrent described above. Then, coming around the eastern corner to turn west along the north coast, the sailor will find an exhilarating run with the current and winds favorable all the way.

The **clockwise** route would leave the sailor with the task of beating into stiff headwinds and currents east of Havana. At a glance the cays along the way might offer protection, but in fact the water inside those cays on the north coast is shallower than first appears and much of the inside route is not navigable by yacht. Along the south coast, journeying west, the winds would to some extent be favorable, but the current would not assist as much as might be hoped.

Conclusion: I would go *anticlockwise*; so that is how the rest of the book will be structured.

A sheltered small-boat refuge at Bahia de Cienfuego.

Photo on previous page, upper left and bottom by Mark Burrell / Zapotech

Photo opposite page and top by Mark/Burrell / Zapotech

TABLE OF WINDS

Compare place names with charts on Pages 94 and 95.

Cabo San Antonio	Jan	Feb	Mar	Apr	May	Jun	Jul	Aug	Sep	Oct	Nov	Dec
wind direction	E	NE	NE	NE	SE	SE	ENE	ENE	NE	NE	ENE	NE
speed	10	15	16	15	16	14	9	9	5	10	13	11
turbulent days	3	2	3	4	8	16	19	23	18	8	4	2

Caibarien	Jan	Feb	Mar	Apr	May	Jun	Jul	Aug	Sep	Oct	Nov	Dec
wind direction	E	NE	ENE	E	ENE	ENE	ENE	ENE	E	NE	NE	E
speed	13	14	15	15	12	11	14	13	11	12	13	12
turbulent days	5	2	1	3	11	12	10	10	13	8	2	1

Punta Maisí	Jan	Feb	Mar	Apr	May	Jun	Jul	Aug	Sep	Oct	Nov	Dec
wind direction	ENE	ENE	ENE	ENE	ENE	E	E	E	E	E	ENE	E
speed	17	16	18	23	20	16	23	20	18	16	22	23
turbulent days	1	1	2	2	6	6	5	4	5	4	1	2

Jucaro	Jan	Feb	Mar	Apr	May	Jun	Jul	Aug	Sep	Oct	Nov	Dec
wind direction	NE	NE	N	NE	S	NE	E	E	NE	NE	NE	NE
speed	24	22	19	21	21	12	16	14	14	17	23	24
turbulent days	0	1	1	3	12	16	20	20	21	12	3	1

Nueva Gerona	Jan	Feb	Mar	Apr	May	Jun	Jul	Aug	Sep	Oct	Nov	Dec
wind direction	E	E	E	E	E	E	E	E	E	E	E	E
speed	14	14	14	14	14	14	14	14	14	14	14	14
turbulent days	0	1	0	0	4	9	10	10	5	2	2	0

CRUISING SECTIONS

| CHAPTER 5 | Havana, Westwards to Cabo San Antonio |

This route will take the reader to the Marina Hemingway in Havana, then on to the cays along the northwest. On the way, the cruiser can stop overnight in Bahía Honda or Mariel, as the cays are too far to allow a daylight run to the first of them. Along those cays, there are docks at two small islands where there are wharves and hotel complexes, allowing an easy introduction to Cuban cruising. Westwards, there are more cays, and you may wish to anchor out overnight, or visit the mainland at a couple of the towns and ports along the way.

Finally, at the western extreme of the island there is the option of returning to Havana, leaving Cuba, or continuing on to the next section.

| CHAPTER 6 | Cabo San Antonio, Eastwards Along the Southwest Shoreline and Cays, to Cayo Largo |

Rounding the cape, this chapter takes the reader along the cliffs east to the bay of Corrientes and the dive resort of Maria La Gorda (Fat Mary). From here, it's an easy run towards a couple of towns on the mainland inside the Gulf of Batabano. Then we divert over to the Isla de Juventud where you might wish to rest for a day or two. Later we visit the stretch of cays ringing the gulf to end up in Cayo Largo, from which you may leave for the Cayman Islands or continue on.

| CHAPTER 7 | Cayo Largo to Cabo Cruz |

Leaving Cayo Largo, there are firstly the ports of Cienfuegos and Casilda. This last harbor serves the beautiful city of Trinidad, one of the two Cuban cities UNESCO has placed on its world heritage list (Old Havana is the other). From here, we cruise the spectacular, huge, deserted area of cays heading east, until we come to the mainland city of Manzanillo, finally stopping at Cabo Cruz.

| CHAPTER 8 | Cabo Cruz to Punta Maisi |

The next stretch is the most impressive in the whole journey, with sheer cliffs and mountains dominating the coast. Halts can be made at secluded ports along the way, stopping for a much longer time at Santiago. From here, the route continues on past the U.S. naval base at Guantanamo (you may even wish to enter the bay) until we round the cape at Punta Maisi on the southeastern tip of Cuba.

| CHAPTER 9 | Punta Maisi to Havana |

The last leg will be the fast northwest run up along the coast, past huge deep water bays with narrow entrances (some with cargo facilities further in). Although largely deserted, there are one or two holiday resorts and complexes dotting the beach-lined cays further along, with more being built. This is Cuba's premier vacation area, and we shall stop awhile in Varadero before the easy run up to Havana to complete our tour.

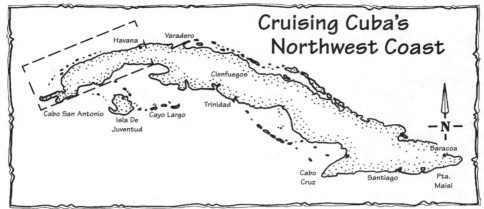

CHAPTER V

Cruising Cuba's
Northwest Coast

HAVANA TO CABO SAN ANTONIO
PASSAGING FROM MIAMI

The Capital and most interesting city in the country, Havana is usually the first port of call for any North American visitor. It isn't really the closest port to the U.S.A. — that distinction is held by Varadero, some 70 miles to the east — but nevertheless, it wins out most of the time, so this guide starts there too.

With the greatest respect to those who arrive from the rest of the West Indies, the majority of visitors to Cuba will at some stage pass through Miami, or at least its sister port Ft. Lauderdale. These are, after all, amongst the last halts on the North American continent where you can get every aspect of your boat seen to professionally. With regard to my earlier remarks on boat preparation, that's not such a bad thing; but nevertheless, much like the mythical Irishman who once responded to a stranger's request for directions by saying, "Well Sor, if I were going there, I wouldn't be going from here!". Neither should you, because a direct journey from Miami will needlessly expose you to endless slogging into the teeth of the Gulf Stream.

Instead, leave the port of Miami sinking under the Biscayne Bay horizon, head for the Florida Keys and make your crossing from Key West. You might as well take the inside route along the Intracoastal Waterway, stopping as you see fit in Marathon's Boot Harbor, Plantation Key, Big Pine, or any one of a dozen snug anchorages along the way. This way you'll get a chance to right whatever wrongs your friendly mechanic may have done you on the last service, before it becomes critical. You can call it a shakedown cruise within a cruise.

The weather forecast is easily obtained from the NOAA transmitters on VHF (the WX channels on your set), and they also give the position and strength of the Gulf Stream which you need for dead-reckoning. In addition, you can go upstairs at the airport in Key West where the cooperative staff will give you not only the latest weather, but a pretty good passage prognosis.

Note: You don't want to be caught with a rising wind in opposition to the stiff current which already exists as it'll only get rougher, so delay your journey if this is your first such crossing, and wait for relatively settled conditions. This can be an awful trip if you get caught out, so heed this advice well. If you encounter strong northeast winds you will also encounter large, square, waves. I have delayed for anything up to a week and never regretted it. On the other hand, in spite of misgivings, I've also sometimes jumped the gun and got walloped.

Your final day in Key West is best spent at dockside making your final checks on the boat. If you haven't filled those extra canisters of fuel I talked about then you can do it here at any of the marinas. Don't leave, as we always do, the fitting of larger bilge-pumps, batteries, and the like, to the last minute; but rather get everything sorted out in advance. Leaving on your first trip is stressful enough as it is.

BUT HAVANA'S *NOT* YOUR REAL PORT OF ENTRY

The first time we went to Cuba we thought the marina was at Havana which is a *big* mistake. In fact, although a direct course from Key West takes you close to the city, all foreign yachts are cleared in approximately nine miles west at the Marina Hemingway (23° 05.4N / 082° 30.6W).

Do not, under any circumstances enter Havana's harbor. It is foul, oily, smelly, and the officials will demand commercial docking fees just like you were some kind of a passenger liner! This is not a joke. I know of several yachtsmen who have been *towed* in and still regret it. Unless it is the direst form of emergency, resist all attempts to drag you there.

U.S. FORMALITIES

OUTWARD CLEARANCE

Over the last couple of years, the U.S. government has waived the necessity for obtaining outward clearance for its citizens, but (at time of writing) they are now temporarily obliged to obtain a permit to depart the "National Security Zone" established around the time of the downing of two light aircraft by Cuba in February, 1996. In spite of its intimidating name this is nevertheless a fairly straightforward process, and the **Key West Coast Guard** can fax you a copy of the form in advance. Contact them at the address or phone below:

The delay involved is about 24 hours, but to simplify matters they will fax you a form in advance. In turn, you may complete the form and fax it back. Conveniently, it will be approved, and kept on file for collection upon your arrival in Key West ready to depart. Attending to this beforehand will be of invaluable assistance if you are waiting on a weather window. It is not clear, at time of writing, just how long this form will be

required, so do not be surprised if by the time you call they just say "Huh?".

Do not worry about mention of being on file, 'cos of all people *I* should be worried, and no one's ever hassled me, and I live right here in the U.S.

For more on this, see my comments on the following pages.

One final point about departure regulations is that it will be of benefit if an American vessel purchases the US Customs User-Fee decal in advance ($25). This will considerably ease your subsequent return as you will probably be allowed to clear back in by 'phone, without the necessity for a formal visit.

A point to note well is that from here on you have **no passengers** and everyone aboard must be listed as crew on *these and all further documents*, both here and in Cuba.

Neglecting this will involve you in countless bureaucratic hassles, so short circuit the whole process by taking the easy way out.

RETURNING TO THE USA

Note: Upon arrival you may go alongside any of the commercial marinas, or even anchor out, without the necessity for calling in to Customs on VHF; but you must contact the authorities as soon as practical. The captain alone is allowed to go ashore to make a phone call to U.S. Customs and

USCG Group Key West
Trumbo Annex, Bldg.102
(*not* Truman Annex)
Key West, FL 33040
Tel. (305) 292-8727

Immigration Service. They will, in all likelihood, merely issue you with telephone clearance, but you may be required to go through a more formal process if they so choose. Either way, they will advise.

All foreign vessels or foreign nationals may follow this procedure too.

The toll-free numbers to call are on the bulletin on the adjoining page.

And equally, the U.S. Customs building is very conveniently downtown at:

U.S. Customs Service, 301 Symonton St., Key West. (Use the toll-free numbers to call).

Be aware though, that to enter the U.S., a foreign national will need a *valid visa* even if he is more accustomed to entering from Europe on the 90-day waiver scheme. Unlike the airlines, your boat is not a signatory to that treaty. You will need to get a visa at the large, supposedly nonexistent U.S. Embassy on the waterfront in downtown Havana. This, I know from experience does not take long (a morning should do it); and I even know U.S. yachtsmen who have received replacements for lost passports there too.

American passports and visas, issued in Havana! Kinda makes you think doesn't it?

Although the most common misconception held by North American yachtsmen surrounds their reception upon return to the U.S.A., I must categorically state that I have never received — or heard of anyone else receiving — anything but the most courteous and friendly treatment by the U.S. authorities in Key West.

Provided you have *no evidence aboard* of spending money in Cuba, both in the form of goods and receipts, no one need fear any reprisals by the authorities. The thousands of yachtsmen who have made the journey since the first publication of *The Cruising Guide to Cuba* in 1994 will attest to that.

Nevertheless, please note that you are *not presently allowed to bring in any Cuban goods at all*. For the sake of all, do not laden your boat with rum and cigars, subsequently get caught, and start to whine. Enough of this behavior will spoil the excellent relations presently enjoyed by Cuba cruisers and those U.S. authorities actually in the trenches. You may even get your boat confiscated for your pains if the quantity is seen to be sufficiently commercially oriented, and you know fully well what I mean by that.

Not should you, as a U.S. citizen, blithely declare that you have been spending money in Cuba. Under all kind of internal political pressures, the Treasury Department presently takes a dim view of this, so just declare that you have only consumed ship's stores and all will be well.

PASSAGE TO HAVANA

THE GULF STREAM

The direct course is 208°M (plus something added for the current) for 91 miles. This takes you from the final channel marker outside Key West, to the first channel mark

Street photographer Frederico Vera poses a couple on a Havana street.

at the marina (23°05.4N / 082°30.6W).

I don't wish to tell anyone how to navigate their boat, but for dead-reckoning you'll need to make some sort of allowance for the direction and strength of the Gulf Stream. Just where it is on any particular day is open to conjecture as you don't always come across it at the same place, but the VHF forecast gives its approximate location several times daily. The current will probably have a course of anything around 70°M, a strength of maybe two-to-four knots, and could be positioned anywhere from five to 40 miles off the Florida coast. This should be checked before making your allowance.

At best, it'll be a guess where you actually begin to be affected, so if you don't have an electronic navigation aid aboard,

DEPARTMENT OF THE TREASURY
U. S. CUSTOMS SERVICE
MIAMI, FLORIDA

MAY 13 1994

VES 4-DD:IC:S BHR

INFORMATION BULLETIN NO. 94-37

To   : Small Vessel Operators, Marina Operators, Other
           Interested Persons

Subject: Small Vessel Reporting Requirements

        Customs Regulations require pleasure vessel operators to
report to U. S. Customs immediately upon arrival in the United
States from a foreign port or place.

        Effective May 9, 1994, the requirement for small vessel
operators in the South Florida area to proceed to one of 28
designated reporting stations has been eliminated. Vessel
operators may now report from any phone they choose. (Note: the
Private Marine VISA Program is now no longer necessary and is also
being rescinded, effective immediately.)

        The following toll-free numbers are provided for use in
reporting arrival from foreign:

                1-800-432-1216   US Immigration Service KW
                1-800-458-4239   305-296-2233
                1-800-451-0393

        Vessel operators are reminded that only the master or owner of
the vessel may disembark to make his report of arrival. All others
must remain on board until clearance has been granted.

        Owners of pleasure vessels 30 feet long or longer must still
purchase a yearly Customs User Fee Decal, if the vessel proceeds to
a foreign port. The decal number will be required at the time of
reporting arrival from foreign. If the decal was not obtained
prior to departure for a foreign port, the vessel operator will be
directed to the nearest Customs office to purchase a decal within
48 hours of arriving in the U. S.

        We appreciate your patience and cooperation as we make this
transition away from designated reporting locations. We feel
confident that this change will be both convenient and functional
for the boating community.

                                        D. Lynn Gordon
                                        District Director

REPLY TO: DISTRICT DIRECTOR OF CUSTOMS, P.O. BOX 025280, MIAMI, FL 33102-5280

Information sheet valid for all foreign re-entries into Florida.

U.S. DEPARTMENT OF AGRICULTURE ANIMAL AND PLANT HEALTH INSPECTION SERVICE PLANT PROTECTION AND QUARANTINE	1. PORT REPORTING	2. FLAG/NAME OF VESSEL	3. DOCK
SHIP INSPECTION REPORT	Key West FL	Britain HOBBES my	Oceanside

4. FROM (Port and Country)	5. VIA		
MARINA HEMINGWAY CUBA			

6. ARRIVAL DATE	7. ARRIVAL TIME	8. INSPECTION DATE	9. INSPECTION TIME
JUNE 20 1996	Actual 0805 ETA	6-20-96	From 2155 To

10. NO. PASSENGERS AND CREW CLEARED	11. NO. PIECES OF BAGGAGE	12. PROPOSED DEPARTURE DATE
4		6-25-96

PROHIBITED AND/OR RESTRICTED AGRICULTURAL MATERIALS

13. COMMODITY	14. LOCATION	15. COUNTRY OF ORIGIN	16. SAFEGUARD AND/OR DISPOSITION PRESCRIBED
POTATOES		Cuba	EMBARGOED BY EXECUTIVE ORDER
TOMATOES			

SAFEGUARD NOTICE: While this vessel is in the territorial limits of the United States, no crew member or other person shall remove any of the following items except by specific permission of an agricultural officer: (1) fruits, vegetables, meats, or other animal products; (2) live plants; (3) live birds; (4) hay, straw, rice hulls, hold sweepings or dunnage; (5) garbage from food materials including rootcrop bags, meat wrappers, and other food containers. GARBAGE MUST BE KEPT IN COVERED, LEAKPROOF CONTAINERS INSIDE THE VESSEL'S RAILINGS AT ALL TIMES.

If any agricultural items are sealed, the seals are not to be broken or removed while this vessel is within territorial limits of the United States or the St. Lawrence Seaway except under direction of an Agricultural Officer.

WARNING NOTICE: The requirements above are specified in 7 CFR 330 and 9 CFR 94 and violations are punishable by fine and imprisonment. (7 U.S.C. 150gg)

17. I Fully Understand the Safeguards Prescribed Above (Signature of Responsible Ship's Officer)	18. TITLE	19. DATE
X	Captain	6-20-96

20. CONDITION OF GARBAGE CONTAINERS WHEN INSPECTED			DEFICIENT CONDITION CORRECTED	21. SHIP AREAS not INSPECTED	HOLDS INSPECTED (Identify)	22. LIVE ANIMALS/BIRDS ABOARD
COVERED	INSIDE RAILING	LEAKPROOF		☐ QUARTERS		☐ YES ☒ NO
☐ YES ☐ NO	☐ YES ☐ NO	☐ YES ☐ NO	☐ YES ☐ NO	☐ DRY STORES		Type:
				☐ PANTRY		Number:

APHIS MARPOL ANNEX V COMPLIANCE CHECKLIST

THE FOLLOWING OBSERVATIONS WERE MADE BY APHIS PERSONNEL AFTER INSPECTING VESSEL'S WASTE HANDLING PROCEDURES AND EQUIPMENT:

23.	☐ YES ☐ NO	Plastic materials requiring disposal are used aboard the vessel.		
24.	☐ YES ☐ NO	There are waste plastics in the vessel's trash for disposal ashore.		
25.	☐ YES ☐ NO	There is a functional incinerator or other disposal method aboard.	TITLE OF REPRESENTATIVE	PPQ BOARDING OFFICER INITIALS
26a.	☐ YES ☐ NO	Responsible vessel representative was requested to show garbage pickup receipt or other evidence of lawful disposal of plastics ashore.		
26b.	☐ YES ☐ NO	Responsible vessel representative produced garbage pickup receipt or other evidence of lawful disposal of plastics ashore.	TITLE OF REPRESENTATIVE	PPQ BOARDING OFFICER INITIALS

ALERT: Report the presence of Honey Bees (swarms or individual bees) to the nearest Agricultural Officer, telephone _____

27. REMARKS

28. SUBSEQUENT PORTS OF CALL (Notified)	NO. PASSENGERS	OFFICER'S SIGNATURE
ST Pete		

PPQ FORM 288   Previous edition may be used.
(JUN 92)

As you can see, "Hobbes'" potatoes and tomatoes were removed by a U.S. Department of Agriculture representative upon arrival in the states.

then you should allow the current to take you east towards Havana. This way, when you hit the coast you can just turn right. If you've never done dead-reckoning in current before, read up on it, and remember that what you allow should take into consideration your anticipated boat speed (haven't you been making notes on this in the various logs?). Don't be surprised if the actual allowance is well over 10 degrees. But plot it all out in advance, even if you do have a GPS set aboard, and enter it in your passage-notes.

One final note on this subject: Your sailboat will come almost to a dead stop as you get right into the heart of the Gulf Stream, with those hourly X's on your chart ever closer to each other. If you're getting nowhere slowly, then bear off to the east and get in close to the Cuban coastline, anywhere. There, you'll usually find a nice little counter current which you can follow in the correct (westerly) direction, right past Havana.

In spite of your apprehensions, no one will bother you if you do this.

KEEP AN UPDATE OF YOUR POSITION

If your boat is not a speedster, set your departure for the morning or early afternoon so that you leave in good light, allocate watches throughout the night, and arrive in the middle of the following day. You will be crossing the Florida Straits, one of the most heavily traversed stretches of water in this part of the world , but with due care there shouldn't be any problem. Any lights however should be closely monitored to ascertain the course and speed of the other vessel. And do not, like we've done before, mistake the rising moon for imminent collision, or falling stars for flares!

We like to update our position every hour, plotting the position on the chart, and especially on long featureless passages this can make for a welcome break in the monotony. If this is your first night passage, you might find it wisest if all watches were double-manned until at least the early hours of daylight when, if you're satisfied that all is well with the world, the crew can go below to nap in turns.

RADIO CONTACT

Having crossed what you believe to be the 12-mile limit, you may begin to call in on VHF channel 16 to the Marina Hemingway. If you receive no reply, merely continue onwards, calling in at regular intervals.

A recent (and most welcome) development is the radio post on the top of the hotel near the marina where someone will have a rudimentary grasp of English. They can see way out past the 12-mile limit, and sometimes even call *you* first, so keep your ears on good buddy. If you are in contact with the marina they'll want you to switch to the working channel 72 where you will be asked a series of questions about your vessel and passengers. They will then contact the various immigration functionaries so that all will be ready upon your arrival — See Chapter Two: *Entering the Country*.

Note: You'll also need to know how to spell the name of your boat in the International Phonetic Alphabet, a copy of which is found on Page 49.

In spite of the foregoing, it is not unknown for radio contact to fail. You will hear countless calls early in the morning on channel 16 to the Havana Morro (the Signal Station in the Castle) from various commercial vessels awaiting pilots, instructions, and the like. *They* rarely seem to receive any reply, so why should you?

Don't worry. No trouble will be made if you finally do arrive unannounced. It just entails a long(er) delay while the officials are being rounded up.

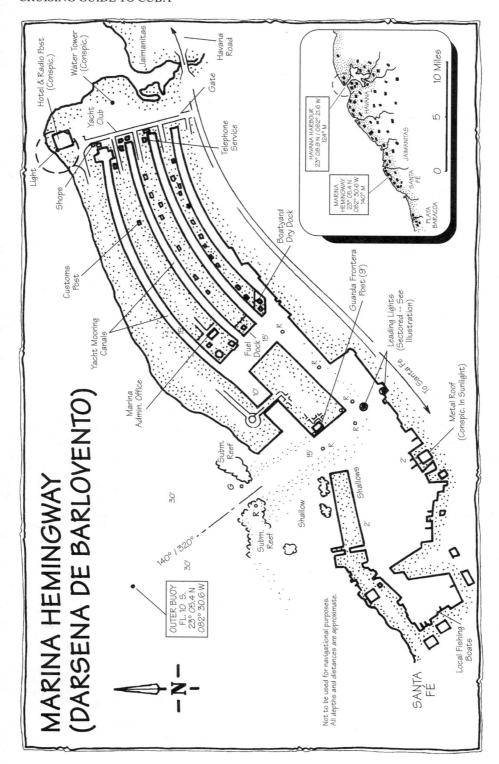

MARINA HEMINGWAY (DARSENA DE BARLOVENTO)

-N-

OUTER BUOY
FL. 10 S.
23° 05.4 N
082° 30.6 W

140° / 320°

30'
30'

Not to be used for navigational purposes.
All depths and distances are approximate.

Light

Shops

Yacht Club

Hotel & Radio Post (Conspic.)

Water Tower (Conspic.)

Jaimanitas

Havana Road

Gate

Telephone Service

Customs Post

Yacht Mooring Canals

Marina Admin. Office

Subm. Reef

Subm. Reef

Shallow

Shallows

Shallow

Fuel Dock

Boatyard Dry Dock

Guarda Frontera Post (9')

Leading Lights (Sectored -- See Illustration)

To Santa Fé

Metal Roof (Conspic. In Sunlight)

SANTA FÉ

Local Fishing Boats

G

R

R

R

R

R

R

R

R

15'

15'

10'

15'

2'

2'

HAVANA HARBOUR
23° 08.9 N / 082° 21.6 W
124° M

MARINA HEMINGWAY
23° 05.4 N
082° 30.6 W
140° M

HAVANA

JAIMANITAS

SANTA FÉ

PLAYA BARACOA

0   5   10 Miles

RECOGNIZING MARINA HEMINGWAY

The Marina Hemingway is situated a mile or so to the west of the Dársena (harbor) of Barlovento at the mouth of the river Jaimanitas, and just east of the town of Santa Fé.

It can be recognized at a distance by the large squat grey-white hotel block with the aforementioned radio post on top, three-quarters of a mile *east* of the marina; and then closer in, by the sun reflecting off a low curved metal roof just to the right inside the entrance. In any case you will be able to see the masts of yachts already docked inside.

While simple enough, the approach is guarded by a submerged reef not a quarter-mile offshore, so look for the large red and white marker-buoy (Fl.10s) at 23°05.4N / 082°30.6W in about 120 feet of water. Despite its size it is not always easy to spot, but it *is* there. Pass it close on your port side, then come in along a course of 140°M. lining up the range-markers inside the harbor, a leading diamond (R) and a trailing post (R/W spiral). This will take you a couple of hundred yards on, between red and green markers marking the gap through the reef. Here, the passage is dredged to about 18-20 feet and is only about 25 yards wide so do not stray off line until you are into the harbor proper.

An additional hazard which you will face are the snorkelers who spearfish around the entrance. Be on the lookout for them, from as far as the outer buoy.

NIGHT ENTRY

At night, the channel is marked by a sectored light which sends a precise, narrow beam, out along your course, *blinking at one second intervals*. If you see the yellowish/white light you're on course, and if you see red then you're too far to port. Equally, the green tells you that you're too far to starboard (see sketch plan).

CAUTIONS

While easy to enter in daylight and in calm conditions, do not attempt to enter the channel in very strong winds as you can surf right up onto the reef as some have done,

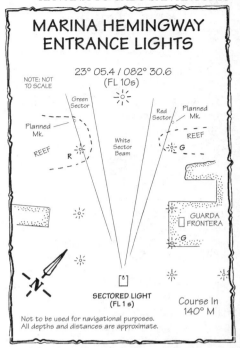

MARINA HEMINGWAY ENTRANCE LIGHTS

23° 05.4 / 082° 30.6 (FL 10s)

NOTE: NOT TO SCALE

Green Sector

Planned Mk.

REEF

R

White Sector Beam

Red Sector

Planned Mk.

REEF

G

GUARDA FRONTERA

G

N

SECTORED LIGHT (FL 1 s)

Course In 140° M

Not to be used for navigational purposes. All depths and distances are approximate.

terminally. Nor should you be confident of any or all of the lights actually being lit at the time. If the outer buoy is unlit it is almost impossible to pick up any of the other lights due to the background clutter at night.

I have entered both in inclement weather at night, and with the lights out, but only in emergency; and I would not willingly repeat either experience. The channel points northwest, and in high winds *large* waves surge in from the stern quarter making for an extremely treacherous passage. Combine that with trying to line up dim, blinking lights, set against backyard and street lighting and you have a recipe for disaster.

Ignore it later, when someone tells you at dockside that he's come in on 30-foot waves. Local characters abound at the marina.

A strange vehicle still in daily use.

ENTERING THE MARINA, CUSTOMS & IMMIGRATION
CHART NO. ICH 11424 (CUBAN)

The Guarda Frontera post is immediately inside on the left, and just past it, a stretch of concrete dock alongside which you can moor using uncertainly secured cleats. The wall here reaches up some five feet above water-level. There is a protruding top lip so you might wish to mount your fenders high; and if there is a swell entering, then station a crewman there to fend off.

You will understandably be a bit nervous, but don't worry, it's all been seen before. If you've earlier been in contact with the marina they will have notified the immigration officials who should already be on their way, and a marina representative will also accompany them to smooth your path. Wait on board for their arrival rather than walking over to the nearby swimming pool and demanding a beer.

You'll probably be tired, and even if you've already read the section on entering the country might not be prepared for the invasion of officials, but don't be alarmed. Handle things with aplomb by having all your documents ready and exhibit a gracious manner.

The whole affair should only take an hour or so if there is no problem, and even if there is, you will find that (unlike *some* foreign ports of call) the officials will try to sort things out as best they can.

Once clearance has been given you may take down the yellow Q-flag and proceed to the marina itself, so call them again on VHF 72 to say you'll be there in three minutes, and depart the dock.

From the Guarda Frontera post proceed slowly, only about 50 yards further on, then turn sharply port between the green shoreside mark on the corner and the large red marker-boxes in the water. Remember to keep a sharp eye out for the hordes of young swimmers who shin up those very structures to dive in from the top.

Turn port (NW) again 200 yards further down the line, and off your starboard bow will be the fuel docks and the marina offices.

You are now at:

MARINA HEMINGWAY
Calle 248 y 5 Avenida, Santa Fé,
Havana, Cuba.
Telephone: (53) 7-331150/56
(You may dial direct from the USA)
Fax. (53) 7-331536, 331149, 331831
(Mark name of yacht & skipper on top)

Sign at the Marina Hemingway gate.

Most foreign yachts dock along the outermost of three concrete-lined canals on the right (the closest to the sea) and heading there you should be especially cautious. There are always curious swimmers, small pleasure craft, and even maniac jet-skis in the basin which is only about 70 yards wide anyway.

The canal itself is narrower (about 60-foot), so enter carefully to starboard, and dock either where indicated by marina personnel or some other available space.

A couple of hints here:

1. If you moor close to the entrance (the *west* end of the canal) you will also be close to the marina's restaurant/disco whose noise will keep you up all night. If possible, move along at least 100 yards or more.

2. Although the canals hold some 15 feet of depth across their width, there are also occasional shallow spots tight alongside the dock walls in some berths. Ensure that your keel is not grazing these when you tie up alongside. Unless it has been recently rectified, this problem is particularly notably closer to the restaurant end, and also in the No.2 (inner) canal.

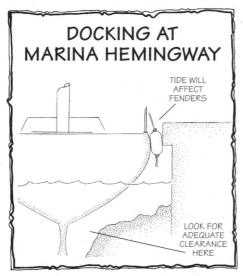

DOCKING AT MARINA HEMINGWAY

TIDE WILL AFFECT FENDERS

LOOK FOR ADEQUATE CLEARANCE HERE

3. Finally, the prevailing winds are from the east so if *your* cabin is aft then turn the boat round so the breezes can enter more easily for cooling. I once carried a max./min. thermometer in our cabin and it showed daytime temperatures of 104°F, and 80°F at night in mid September, although it is much cooler in winter.

Make up some cunning, skipper-like excuse to the rest of the crew in front who will not be aware of what you're doing, and tie up to the impressive cast-iron cleats.

Don't fret, because although the No.1 canal is about half-a-mile long, it has a turning basin at the far end if you don't feel like turning round in the channel.

Something else to look out for: The cleats are set back about a foot from the edge of the wall, so if there's a low tide with a bit of movement you can find your ropes being frayed where they run over the lip and down to your boat. Chafe-guards are called for.

THE MARINA STAFF

The first contact you will usually have with the marina staff in person will probably be the gentleman who indicates your dock space, takes your lines, sorts out all the power/water connections at dockside, and handles local gossip. Standard U.S. connections will probably be at variance with those used in Cuba so be prepared for your hose to leak, and for a rat's nest of bare electric connections to steam in the rain.

The marina will sometimes provide a dockside welcoming committee of sorts whose job it is to give you as much information as possible about the services offered. They are wonderfully friendly; but take everything they say with a grain of salt as they tend to make light of sometimes perfectly obvious problems and — certainly within each other's earshot — spout the official party line.

It is also, not unusual to receive a further visit from the medical staff or the local customs officials who are stationed in the marina. The medicos are letting you know they're there on call if you need them, and the customs are just bored. They too are a happy, friendly bunch, passing many an idle hour chatting with yachtsmen. No one stands on their dignity here, and if you are at all comfortable with Spanish this is where you're going to get a lot of handy information you wouldn't get elsewhere.

MARINA CHARGES AND SERVICES

Marina charges in mid-1997 were 40 cents/foot for dockage. Additionally there is a metered charge of 5 cents/gallon for water and 30 cents/Kw for electricity.

There is fuel available at around 65 cents/litre for diesel, 90 cents/litre for gasoline, and oil was $1.75/litre. For this, you have to move alongside the fuel dock to the south of the offices.

There are telephone hookups available too, and an increasing amount of yachtsmen are taking advantage of this. Those using this service receive their own extension number from the marina switchboard. You may even obtain cellular phone service if you've already brought your own 'phone!

You will, if cruising further afield, be expected to purchase a six-month Cruising Permit/Safety Certificate too for a sliding scale ranging from $25 for a 33-foot yacht to $100 for a 100-foot super yacht. The marina will handle all your requirements as regards documentation. Let the current take you lazily along and don't fight it. As mentioned before, you'll need a *Guia de Recalas* (list of stops). Remember it is not limited by

A rainy day in Havana.

time, so don't make it into a regid schedule, but rather just a vague route you'll be following, then hand it in to the marina office. This service is free to all.

Arrival of your documents will take about two days so start the process *at once* if planning to cruise the cays.

Note: Recently, a 10 percent gratuity has been showing up on your bill. This, tacked onto the total, is entirely optional at present and may be declined if you feel hard done by for some reason.

There is too, a six percent surcharge for paying by credit card (see earlier advice about cards), so try to pay in cash.

LEAVING THE COUNTRY

There are no exit fees:. You merely need to clear your bill then go back to the Guarda Frontera post to clear Customs and Immigration on the way out. No advance documentation is required, many skippers making the decision depending on last-minute weather judgements; but adequate notice will ensure that officials are actually there when you want them. Hang on to your Cuban outwards clearance document (the Zarpe) for U.S. inward clearance, and get rid of all others. Remember that to comply with regulations, no U.S. citizens on your crew should have any evidence of spending money in Cuba (goods or receipts) aboard.

A DESCRIPTION OF THE MARINA OPERATIONS

This is the first stop for the majority of visitors, so at the risk of burdening the reader who may want to get on with it, I'll give a somewhat expansive description of things in and around the marina. Other ports, later on down the line, will get gradually lesser versions as the reader becomes more familiar with things and how they work in Cuba.

In contrast to the six or seven foreign boats of a couple of years ago, when the first edition of this book was released, there are usually some 40-to-50 yachts moored along the canals now, along with a couple of Cuban sportfishermen which moor there between day-charters. Larger, super-yachts, which are visiting in increasing numbers, are usually berthed in the second canal from the sea, and the smaller transient boats on the outer canal when there is space.

The marina's office is open until 9.30 p.m. and situated between the outermost canals near the outdoor restaurant you passed on your way in.

Here, all aspects of your stay may be dealt with, including the documentation required for cruising. The amiable staff will order taxis for you and can advise on further travel inland if you so desire. We once had to leave our boat here for a month, and they were happy to hold our keys to enable the boat's bilges etc. be periodically checked. In fact you will be surprised to find how many boats are left there unattended with mechanics carrying out routine maintenance for absent owners. Over the last few years too, there has also been an increase in the amount of what might loosely be considered resident, live-aboard, foreign boat crews.

WEATHER CHART

Inside the corner office you will also find a full weather forecast and a chart of the Caribbean areas with all isobars, fronts etc. drawn in daily. This is a handy addition to the southwest and Wx forecasts available on your own boat radios.

THE HEMINGWAY YACHT CLUB

One of the best features of the marina now is the excellent new yacht club. The *Club Nautico Internacional Hemingway*, offers a host of benefits. Members receive a substantial discount on their dockage, and the spotless bar is comfortable, air-conditioned, satellite TV'ed, and pool-tabled. The staff upstairs will arrange any documents you require, and the club also now sells all charts you might need for further travel along the coast.

The club hosts an increasing number of fishing and sailing regattas too (ask if *your* commodore has received any communication), and more and more U.S. yachtsmen are participating in these. Entrants usually receive temporary membership, and usually dockage fees are waived.

In the event too, of problems, then the club director and original inspiration, Sr. J. M. Escrich will attend to these on behalf of members. Membership of this club, while not cheap, strikes me as being a sound investment and must be recommended. If you care about such things, in years to come, it'll have a lot of prestige.

The club can be contacted by phone at (53) 7-801336, and faxed at (53) 7-331689.

The yacht club premises viewed from Canal No.2.

There is a medical post (near the drydock, two canals in), with a rotating staff of doctors on call. Here, all manner of minor ailments can be attended to. If you prefer, they will attend to you aboard, or if anything serious crops up they will even accompany you to a local hospital. I have nothing but praise for this service which we have regularly used, from back problems to (judgement-impaired) falls from bicycles. The medical staff stress that this service is free to all, but it would be nice if you could show your gratitude by donating any medical supplies you have to spare. For reasons not under its own control, this admirable system is under severe stress.

Over the last two years a splendid bath/laundry-room building has been constructed. We all felt privileged to witness the awesome sloth with which it was constructed, and amazed to see it eventually finished. It's at the west end of the docks near two tennis courts. Laundry charges are complicated, so it's best to hand over a full black plastic-bag which will all get washed dried and folded overnight by the attendant at the desk in the bathhouse. Charges vary depending on the load but La Fiona says it's still worth it. Don't be shy!

There's a scuba depot halfway along the main avenue leading out of the marina and I've been able to get air-fills there. You rarely see much overt signs of activity, but I know they offer dive-trips out along the reef. It's clearly marked by a large red and white scuba flag painted on the wall and an illuminated sign.

WATER AND ELECTRICITY

The 110V electrical hookups are via supply-boxes at dockside, much like anywhere else except that your connection won't fit. The man who gets all things done, will sort you out, using a pair of pliers, bare wires, and lots of electrical tape. Be careful of the resultant sticky tangle.

Neither does the recent fitting of water meters to the supply points on dockside boxes mean that your U.S. fittings will fit. Instead you'll just about get a couple of threads onto the pipe. Never mind, that's the least of your worries. Actually *getting* water is your biggest problem, as despite all reassurances to the contrary, it has always been difficult for marina residents to get water daily — And then, only at odd and completely unpredictable times. Fill your tanks, and clean your boat whenever you see your neighbor's pipe leaking. The water won't be there long.

Go to the showers early in the mornings and you'll have a reasonable chance, but

View along the wide expanses of the canal docks at Marina Hemingway.

don't try it later.

If you're persistent enough, refusing to accept obvious evasiveness, you may get a reduction in your bill. After all, the marina does contract with you to supply water, electricity, and security.

We'll talk about the security later.

In the middle of 1993 the first yacht service was introduced whereby a van came around taking orders for supplies of groceries and vegetables, etc. at wholesale prices. Most of what one ordered never arrived and as you may imagine, the enterprise never survived long.

Now, another is in place with offices near the office complex at the end of the canal. Its prices are excellent, but only time will tell if this one survives. Ask at the office for the "ships' chandlers." Ice is available here.

MARINA SHOPPING COMPLEX

At the end of the avenue leading out is the small complex containing some five or six shops which accept foreign currency for provisions and rather tacky items of clothing. Further along, at the head of the next canal there is a telephone-office where you can call, or send/receive faxes; and if you turn right at the office you come across two official restaurants.

The only place you'll get any service worthy of the name is the *Fiesta*, along the middle canal some 200 yards down on the right. Their food, unusually in the official scheme of things, seems to have been inspected both before and after cooking, and actually served warm! Nevertheless, unless you're looking for something posh and overpriced you'd still be crazed to eat anywhere other than a private paladar restaurant. These are littered all over Jaimanitas and Santa Fé not five minutes walk from your boat.

And then there's the *PizzaNova*, near the

Security or watcher?

exit. This place, a Canadian chain, serves up quite acceptable pizzas and will even deliver to your boat if, like some, you've taken up the option of having a phone installed by the marina.

There are discotheques both at the shopping complex (this one was temporarily closed in '96) and at the marina proper (Papa's). If this is your first experience of Cuban dancing, it will knock you out. The one at the far end of the avenue got closed down 'cos it got out of hand, and who knows when it'll be reopened. Incidentally, the girls from the marina discos used to tap lightly on the side your yacht at night, but all that foolishness has been stopped now.

SECURITY

This brings us to the delicate subject of security. I can categorically state that in all my traveling in and around Cuba, I have never ever had anything stolen . This holds as true for the farthermost and most miserable, unattended mooring as it does for the Marina Hemingway. The one time I could have sworn my flip-flops had been hijacked they turned up by post five days later, having been left aboard *Aphrodite* the night it sailed for Varadero. Nevertheless, there were some very occasional reports of petty theft in 1995/96. To counter this, and in an attempt to stamp out the worst excesses of some of the more shameless sailors (perhaps the two were closely linked), there has recently been a tightening up of the regulations governing the marina. You are presently not allowed to bring visitors aboard unless they have a pass issued by the office. Thankfully, this has stamped out much of the more offensive behavior which was blackening the names of both the marina, and the yachting community. There has been a commensurate increase in the staff which has turned out a mixed blessing.

Unfortunately, those very personnel now hang around, seemingly more interested in prying into your affairs than anything else. Some indeed, have taken to sitting at fifty yard intervals, close to your boat, staring *in* at you. The more barefaced, stand right next to you while you hold private conversations.

The way to react, of course, is *not* politely.

BOAT REPAIRS

There is a dry-dock between the first two canals closest to the main road. Boats are attended to on the concrete apron where they can haul anything up to 6.35 tons using the marriage of a Japanese telescopic-boom crane with Russian controls; or a 20-ton crane available on call. When I first visited, the mechanics there assured me they could handle almost anything, eg. keel repairs, engine overhauls, fiberglass work, etc. Now, more and more foreign boats are taking advantage of excellent workmanship for everything from full blister jobs and topside renovation, to straightening prop shafts and the like. Don't expect the job to be done at once, but they do stick to their quote; and if you wish, you may bring in your own materials from abroad.

ASHORE

At the entrance to the marina is the main Havana road. Turn left and take your bike if you want a work-out. It's about six or seven

Waiting for a ride.

miles into the center of the city, but worth every inch. Just a hundred yards along as you come to the first bridge, stop and look out towards the north. It'll be your first view of a small local Cuban harbor — Only a tiny pool, but full of the most fascinating boats. The small barrio of Jaimanitas here is full of extremely good Paladars (small family restaurants). Both here and Santa Fé (on the other side of the marina, to the west) are where you should plan most of your meals. Just ask any yachtsman in the marina for advice on who's currently hot.

Continuing on your work-out, if you follow the road (5th Ave.), it will take you all the way into the center of Havana. To get there, you pass along broad shady avenues, through a deep tunnel beneath the river Almendares, then past the beautiful district of Vedado and along the famed Malecon or seawall road. When the Moro castle looms and the road swings right, you are at the ancient city of Old Havana along the entrance to the bay. One of the most entrancing cities you will visit. The stupendous architecture is decaying perhaps, but maybe that's what's saving it. At least it gets used by and for those whom a city should be — people.

If you just want a nice ride, then a mile from the entrance to the marina take the turnoff diagonally to the right where the sign directs you towards the New Latin-American Cinema. Here you'll enjoy a wonderful ride down dim avenues, perfectly shaded in the middle of the day by huge overhanging banyan or bearded fig trees and lined by amazing old houses. Dark and cool even in the scorching heat of a midday sun.

PRODUCE MARKETS

In the event of requiring provisions for your stay, there is now a convenient agricultural market in the town of Santa Fé, not ten minutes ride by bicycle from the marina. For the more timid, prices for all agricultural items are prominently posted so you do not have to bargain for goods. Ask around for directions, and don't be put off when the marina staff says it's not worth it, or it doesn't exist. They have their own

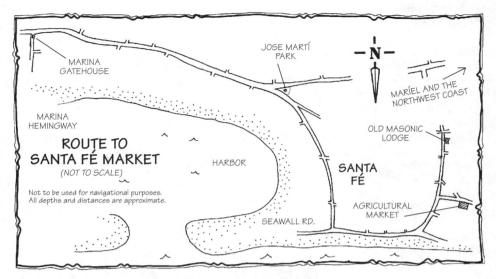

ROUTE TO SANTA FÉ MARKET
(NOT TO SCALE)

Not to be used for navigational purposes.
All depths and distances are approximate.

agenda, which most definitely is not yours.

Downtown Havana also has a larger, more busy market, which is also worth checking out. It is called *El Mercado Libre Campesino de La Habana* and is situated in Calle (street) Monte.

Do not worry, you may discreetly change currency anywhere outside these markets.

AUTOMOBILE TRANSPORT

A taxi, called for you by the staff at the marina will set you back about $20 to get into Havana, but you can do better by dealing with the unofficial cars which ply for hire near the entrance. If you plan your day properly, most people find it best to make an arrangement for the entire day's use of the car (say $25 plus cost of fuel used). You won't forgive yourself if you miss spending an afternoon in Old Havana (Habana Vieja), one of the two Cuban cities placed on UNESCO's World Heritage list, worth every minute you spend there. And check out the surrounding streets, there are nuggets among the decaying structures.

Your driver will be invaluable here.

For the fabulously wealthy, there is a car rental agency (Cubanacan) just opposite your moorings, near the Hotel *El Viejo y el Mar* (The Old Man and the Sea). Take gold, diamonds, and your richest aunt too.

CHARTS/MAPS

Conveniently, *El Navigante* (the shop where you can buy all necessary nautical charts) is right there in Old Havana, so you might wish to drop in there to obtain what you need.

Tienda "El Navegante"
Mercaderes #115
(between Obispo and Obrapia)
Old Havana
Tel: (53) 7-613625

Before selling you the chart, the ever helpful Sr. Rosales or his delightful assistant will correct it to the absolutely latest information. The process takes some fifteen minutes per chart, so while they're doing this you can take in the sights, afternoon tea just around the corner, or even a Chinese meal next door!

Maps of all the major Cuban cities are also sold here in the shop.

It is beyond the intended scope of this book to function as a shoreside travel guide, but be prepared for a certain amount of culture-shock. If you've never before visited a Latin American city your conception of noise and crowd etiquette may be at variance with normal practice, so get a good guidebook in Havana or order one or two in advance of your visit.

TEMPORARY LEAVE
OF ABSENCE

You may, for one reason or the other, need to leave the country by air. As mentioned before, you can leave the keys to your boat with the marina whose staff will need to know of your plans; and if you wish you can make an arrangement to bring in any needed spares for your boat in your luggage. Ask the customs officers at the marina. They will only be too happy to give you a letter stating that you have a vessel docked there which will help with any overenthusiastic airport customs officials when you return. If you're doing this, why not ask around at the office to see if they need any bits and pieces which you could bring in for them?

Normally you have to show a return ticket when entering Cuba by air, but if the original ticket has been bought in Havana, or you have a boat there, they won't put up a fight over this. If going to the USA, you may find it discreet to fly to the Bahamas and then cross over to Ft. Lauderdale. Tickets are available through Havanatur at around $145 return, and the trip from Nassau is around $60. No one knows it, but you can get a entry-visa for Cuba at the airport in Nassau just by showing up.

In that discreet vein, remember your passport will not be stamped upon entry or departure.

Flights are also available to Mexico, Jamaica, Ireland, Spain, etc. and the airport ride will cost you around $20 by taxi.

LEAVING HAVANA FOR THE COAST
CHART NO. ICH 1124 (CUBAN)

It is important to have arranged all aspects of this procedure as far in advance as possible, so you should have already notified the marina staff in the office about your plans. In addition to everything else they are always extremely helpful and efficient.

Presuming you are cruising the cays, then you should have already researched your probable route. Following the guidelines given before (Chapter Two: Leaving Port), ask for documentation allowing a certain flexibility, and do it at least two days in advance.

To ensure that all is right, make sure you've been issued with the cruising permit /safety certificate and guia de recala (the permit with your route), at least the night before leaving.

Once you have these, speak with the marina representatives or local customs officials at their post halfway along the avenue in the marina. Assure them that you wish to leave early next morning. Seven o'clock will probably be a good time, and you should emphasize that your plans are not at all flexible in this regard. Of course, if you're doing an overnight run then give them that planned departure time.

If you need to top up your tanks, then inform the staff and take your vessel round to the docks opposite the offices where the splendidly color-coded supply lines deliver clean fuel. Do not delay this operation until departure as the immigration officers quite rightly won't wait long at the Guarda Frontera post twiddling their thumbs.

On that subject, be firm when requesting their presence at seven o'clock. Failure to emphasize your departure time can result in a three or four hour delay as I have witnessed several times.

And make sure you have a dockage receipt from the office in case anyone asks about it in the morning and the office is closed.

Mind, you need to be sure that you're actually leaving, and not just sticking your head out to see what the conditions are like outside. A couple of years ago we tried three times to leave the harbor, each time arranging visits from all and sundry, only to abort in the face of the stiff northeast wind that had cooped us up for a week, as it drove heavy swells over the sea defenses. They'd come down to the boat, and we'd be so embarrassed.

We actually did manage to leave once, but were driven back in two hours, as the boat was on its beam ends all the time. Returning, we had to go through the whole check-in procedure all over again, but this time accompanied by jeers!

Mind you, we're not ashamed to be called "chicken" — that's just another word for wise.

LEAVING PROCEDURE

Morning departures: Having crawled out of bed at 5 a.m. to prep the boat, and taken it round to the Guarda Frontera post at the entrance, you will be understandably disgruntled when 7 a.m. passes without a visit from the customs or immigration officers, but never mind. This seems to happen to everyone, so insist that they be 'phoned at once.

Sooner or later they'll show up grumbling and muttering, but otherwise in a cooperative enough frame of mind. Sometimes too, if they're bored they'll even cadge a lift on your boat for the ride round to the Guarda Frontera post. This is good, so bring them aboard, slip your lines and depart rejoicing.

At the mouth of the harbor where you stop, you will be boarded by all the officials in turn, your vessel will receive a quick search, and they'll clear you outwards.

The Guarda Frontera too will have their say in the matter before you get the final all-important despacho (the permit to actually leave port), but if as before you've put all your relevant documents in their folder there won't be much trouble. Don't expect much change out of three-quarters of an hour though for the whole sheebang.

Infuriatingly, this process is the same whether you're traveling 10 miles up the coast or going foreign, so be prepared for the delay. Just make sure you have the following documents:

1. Safety/cruising permit (from the marina)

2. Guia de recalas (from customs)

3. Despacho (from the Guarda Frontera)

And now, you may heave your marina receipt over the side, and leave.

Night departures: It is often wiser to depart in the night, or even in the very early hours of morning. On the one hand, this may enable you to take advantage of the calm conditions which always exist at these times, and on the other, it may enable you to reach somewhere like Cayo Levisa, 60 miles up the coast, in sunlight the next day.

The procedure is much as above, except that you should be through sometime in the early evening (say 7 p.m.) while the port officials are still on duty. But remain tied up to the Guarda Frontera dock until you are actually ready to leave the harbor during the hours of darkness. This arrangement, practiced by many of the old hands, seems much better than a frantic day trip up the coast and a reef entrance in failing light.

Exiting the channel is straightforward. Steer 320°M with attention being paid to the channel width and the existence of snorkelers who will be in evidence as far as the outer marker; but as soon as you've cleared it you'll be in deeper water and can set course for Bahía Honda or Key west.

A ferry boat departs the cays.

117

PASSAGE WEST TO THE COAST AND CAYS
CHART NO. ICH 11424 (CUBAN)

If you leave in a north wind of any strength you're likely to be in for a rough passage as the seas will be on the beam. Hopefully though, you've scheduled things for a more easterly wind, and even if it's blowing a bit outside the seas will be calm in the land's wind-shadow where you will find only a gentle swell pushing you down the coast. Tucked close in you can also take advantage of the westerly countercurrent which seems to add a fair bit to your speed, and it will be a visual course all the way.

Night sailing note: While the above is all very well on a fine moonlit night, be careful if there is no moon as there are likely to be few house or street lights ashore later on, and you will have to rely on navigational aids. The wall here is steep and close inshore without much warning of shoal waters, so let caution rule. For a dark moonless overnight run along the coast, you can set a course of 268°M for about 40 miles while staying two or three miles offshore.

At around longitude 083°15.00W, you'll be coming up on the cays and can begin to veer further round to the south. If it's still dark, then you may steer 250°M for the next 10 miles, whereupon it should be light and you should be ready to pick your way through the reef into Cayo Paraíso or Cayo Levisa.

If, however, you're doing your first run in daylight, then an early departure should at least get you into Bahía Honda in good time, as it's only some 36 miles away. Position yourself a mile or so offshore, and you can make a visual passage all the way along a coast largely free of dangers.

Close inshore there won't be much in the way of current to slow you down, and you'll even get a little lift from a slight countercurrent heading west southwest down the coast.

Along here the terrain is generally flat with lots of houses around Playa Baraco which gives way to green open spaces further along and a large flat topped hill, the Mesa de Mariel some five miles inland.

Your first notable landmarks will be the cement plant's chimneys smoking away, some 15 miles further along the coast at Mariel, the port made famous by its boatlift to the U.S. some years ago.

MARIEL & CABAÑAS:

Mariel: It's a bit close to the Marina Hemingway, but if you wish to stop you may do so, provided you remember to check in at the Guarda Frontera dock just at the entrance on the eastern side.

It's a busy port (400 boats annually) inside a deep protected bay with a well marked, dredged entrance, suitable for the deepest keel, and wide enough for all tastes.

Within the bay it is forbidden to approach to Angosta Peninsula with its disused airstrip, or the Laza Harbor (both southwest from the entrance), but you may proceed to the other large docks for instructions. The port is notable only for the boatlift, and there's not a lot of reason presently to visit unless you are fascinated by cement works and the dust they spread, but it does appear to be a good shelter from a storm even if it meant abandoning Marina Hemingway. If, like some, you have travelled to Cuba with a motorcycle or scooter aboard then it is easier to visit by road from Havana for a look-see first.

Cabañas: Further down the coast you come to the Bay of Cabañas. This naval base is off-limits to commercial traffic or cruisers, and additionally it is prohibited to anchor along the coast between longitudes 082° 57 W and 083°00 W. Ashore you'll see evidence of military training with the occasional beach defended by anti landing-craft devices, so I'd pass by unless I were interested in a really long-term stay. Around here too, you may encounter your first patrol boats scooting by.

The entrance for those who absolutely need it, is well marked (R/G's), and takes

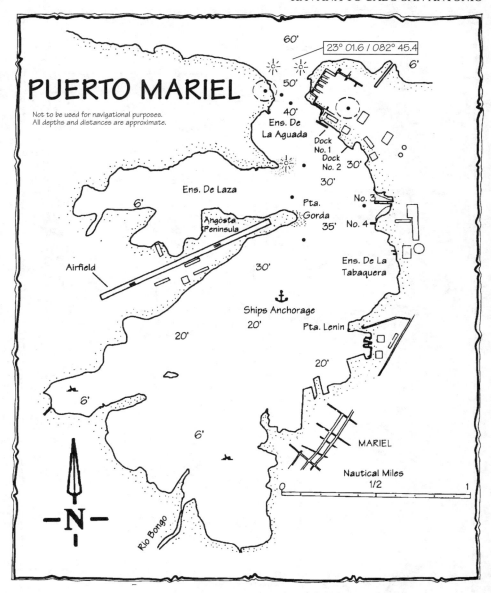

PUERTO MARIEL

Not to be used for navigational purposes.
All depths and distances are approximate.

23° 01.6 / 082° 45.4

60'
6'
50'
40'
Ens. De La Aguada
Dock No. 1
Dock No. 2
30'
30'
No. 3
Ens. De Laza
6'
Pta. Gorda
35'
No. 4
Angosta Peninsula
Airfield
30'
Ens. De La Tabaquera
Ships Anchorage
20'
Pta. Lenin
20'
20'
6'
6'
MARIEL
6'
Nautical Miles
1/2
0
1

-N-

Rio Bongo

you through on the western side of the neck, close to shore. There are strange t-shaped electricity pylons stretching across too, but not in your way. This is an extremely well protected harbor, and one which in the event of a major storm, might well be made available for emergency use. Just don't count on it until things change.

The terrain is still low-lying with slight escarpments on the western side of this extremely large bay, but right inland we begin to see the first glimpses of the Sierras de Rosario which may be strange for a North American visitor more accustomed to the flat Florida coastline.

119

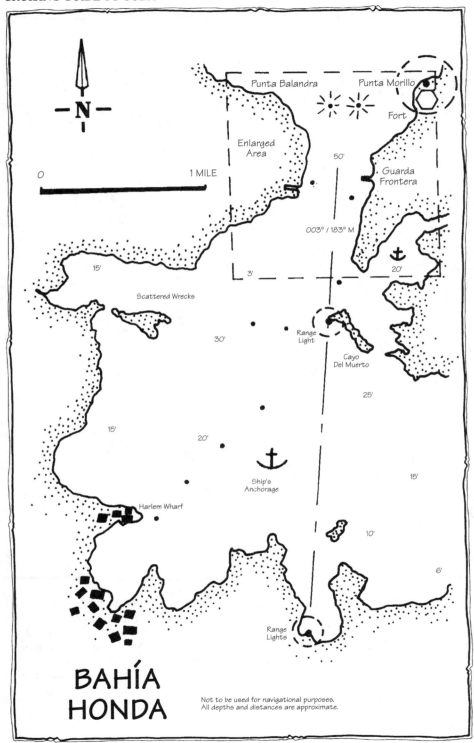

—N—

0   1 MILE

Punta Balandra

Punta Morillo

Fort

Enlarged
Area

50'

Guarda
Frontera

003° / 183° M

15'

3'

20'

Scattered Wrecks

30'

Range
Light

Cayo
Del Muerto

25'

15'

20'

15'

Ship's
Anchorage

10'

Harlem Wharf

6'

Range
Lights

BAHÍA
HONDA

Not to be used for navigational purposes.
All depths and distances are approximate.

BAHIA HONDA

Among other things, a grave-yard for boats, this is where old or damaged commercial vessels are brought to be decommissioned and stripped for salvage. This is a point not lost on the cruiser, in light of the amount of wreckage he will see along the coasts.

Approaching the Bahia Honda from Havana, you first see a prominent lighthouse (visible almost 8 miles.) and closer in, a large crane on the western side in from the entrance where there used to be a wreck run aground

Light on west side of Bahia Honda.

in the shallows. The eastern side has a small hill with conspicuous trees completely overgrowing the old fort of San Fernando, and in front of this a short light-beacon pylon partly concealed by vegetation.

Waves break inshore on the shallow fringing reefs, so you should remain a mile or so off (just along the wall and no closer than

23° 00.0N), then after the fort, curve round gradually into the mouth. Around 083° 09.5W, or when you come into line with the range-marks and buoys in the channel, turn south heading 183°M.

If you're coming in along the wall from the west, approach no closer than 23° 00.3N as you pass the lighthouse. Once past, keeping well outside the conspicuous shallows, take up a heading towards the hill with the invisible fort and the barely visible light, then turn with the markers in line.

Inside to your port, just a few hundred yards past the fort's elevation, you will see a small dock with a shed on the end and fishing boats moored all round. A patrol boat stationed there gives the clue. This is the Guarda Frontera post that you need to contact.

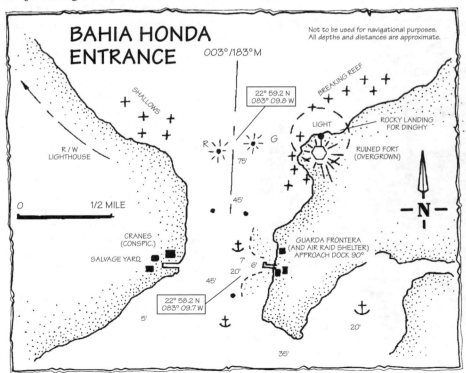

Alongside the spindly little wharf, there is a small beach and a couple of scattered buildings painted drab grey, near the pink Guarda Frontera hut with its antenna and flag.

Trickle in at 90°M towards the rickety dock, carefully, because the depth is extremely shallow anywhere off line, and pull alongside the left of the low wharf, ensuring your fenders are properly positioned equally low-down in advance.

The passage from the main ship's channel is quite narrow, perhaps no more than 20 feet wide and four or five feet deep, all the way over soft mud, but can be accomplished without drama. If you prefer, you may even drop anchor and dinghy your papers over to the dock.

There will be masses of spectators slack-jawed at your approach; old fishermen, girls scratching their bellies, naked children and hurrying Guards Frontera. We once found them openly butchering a cow on the dock as we docked there, throwing the offal into the water off the end. Nevertheless, more and more cruisers are stopping here, so there won't be too much hassle with your papers.

As always, it is important to inform the Guarda Frontera that you are going to be using your dinghy later on, and once your papers have been attended to, you should pull away carefully towards deeper water.

If you wish to be near the fort, you can anchor northeast of the large green buoy to the south of the dock in about 20-40 feet, or wherever the press of fishing boats allow.

On the other side, opposite your dock, there is a concrete harbor facility (the Dársena Ciro Redondo) with cranes and other equipment for stripping vessels. While it has the appearance of disuse, it is still in operation, but as confirmed by local fishermen, some of the six or seven wrecks around here were sunk before they could be attended to. In fact, given the relative newness of some, I doubt that they all actually arrived with this attention in mind.

At the bottom end of the bay you will see the port of Harlem with its square housing blocks (eastern block architecture prevailing over good taste), watched over by the Sierra del Rosario.

THE FORT AND THE MOUNTAINS

The fort can be approached by road from the dock, but you may find it easier to use the dinghy, going round the point to a protected, if shallow, landing area northeast of the hill. The hill is seriously overgrown, and the mosquitos are going to thank you for your visit, but isn't this what you've come to Cuba for? Entering, you'll have to scale the walls, using vines, if you can't find the breach in the northeast corner.

After this you can take the dinghy further in towards the south of the bay and cruise around the cays inside. There are beaches on the Cayo del Muerto (Hmm...), near the first range-mark at Punta Difuntos, and if you prefer this environment, you can ask the Guarda Frontera if you may moor there instead of near the dock. Although they really shouldn't give you any trouble about this you may have to press the point sometimes. Don't believe all that guff about "It's for your security, señor". It isn't.

Waterfall at Soroa.

It's worth being insistent here, because the town at Bahia Honda is really quite nice and well worth a visit by dinghy. In addition, you may take a car up into the lovely mountains (the Sierras del Rosario) which loom to the south. Here, at a place called *Soroa*, surrounded by striking views, you will find an outdoor restaurant with musicians and massages, complete with a picturesque waterfall nearby, around whose delicious base you may bathe.

If you wish to leave your tender in the water overnight, attach it carefully with regard to security, and in the morning when you're ready to resume your cruise, take it in to the dock to collect your despacho rather than maneuver alongside. It's always quicker this way.

When leaving, follow the line of the range-marks (003°M) at least 200 yards past the outer mark. If you turn west along the coast too soon you'll be in shallow water in no time at all. Make your turn along the coast when abreast of the light or the low wooded headland, and follow the wall a half-mile off the breakers on the reef. If you do stray in over the wall, you'll still find 50-to-70 feet of water, which is good enough for me, and as with all coastal navigation around here, if you can't see anything below you're "off the wall."

COURSE TO CAYO PARAÍSO
CHART NO. ICH 11424 (CUBAN)

It's only a 15-mile run further down the coast to the first of our stops along the cays, but it's best to leave early in the morning so the sun will be high for your first real reef entrance. When you're at the cay, you'll also have time for some exploring, or maybe a sunlit wreck-dive in shallow water.

By now the coastline has begun to curve gradually towards the west southwest, bringing it into the lee of the prevailing easterlies, and the waters should exhibit only a gentle swell as you fishtail along with the genoa boomed right out.

Remain closer in over the wall at whatever depth keeps you happy, and you'll gain at least a knot by staying out of the northeast current. For the first couple of miles the bottom will become dark green at around 30-40 feet from the turtle grass which grows in such depths.

After you pass the small harbor of Morillo (eight miles along, around 083° 19.0W), you'll begin to see the cays and the Colorados Reef, which will now extend all the way along the coast as far as the western tip of Cuba and the first of

those cays is Cayo Paraíso.

From the east, there are two entrances to this cay, the first slightly deeper entrance is at the Pasa de La Mulata about four miles past Morillo, and second just 200-300 yards before the island itself. Both entrances are described on the following page. If taking the second then remain a bit further off any breakers along the reef now (about 500 yards) in 30-40 feet of water, as closer to Cayo Paraiso there are scattered heads of elkhorn coral in 15-20 feet, and these reach up to within a foot or two of the surface. The waves this far in from the wall may not be strong enough to cause breakers, so look out for the other clues, such as swells or color change (orange/olive tinge).

A beached vessel. (LaFé northwest coast)

CAYO PARAÍSO (PARADISE CAY)

For some reason, the authorities in Havana occasionally like to pretend that Paraíso doesn't exist, but pay no attention to this nonsense. It most definitely does, no matter what they say. Although being slowly eroded by the elements, it's a perfectly delightful place.

Cayo Paraíso is a small cay shaped much like an inverted crescent with a widening gap in the middle. A couple of years back it underwent a rather halfhearted refurbishment with a view to installing facilities for tourists and yachts, but the work progressed in such a desultory fashion that most of whatever got done just collapsed or blew away. What do you expect when there are only two people on the island.

I wouldn't hold out too many hopes that it will be still be there when you arrive, but there was a small restaurant on the western side. The dock was looking decidedly sorry for itself, but surprisingly, the tiki hut on the end was still standing. Mind you Cuba is still full of occasional surprises.

Nevertheless, in spite of all the above, the very absence of development has contributed to its attraction and the clean blue waters surrounding the cay are absolutely lovely. I think it's a great spot to hang out.

Be aware that you are not the first to visit this delightful little spot. Ernest Hemingway beat us all to it some 50 years ago, making it his cruising base for quite some time, even to the extent of conducting naval operations from there during the second world war!

Cayo Paraíso from the East:

One: The first entrance we come across is at the *Pasa de La Mulata* just after Morillo. This entry is best shown in the sketch chart on Pg. 127.

Follow the line of coral until you come to a large, concrete barrel-type marker at 22°56.9N / 083°23.2W.

It is imperative that you pass this to port (to the west of the mark) as it sits directly upon the reef. Come in due south in waters varying from 25-70 feet depending on the depressions you cross. Once inside, do not immediately head in a direct route to the cay, but rather take up a gentle arc, beginning more or less 210°M and coming round gradually to 235°M. This route will take you over the flats in about 9-to-12 feet of water. You can see Cayo Paraíso across the way so aim finally at the bottom corner where there are two stakes marking the southeast channel into the sound at 22°55.2'N/083°25.9'W (see Cayo Paraíso sketch).

Two: The second entrance also requires some care, so study the drawing below and opposite, which give very subjective im-

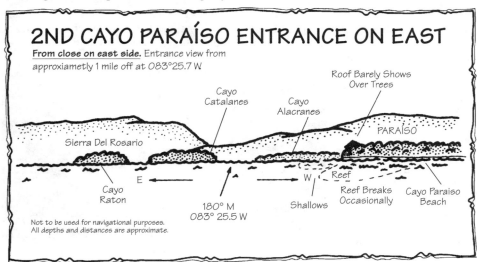

2ND CAYO PARAÍSO ENTRANCE ON EAST

From close on east side. Entrance view from approxiametly 1 mile off at 083°25.7 W

Roof Barely Shows Over Trees

Cayo Catalanes

Cayo Alacranes

PARAÍSO

Sierra Del Rosario

Cayo Raton

E ←

180° M
083° 25.5 W

Shallows

→ W

Reef

Reef Breaks Occasionally

Cayo Paraiso Beach

Not to be used for navigational purposes.
All depths and distances are approximate.

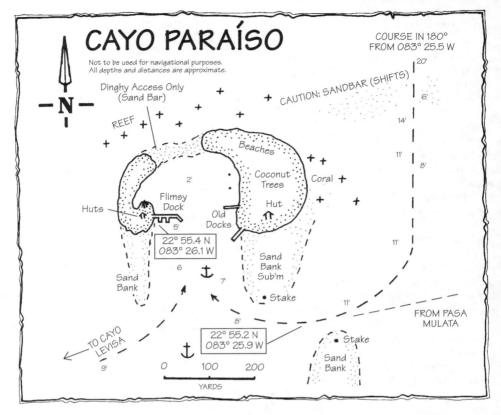

CAYO PARAÍSO

COURSE IN 180°
FROM 083° 25.5 W

Not to be used for navigational purposes.
All depths and distances are approximate.

−N−

Dinghy Access Only
(Sand Bar)

CAUTION: SANDBAR (SHIFTS)

20'

6'

REEF

14'

Beaches

11'

8'

Coconut
Trees

Coral

2'

Flimsy
Dock

Hut

Huts

Old
Docks

11'

5'

22° 55.4 N
083° 26.1 W

Sand
Bank
Sub'm

Sand
Bank

6

7

Stake

11'

Stake

FROM PASA
MULATA

8'

22° 55.2 N
083° 25.9 W

Stake

TO CAYO
LEVISA

Sand
Bank

9'

0   100   200

YARDS

pressions of both this entrance and the layout of the cay itself.

As you cruise west parallel to the reef, make your turn 180°M south some 300 yards east of the cay at about 083°25.50W (roughly as shown). As noted before, there are elkhorn coral patches below the water approximately one-quarter-mile east of this longitude, so be on the lookout, and if you've come within 200 yards of the island, you've come too far west also.

Enter along your course, being aware of a sandy bar northeast of the tip, which reaches to six feet but can easily be wriggled around. Past that, be aware of the shoals close to the island on your right and aim to the left of a turquoise patch of sand ahead where the water is too shallow for safety. At this stage, paralleling the eastern side of the island, the depth will be 10-12 feet, and

continuing on you can begin to make a gradual right turn through two sandbanks off the southeast tip. One of the sand banks extends some 300 feet out from the island, but both are quite obvious through the water and are also marked by stakes or whithies between which you pass (22°55.2N / 083°25.9W) going west.

Paraíso won't look like this now.

Once into the underbelly of the island in 10 feet of water you can anchor or ease up (it gets shallower) to any of the narrow docks extending from the left side near the surviving thatch huts, and go about your business unmolested by any form of officialdom or Guarda Frontera.

As evidence of the veneration in which Ernest Hemingway is held by literate Cuba, there is a small monument placed close to the dock on the southwest end of the island. It is translated roughly into English in the adjoining box.

There is a small diesel generator behind the huts, so perhaps when you get there the island will have electricity, but I for one certainly wouldn't bet on it. In any case you will find this an ideal spot for a short stay in peaceful surroundings. You may walk around the island in 20 minutes using the beaches and an internal track through the trees, but if you prefer not to wade across the low lying area between the two halves, then take the dinghy across to the eastern side.

If you feel like a swim, dinghy out towards the reef to hunt lobster (lots around here), or northeast of the island where there are the flattened remains of an old iron vessel wrecked in about 15 or 20 feet of water. Anyone on the island can tell you where it is, but if you have a hand-held GPS the coordinates are 22°56.3N / 083°25.2W. In any case, the wreckage is spread about over an area the size of two tennis courts,

> *"From the beginning of the 1940's, this place was the refuge of the great North American author Ernest Hemingway who visited it assiduously, sometimes remaining on the cay for up to 20 days at a time. Here he wrote, rested, roamed the beach, swam, and loved it so much he used it as a base for antisubmarine operations from his yacht "El Pilar" during the Second World War".*
> *— In his memory, on the 90th anniversary of his birth*
> —
> **Provincial Commission of Monuments, Piñar del Rio, 21 July, 1989**

and it can be clearly seen from the surface. So if you wish you can prospect for it from the dinghy and snorkel down over the wreck.

In early evening, the already considerable insect noise will rise somewhat, and you'd better be ready with the repellant. This will probably be your first real onslaught.

CAYO LEVISA

This is a larger (but still relatively small) cay not more than five or six miles to the west of Paraíso and visible from your overnight mooring. For those without deep keels, it's a straightforward, if occasionally shallow, inside run across a calm sound, and if you leave in the morning you can find yourself enjoying a wide variety of cocktails by midday. I would recommend that if you draw more than six or seven feet you go back out the way you came in and make your reef entry further along.

Inner Route: Using the shallower inside route, leave Cayo Paraíso past the sandbank, which extends out from the southwest tip, and take up a visual course (250° M) towards the northern edge of Cayo Levisa where you may faintly make outbuildings and huts. Along this inside route the water is largely free of danger and usually more than eight feet, except close to Cayo Alacranes just to the south. Over by the reef too, you will see bright turquoise patches denoting shallow sand.

Coming up on the protruding end of Cayo Alacranes to your left, the water will shelve to six feet for a second if you go too close, so hold your course looking back frequently to see that you are still in line with the southwest tip of Paraíso and continue to-

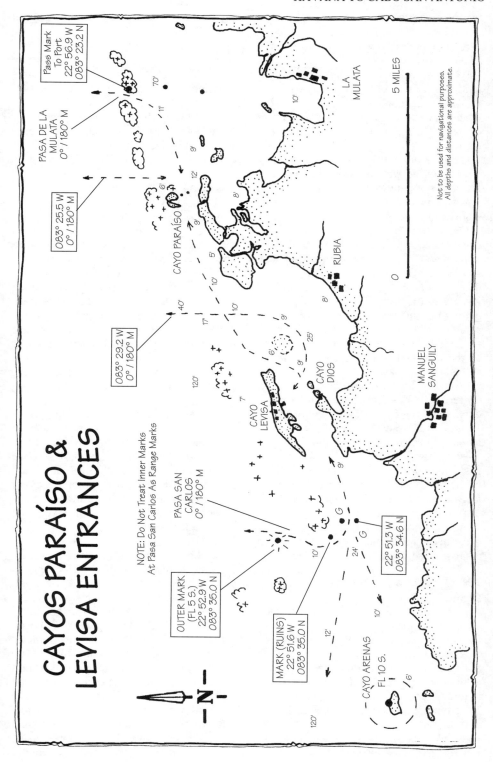

CAYOS PARAÍSO &
LEVISA ENTRANCES

Pass Mark
To Port
22° 56.9 W
083° 23.2 N

PASA DE LA
MULATA
0° / 180° M

083° 25.5 W
0° / 180° M

083° 29.2 W
0° / 180° M

LA
MULATA

RUBIA

MANUEL
SANGUILY

CAYO PARAÍSO

CAYO
LEVISA

CAYO
DIOS

NOTE: Do Not Treat Inner Marks
At Pasa San Carlos As Range Marks

PASA SAN
CARLOS
0° / 180° M

OUTER MARK
(FL 5 S.)
22° 52.9 W
083° 35.0 N

MARK (RUINS)
22° 51.6 W
083° 35.0 N

22° 51.3 W
083° 34.6 N

CAYO ARENAS
FL 10 S.

Not to be used for navigational purposes.
All depths and distances are approximate.

5 MILES

0

-N-

127

wards the northern edge of Levisa.

Begin to veer left about half-a-mile off Levisa (at 083°30.0 W), taking a course of 212° M towards the northeastern tip of Cayo Dios, which sticks out from the mainland over to the southwest. This will take you past a sandbank on the eastern tip of the island and round underneath it, but be aware of the six-to-seven- foot depths along this stretch.

Once clear of the sandbank, you may once again go west between the two cays towards the derelict barge and the wharf now showing halfway along the bottom edge of Levisa.

Outer Route: This necessitates going back outside the reef via any of the entrances you used to enter in the first place, so you may find it best to use the closer of the two and to wriggle out past the sand bar just above the tip of Paraíso. Don't worry, getting out this way's not as difficult as it sounds, and I know several boats drawing 8 -9 ft. which have done this. Failing that, go all the way back to the Pasa de La Mulata and leave that way.

Once past Paraíso, come back in through the reef at 083°29.2W heading due south in depths varying from 10 - 20 feet of water. At around 22° 54.0N it gets slightly shallower, and you may begin to veer slightly to the west (say 212° M). This should take you past and under the sandbank shown on the chart, then when you're about level with the far southwest corner of Cayo Levisa you can head due west in deeper water now. It should be noted that both of the routes described require that you pay attention to what's ahead, and not to get carried away.

AN ALTERNATE ROUTE
(From The West)

If you don't feel confident about such shallow sandbank navigation as is available on the eastern side, then you will find a deep and wide marked channel, the Pasa San Carlos, about two miles west of the cay at longitude 083°35.0W. This way you could quite easily take the outside route there and back round. Enter the marked channel along 180° M, pass the ruined inner mark to port, and make your turn east between the following green marks when Cayo Levisa

shows well clear of the mainland cays at Punta Purgatorio.

A warning: Whatever else you do in this world (unless your premiums are up to date), do not treat these inside green marks as range marks when coming in from outside, but rather, pass between them.

Once through the channel, stick well over to the southern (mainland) side for deeper water, and again pay attention to what's coming up.

A STRAIGHTFORWARD APPROACH

An increasingly popular stopover for yachts, Cayo Levisa has a sturdy dock on the south. The approach is straightforward apart from a shallow patch southwest of the wharf, and you can come in from almost head on. The depth is anything up to 20 feet, but the various boats which bring in fresh water and supplies to the island use the outer end, so (except temporarily) you take the western edge where it is a bit shallower (up to six feet near the outer end). Unless you have a power boat, avoid the eastern side where it is only four-foot deep alongside.

A couple of curious sailors might assist with your lines, but as there are no cleats in use, find a gap or two in the planks and thread your line round a support beam like everyone else is doing. You will be visited by a young Guarda Frontera to inspect your papers (a recent and rather unfortunate development this), but apart from that you can just wander in and about the island at your leisure.

Anchoring: If you're going to anchor off, then there are a couple of deep lagoons available to the west of the dock. Here you will be secure from almost anything nature can throw your way. Check the sketch and note the course in. Once again, don't be put off from using these very safe anchorages.

The dock is about eight feet wide and 100 feet long, with quaint lamps along its length and a green light at the outer end (which will shine in your windows). Following the elevated wooden walkway 200-300 feet through the mangroves will bring you to the hotel complex over on the north coast, where you might as well have a couple of

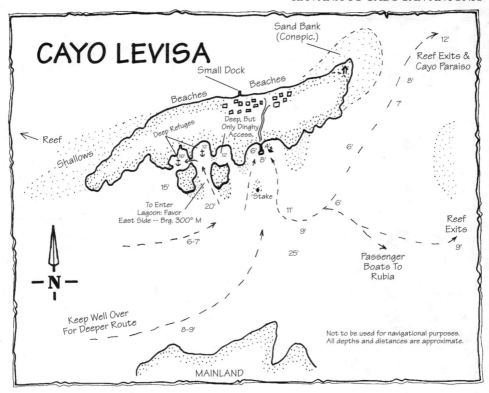

CAYO LEVISA

Sand Bank (Conspic.)

12'

Reef Exits & Cayo Paraiso

Small Dock

Beaches

8'

Beaches

7

Deep, But Only Dinghy Access.

Reef

Deep Refuges

Shallows

16' 12' 12'

6'

6'

8'

15'

To Enter Lagoon: Favor East Side -- Brg. 300° M

20'

Stake

11'

6'

Reef Exits

9'

6-7

25'

9'

Passenger Boats To Rubia

– N –

Keep Well Over For Deeper Route

8-9'

Not to be used for navigational purposes. All depths and distances are approximate.

MAINLAND

stiff ones at the outside bar while getting the lay of the land.

The hotel complex is now a Cuban / Italian partnership (Gran Caribe), entirely Cuban operated, and has a bar (naturally), restaurant, bakery, scuba shop, and some 20 cabanas. Visitors are ferried in from the mainland to the dock, and if you're there when anyone arrives in the off-season, you might see the congregated staff singing songs of welcome with guitars twanging, maracas shaking, much shouting, back slapping, and bags held high overhead as they're carried along the duckboards.

Emotional yes, but what a way to arrive. And no, it does not seem some propaganda-show staged by the government. The hotel also has a VHF base station, "Cayo Levisa" on 19, if you fancy a similar welcome.

Water, and any services you might conceivably require are available by asking any of the local sailors lounging about on the docks. You can even obtain bread and the like from the hotel kitchen.

Tours are offered to the mainland, which

might be one way of taking in as much of the rugged hinterland as possible, without having to rent cars. You can visit tobacco factories and rum distilleries; and there are boat tours offering submerged rivers through the caverns near Pinar del Rio in the mountains or out to the cays where you can cook your own fresh-caught lobster.

Tourism is mainly concentrated in the winter when a lot of visitors arrive, but off-season the place is likely to be quite deserted, and you will have a mile or more of white sandy beaches to yourself. You can play with the hotel's Hobie-Cats and catch up on really quick responsive boats, like the ones you used to sail.

When we were last here there were about 20 guests, mainly engaged it seems in diving. Compressed air is available at the end of the dock and there are lots of scuba sites around here. Some, such as the forests of black-coral along the walls at Pasa San Carlos, are quite spectacular, especially when compared with the Florida Keys not 90 miles away to the north!

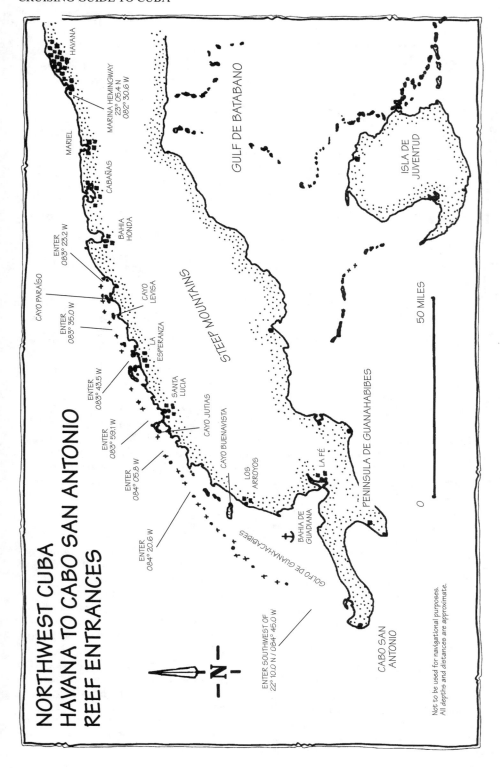

NORTHWEST CUBA
HAVANA TO CABO SAN ANTONIO
REEF ENTRANCES

HAVANA

MARINA HEMINGWAY
23° 05.4 N
082° 30.6 W

MARIEL

CABAÑAS

BAHIA
HONDA

ENTER
083° 23.2 W

CAYO PARAÍSO

ENTER
083° 35.0 W

CAYO
LEVISA

LA
ESPERANZA

ENTER
083° 43.5 W

SANTA
LUCIA

ENTER
083° 59.1 W

CAYO JUTIAS

ENTER
084° 05.8 W

CAYO BUENAVISTA

ENTER
084° 20.6 W

LOS
ARROYOS

LA FÉ

BAHIA DE
GUADIANA

GOLFO DE GUANAHACABIBES

ENTER SOUTHWEST OF
22° 10.0 N / 084° 45.0 W

CABO SAN
ANTONIO

PENÍNSULA DE GUANAHABIBES

STEEP MOUNTAINS

GULF DE BATABANO

ISLA DE
JUVENTUD

50 MILES

0

-N-

Not to be used for navigational purposes.
All depths and distances are approximate.

130

It's well worth taking supper at the resort, both for the break, and also to give something back to the local economy. Dining is often buffet style, and considerably better (for less too) than anything offered in the cities like Havana. A local idiosyncrasy here used to be the custom of occasionally weaving your name into the various songs you'll be serenaded with during supper. Be prepared for anything.

Various members of the staff also eat in the communal dining room, serving themselves along with the guests, and this brings up another point with which the visitor may not be as yet familiar.

Perhaps in part due to your being a bit weird (all cruisers are), and perhaps in part due to Cuban egalitarianism, a staff member with whom you have been earlier chatting (we always chatter away with everyone), may well catch your eye and bring his plate over to accompany you at your table during your meal. As long as you're not deliberately looking for solitude that evening, it's a great way to dine.

We always end up eating with delightful people, and loving it.

We've done a lot of fishing in and among the mangroves off to the west of the dock, and I still treasure the sight of a local tarpon arcing skyward while snapping my line contemptuously. Mainly however, you'll get snapper and jacks in the deep lagoons. Then too, there was the surprising sight of a couple of Jutías (a local rodent much sought after for its delicious meat) rooting around in the mangroves just nearby.

Leaving Cayo Levisa for the west is merely a matter of watching out for the shallow patch off to the southwest of the dock, and remembering that the deeper water is available over to the *mainland* side. Head towards the inner green marks at the Pasa San Carlos along a course of roughly 250°M once past the island, and pass between them (see earlier sketch on Pg. 127). From there you can head on towards La Esperanza, Santa Lucia, or Cayo Jutías along the outer route. Mind you, if you'd prefer to be more adventurous with your piloting you can take the inner passage most of the way.

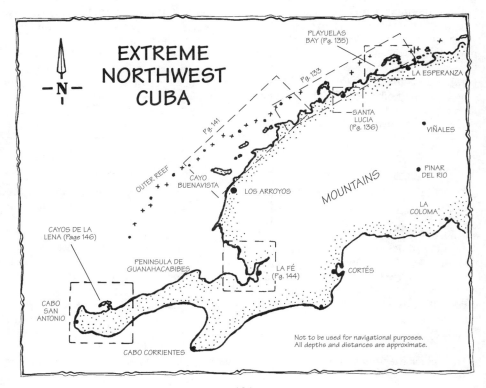

EXTREME NORTHWEST CUBA

-N-

PLAYUELAS BAY (Pg. 135)

LA ESPERANZA

Pg. 133

Pg. 141

SANTA LUCIA (Pg. 136)

VIÑALES

OUTER REEF

CAYO BUENAVISTA

LOS ARROYOS

MOUNTAINS

PINAR DEL RIO

LA COLOMA

CAYOS DE LA LENA (Page 146)

PENINSULA DE GUANAHACABIBES

LA FÉ (Pg. 144)

CORTÉS

CABO SAN ANTONIO

Not to be used for navigational purposes. All depths and distances are approximate.

CABO CORRIENTES

131

LEVISA TO SANTA LUCIA
CHART NO. ICH 11423 (CUBAN)

There is no substitute for the correct charts here if you wish peace of mind along the inside, so if you do not have the Cuban charts, then it will be best to take the outer route, only entering along marked channels. The older large-scale U.S. charts don't have the required detail for much more.

No matter which route you do in fact take, there will nevertheless be a marvellous view of the Sierra de Los Organos running the length of the mainland here. This crushed velvet range of steep-sided mountains makes a beautiful inland backdrop, with a slanting sun shadowing valleys into the deepest green, rather like the mountains of Macchu Picchu or Rio de Janeiro. They are not enormously high, but perfectly amazing, especially if you're coming in from somewhere low-lying like the Gulf or East Coast of the U.S.

Outer Route:

From the inner marks you should head out approximately 280°M over the wall some four miles away, or if you prefer, due north through the main channel at Pasa San Carlos (083° 35.0W). From either of these, parallel the wall outside the reef, following your usual method of coasting until coming to the marked entrances.

Quebrado San Cayetano for La Esperanza

(enter around 083°43.5W and go just slightly west of south after entering).

Pasa Honda for Santa Lucía (wide and clearly marked at 22°43.9N / 083°59.1W).

Quebrado la Galera west of Cayo Jutías (at 22° 40.7N / 084°05.8W), for points further southwest inside reef.

These entrances are sometimes a bit vague on the charts, but on approach they become quite obvious and combined with any sort of vigilance, you will have no trouble at all nipping in and out through the reef. In fact the charts, even the most up to date revisions, do not show always the recent buoyage through the above channels.

Inner Route:

From the inner markers at San Carlos pass, head approximately 245°M to pass between two small cays (Arenas and Verracos) some 4.5 miles across the bay at 22°51.0N / 083°35.lW. Best used by a powerboat, this route can be quite shallow between these cays so be careful to steer round the shoal spots which in any case are only five-to-six feet deep. If this hasn't put you off, it gets easier the rest of the way to La Esperanza, or if you're not stopping there you can aim outside of the outermost cays another seven miles west in better water the closer to the reef you go.

LA ESPERANZA

A small fishing port receiving more and more boats lately, the entrance is straightforward once you have come in over the wall at 083°43.5W, or rounded the cays just about three miles past Cayo Arenas. Just remember to give a wide berth to the shallow bank which extends west of the cays on the eastern side of the bay, and head directly towards the town deep within the bay. The tall concrete dock on the eastern side of the town (22°46.5N / 083°43.7W) carries some 11 feet of water alongside and is protected by large black tires, but surprisingly, has no

cleats. Attach your ropes to the railway lines up top and if there is a swell then put some sort of chafe guards on them. The Guarda Frontera will most definitely come over to you (their buildings are, after all, just next door) and once cleared in they'll probably prefer that you moor a short distance to the northwest. The port is used by fishing boats, and is open to the north. If there are any spare permanent moorings then ask permission to use them. The one I last used had a nice thick barnacled cable and held beautifully in a worrying norther.

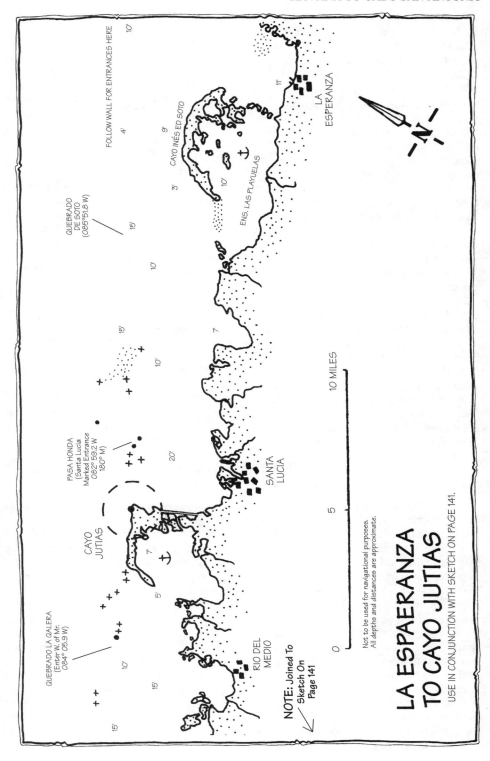

LA ESPAERANZA
TO CAYO JUTIAS

USE IN CONJUNCTION WITH SKETCH ON PAGE 141.

Not to be used for navigational purposes.
All depths and distances are approximate.

10 MILES

0   5

Otherwise drop the hook and set it well against the freely entering swells. You may take the dinghy ashore, leaving it on the shore next to the dock where it will be safe.

Set against a lovely backdrop of mountains, the town is surprisingly attractive. So much so that I know of one American sailor who brought his flat-bottomed (and very homemade) Chesapeake Bay oyster boat on a passing visit and ended up staying six months. He used up every excuse in the book, thwarting all attempts to move him on, and even lodging for a while in a private house. Close to the dock, and owned by a wonderfully spunky woman, this casual establishment also feeds hungry yachtsmen who write their messages of appreciation all over the walls of the dining room. There will likely be more of these by the time you get here.

From your landing spot, leave the compound and head west to see what else the town has to offer. There are clean streets, crowded by tiny houses, and a broad central avenue leading off towards the mountains behind. Along this avenue, there are just a few local enterprises, but the whole place is pervaded by a friendly atmosphere, making it a pleasant layover for anyone wishing to get away from it all. There is also a convenient slipway alongside the dock if such things are of pressing importance or if you wish an excuse to stay.

The Guarda Frontera office is housed in a white building on the west of the dock. To get there, walk through a small woodworking shop, cross the rails of the slipway, and enter through a gate. Once informed about your departure plans they will row out to you, saving you the problem of having to come alongside again. All in all, you too might get a buzz out of La Esperanza.

There are two westerly inside routes further on, both requiring care. One goes between the outer portion of the nearby cays and the reef; while the other, more interesting, takes you through a narrow channel in the southwest corner of the bay of Playuelas. This last route is also a great anchorage if you had to take refuge in a serious blow.

Note that there are scattered shallows between the Ines de Soto Cays and the reef; so you may choose to exit the reef north of Esperanza, re-entering around 083° 51.8 W at Quebrado de Soto; or even further along if you prefer. The alternate route is to use the enclosed Playuelas Bay, just west of La Esperanza. For this remain about 400 yards offshore, parallel to the coast until you're almost sure you're going to run into the cays then swerve south into the very corner where they meet the mainland.

PLAYUELAS BAY & ANCHORAGE

The entrance will suddenly open up right in the corner at 22°46.3N / 083°45.3W presenting a short (east/west) channel which is marked by whithies (rough stakes). It is 30 yards wide and has good deep water if you keep to the southern bank.

Having passed through the passage, veer slightly north, and you will find yourself in a secure, totally enclosed bay some two miles wide with a barrier of cays curving round to the north. The other exit is four miles over to the other side, right at the tip of the cays reaching out from the land on a course of 260°M. Ignore the fishing boats which take the direct route straight across the bay — they only draw four feet and stir up a trail of mud over the shallows — but rather make a nice gentle arc to the north.

This way you'll find 10-to-15-foot of water over a soft bottom.

The western exit is narrower than shown on the charts due to a spit of sand extending down southwest from the end of the northern cays at Punta Hicacal. It is not clearly marked on charts, but again the bank is quite obvious and the passage is marked by whithies. Approach the gap from the northeast, and once there you can take up a course of roughly 300°M out through a short staked channel 50 yards wide at 22°45.7N / 083°50.6W. The shallows here shift about a bit, but you'll be all right when you exit if you swerve slightly north in the darker green waters which show just outside the channel.

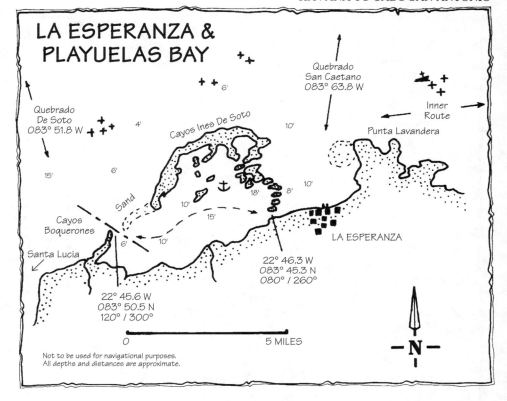

LA ESPERANZA & PLAYUELAS BAY

Quebrado San Caetano
083° 63.8 W

Inner Route

Punta Lavandera

Quebrado De Soto
083° 51.8 W

Cayos Ines De Soto

Quebrado San Caetano

Cayos Boquerones

Santa Lucia

LA ESPERANZA

Sand

22° 46.3 W
083° 45.3 N
080° / 260°

22° 45.6 W
083° 50.5 N
120° / 300°

0   5 MILES

Not to be used for navigational purposes.
All depths and distances are approximate.

– N –

Once back into the main sound inside the Colorados reef, Cayo Jutías will be visible 10 miles away where it sticks out from the land just past Santa Lucia. So you have time to make your decision about your destination over the next hour or two.

SANTA LUCIA

Santa Lucia is a small port catering to the shipment of mineral ores, offering repair and towing facilities for vessels in difficulties. It actually is a sub-port of Mariel and comes under the administration of the port of La Coloma over on the other side of the peninsula. It is worth noting that you can clear in and out of Cuba here, which is handy for anyone contemplating a passage to or from Mexico. I used to think there wasn't a lot here, and the facilities *are* presently a bit run down, but I have unreservedly changed my opinion over the last couple of years.

Coming in from outside the reef, there is a marked channel (0°/180°M past the R/G buoys) through the reef, two miles east of Cayo Jutías at 22°43.9N / 083°59.1W, and from there it's 165°M for 2.5 miles to the port, passing a mid-channel marker (R) along the way in 35 feet.

The town itself is set back inside a channel through the mangroves, as per the adjacent drawing, and upon entering, buoys mark the way to the Guarda Frontera post. You'll easily recognize the dock as it's situated in front of an amazing old wooden ore-loading plant which dominates the view.

Moor where directed, and present your papers to the local Guarda Frontera. We certainly, were made to feel most welcome here by all the officials we met on our last visit, and most laudably, a phamplet showing the port regulations was given to us by the helpful dock manager (See next page).

Tug boats moor here too, but provided

135

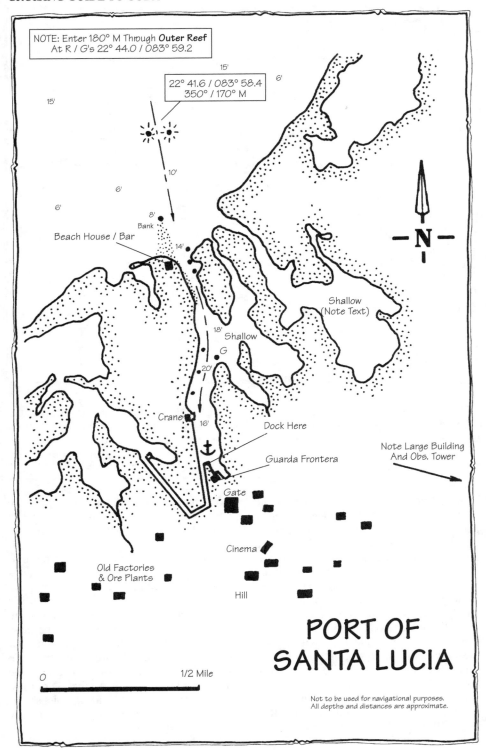

NOTE: Enter 180° M Through **Outer Reef**
At R / G's 22° 44.0 / 083° 59.2

22° 41.6 / 083° 58.4
350° / 170° M

15'

6'

15'

15'

10'

6'

6'

8'
Bank

Beach House / Bar

14'

Shallow
(Note Text)

18'
Shallow

G

20'

Crane

16'

Dock Here

Guarda Frontera

Note Large Building
And Obs. Tower

Gate

Cinema

Old Factories
& Ore Plants

Hill

PORT OF
SANTA LUCIA

Not to be used for navigational purposes.
All depths and distances are approximate.

0   1/2 Mile

136

1996 Santa Lucia Port Regulations.

WELCOME TO SANTA LUCIA

Welcome to Santa Lucia, Cuba. Our port is open to all visiting yachtsmen who possess valid Cuban Visas and Cruising Permits from the Guarda Frontera.

You may tie alongside the concrete wharf, preferably on the south side. You may also anchor out of the main channel in a cove surrounded by mangroves, There is no charge for checking in or out of the port. There is a charge for dockage at the rate of $ _6_ USD for the first three days. Thereafter the charge may be reduced.

You are requested to pass through the Guarda Frontera Base and Gate when visiting town. Other gates are for Cuban workers. Cuban visitors are not allowed on foreign yachts. Only an official from the Guarda Frontera will board your vessel under normal conditions.

Your safety and security are our primary concern. We take our responsibility seriously, and we request your cooperation.

While you are here we offer potable water dockside. Electricity is available at no additional charge if requested. As supply conditions.permit, you.may buy diesel fuel at the prevaling price per litre.

We sincerely hope you will enjoy your visit with us. Please do not hesitate to ask for any sort of assistance. We will do our best to help you.

THANK YOU!

BIENVENIDOS A SANTA LUCIA.

Bienvenidos a Santa Lucía, Cuba. Nuestro Puerto está abierto a todos los yatistas que posean visas y permisos de salida de Guarda Frontera.

Pueden hacer firmes al muelle de concreto preferiblemente por el lado Sur. También se puede anclar fuera del canal principal en la Ensenada rodeada de mangles. No hay costos de entradas ni de salidas del puerto, hay una tarifa de $—— para los primeros tres días. Después el costo puede ser reducido.

Le pedimos que pase por la base de Guarda Frontera.cuando visite al pueblo. Las otras salidas son para los trabajadores cubanos. Los huéspedes cubanos no deben visitar los yates extranjeros; sólo un oficial de Guarda Frontera puede abordarlo bajo condiciones normales.

Su salud y seguridad son nuestra principal preocupación. Tenemos seriamente la responsabilidad y pedimos su colaboración.

Mientras esté en el Puerto ofrecemos agua potable cerca, si desea electricidad está disponible sin costo. Como suministro puede comprar combustible al precio establecido.

Deseamos sinceramente que disfrute su estancia con nosotros. Por favor no vacile en pedir cualquier servicio. Trataremos de ayudarlo.

¡MUCHAS GRACIAS!

there is room you may tie up along either side of the dock. In fact, although the dock area here is a bit primitive, both water and electricity are supplied. Fuel and the like is also available.

Suggestions may be made about anchoring away from the actual docks themselves, but if you do this, you'd best lock up, as a friend of ours once discovered several years ago.

They were moored inside the harbor, working on a burned-out alternator below with a couple of officials actually aboard, when someone attempted to climb on quietly.

As a counterpoint, I must stress that certainly nothing of the sort has *ever* happened to us anywhere in Cuba, and additionally, we felt absolutely at ease upon our last visit to this pleasant spot.

Fascinating ore loading site at Santa Lucia dock.

The town makes its living from the refining of various minerals, with a tiny overhead ore-carrier just outside the gates. Around here you will find a tiny park with benches and a little Madonna and child painted silver. Following the main drag up from here, there is a small market and a

dollar-only shop (fishermen get a percentage of their wages in convertible currency now). There is a cinema showing old British and French films, and further along there's even a quaint hotel. It's seen better days, and looks rather like it should be appearing in those very films.

Around here too, you'll probably be intercepted by runners acting for local Paladars. Follow along, 'cos this is why you're in Cuba. It's not Havana, so be prepared to be entertained in someone's living room by the flickering light of a television soap opera, but you'll still get good value. Especially when you consider the handicaps they operate under — and when you think of washing up after a good meal in your own tiny galley it's even better value.

Finally, there are lots and lots of small private fishing boats in the area; so if you want an eternal friend, then remember the magic words "How about some of them coconuts for these here fishing hooks and this line?".

Yeah, you can tell I got a good feel from Santa Lucia.

CAYO JUTÍAS & THE WESTERN REEF ENTRANCES

If you wish to anchor out, then you may seek shelter over to the cays a mile or two northwest of the port, on one side or the other of Cayo Jutías. Unless you wish to search for space amongst the creeks at the northern end, the best shelter is available on the other side, over to the west. This is a long outer cay, stretched along the line of the coast, and joined to it by a loose series of smaller cays, with a rock causeway, or *pedraplén* giving access (See Pg. 133).

You can exit the reef at the well-marked channel north of Santa Lucia through the Pasa Honda, two miles east of the light on the cay, then continue on until the next entrances, just past the reefs west of Jutías at Quebrada La Galera. If you're coming from further away along the outer routes you can recognize Jutías by the large yellow and black lighthouse and the beach which is bound to see a lot of development now. The water here is crystal clear, with the sunlight casting variegated patterns on the bottom. Makes you indeed want to

throw yourself over the side.

The easy route back inside the reef: There is a green buoy which shows you the way through at 22°40.7N / 084°05.9W in 25 feet. Apply normal precautions when entering on a course of 120°M, passing the mark to port, and following the bright turquoise sand path until well inside before turning westwards or back under Cayo Jutías for the night. Inside these entrances, the water is as clear as anything you've ever seen, with what coral patches there are standing out perfectly against the contrasting bottom. Ashore too, the mountains are giving way to hills, with their neatly cultivated slopes giving you a picture postcard view.

There is also an earlier, slightly more easterly, unmarked, but still safe entrance just past Jutías at 22°41.65N / 083°05.7W with 15-to-25 feet. of clear water over the sand. Coming through at 150°M will take you to the beautifully sheltered bay inside Jutías at the anchorage Nombre de Dios, but it is important to note that there is a soft bar some five feet deep in places extending from the tip of Jutías towards the small protruding landside cay. If you prefer not to have to wind your way past this, then progress on to the shelter at Rio del Medio five miles southwest of the entrance instead. If however, you do enter, then this will allow you to moor in good waters up to 10 feet deep, and to explore the labyrinthine waterways between the cays and the mainland.

Anchor anywhere you want in Nombre de Dios Bay. Around here, you sometimes see the most marvelous jellyfish pulsing along their way just below the surface, and flights of herons or cranes gliding above with extended necks and inquisitive beaks. The mosquitos here can be fierce in the evening and morning during summer, so you may prefer to remain further away from the cays. Remember this exposes you more, so check the anchor's holding.

In the bay here, I remember the mosquitos were relatively invisible during the day, later descending in an avalanche of lust at some secret signal in the early evening and dawn. Your screens had better be tight-fitting, as in the morning you might just see 30-40 of them gazing in hungrily at you.

FOR THE RECKLESS SPIRIT

While the causeway was under construction, there used to be an exciting and tricky way through the cays joining Jutias to the mainland. Coming directly from Santa Lucia it could be done with a shallow draft vessel and an adventurous spirit, but now alas, it seems to have been blocked off. Nevertheless, if you are using your dinghy you may still find it.

If the following appears a bit imaginative, we nevertheless did it with no instructions or guidance, using our 34-foot trawler, a vague rumor and nothing else. Maybe you can too.

From Santa Lucia: Coming through any existing gap in the causeway, turn back to the south into sometimes not much more than four-to-five feet, (over turtle-grass) while looking for a couple of whithies marking the channel through. Remain in the exact center between the causeway and the

cays, while trickling along until at 22°41.5N, then suddenly in seven feet of water, you can turn west towards the two small whithies, marking an extremely narrow (no more than 35-40 feet) channel, with no obvious exit.

The channel at first narrows after the entrance (at 22°41.5 N / 084°00.7 W), and you'll be so close to the banks that overhanging trees will sometimes brush your rigging, leaving small branches and twigs all over the decks.

I won't track all the twists of this amazing labyrinth of tributaries surrounded by the cry of birds, leaping needlefish, and tightly closed in on all sides (including above), but make progress generally westwards, and look for the current at the forks where there is no obvious indication of the correct channel.

Note the current inside the first few yards and remember the direction. It will likely be flowing through from one side of the cays to the other, so if the tide is moving the reeds below in the correct direction, then you are likely on the right track. Slack water in one tributary compared with another, can be an indication of no exit that way.

So, press on (okay, if you have to use directions then take the first fork right, and the next is a left) for half-a-mile, and after the most amazing passage, you'll burst out into the full light of day again. Stakes mark the western end at 22°40.9 N / 084°01.1W, and you can now head over to the anchorage in the snug shelter of Nombre de Dios bay.

If you can't manage the shallows near the causeway, but can still get round into Nombre de Dios, then a dinghy ride into the maze here will be a welcome diversion.

I still remember every minute of my time here.

La Esperanza

ROUTES TO LA FÉ AND CABO SAN ANTONIO
CHART NO. ICH 11422 & 11423 (CUBAN)

This route will take you along the Clorados reef, past the end of the Sierras de Los Organos and into the Gulf of Guanahacabibes (you'll need to practice saying this one), where continuing as far as the tip of the peninsula at Cabo San Antonio the land becomes progressively more uninhabited. The Peninsula de Guanahacabibes is lined with mangrove along the northern shoreline, but for the rest is largely covered with scrub. It is more or less a nature reserve now, with a few buildings at the extreme west where there are facilities for tending the lighthouse and pilot services.

LEAVING THE BAY OF NOMBRE DE DIOS

Leaving the bay of Nombre de Dios, pay attention to the bar which exists at the western end, then steer about 238°M to clear the tip of the little cay Alonso Rojas, six miles away. There are a couple of buoys (uncharted) just off the cay, so continue on outside them towards Punta Tabaco, the next cay, another five miles across the bay. These buoys also mark a convenient pass through the reef to the outside at Pasa Roncadora.

Caution: About two miles north of Punta Tabaco, and east of the large white-girdered lighthouse, there is a charted reef which seems to have grown considerably since survey. It now has trees growing there and extends eastwards with scattered obstructions below the surface to 22°36.0N / 084°12.5W.

The lights erected on the reef grow more numerous along this stretch, but judging by the scattered wrecks near any of a dozen lights around the coast, I'd not be attracted to them at night like a moth, but rather use them as warnings to stay away. Passing about three-quarters-of-a-mile below the light at Punta Tabaco, you can see the breakers along the reef, and even though it may be mirror-calm inside, you'll be surprised to see the amount of waves over on the horizon outside the sound. There is also another new cay which has grown since the original charts were made. It is at 22°33.3N / 084°15.7W and is trailed west by a long shallow bank which, depending on the humor of the local fishermen is sometimes marked by stakes. No matter, even if they're not there, you can easily steer outside of the bank. Again, keep closer to the reef for better depths. A lot of the reefs in Cuba are like the girls your parents warned you about. Too close and you get burned, but just close enough and you're nicely warmed. Whatever, just like the girls, you've always got to keep your eyes on them.

By now there should be a collection of cays (Rapados Grande and Chico) coming up ahead of you, and first steering close to the light at Cabezo Seco, you can approach them from the north. Here you will come across the first of the *Acopio* wharfs, which are a feature of Cuban fishing practice.

These freestanding wharfs are not necessarily connected to any body of land, but rather built onto pilings in water deep enough to enable fishing craft to moor alongside. Here, the catch is landed temporarily, stores taken on, and the crews may rest a few days. For a description of these acopios, see my later remarks in the section dealing with the Cayos de La Lena towards the end of the chapter.

If you wish to anchor overnight around here, you may find the best shelter is available in the lee of these cays, or even a mile or two on at Cayo Buenavista. We've used them all in bad weather, dodging from one to the other depending on wind-shifts.

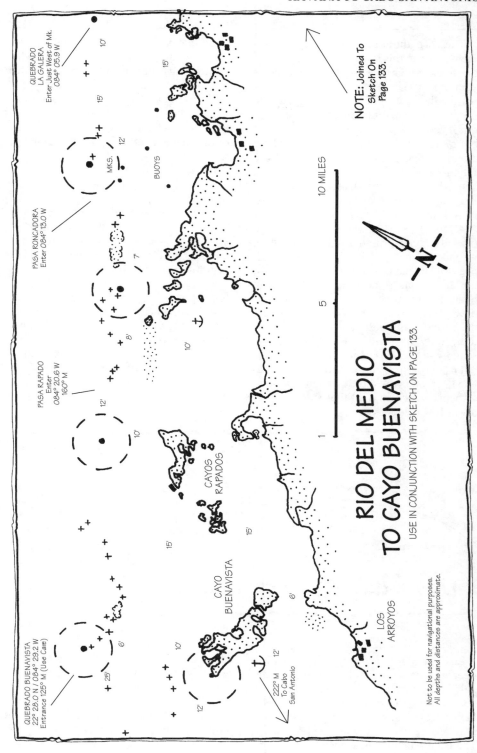

RIO DEL MEDIO
TO CAYO BUENAVISTA

USE IN CONJUNCTION WITH SKETCH ON PAGE 133.

NOTE: Joined To
Sketch On
Page 133.

QUEBRADO
LA GALERA
Enter Just West of Mk.
084° 05.9 W

PASA RONCADORA
Enter 084° 13.0 W

PASA RAPADO
Enter
084° 20.6 W
160° M

QUEBRADO BUENAVISTA
22° 28.0 N / 084° 29.2 W
Entrance 125° M (Use Care)

MKS.

BUOYS

CAYOS
RAPADOS

CAYO
BUENAVISTA

LOS
ARROYOS

222° M
To Cabo
San Antonio

10 MILES

N

Not to be used for navigational purposes.
All depths and distances are approximate.

141

CAYO BUENAVISTA

The last of the larger cays encountered on the way west, this is a handy place to drop the hook, so choose whatever side takes your fancy. There is a series of lagoons within the cay, with an entrance to the northwest just before the light, but don't try this if you draw more than four-to-five-foot but rather go round to the west anywhere around 22°23.7N / 084°26.0W where we've found the holding to be excellent. Pelicans and fishermen catch fish close to the shoreline and you may even get a visit later, which isn't at all bad.

A few of years ago (having arrived dog-tired after an overnight run from Havana), we moored in the shallow bay on the north coast of Buenavista and fell asleep early in the afternoon. Some time later a fishing boat (but this time with uniforms aboard) drew close alongside. We were roused, naked and as ill-natured as you'd expect us to be, only to find that they didn't want to see any documents. They'd only come to tell us they expected the northeast wind to rise later, and why didn't we move around to better water on the other side, or over towards Rapado Chico.

On that occasion, we showed our papers only *once* after Havana, and that was when clearing out from Cayo Largo halfway down the south coast near the Bay of Pigs!

Going round Buenavista can best be done outside the cay, between it and the reef as there are uncharted shoals just to the south of the island and the depths in the channel seem to be five-to-six feet

If passing through tha shallower inside passage, keep in the center of the Santa Maria channel, and beware an even shallower patch protruding slightly west southwest of that shown on the charts at Punta Las Orillas. The water around there is crystal clear, and this at least makes for good vision to the bottom. My records, in fact, say that we could see, "Every blade of turtle-grass, every starfish, every urchin..." and we still ran aground adding our propeller tracks to those already scarring the bottom off the point.

If going to Los Arroyos behind Buenavista, the best approach would be made from the northwest, head on in 10 feet of water.

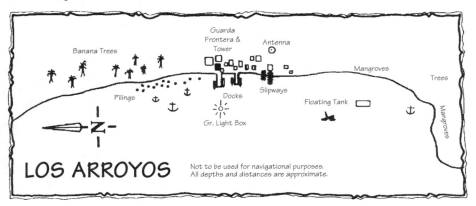

LOS ARROYOS — Not to be used for navigational purposes. All depths and distances are approximate.

LOS ARROYOS

Los Arroyos is a fishing village with a fleet of some 50-60 small craft working the gulfs of Mexico and Guanahacabibes. The boats anchor off the port, having discharged their catches alongside the two small docks, so exercise caution when approaching. There is a watchtower, a green light guiding

you in, and two small slipways here too, which you could use in an emergency. It's surrounded by banana trees and connected by road to the nearby town of Mantua, but you're still going to be a long way off from any good highways elsewhere.

The author and "Hobbes".

THE WIDENING INNER GULF

The Gulf of Guanahacabibes now begins to widen considerably, with depths dropping gradually down to 60 feet, and crisscrossed with deep stands of coral separated by sand. A scuba diver or snorkeler can spend a lot of time there, or along the outer reef with the wall only a few yards further off. The waters are crystal clear, and the abundance of marine life is a tribute to benign neglect.

Your loran too, will still be giving excellent information, so it can be relied on where there are no landmarks or buoyed channels (we've checked this as far south as the Caymans)

On the other hand, if you prefer to remain close in to land, you may set a visual course all along the coastline from now on, remaining a few hundred yards off in whatever depth you choose.

Continuing on from Arroyos, the coastline veers south, and the inland terrain becomes flatter with slight hillocks and open areas dotted by isolated trees.

Along here, you may see smoke quietly rising from the sugarcane fields as they burn off the leaves and scatter the snakes prior to harvesting, and you might occasionally also hear loud explosions too, with its own distinct type of smoke. We once thought it was from quarrying, but one of the local officials informed me it was from army maneuvers.

The Ensenada de Guardiana is a deep bay east of the widest point of the gulf, itself containing a smaller bay further in the extreme eastern corner. This is the bay of Juan Lopez, with the town of La Fé nestled inside at the entrance to the river Guardiana.

The first part of the river is navigable by shallow draft boats and is used as a refuge in times of really bad weather, but in any case the whole bay at Juan Lopez is enclosed on most sides.

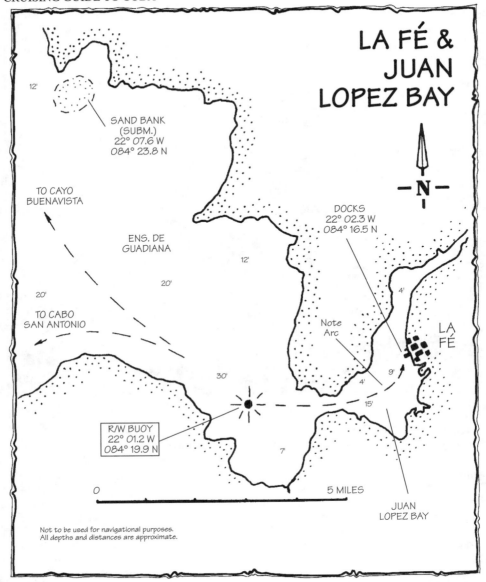

LA FÉ &
JUAN
LOPEZ BAY

-N-

12'

SAND BANK
(SUBM.)
22° 07.6 W
084° 23.8 N

TO CAYO
BUENAVISTA

DOCKS
22° 02.3 W
084° 16.5 N

ENS. DE
GUADIANA

12'

20'

20'

4'

TO CABO
SAN ANTONIO

Note
Arc

LA
FÉ

9'

30'

4'

R/W BUOY
22° 01.2 W
084° 19.9 N

15'

7'

0   5 MILES

JUAN
LOPEZ BAY

Not to be used for navigational purposes.
All depths and distances are approximate.

LA FÉ & JUAN LOPEZ BAY

The entrance is marked by a large red/white buoy (22º01.2N /084º19.9W), which is in fact, now only white with accumulated bird-droppings. The other outer mark shown on some charts is no longer there, but this is a perfectly straightforward entrance which needs no aids to navigation at all.

Enter via the center of the channel, and you can make a southerly arc across the bay on a general course of 60ºM towards La Fé, which will be visible two miles away against a lovely backdrop of hills.

It's a tiny picturesque little place with red-roofed white buildings, a red and white antenna and a watchtower looking suspiciously over the bay, in case the enemy ever does arrive (Here? Why here?). The better buildings tend to be along the northern end of the town, with more humble affairs closer to the only wharf on the south side.

Approach the sturdy Russian-built concrete wharf only on its left (north). Although there are tire fenders strung along the right side, the bottom there is fouled by debris jettisoned over the edge. Slip between the mooring post off the end and the wharf itself (the gap is about 20 feet), and moor alongside.

There is a slipway right next to the dock with a couple of yards depth outside, and in spite of its rather dilapidated appearance we have been told it could handle our boat if necessary.

The Guarda Frontera barracks is a grey building 100 yards to the north, and they'll come out to the wharf as soon as you approach, but do not allow them to remove your documents. They do not get much in the line of visitors here, and may even request that you don't take the dirt roads far inland, but the local inhabitants are friendly in the extreme. Your vessel will be the center of attention, and what appears to be a goodly proportion of them will find themselves out to the end of the dock, where they'll sit with their legs dangling and stare curiously inside your cabin.

PLANNER'S THEORY BREAKDOWN

You may notice along the coasts out here that the centralized distribution and grandi-

A small boat shed at Santa Fé.

ose theories of the planners has somewhat broken down. The townships along here are more obviously deprived, compared to what might pass for basics in the more privileged (yes, privilege does exist in Cuba) areas of Havana, but the people who actually have to live with it are still remarkably friendly, in spite of it all.

In the morning you may be roused by large black vultures coughing and flapping their wings as they strut the wharf outside. So, having collected your despacho (remember that one?) and departed the southeast corner of the Gulf of Guanahacabibes, you are left with an easy run along the low coastline to the west. Navigation along here is purely visual along an unremarkable shore for the next 30 miles, whereupon Los Cayos de Ia Leña (firewood cays) stand out from the peninsula and offer an enclosed shelter.

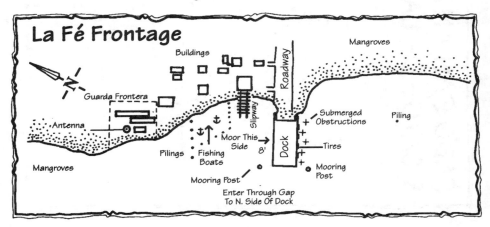

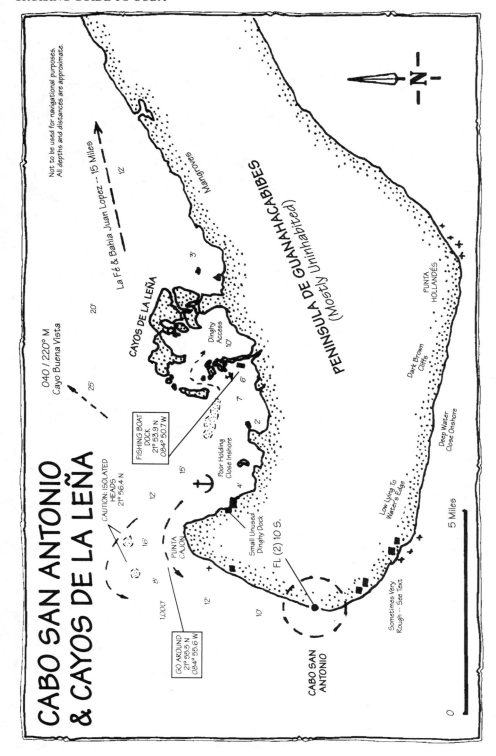

CABO SAN ANTONIO & CAYOS DE LA LEÑA

Not to be used for navigational purposes.
All depths and distances are approximate.

La Fé & Bahia Juan Lopez -- 15 Miles

12'

Manbroves

20'

CAYOS DE LA LEÑA

Dinghy
Access
10'

3'

PENINSULA DE GUANAHACABIBES
(Mostly Uninhabited)

040 / 220° M
Cayo Buena Vista

25'

CAUTION: ISOLATED
HEADS
21° 56.4 N

FISHING BOAT
DOCK
21° 53.9 N
084° 50.7 W

6'

7'

2'

Poor Holding
Close Inshore

15'

12'

16'

8'

1,000'

PUNTA
CAJON

GO AROUND
21° 55.5 N
084° 55.6 W

12'

4'

Small Unused
Dinghy Dock

FL (2) 10 S.

10'

Sometimes Very
Rough -- See Text

Low Lying To
Water's Edge

Dark Brown
Cliffs

Deep Water
Close Onshore

PUNTA
HOLLANDÉS

CABO SAN
ANTONIO

5 Miles

0

146

CABO SAN ANTONIO AND THE CAYOS DE LA LENA
CHART NO. ICH 11422 (CUBAN)

The tip of the northwest coast of Cuba is your final destination on this leg. It's the place from which you start your return journey back up the coast, or where you rest up for an early morning trip round the cape and on towards the southeast.

As you can see from the chart showing Cabo San Antonio, these cays offer excellent shelter within the bight, while still remaining close to the cape. A little distance off the western side there is a small dock offering facilities for local fishing vessels, and it may be approached along a direct line from the tip of Punta Cajón over to the west or by coming round the top of the actual cays. If coming in on the latter, then be aware of the shallow bank which exists just west of the cays so give them a wider berth. The depths closer to the docks are not always suitable for deeper keels either, so if you draw more than six feet be prepared to anchor about two hundred yards off.

The fishermen here are amongst the nicest you will meet on your entire journey, thankfully free (so far) of official watchdogs, and we make it a point to pause here whenever we can. Not only for the rest stop it offers, but also for the good cheer and company. It's great at the Cayos de La Leña.

We have always been invited (request permission before docking) to remain a day or two, waiting on suitable weather for rounding the cape, and have enjoyed tremendous hospitality from the simplest of people here.

The dock, at a position of 21°53.9N / 084°50.7W, is constructed of wooden pilings and situated well away from land to allow access by various types of small fishing vessels. There is a small shed at one end with an ancient diesel generator supplying power to the main building, and there are living quarters for the four or five workers who call it home. When we were there once we saw a litter of piglets suckling noisily away in the back room, but now only a cat seems to be allowed. Apparently the dogs molest the lobster and turtles on the dock.

At the front in the main room, which doubles as an office, there used to be the most fascinating posters depicting a smartly dressed group of middle class citizens, complete with shirts, ties, and creased trousers, calmly leading frocked children to the safety of a bunker while a mushroom cloud rose behind in the background. Meanwhile, Che Guevarra smiled benignly down from the walls, a cigarette dangling negligently between his fingers.

If you dock at the southern end, you'll be out of the way, well placed to observe a life which few people are even aware of, and if you're at all sociable your boat will be the scene of much friendly coming and going.

There is casual tarpon fishing right off the dock, and I have actually witnessed an epic battle between one of those fighting monsters and an elderly Cuban gentleman with a *handline!* You should have seen the state of his hands by the time the heroic fish

147

broke free, but to tell you the truth I was rooting for the fish under my breath.

A wire netting cage in the water can, rather unfortunately, sometimes contain either live turtles or empty turtle shells being naturally cleaned of bloody shreds by fish. Sad, but that's how it goes.

A portion of the catch is salted here too, so you may want to bargain for some which can be prepared in a variety of delicious ways particular to the Caribbean. Try it in fish-cakes, or even in a coconut and tomato sauce (a Bahiána, Brazilian style). And if any of the fishermen here offer you trunkfish (yes, trunkfish), take it in spite of all your misgivings. Breaded and shallow fried it is absolutely delicious. Easily the equal of the

Loading the sugar cane harvest.

Colonel's Southern fried chicken. Just don't show up when they're filleting it if you're squeamish or if you have any sort of a conscience.

Finally, ice is kept there in an insulated storeroom off the main building, and if your boat is running a bit low it's a good place to stock up.

If you choose instead to anchor a mile or two closer to the cape, in the wide open bay of Cajón, then be careful of the holding near shore. The bottom here close to the shoreline can be smooth rock in places, offering little or no grip, and the northeasterlies can set up swells which are capable of dislodging an anchor only half-set on one fluke. Better to moor a little further out where the grip is better.

Interestingly, the water close inside this area of the coast is extremely dark, obscuring the flat, shallow bottom in a few feet, whereas off the desolate tip of Cajón the waters again become as clear as a fine vodka, and half a mile or so northeast of the point the bottom is

scored with deep ravines.

Along the coastline where it swings northwards at Los Morros, there are a couple of small landing areas, and there's's even a tiny concrete step at the waterside where you can moor a dinghy if you wish to trek into the peninsula.

Mostly, however, the area is pretty much deserted following a rehousing program which transplanted the population some time ago. We've met loyal Cubans who just love to tell you how the original inhabitants have wonderful housing now, in big concrete apartment blocks with televisions, occasional electricity and water... Ha!

If you're going on, then this is the place to prepare for rounding Cabo San Antonio on your way to visiting the southern coastlines and the much larger cays along that side. But if you're going to be returning to Havana, then this is the end of the line.

Whichever way you go, by now you have quite enough experience to take up your own route. So have fun.

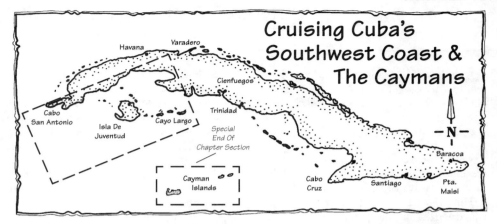

CHAPTER VI

Cruising Cuba's
Southwest Coast &
The Caymans

—N—

CABO SAN ANTONIO TO CAYO LARGO

T his is a fairly straightforward cruise, along the mainland at the western end of Cuba then through the cays as far as Cayo Largo, 200 miles to the east on the outer reef.

The land along the northern (top) edge of the gulf is low-lying, but within the gulf, depths are more than adequate to allow most transits. There is a ring of cays along most of the southern edge forming a protective barrier against the seas, and additionally there is a large island (the Isle of Pines, or more recently the Isle of "Youth") more or less half way along, giving even more shelter and opportunity for landside exploring.

The waters inside the cays are deep enough for most purposes (large ships use the gulf), and the bottom is usually turtle grass over sand. Along the outside of the cays, we usually find white beaches and much clearer water, with visibility all the way down

Dr. Mauriz's front porch: The perfect waiting room.

to 100 feet. in places.

Finally, there are several passes through the ring of outer cays, making for easy entrances and exits across that barrier.

CHARTS

Once again the best charts to use are the most recent updates of the official Cuban ICH series.

If they are not available to you then any of the best DMA or Admiralty charts will have to do, but as these are produced from different sources and to a different scale, be more cautious in your interpretation of the data.

If you do have the opportunity to purchase ICH charts in advance of your trip (Bluewater Books & Charts in Ft. Lauderdale is best for copies, or Havana itself for originals) then the numbers you need for the gulf are as follows: ICH1147,1146,1145, 1144,1143. Plus of course, ICH 11422 (which deals with Cabo San Antonio).

ROUNDING CABO SAN ANTONIO
CHART NO. ICH 1122 (CUBAN)

A doddle if it's done right, or a serious bummer if you get it wrong.

If you are using a larger scale U.S. chart you might wonder about the nifty little waves which are drawn on it. They're there for a reason.

And if you've got the Cuban charts, well, the annotation "Perpetua Rpte" on the point means "Always Breaking!"

This, the narrowest point between the island and the Yucatan peninsula in Mexico, is where all that water coming up from the Caribbean Basin gets squeezed down. It then meets all those minor countercurrents which confuse it into a state of nervous agitation, and it only needs one little thing to set it off... a southeast wind.

Squalls too, whip themselves up out of nowhere, and we have been calmly cruising round the point under fair skies when suddenly huge waves have appeared on the horizon and borne straight down on us. We once made this trip in an unfavorable southeast wind, and it was a miserable time, mostly spent clinging on as the boat rolled onto its beam-ends or submarined into vertical walls of water.

But on the other hand if you wait for a northeast wind, then protected by the mainland, you're subject to little more than a gentle rolling motion. This then, is the secret.

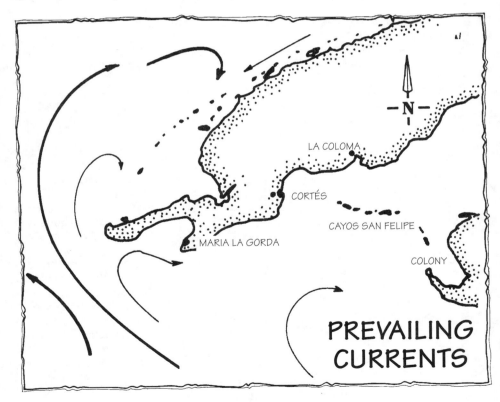

LA COLOMA

CORTÉS

CAYOS SAN FELIPE

MARIA LA GORDA

COLONY

PREVAILING CURRENTS

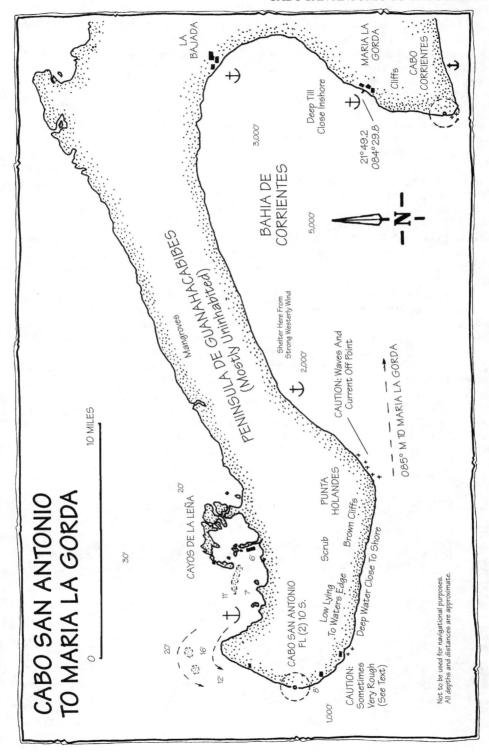

CABO SAN ANTONIO TO MARIA LA GORDA

10 MILES

0

LA BAJADA

MARIA LA GORDA

CABO CORRIENTES

Deep Till Close Inshore

3,000'

21° 49.2
084° 29.8

BAHIA DE CORRIENTES

5,000'

-N-

Cliffs

PENINSULA DE GUANAHACABIBES
(Mostly Uninhabited)

Mangroves

Shelter Here From Strong Westerly Wind

2,000'

CAUTION: Waves And Current Off Point

085° M TO MARIA LA GORDA

CAYOS DE LA LEÑA

20'

20'

30'

PUNTA HOLANDES

Scrub

Brown Cliffs

Low Lying To Water's Edge

Deep Water Close To Shore

6'

7'

8'

11'

12'

16'

20'

CABO SAN ANTONIO
FL (2) 10 S.

1,000'

CAUTION: Sometimes Very Rough (See Text)

Not to be used for navigational purposes.
All depths and distances are approximate.

151

Prepare the vessel overnight by bringing down and furling the Bimini, wedging loose objects with cushions, and in general readying the boat for an early departure. If all notes, charts, instruments, engine-checks, etc., are sorted out the night before, then you can be on your way by sunup, when the winds are likely to be at their lowest. The forecast should be listened to, but you should have a pretty good feel for it by now, and if you've been anchored near the tip, then you'll pretty much know what the wind is up to overnight. All you want is a day's worth of any wind out of the north or northeastern quarter.

SHALLOWS AND A WRECK

There are a couple of shallower spots, with a submerged wreck a bit north of Punta Cajon, so you can go round at 21°57.0 N to avoid these. But you might equally choose to pass between them and the mainland at around 21°55.5N, heading east from your anchorage, then turning south whenever you feel comfortable with the depth. A half-mile or so offshore should have you in about 10 feet, and you'll be out of any unfavorable swells.

Passing the well-built light and radar station at Cabo San Antonio, swing outside the shallows at Los Cayuelas and the beaches at Caleta Larga (21°49.9N / 084°56.0W),

then once the coast has curved east you can come in close again. Don't be surprised if the lighthouse calls you up on the VHF to check you out, so once again keep your radio on.

Provided you've been lucky with the weather, you'll have been rewarded with a gentle run in the morning sunlight, but in the event that your schedule has not allowed you to pick and choose your time, then stay a bit further offshore to give yourself some sea-room. In unfavorable conditions there can be some dangerous onshore currents, so be careful to note your position and heading. It's not a long run, but it can be a bit uncomfortable.

The deserted coastline continues some 10 miles east to the cliffs at Punta Holandés, dead into a blinding low sun which is also reflected into your face by the water. Your darkest glasses will help, but they will reflect even more light back onto your long-suffering nose. Remember to slather on the strongest sunscreen you have, or the next few days are not going to be too pleasant.

Low black cliffs mark the approach to Punta. Holandés, and the base of the point is surrounded by a shallow bank extending out a mile, so give it a bit of room as you come out of the protection of the land and into the Bahía de Corrientes (the Bay of Currents).

Maria La Gorda

EXTRAORDINARY WATERS

From Punta Holandés, set a course of 85°M across the bay towards the resort of Maria La Gorda (16 miles), and revel in the deepest indigo-blue water which now extends on all sides. Within this extraordinary bay, frigate-birds will soar, and the sea-gulls take up station overhead looking out for any flying fish that panic at your approach. You might even see hunting packs of tuna or dolphin rounding up other smaller fish and herding them into small compact schools before the feeding frenzy whips the water on the surface. The bay is also host to the occasional whale-shark too so look out for the disturbances as its huge spotted body slowly passes close to the surface.

At about half distance across the bay, you'll begin to see a small promontory ahead of you on the other side, so adjust your course to the left of this where a small group of red roofed buildings will soon become visible.

MARIA LA GORDA (FAT MARIA)

A dive resort, situated on the eastern shoreline of the Bahia de Corrientes, this lovely spot is surrounded by deserted wilderness and co-conut strewn beaches. The waters within the bay are of unparalleled clarity, and host to an amazing variety of fish. I will even go out on a limb to say that I have never dived in a more beautiful environment below the surface.

At 21°49.2N / 084°29.8W, the white-painted concrete dock is about 150 feet long and 10 feet wide, with some six or seven feet at the end. Temporarily, you should moor along the southern edge to leave the local dive-boat its usual berth across the way. Use the bollards, even if they are on the other side, and do not attach your lines to the light-posts on the end. When last seen they were only sitting on concrete blocks and could be easily dragged over and onto your deck.

Checking-in here is an informal process and should only take five minutes if the dock manager's around. If not, you may have to wait until he get's in from fishing with the rest of the guys.

Note: I have seen sailboats clearing-in from Mexico here, but it takes forever for the officials to arrive from the interior, and you are charged an extra $25 for this (which is not at all bad when you consider). Just remember though, the last crew I saw doing this had to wait a day and a half (on board) to finally complete all the for-malities.

Having cleared-in, you will probably be expected to moor some 50 yards off to the north-west of the dock in about 30-40 feet where there are a couple of small buoys you might tie up to. Later you can bring your dinghy to the dock at any point along its length.

If the moorings are occu-pied and you have to anchor, remember that the bay is to-tally open to anything that comes out of the west. Be very careful to put out a lot of scope, set your heaviest anchor as best you can, and finally dive it. The bottom is hard sand and the point will not easily penetrate unless forced in by hand.

The hotel has about 48 beds in a collec-tion of neat concrete cabins fronted by tended periwinkle flower-beds, and the res-taurant serves a great variety of well-cooked food at around $15 per plate. Just ask Juanito in the kitchen for Lo que hay ("Whatever there is"), and you'll be glad... okay, in this happy day of the paladar restaurant it's not all that cheap, but you do get soup, dessert, and all the trimmings.

Although the resort is largely dedicated to scuba diving, it does arrange tours into the hinterland of Guanacabibes if you wish. Rental cars are available, but they need to be booked the day before as they have to be delivered some distance to the hotel. Look at the map to see just how isolated this place is.

There are more than 20 superb dive-sites along the wall just in front of the hotel and within 2-3 miles of the dock, with tunnels, caves, vertical drop-offs, and fronds of wisteria-like ferns hanging down into the depths from the coral towers. Those dives I have done here will remain engraved on my mind forever.

If you're going to dive with the resort boats, remove at least four or five pounds from your normal weightbelt to compensate for the heavy steel cylinders they issue to divers. They're well over 100 cubic feet capacity, compared to the U.S. norm of 80 cubic feet.

Unfortunately, it must be said, there has been a subtle change in the treatment recently afforded to cruisers — if they themselves are divers. In contrast to previous years, when we were always made most welcome, the resort has taken to threatening boaters with all kinds of harassment if they have the nerve to go diving on their own.

You are now told that you have to pay diving fees, even if you dive from your own boat with your own equipment; and you have to be accompanied by the resort divemasters!

While discussing this on my most recent visit, I was told in an somewhat offhand way that they considered they owned the rights to diving in the bay. Supervision, it was claimed, was needed to safeguard the visitors from injury and more importantly, to stop them stealing all the black coral. Rich indeed, coming from one who was at the time festooned with the stuff, and even richer when the shop there is busily engaged in selling jewelry made from it (as do all hotels along the coast). To make matters worse, there is a large bronze monument to Ludo, a divemaster (and son of the French resort operator) who died there while diving to over 350 feet on compressed air! Yep, *great* examples of safety to us all.

If you think I'm being a bit harsh, well I too, used to make my living as a divemaster/instructor in the Caribbean and I've not heard of this sort of treatment being meted out anywhere else.

If you are here during times of bad weather, you may have to seek shelter over on the west or even the north side of the bay around the small village of La Bajada. Again, unfortunately, there have been the very occasional reports of boats receiving a less than friendly reception here, with one that I know of being made to leave shelter in a bad norther. In this event, the answer was to go all the way round (five miles) to the lee of the cliffs south of Maria La Gorda and to anchor close inshore. In any case, the whole bay is somewhat unprotected, so if *really* bad weather is expected then the only answer is to leave the area the day before.

Perhaps the resort still does wish pretty yachts to moor off the beach for the benefit of the land-based visitors, but alas, this is one of the places in Cuba whose performance has declined over the last few years. A pity, because it is a really lovely place to spend a few days relaxing, and the fishermen and most of the other staff members of the resort are super-nice.

Departure is a simple affair, visual past the Tetas de Maria (no, I shall not translate), two protuberances out from the cliffs at Punta Caiman two miles south of the dock, and on to Cabo Corrientes in water of cutglass transparency. Just keep the pale-blue stuff to your left, the dark-blue stuff to your right, and cruise along the wall 200 yards offshore, go round the corner and truck on eastwards to Cabo Francés about 30 miles away.

This is a straightforward run along desolate scrub-lined escarpments with rocky undercut cliffs. There are no offshore reefs and you may tack freely along the first section, but there is a shallow shelf extending well out from the buildings and the light at Punta Francés (084°02.OW). This can get you into trouble as it's quite abrupt and there's no real warning, so go wide round the point there and remain at least a mile offshore.

From here, half a dozen places beckon, among which we find Cayo Reál and the San Felipe cays, The Laguna de Cortés, The Isla de Juventud, and even the town of La Coloma right up there on the north coast of the Gulf of Batábano.

HEADING FOR THE ISLA DE JUVENTUD

If you wish to go straight across to the Isla de Juventud from Cabo Frances, then head to Cayo Reál and follow the cays (see following text). For a new experience along the way, take a dive along the wall just south of the westernmost point of the San Felipe cays to confirm the existence of undersea freshwater springs.

Be very careful, however, of the Canal de Los Indios just after those cays when you're coming in through to the inside near Juventud. Although this looks like the logical place to enter, there is a substantial reefy bar across that entrance, and care is required to pass through. A deep finned sailboat will find it as easier to continue down past the Cayos de Los Indios towards the

southwest corner of the island. After safely passing all the cays and their associated banks, good water will be found between latitudes 21°43.0N and 21°39.5N., and you can then come in through the major channel there.

On the other hand, if you wish to remain awhile on the mainland of Cuba, then go to Cortés or Coloma along the way (see sketch).

CAYO REÁL & THE CAYOS SAN FELIPE

Cayo Reál is the first cay along the Cayos San Felipe, and a great spot to spend a day or two, either snorkeling or just plain poodling about in the dinghy looking for an abundance of lobster. But anywhere along the south side of this archipelago is going to be a delight to the eye, with clean blue waters edging uninhabited white beaches. And they're on the leeward side so you can normally anchor-off as you wish.

Remember, it's a total of 50 - 55 miles, into the wind, from Maria La Gorda to Cayo Reál; so leave early if you're planning on making it in one go. The journey is straight-forward enough, east along the coast then 80°M for 23 miles from the tip of the mainland at Cabo Francés. It can be a bit of a bear in a strong easterly, so be prepared to slog it out until you reach the shelter of the cays. Although you might think there is an alter-

ROUTES: MARIA LA GORDA TO ISLA DE JUVENTUD

Not to be used for navigational purposes.
All depths and distances are approximate.

native route available by traveling on the northern side and following the shallower waters in the gulf of Batabáno, I have found that the waters there don't really deliver on their promise.

To pass a pleasant time surrounded by clear, clean waters and lobster, try mooring off the western tip of Cayo Reál anywhere around 21°58.6N / 083°37.4W; or wherever your anchor will grip and the bottom is deep enough. That caveat about the anchor is important, because the floor there is a covering of sand over flat corals and you may have to hunt around for a good spot. Look out too for some heads which might cause a problem at 21°58.1N / 083°37.9W.

If you were faced with a wind out of the south, then shelter can be found over on the other side of the cays, but be careful how you get there. There's a shallow area northwest of the island extending anything up to six miles from the tip, and you'll have to pass through this if you don't want to go all the way round. Nevertheless, you can find

a shorter route through to the north by going to 22°01.5N / 083°41.8W and heading across on a bearing of 45°M in 10 feet all the way. That's about two miles west of the Acopio (the freestanding fishing boat dock) off the tip of the island.

The holding is not great on that side of the cays though, so a great deal of care is required when anchoring. We did this once in a hard southeasterly and had to visit several shallow bays before we could feel comfortable, on the north side of Cayo Perro. Be on the lookout for fishing nets too, strung along poles and sitting anything up to a quarter of a mile offshore.

All in all, the southern side is a better prospect, and luckily, the prevailing winds favor that side. There is a shelf which reaches out some way from the actual cays and it's easy to find lovely bays and beautiful beaches along this stretch. We certainly noted these Cays as among the most attractive in the whole of Cuba.

LAGUNA DE CORTÉS
(45 MILES FROM M. LA GORDA)
CHART NOS. ICH 1122 & 1147 (CUBAN)

On the mainland itself, this a large enclosed lagoon with a tricky entrance about ten miles north/northeast of Cabo Francés. It offers shelter from all sides, and is a placid overnight stop if you can get in, especially if any winds are expected later. Once again, there's not a lot of shelter along

the way, so to get here comfortably from Maria La Gorda you've got to leave early in the morning.

Note: Do not attempt this entrance if you have a deep-keeled yacht (6 feet), but rather anchor in the wide bight of the Ensenda de Corte's a few miles further on.

There are two entrances to the lagoon as shown on the charts, but on no account should you try the wider, more northerly of these. It is barred by a shallow bank and you will ground.

As a matter of fact, I ran aground there repeatedly before I found the right way in myself, on a visit two years later.

Follow the sketches for the entry route, paralleling the coastline northbound at least a mile or two out to avoid the shallows close inshore, and remembering not to aim straight at the entry channel when you make your turn back west.

Rather, come in from slightly below the first gap (say 22°02.6N) heading west to-

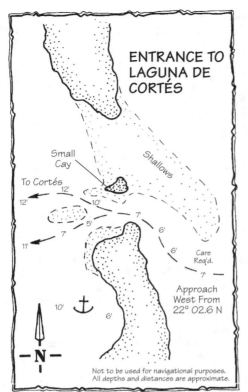

ENTRANCE TO
LAGUNA DE
CORTÉS

Small
Cay

Shallows

To Cortés

12'   12'   10'
5'   7'
7   6'
11'   6'   Care
Req'd.
7 —
Approach
West From
10'   6'   22° 02.6 N

— N —

Not to be used for navigational purposes.
All depths and distances are approximate.

Anchored across here, you'll be rewarded with lovely views of the sun slowly dropping in a red ball of fire over the town of Cortés — and if you do this in March, when they burn the canefields prior to harvesting, then the smoke will lend an eery, fantastic, tone to the whole affair.

The town's a picturesque little spot some two miles away on the western edge of the lagoon, with 20-30 medium-sized fishing vessels, a working dry-dock and lots of roofs nestling amongst a multitude of trees. I've even come across a treasure hunting or underwater archeology vessel there, all kitted up with prop-wash deflectors and the like.

The Guarda Frontera post seems to double as the ice house on the central wharf where the fishing boats cluster, and you should approach this on the left side. If there are any patrol-boats there then draw up a few feet away and shout over for instructions. The wharf is usually crowded, and they will doubtless wish you to anchor in front of the dock so find a clear spot among the fishing

wards a point about 200-300 yards south of the entrance. By now, the sun will be setting, so exercise caution as you approach, shade your eyes and be ready to back up in the event of any unexpected shallows ahead.

When 80-100 yards offshore, turn approximately 300°M, and continue slowly towards the mouth and through the confusion of small markers. Having come round the point, it is shallower in the center, so remain close to the left bank (50 yards) all the way through where you will find some seven feet of water. There is another obstruction just after clearing the entrance inside so steer round it, either north or south as shown. At this point, you may either choose to anchor close to the entrance or to go over to the town across the way.

If anchoring out, then there is shelter with extremely good holding in a small bay just a couple of hundred yards south of the entrance channel. The bottom is thick heavy mud though, so be prepared to wash down for at least twenty minutes after you pull away in the morning.

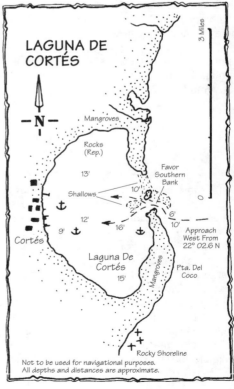

LAGUNA DE
CORTÉS

3 Miles

— N —

Mangroves

Rocks
(Rep.)

13'

Favor
Southern
Bank

Shallows   10'

12'   16'   10'   6'   10'

Cortés   9'

Approach
West From
22° 02.6 N

Laguna De
Cortés

Mangroves

Pta. Del
Coco

15'

Rocky Shoreline

Not to be used for navigational purposes.
All depths and distances are approximate.

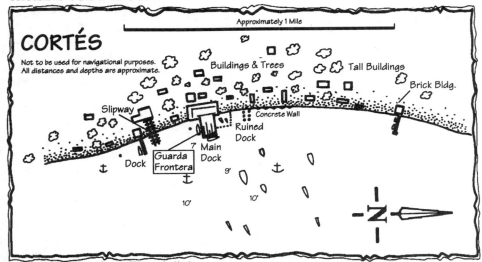

boats and anchor there. There is little wave-action within the bay and the holding is good, so let out just enough rode for security (but not so much that you swing into the other boats), and await the small boat which will bring out the official. They rarely used to get foreign boats here but documentation will only take a couple of minutes if your technique and your papers are right, which they should be by now.

If you're coming in from Mexico, this is not an international port so don't even think about it. Instead, go on to the Isla de Juventud.

Early in the morning you'll see the crews being rowed out to the fishing boats which then go alongside the wharf to collect their despachos and other necessities before streaming out of the bay. As luck will have it, the morning sun will be in your eyes now, so note the direction the fishing-boats take and hunt down the dark glasses again for your departure.

Remember the dangers coming up to the mouth and keep close to the right bank when going through, then having made your exit along the coast go east towards deeper water.

ROUTE TO LA COLOMA
(26 MILES FROM CORTÉS)
CHART NO. ICH 1147 (CUBAN)

A short, easy run to a larger town along the northern coastline of the gulf, this passage can be made directly across from Cortés, or if you prefer, along the low coastline. When going directly over, the most convenient starting waypoint is the large marker 4 miles east southeast of the exit at Cortés.

From here a course of 70°M will put you off Punta Santo Domingo, and further on between the marks leading into the harbor at La Coloma (see La Coloma waypoint sketch on Pg. 160). A jolting ride some-

times, reminding you that the gulf is quite large enough to have waves of its own.

Along the way you are likely to see a variety of the grey rust-stained ferrocement fishing boats typical of the southern side of Cuba. Steered from a position on the stern, they contain a large hold up front and favor carrying their cargo of empty lobster traps on the roof of the main cabin. A friendly lot, these fishermen, and we have even been halted by one vessel which despatched a crewmember in a skiff to present us with a bucket of live blue crabs!

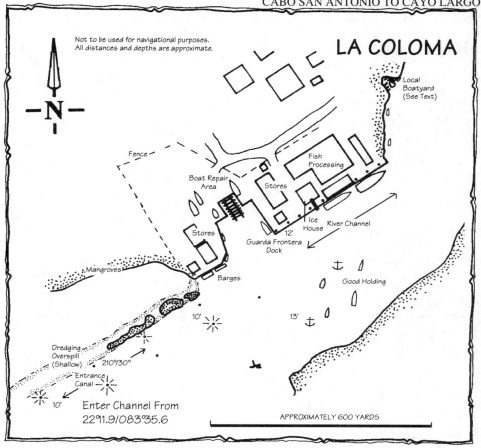

Not to be used for navigational purposes.
All distances and depths are approximate.

-N-

LA COLOMA

Local Boatyard (See Text)

Fence

Fish Processing

Boat Repair Area

Stores

Ice House   River Channel

Stores

12'

Guarda Frontera Dock

Mangroves

Barges

Good Holding

10'

13'

Dredging Overspill (Shallow)   210°/30°

Entrance Canal

10'   Enter Channel From
22°11.9/083°35.6

APPROXIMATELY 600 YARDS

LA COLOMA

Situated at the mouth of the river Coloma, the town's principal commerce is fishing and other associated industries. It can be seen clearly on any sunny day by the white reflections from the warehouses, the tall ice-making plant, apartment buildings, and the large mushroom-shaped water tower behind the docks.

The town also serves as a transport hub for passengers and freight travelling by water to the Isla de Juventud, and overland to the city of Pinar del Rio in the mountains to the north.

In the case of a major storm the river is navigable for some distance if you need to seek refuge.

From points south, the outer Santo Domingo light is at position 22°09.5N / 083°36.5W, and then you head 20°M for 2.5

miles to the dredged channel into port.

Enter the canal itself along a course of 30°M at position 22°11.9N / 083°35.6W, slightly south of the beaches at Las Cañas, themselves visible from well off with their cabanas, white sand, and other buildings. (See following sketch.)

The 2.5 miles long channel is 40 yards wide and 10 feet deep but keep to the center as it is shallower at the sides. It is marked by large sentry-box type lights on alternate sides so look back frequently to see that you are still in line between the markers, and on no account stray too far left as the dredged overspill has been deposited there.

Once inside, the easily-recognized Guarda Frontera post is on the far outer corner of the first basin which also houses wharfs and shipyards. The dock is a well-built affair which contains the ice-plant and a number of buildings comprising the fishing fleet's base and warehouses.

Moor alongside the guardhouse at the base of the flagpole and present your papers. The last time we were here, checking-in took not more than five minutes and we were given permission to depart in the morning without having to return to the dock, so request this facility.

Although I do have reports of some boaters being recently met with puzzled looks, we ourselves have been offered all kinds of assistance by the authorities here, and our logbook once noted that they were the most helpful officials we'd met.

You will probably be asked to moor a little way out from the dock and among the other fishing boats at anchor. The holding is excellent anywhere in the harbor so just make sure you're out of the main channel,

and dinghy back ashore to have a look around.

Leave the tender at the dock, walk between the warehouses near the Guarda Frontera post to the main gate and let the gateman know you're leaving. Strange sights await you following the road round to the right.

Grim Eastern-Block concrete apartment-buildings, miserable huts, nicer streets with neat dwellings, a baseball stadium, and squealing pigs contrasting with children playing happily at the side of the road.

The walls of the more primitive huts among the mangroves are made of roots bound into wall-sections and they are peopled by charcoal-burners using only the most rudimentary of techniques (they don't exclude the oxygen). There's even a tiny rural boatyard where you'll see boats being carvel-planked at the side of the road.

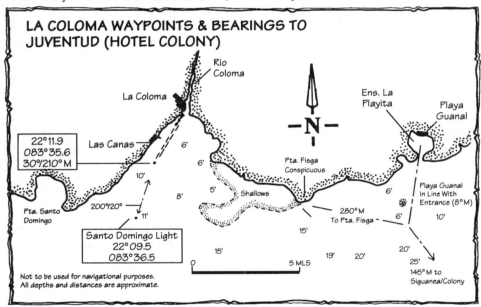

LA COLOMA WAYPOINTS & BEARINGS TO JUVENTUD (HOTEL COLONY)

Not to be used for navigational purposes.
All depths and distances are approximate.

ROUTE TO DARSENA DE SIGUANEA (ISLA DE JUVENTUD)
CHART NOS. ICH 1147 & 1145 (CUBAN)

It is important to note here that you cannot travel in a straight line all 48 miles southeast from Coloma to Siguanea, the small harbor near the hotel *Colony* in Juventud. The shallows of the San Felipe and Los Indios cays intrude slightly on the course making it necessary to take a gentle eastern arc on the journey.

If you don't wish to skirt those cays visually, you can go east along the mainland for some 12 miles after the outer light and steer a direct compass course from there. Avoid the shallows just southeast of Coloma by going out to the outer Santo Domingo light and then going east, following the 15-foot contour. When the prominent Punta Fisga headland bears 280°M and you can just see the village of Playa Guanal through the mouth of its bay (say 008°M), then a direct course of 145°M should take you to the Punta Buenavista marker off the west coast of Juventud. You can now go south/southeast, paralleling to the coast for about 10 miles to the harbor.

Otherwise, just use whatever electronic aid you have aboard in order to get to a point 21°37.0N / 82°59.2W where the Siguanea entry channel begins.

On the latter stages of this run you are likely to come across a haphazard multitude of lobster-pots. It would be a bit of a pity for you to blot your copy book and be towed ignominiously into some village harbor in your shiny white boat, so keep an eye out for them. The assorted dinghies attached to the major fishing-boats tend the pots, but only God knows just how they find all these scattered cages below the surface. We've looked down with snorkel and masks and found the cages absolutely packed with lobster... do not molest.

Be especially aware if you see dinghies fussing about close to the mother-boat as they may be laying out nets. They seem totally unconcerned by your presence and will gaily watch your approach until the last minute and then begin to lay their lines directly across your path.

Meanwhile just to let you know it's not personal, they're waving happily all the time. Oddly enough, the fishermen on the northeastern side of Cuba are not as demonstrative, and perhaps this is a natural outcome of the officially encouraged paranoia over there.

But there is also a lot more evidence of needlefish, leaping hound-fish, playful dolphins and the like on this side too. Are the two features connected?

ISLA DE JUVENTUD

This island (population 100,000) has had other names since it was discovered by Columbus on his second journey to the New World in 1494. He called it La Evangelista then, and it was once even called La Isla de Tesoro (Treasure Island) and may even have been used as an inspiration for R L Stevenson's book of the same name (well, *everyone* claims this one). Later still, it was called the Isle of Pines, by which name it is still known in some places.

In 1978 the name was changed to the present "Isle of Youth" after the agricultural facilities dedicated to training young

A fisherman aboard a make-shift raft outside La Coloma.

Smiles abound in Cuba.

people from all over the socialist world.

Previous to Columbus' arrival however, it was home to other groups of indigenous Cubans like the Ciboney Indians who left their marks on the walls of caves in the south and at various other sites inland.

The island was colonized by the Spanish between 1494 and 1898 and after the Spanish-American war the North Americans had bought up half of the total land area, excluding most Cubans from the territories by 1925!

During 1870, the Cuban patriot José Martí (whose name is still invoked by both sides of the political debate) was deported here, and in the early 1950's Fidel Castro too was imprisoned near the capital Nuevo Gerona.

Although the island is relatively flat (the highest point is 950 feet) the mountains which do exist are close and easily seen from the coast, making the place look most impressive from some angles.

The island has several anchorages, one large port and one marina.

OVERNIGHT OPTIONS
AROUND JUVENTUD

For vessels drawing up to eight feet, especially good shelter from the prevailing wind is to be found in the Ensenada de Barcos just on the northwest tip of the island. Enter northeast from anywhere around 21°54.0N / 083°01.0W, and anchor where your echo sounder indicates.

Again, for deeper waters, you could find refuge amongst the cays to the NE of the island (Los Inglesitos) if you make sure your anchor has gripped.

There is a large sheltered bay, protected by a long string of cays down on the southeast corner. It has a well marked and wide entrance at 21°32.8N / 082°30.6W and depths inside of 10-12 feet. Really large vessels (15-foot draft) can shelter just south of the light nearby (Punta del Este on the mainland), but they will have to be careful to enter west of the reef there and come in from that side at 82°34.5W.

And again (subject to the warnings below) there is the bay of Siguanea along the west coast.

There is too, the main island port of Nueva Gerona which handles large vessels, and finally the marina near the hotel *Colony* (the Darsena) which can take yachts drawing up to nine feet.

DÁRSENA DE SIGUANEA / HOTEL COLONY
CHART NO. ICH 1145 (CUBAN)

Merely a notch in the coast immediately above the bay of San Pedro, this small but sheltered harbor serves the hotel Colony, originally built for the exclusive use of the North Americans who controlled the island before the revolution. In addition, it is near the site of one of Columbus' original landings in 1894.

Perhaps conveniently for some, this tiny harbor can handle international arrivals even though you may have to wait some time for the officials to arrive from the main port of

Nueva Gerona 30 miles away by road.

On your approach to the harbor you will see the hotel a mile or so north. The hotel (itself a mile or two south of a couple of iron wrecks), is easily recognized being a large white flat-roofed two-story building with a long narrow walkway leading out to a pavilion dance floor 100 yards from shore.

Do not be tempted to approach the pier as the water there is just barely enough for shallow-draft boats. We've found less than four-foot on the approach and even the

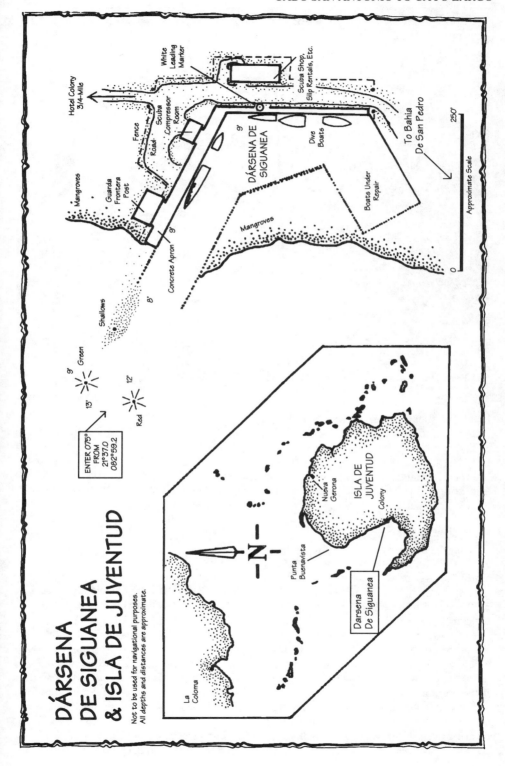

DÁRSENA DE SIGUANEA & ISLA DE JUVENTUD

Not to be used for navigational purposes.
All depths and distances are approximate.

ENTER 075°
FROM
21°37.0
082°59.2

13' 9' Green

12' Red

-N-

Mangroves

Guarda
Frontera
Post

Fence

Road

Scuba
Compressor
Room

Scuba

White
Leading
Marker

Hotel Colony
3/4-Mile

Scuba Shop,
Slip Rentals, Etc.

DÁRSENA DE
SIGUANEA

Dive
Boats

To Bahía
De San Pedro

Boats Under
Repair

Mangroves

9'

Concrete Apron

9'

8'

Shallows

Mangroves

Approximate Scale

250'

0

La
Coloma

Punta
Buenavista

Nueva
Gerona

ISLA DE
JUVENTUD

Colony

Dársena
De Siguanea

163

A typical south Cuba fishing harbor.

hotel dive-boats collect their divers from the harbor down the road.

The hotel caters mainly to scuba-divers from Germany and France, but the harbor is also a convenient cruising base from which transport and other inland tours can be readily arranged.

ENTERING THE MARINA

Enter the marked channel from position. 21°37.0N / 082°59.2W steering 075°M towards the large white "screw" on the inside. You'll know it when you see it, but it's really meant to be a locally-found prehistoric shell.

Keep to the right of the channel until inside, where the staves hold back the banks, and dock at the Guarda Frontera wharf immediately on the left where the large patrol-boat usually moors.

The Guarda Frontera are friendly enough (if you play the game), but it seems that clearing in is taking longer and longer compared with a couple of years ago, so be prepared for a long delay.

The marina supervisor's office is in the building alongside the eastern edge of the dock and also serves as a storeroom for marine supplies and the dive-shop. Marina charges are about .45 cents/foot and electricity is available by twisting the bare ends of a supply line onto your plug. Water is supplied from the dockside tap by your boat, but the water itself is of dubious quality.

WARNING: STAYING HERE MAY BE INJURIOUS TO YOUR POCKET AND YOUR HUMOR

I seem to have a growing list of complaints in my notebooks from other cruisers who have visited this marina over the last year, and even if the following seems to be an excessively gloomy report, it is obvious that all is not well with this particular marina.

The first thing to look out for is additional charges for bringing customs officers from

Nueva Gerona to inspect you upon entry. If you're already legally in the country, no such charges should apply as you have already cleared customs. You do have all your original documents and receipts don't you?

Most of the diving takes place off the western tip of the island (the tail of the comma) but the area is also claimed to be a submarine preservation site, and in yet another scandalous effort to extort money from you a guide is required to accompany you from the dock. It seems to cost much the same if you take one of the organized dives, but the $56 fee (two tanks, with a beach-lunch) might be a bit over-the-top for a cruiser with his own boat, all the gear, and hundreds of miles of unsupervised diving immediately behind or ahead of him. Especially when you consider that you could get a package tour rate of just a bit over $30 per day (room, food and diving), when booked overseas.

Unfortunately too, again I have to write that reports are regularly coming in of problems being made for yachts actually moored *outside* the confines of the harbor. I know of more than one which was threatened by various dive-boats who demanded fees from

them, even when they weren't diving. Demanding to see authorization with a proper receipt book has been known to deter this sort of behavior, and there can be no complaint if you refuse to pay anyone not duly authorized.

Another black mark (when anchoring out in the bay) is that the Guarda Frontera try to make you moor where they can see you, and want you to pay .35 cents/foot for the privileged of being watched. As usual, "It's for your security, Señor", but once again we all know it isn't. To my certain knowledge, refusing to pay this charge led to one yacht being forced from the shelter of the bay in a storm.

Be careful too of yet another little dodge, that of trying to charge you an extra $20 for Customs clearance *out* of the port when leaving. The authorities in Havana and elsewhere have repeatedly stressed that there is a one-time customs fee upon entry into the country itself, and that it is not repeated anywhere else once you're legally in.

Finally, neither should you pay for a second Cruising Permit/Safety Certificate, like the one you got in Havana. That one has a full six month life-span, valid even though you've left the country and returned.

The crew of a Cuban patrol boat waves in Siguanea Harbor.

With the increased traffic along the coast seems to have come an increased aggravation factor, and this port seems to be host to all the worst practices.

As a result of all the above, some yachts are finding that it's just as convenient to anchor out further round the SW tip of the island where no one can charge you, where the view and the waters are as good, if not better, and where the only soaking you get is in the sea.

Hopefully, things at Siguanea will have changed by the time you get here, again returning to the old friendly ways we used to be accustomed to.

DIVE ORIENTED HOTEL

The 54 room hotel is crowded with regimented German divers (upwards of 150 when we were last there) who arrive on package holidays. Weirdly (to this more relaxed Caribbean diver), they are allocated cards which are subsequently clipped every time they dive to ensure they don't do more than the package allows.

In the mornings you will be woken by trucks bringing the divers to the docks where they board the boats. Check out the compressor system near the gate. It's the most sophisticated I've ever seen in daily use anywhere in the West Indies. And to cap it all off, the resort has its own recompression chamber at dockside!

The hotel is a mile away down a straight road. You know you need the walk, but rub on lots and lots of repellant. Tours to the decorated caves at Punta del Este (once

again you must be accompanied), rental cars and other island transport can be arranged there.

For those who need it, an air ticket to Havana cost $17.00 in 1996, and it'll cost an extra $20.00 for the bus from the hotel Colony to the airport.

The restaurant is particularly good and there is a game room for any bored children on board.

Quite apart from all the problems in the marina (and maybe they haven't applied to you), one can have quite a good night here, and if you're at all sociable you will have already been befriended by people at dockside, some of whom may have also come from Havana or up from the southeast coast and thus may already know you. Some will doubtless encounter you somewhere near the bar/game room of the hotel and when that environment palls the party can move to the pavilion at the end of the pier. Purchase your booze by the bottle in the hotel store early so as not to have to drink expensive shots at the bar later on. You can keep it at your table, and in any case you'll need to be a bit merry to survive the mosquitos on the walk back.

There is also the sound of the watchman patrolling on the concrete outside your window all night. As is the norm in Cuba, he peers in unashamed at every opportunity until he gets bored and slips away to sleep.

DELAY CLEARANCE UNTIL DIVERS DEPART

Clearance out is best delayed until the divers have left at 9:15 a.m., but you should be ready to leave immediately afterwards. Whatever, ensure that your bill is paid well before the last minute, and double check it, especially the additions and extras. There is likely to be a long delay with little or no explanation at the guard post. Don't let it spoil you humor; after all, you're leaving.

There are two potential routes east from here. One will take you over the top of the island via the port of Nueva Gerona, and the other allows you to take the outer route along the south coast of Juventud and along the cays. If you draw more than eight-foot take the southern route (see Canal de Rosario).

SOUTHERN (OUTER) ROUTE BELOW JUVENTUD
CHART NO. ICH 1145 (CUBAN)

Head for the point which you can see 13 miles away due west and come round along the bottom edge of the island. Do not pass too close to the point itself as it is shallow there, but pass some two miles north of it, or even by the main entrance channel around 21°40.6N / 083°12.4W.

The 44-mile southern coastline is rocky and sloped. but sometimes, due to the trees, it can appear to be an escarpment.

There are few natural harbors along here but if you don't draw more than five-to-six feet you might be able to use Caleta Grande at 21°31.0N / 083°07.OW. There is a small dock inside serving the tiny villages of Cocodrillo and Jacksonville, originally settled by Cayman Islanders in the early part of this century. English is still occasionally spoken here as a result, and family ties loosely bind the two regions.

The eastern half of the coastline is mainly beach protected by an offshore reef, but once past that you can come into the large enclosed sound (10 -15 feet inside) on the southeast corner of the island just past Punta del Este.

Enter around a position of 21°32.8N / 082°30.5W and anchor inside, anywhere you see fit. The bay here is wide, and shelter can be found from any angle of wind.

As mentioned before, you can also come round from the west, behind the reef off Punta del Este and anchor offshore.

We have in the past found a passage in to a small dock which lies in some six-to-eight feet of water at 21°33.6 / 082°32.8, but access is too tricky to be recommended for anything other than a shallow draft vessel (keep west of the stakes marking the way). In any case, if you do venture ashore by dinghy there are impressive Indian designs all over the walls of some prehistoric caves in the immediate vicinity.

Further along, you can anchor off any of the cays which offer protection, but make sure you have entered through the reef *west* of Cayo Avalo at 82°10.0W if you're going to take up this option.

NORTHERN ROUTE TO NUEVA GERONA
CHART NO. ICH 1145 (CUBAN)

This 35-mile passage is a visual run north from Colony along the coast, round the northwest corner, then east to the mouth of the Las Casas river where the port is situated a mile or two in.

Prior to that however there is the convenient shelter inside the cays just off the tip at the Ensenada de Los Barcos where you

Nueva Gerona Harbor downtown.

could stop overnight if you weren't headed for Nueva Gerona but merely travelling east along the inside of the cays.

The above harbor, while giving ample shelter from most of the winds is open to the southwest. If you're faced with a south wind, then this coastline can become quite squally and shelter will have to be found somewhere along the northern edge of the island, but be especially careful about your holding, along here.

The mouth of the Las Casas river lies one-mile west of Punta Coloma, a narrow point made up of steep mountains which sweep right down to the sea. The point can be identified by a tiny island just in front of it, and large commercial vessels use the bay formed there to anchor while awaiting attention within the harbor.

Note: Going east, it's ahead of the first promontory you meet, and if you're *coming* east from the Pasa de Quitasol then the river lies after the second (larger) of the two promontories you'll meet. In the morning sunlight it can be an especially impressive sight.

NUEVA GERONA

Just inside the mouth of the river Las Casas and specializing mainly in the export of grapefruit and other citrus products, this commercial port has all Customs and Immigration facilities for international entry or departure.

From outside, at 21°55.5N / 082°47.8W, markers lead in along a course of 218°M through a channel dredged to about 20 feet. Do not venture to the west of the channel as the dredged soil has been deposited into a bank there. Sometimes too, that very dredger and its barges are moored there.

As you come in, be ready to avoid the large hydrofoils which speed in and out of the river delivering passengers to the other side of the gulf of Batabano. These amazing Russian-built craft (Kometas), looking rather like something out of "The War of the Worlds," rise up on thin foils as they accelerate through the channel until they are some ten feet out of the water and travelling at a ferocious speed. Snorkelers in the channel (another thing to be aware of) take one startled look and dive, dive, dive; abandoning their rubber-tire rafts in a serious hurry to preserve life and limb.

There is a Guarda Frontera post at the end of the markers in a collection of low white buildings dead ahead and on the right-hand bank. There isn't anywhere to moor, so draw up as close as you can and shout across for permission to enter.

You will be directed to the main post some way in so continue slowly about one-

Russian hydrofoil leaving North Gerona.

mile along the narrow river just off the large concrete wharfs, marine repair facilities, and the roadway.

A MOST BEAUTIFUL SURPRISE

Passing here in 1993 we received a most beautiful surprise when we encountered a group of about 15 tiny schoolchildren casually walking the road alongside the river bank, all beautifully neat in clean white shirts, red neckerchiefs, skirts and shorts. They immediately formed up a hurriedly measured arms length from each other, and in front of a beaming teacher they sang to us as we passed slowly in our boat!

Sometimes, just sometimes, life is so sweet.

THE PORT CAPTAIN'S OFFICE

The first major building after the open

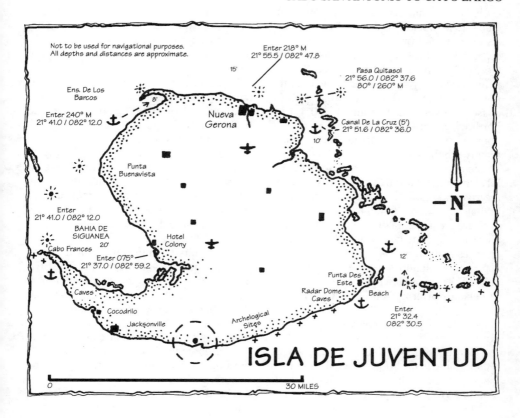

Not to be used for navigational purposes.
All depths and distances are approximate.

Enter 218° M
21° 55.5 / 082° 47.8

15'

Pasa Quitasol
21° 56.0 / 082° 37.6
80° / 260° M

Ens. De Los
Barcos

Enter 240° M
21° 41.0 / 082° 12.0

8'

Nueva
Gerona

Canal De La Cruz (5')
21° 51.6 / 082° 36.0

10'

Punta
Buenavista

Enter
21° 41.0 / 082° 12.0

BAHIA DE
SIGUANEA

Hotel
Colony

Cabo Frances

20'

Enter 075°
21° 37.0 / 082° 59.2

12'

Caves

Cocodrilo

Jacksonville

Punta Des
Este

Radar Dome
Caves

Beach

Archelogical
Sites

Enter
21° 32.4
082° 30.5

—N—

ISLA DE JUVENTUD

0   30 MILES

areas which follow the commercial wharfs is the capitanfa (the port captain's office), so pull up on the right at a filthy, rundown wooden dock at 21°53.4N / 082°42.0W and explain your presence here.

Despite that other sweeter welcome, the officials here can be a bit brusque, wondering just why you've chosen to interrupt their routine. Don't be fobbed off with excuses (no space/security), but present your papers showing your route with this stop mentioned. Indicate you'll be responsible for your own boat if something runs into it and you should be permitted to continue on to somewhere past the hydrofoil terminal on the right, a few hundred yards ahead of the bridge.

In this instance, the officials are probably correct, there really isn't much space. But what's a little crowding among friends?

Raft alongside the tugboats pressing together and settle in for your stay. Doubtless another official will show up to check on

your final berth, but he will also be able to advise on the city so don't despair. They get very few private boats here, and you're probably the only entertainment they've had in a while.

The river here is rather dirty, with small carcasses and empty grapefruit skins drifting idly downstream, but your neighbors will make you welcome, and as usual you will likely be taken on board various other vessels to visit. One rather unfortunate feature of the port is the incessant broadcasting of local radio stations over crackly speakers mounted on one of the larger boats nearby. You will not be happy after having to listen to the sugarcane harvest statistics for each province, random speeches by/to the local women's group, soap-operas, and dissertations on Congolese folk art.

Immediately ashore you will find the large ancient ferryboat *El Pinero* used to transport Fidel Castro to prison on the island. Now up on blocks and scheduled someday (as much as anything ever is in Cuba) to be opened to the public, it makes a strange backdrop to a crowded mooring, especially contrasted with the rather "Flash Gordon" hydrofoils just downstream.

Incidentally, you can take a ride over to the Cuban mainland on one of these: Purchase a ticket at the terminal 300 yards north of the bridge. They leave at three-hour intervals and the trip takes a bit more than two hours.

The busiest part of town runs from Calle 32 at the bridge, north to Calle 18, between the riverside and the Calle 41. Note: The odd numbers run parallel to the river.

There are a couple of official restaurants close to the center of town, but constant changes make it almost impossible to give a recommendation so make inquiries locally. There should in any case be a couple of paladars offering better value near your mooring site.

Despite its rather flyblown aspect, the city is a friendly enough place, perhaps due to the influx of foreign students who made it their home in the boom years of Communism and the multitude of "International Youth Brigades" it spawned. Spend a day wandering aimlessly and you are bound to be kidnapped by someone or the other who invites you back (sometimes to a different town altogether) for tea.

Transport around town can best be done by flagging down and sharing any of the horse-drawn carriages which ply the streets. They're also available for hire around the Parque Central at the junction of Calles 28/39, which is the best place to hang out in any case.

If you wish to rent a car to tour the island then you can obtain one at the hotel some three quarters of a mile upstream under the bridge (go by dinghy).

Crossing the bridge will take you to the old prison (the Presidio Modelo) some two-to-three miles east of town. Modelled on a prison in Illinois and now a museum, this is where Fidel Castro was imprisoned after the unsuccessful 1953 assault on the Moncado Barracks in Santiago.

When clearing out, you will have to proceed one-quarter-mile upstream again to the Capitanía for your despacho. The officials here are more accustomed to commercial vessels with more rigid schedules and their relative inexperience in matters concerning private boats will show. Stress that you cannot guarantee your exact schedule further down the line (you'll be anchoring out in the cays) and they'll finally get the picture.

There is a "provedor" establishment (ship's chandlers) at the next major wharf along your route, so stop there on your way to the entrance if you need supplies for the next leg. It's the wharf with the big crane, where they haul-out the hydrofoils for maintenance.

Hydrofoil drydocks at Nueva Gerona.

Fishing boats laden with traps.

ROUTE TO CAYO LARGO
CHART NOS. ICH 1145 & 1143

Once again, there are reports that the officials in the island are up to some new tricks. In contrast to elsewhere in Cuba the officials here will try to stiff you for clearance outwards, even if you are traveling within the country. Some yachts have been charged $10.00, so be prepared, and as before, don't lose your temper.

Delay your departure until the afternoon and you will be able to find a sheltered anchorage dead east of North Gerona near the Pasa de Quitasol by early evening. The following leg is somewhat longer than desirable and an early start through the canal can enable you to make the passage without an intermediate stop.

CAYOS DE LOS INGLESITOS (KEYS OF THE LITTLE ENGLISHMEN)

Close to the dredged canal going through to the other side of the cays, this offers shelter from the east and northeast even if the holding is somewhat poor.

Anchor as near to the edge of the cays as your keel allows, but do check your mooring carefully as the bottom is a thick mat of turtle-grass. If there is any chance of the wind rising you should double-check by diving and force it in manually if necessary

(see earlier chapter for our experiences here).

In spite of the windbreak provided by Cayo Inglés we once carelessly allowed ourselves to drag over half a mile in the space of two hours when the wind got up to 25 knots. Luckily for us, we blew westwards into the bay instead of going ashore.

PASA QUITASOL

Prior to sunup you can make your way round to the western end of the canal at Quitasol and by the time the light is good you will be poised to go through from a position of 21°55.8N / 082°39.4W.

Clearly marked, the canal runs 80°/260°M with a depth of 13 feet along its 1.5-mile length, and we have experienced strong through-currents on occasion. There is a freestanding wharf halfway along and some 400 yards north of the canal but otherwise the water is shallow on both sides.

From the eastern end of the canal at 21°56.1N/082°37.6W the Gulf of Batabano opens wider still and you are over 30 miles away from the moderating influence of the mainland. Choose your route further on with regard to the forecast and wind direction.

You may wish to make your way directly

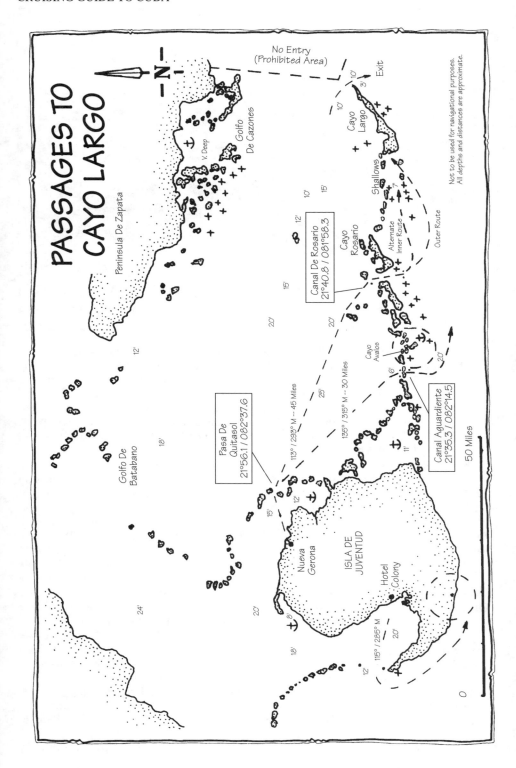

PASSAGES TO CAYO LARGO

Peninsula De Zapata

Golfo De Cazones

V. Deep

No Entry (Prohibited Area)

Exit

Cayo Largo

10'

3'

10'

10'

15'

Shallows

10'

12'

Canal De Rosario
21°40.8 / 081°58.3

15'

Cayo Rosario

Alternate Inner Route

Outer Route

Not to be used for navigational purposes.
All depths and distances are approximate.

20'

20'

20'

Cayo Avalos

Golfo De Batabano

18'

12'

Pasa De Quitasol
21°56.1 / 082°37.6

113° / 293° M -- 45 Miles

25'

135° / 315° M -- 30 Miles

6'

Canal Aguardiente
21°35.3 / 082°4.5

15'

12'

11'

50 Miles

24'

ISLA DE JUVENTUD

Nueva Gerona

Hotel Colony

20'

8'

18'

20'

115° / 285° M

12'

20'

0

across to the major exit through the outer keys at Cayo Rosario and while we have made this 45-mile run in perfect weather, this open run can also be subject to high winds. Our depth-sounder once drew pictures showing 8-10 feet waves over what was nominally only 16 feet of water.

With the exception of the shallow passage through the cays at Aguardiente (follows) there are few closer outlets, and little real shelter before the main exit at Rosario, even if you can hide from the wind just west of the pass itself near the islands which extend northwards from Cayo Cantilles to Tabalones.

CANALIZO AGUARDIENTE

An extremely convenient route through the chain of cays, and some 16 miles west of the Canal de Rosario, this well-marked pass is unfortunately limited by bars at both ends to vessels drawing six feet or less. From the north you may enter at 21°35.3N / 082°14.5W (160º/340ºM) and once inside you will find a fantastic world of low mangrove, herons, diving cormorants, wading egrets, and creeks leading off the main channel. The canal itself is a bit less than a mile long, 200 yards wide and some 10 - 20 feet deep in places.

The southern end is at 21°33.9N / 082°14.5W (10º/190ºM) and is marked by a concrete post with a rickety red triangle on top. As the water from within the gulf spills out, it seems to have scoured the bottom and the sands consequently are distinctly marked in a much lighter shade than the surrounding waters. Once again, there is a shallow bar here, but the water is clear and a boat drawing six feet or less can get through with care.

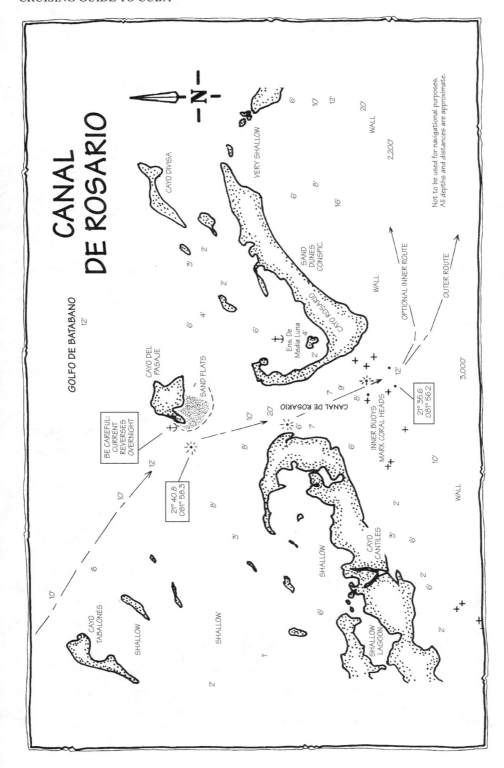

CANAL
DE ROSARIO

GOLFO DE BATABANO

CAYO DIVISA

VERY SHALLOW

SAND DUNES CONSPIC.

CAYO ROSARIO

Ens. De Media Luna

WALL

WALL

2,200'

OPTIONAL INNER ROUTE

OUTER ROUTE

3,000'

Not to be used for navigational purposes.
All depths and distances are approximate.

CAYO DEL PASAJE

SAND FLATS

BE CAREFUL: CURRENT REVERSES OVERNIGHT

21° 40.8
081° 58.3

CANAL DE ROSARIO

21° 35.6
081° 56.2

INNER BUOYS MARK CORAL HEADS

CAYO TABALONES

SHALLOW

SHALLOW

SHALLOW

CAYO CANTILES

SHALLOW LAGOON

CANAL DE ROSARIO

Carrying waters of eight feet, this is the main entrance/exit through the cays along the southeast gulf here. Due to the shallows further east the only way to Cayo Largo is via the outside of the cays. This is the last chance to anchor overnight on the inside.

Going the other way, vessels requiring nine feet had better resign themselves to using the outer route as far as the Isla de Juventud unless they are willing to spend some time picking through the shallows off the inner cay at Pasajes. If however, they make it past here, there is adequate water all the way northwest to the Pasa Quitasol and through into the Gulf of Batábano.

A course of 113°M from Quitasol should

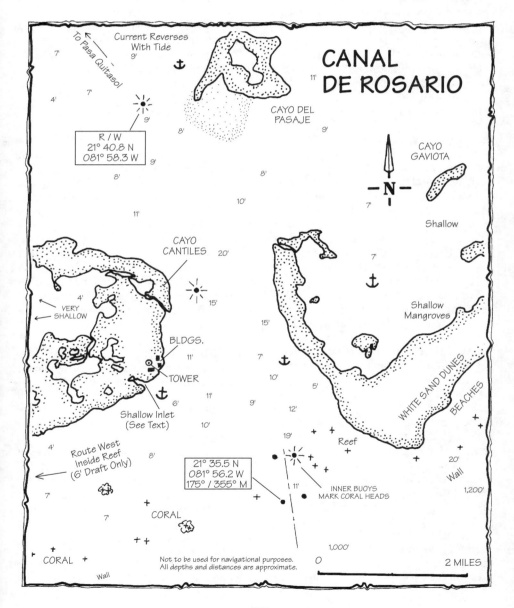

Current Reverses With Tide

To Pasa Quitasol

9'

7'

7'

4'

R / W
21° 40.8 N
081° 58.3 W

9'

8'

9'

8'

11'

CANAL
DE ROSARIO

11'

CAYO DEL
PASAJE

9'

8'

10'

CAYO
GAVIOTA

–N–

7'

Shallow

CAYO
CANTILES   20'

15'

4'
VERY
SHALLOW

15'

Shallow
Mangroves

BLDGS.

11'

7'

TOWER

6'

11'

9'

Shallow Inlet
(See Text)   10'

10'

5'

12'

19'

Reef

WHITE SAND DUNES

BEACHES

Route West
Inside Reef
(6' Draft Only)

4'

8'

21° 35.5 N
081° 56.2 W
175° / 355° M

11'

INNER BUOYS
MARK CORAL HEADS

20'

Wall

1,200'

7'

7'

CORAL

Not to be used for navigational purposes.
All depths and distances are approximate.

1,000'

O

2 MILES

CORAL

Wall

175

take you about a mile north of Cayo Tablones, then five miles further southeast to the Rosario Canal marker which will begin to show just southwest of Cayo Pasaje.

That inner light, marking the beginning of the canal, is at 21°40.8N / 081°58.3W, and despite its size bird droppings make it difficult to see from the northwest when the light is not working.

You may anchor overnight, either side of Cayo Pasaje, but as before check the anchor carefully. Again, the bottom here is a mat of poor-holding grass and I have had to swim down to forcefully reposition the hook in a gully for additional grip.

Note: The current through the canal can change direction 180° according to the tide, so make sure the hook cannot wriggle loose.

In the more unusual event of a southeast wind then you can also enter the Media Luna lagoon inside Cayo Rosario itself. There is good bonefishing to be had there, but be careful about the wind swinging later, and pay close attention to your depth.

A few years ago we came in here to anchor overnight in this lagoon and encountered a large flock of pink flamingos wading in the shallows just south of Cayo Pasaje. Before that, the only other flamingos I'd seen were plastic, and lived on blue-rinse suburban lawns in Miami.

The final 25-mile run to Cayo Largo can be accomplished only via the outside of the keys, so follow the lights out through the wide canal and turn east. The canal itself is quite wide, but the inner entrance/exit marks (21°35.9/081°56.3) denote a reef on either side and are set closer together, with the red inner marker on the eastern side standing directly on the reef. Although it is generally deeper, as before, if you draw more than eight feet, then exercise caution here with someone looking forwards and down at all time. For the best water stay closer to the eastern side of the channel.

Go through the middle along 175°M to the two outer buoys 500 yards further on (21°35.5 N / 081°56.2W) before making your turn.

Note: When a storm is expected, this area is occasionally used as a shelter for boats moored at Cayo Largo 25 miles away.

They tend to moor off Cayo Cantiles just to the south of the eastern entrance bank, where the land offers some protection. There is a small totally enclosed cove there too, at 21°36.9/081°58.3, but it only has anchor-room for one (or at most two), and is limited by depths of five feet at the entrance. If you can use this, as we've done in a northeaster, then get here early. The area is becoming more and more popular with cruisers, and that time we were amused to see at least seven or eight boats of all descriptions, ranging from charter cats and long-distance cruisers from Canada, to local ferrocement fishermen. A year or two previously there would only have been the latter.

Around here too there are likely to be lots of occasions for bargaining for seafood and the like from passing craft.

ONWARDS

Under normal conditions the sea will generally be quite calm and you can make the entire run from here to Cayo Largo in deep water, but in the event of a southeast wind the waves can easily be steep enough to persuade you to make this easterly passage through the shallower waters above and inside the wall.

In the latter case you should exercise caution all the way. Although this is an easy run over sand, it *is* shallow in places and there are occasional coral banks, usually quite visible through the water.

INNER ROUTE:

Along this route, you will notice that all of a sudden there are pleasure craft of all descriptions using the sound, and if you are sufficiently aware and do not draw more than six or seven feet then you should have no trouble.

Keep your depth-alarm turned up to loud and remain about a mile or two off the beaches. Look out particularly for the very obvious shoals south of the two small islets on the western tip of the Perases Cays. Just stay in the light green stuff, but avoid it if it gets *too* pale.

As you begin to see huts, cabanas, and semi-naked bodies, you are nearing the resort area. Turn north when you approach

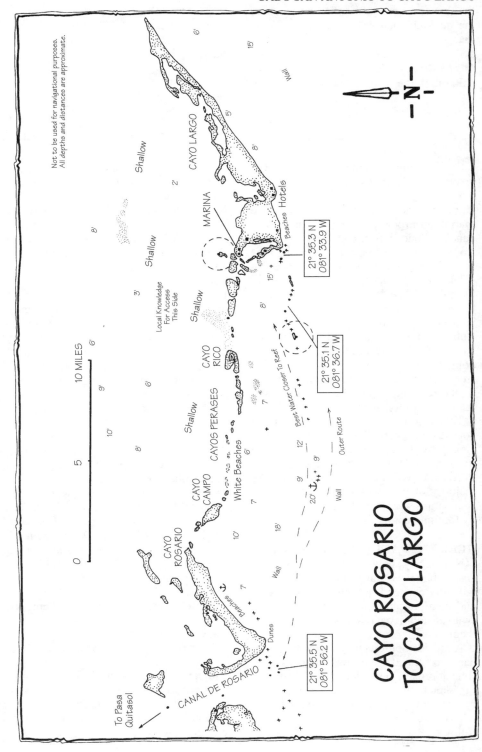

Not to be used for navigational purposes.
All depths and distances are approximate.

-N-

10 MILES

0   5

6'

15'

Wall

CAYO LARGO

5'

8'

Shallow

2'

MARINA

Hotels

Beaches

21° 35.3 N
081° 33.9 W

Shallow

8'

Shallow

3'

Local Knowledge
For Access
This Side

Shallow

6'

8'

15'

9'

6'

CAYO
RICO

10'

8'

Best Water Closer To Reef

21° 35.1 N
081° 36.7 W

CAYOS PERASES

Shallow

7'

Outer Route

Shallow

6'

12'

9'

9'

CAYO
CAMPO

White Beaches

7'

20'

Wall

18'

10'

CAYO
ROSARIO

7'

Beaches

Wall

Dunes

CANAL DE ROSARIO

21° 35.5 N
081° 56.2 W

To Pasa
Quitasol

CAYO ROSARIO
TO CAYO LARGO

the western shores of La Sirena beach and the marked canal will take you in to the marina.

OUTER ROUTE:
Parallel the wall at anything around 21°32.5N until you're past the light at the western end of Cayo de Los Ballenatos. The various entries will follow 1.5 miles later.

CAYO LARGO
(A MARINA TO RESTORE YOUR FAITH)

This is Cuba's premiere foreign tourist resort along the southern cays. Completely isolated and some 25 miles from the mainland, it consists of an excellent full-service marina, an airport, three or four hotels, wild dancing, loud music, and little else apart from superb white beaches, sparkling blue seas, fishing, and wonderful cruising.

Due to it's distance from the coast it is not the place to go if you want mainstream Cuban life, but what it does offer the cruiser is possibly the best operated marina in Cuba; making it an extremely civilized base for further exploration and a jump-off point to the eastern half of the country. Accolades must be offered to the staff here for their cooperative attitude to cruisers and their concern for them.

This is one of the ports where some considerable charter business is done, principally by the K.P.Winter concern which has entered into a partnership with PuertoSol, the Cuban tourist enterprise. The majority of the boats in use are cruising catamarans, chartered for a week or more by foreign visitors.

REEF ENTRANCES (From Outside)
Not clearly shown on the normally precise Cuban ICH charts, this entry has been radically changed over the last two years and there are now two marked entrances (with an additional unmarked one between them).

A considerable quantity of dredging spoil has also created a shallow bank before the final approach to the docks, so the following sketch chart should be consulted and my previous instructions (in the original edition of this guide) should be modified as follows...

Western: The main western channel-markers are 1.5 miles east of the light and consist of two R/G lighted buoys at 21°35.1 N / 081°36.7W some 500 yards apart.

Enter in 35 ft., then aim 55°M over an undulating bottom of corals and sand to the end of a submerged (but visible) bank consisting of the spoil from earlier dredging operations. Pass round the southern tip of this bank and head 40°M to the entry marks at the marina canal. On this final approach, if the spoil bank has been further extended, aim to miss the coral head at 21°36.4/081°34.6 and pass between it and the red mark closer to the eastern shore.

Eastern: Just west of the large main island of Cayo Largo, is a new marked entrance consisting of two lighted buoys at 21°35.3N / 081°33.9W. This carries 25 feet of water and should be entered on a northerly course. Immediately upon entering, take up a course of 335°M to pass east of a mark sitting on a coral head at 21°35.8/081°34.2 by which time the depth will be around 14 feet. Continue on 320°M for a short distance to another mark over a coral head at 21°36.4/081°34.6, whereupon you can swerve round the spit of sand coming out from the shoreline and proceed to the entry mark for the marina channel just to the northeast.

Middle Entrance: This is an unmarked entry, but occasionally it is convenient and I have used it several times.

It is situated at 081°34.5 W and you come in from outside along a north/south course straight for the marina canal. You must look out for any unexpected surprises below, but having said that, with care you should find at least 10 feet minimum depth along this route.

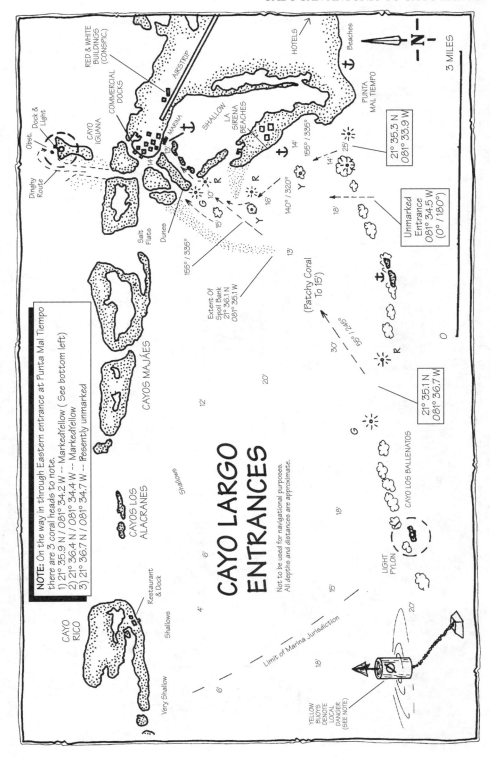

CAYO LARGO
ENTRANCES

Not to be used for navigational purposes.
All depths and distances are approximate.

NOTE: On the way in through Eastern entrance at Punta Mal Tiempo there are 3 coral heads to note.
1) 21° 35.9 N / 081° 34.2 W -- Marked Yellow (See bottom left)
2) 21° 36.4 N / 081° 34.4 W -- Marked Yellow
3) 21° 36.7 N / 081° 34.7 W -- Presently unmarked

CAYO RICO

CAYOS LOS ALACRANES

CAYOS MAJÁES

Restaurant & Dock

Very Shallow

Shallows

Shallows

6'

4'

6'

15'

18'

20'

12'

18'

13'

20'

30'

Limit of Marina Jurisdiction

YELLOW BUOYS DENOTE LOCAL DANGER (SEE NOTE)

LIGHT PYLON

CAYO LOS BALLENATOS

G

R

55° / 235°

21° 35.1 N
081° 36.7 W

(Patchy Coral To 15')

Extent Of Spoil Bank
21° 36.1 N
081° 35.1 W

Unmarked Entrance
081° 34.5 W
(0° / 180°)

21° 35.3 N
081° 33.9 W

14'

14'

25'

16'

18'

140° / 320°

155° / 335°

155° / 335°

Y

Y

R

R

G

10'

15'

13'

PUNTA MAL TIEMPO

Beaches

HOTELS

LA SIRENA BEACHES

SHALLOW

MARINA

AIRSTRIP

COMMERCIAL DOCKS

RED & WHITE BUILDINGS (CONSPIC.)

CAYO IGUANA

Obst.

Dock & Light

Dinghy Route

Salt Flats

Dunes

14'

13'

N

3 MILES

FINAL APPROACH AND DOCKING

Hidden by dunes and vegetation, you cannot see the marina from outside, but there are two large sentry-box markers at position 21°36.9N / 081°34.4W in 15 feet of water. These mark the final short canal passing between a sandy cay to port and some shallows to the starboard. Depths along this route are some 13 feet and at the far end you will see the docks immediately ahead over to the starboard.

If you have previously been in contact (advisable) on VHF channels 16/19 there will be someone waiting at dockside with assistance and instructions. If not, then approach the docks carefully (there is good deep water here) and shout over to any of a couple of dozen yachts or power boats here. Someone will certainly give you a hand with the docking.

The dock area immediately in front of the large thatched bar/restaurant is usually occupied by tourist canoes and the like, but during the day it is usually vacant, and if so

you may be able to moor there temporarily while sorting out your documents.

The marina is likely to be crowded by a mixture of charter and foreign sailboats, all jammed together in a cheerful rabble. And of course, interspersed among them will be a number of local dive and fishing boats, not to mention the large Polynesian-style outrigger canoes which take the hotels' tourists over to the various cays for the day.

Far from the miserly twenty boats a year it used to attract in the years before 1995, the last time I stayed there (just prior to beginning this edition) I counted some 35 boats moored alongside, and about 10 more at anchor in the canal just in front of the docks.

When a berth is available, you will almost certainly be required to Med-Moor (i.e. moor stern-on to the dock) which is a thrill if you haven't done it before.

Med-Mooring: With ample fenders hung on both sides, come to a halt some 30 - 40 yards off your intended docking space and

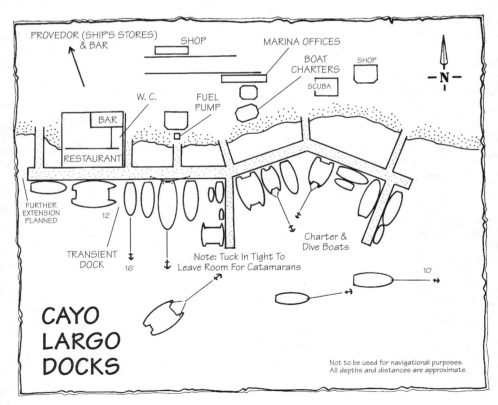

CAYO LARGO DOCKS

Not to be used for navigational purposes.
All depths and distances are approximate.

Feeding iguana.

spin your craft into a 180° turn so that the stern points directly at the spot where you wish to tie up. Lower the bow-anchor at this point, and with the rode (anchor-line) playing out freely, reverse slowly, making frequent corrections to ensure you're not biased to one side or the other. When you're a comfortable distance from the dock throw a pair of stern lines to the helpers ashore and hurry forwards to snub up the main anchor line. Allow those ashore to pull you in against the resistance of the anchor digging in, and if you've got it right you will remain a foot or two off the dock but still firmly held fore and aft. At this point the various lines should be adjusted for fit and the stern lines crossed.

It's always a blast when you get it right, and with care it's not half so difficult as it sounds.

Note: If the docks are too crowded then you may have to anchor out in the channel among the other boats there. The holding is good in the channel, but does consist of soft mud on top, so use the anchor best suited to the task. A Danforth or some such hook, with nice wide flukes, is best here. In a strong easterly I have seen a new arrival

drift back some fifty yards or more before he got a good grip on the bottom.

CONVENIENT FOR CLEARANCE

The marina monitors the VHF on Channel 16, or more usually 19, which is their working channel. They will send a boat to escort you through if you are not familiar with the reef, and if coming from abroad they will arrange for the officials to be ready when you dock.

The first person you are likely to meet is the official marina representative. At time of writing, this is the youthful looking and very efficient Sr. J.M. Cíd, better known as simply Piré. Consider him your go-to guy and you can't be far wrong. Over the several years of our acquaintance, I have seen him go far out of his way to make the cruiser's stay as pleasant as possible; even for those who need such miracles, to the extent of wangling departing crewmembers onto a difficult (and ostensibly overbooked) flight out of the country. He, or his successor will sort out extensions on your visa, documentation for further travel inside Cuba, or any marina services you require.

Customs and immigration are represented here, and the authorities are thoroughly familiar with all aspects of international documentation, making it a convenient spot to clear in or out of the country.

So efficient are they here that we once (albeit a long time ago) managed to clear into Cayo Largo and out of Cuba, *both* at the same time, and in less than 10 minutes! In fact you will find that *all* the officials at this marina have a positive attitude to the cruiser which can only bode well for the future.

I should mention that there is an increased use of sniffer dogs at this port (and indeed throughout Cuba), so don't be surprised when a Cocker Spaniel is brought aboard. Coincidentally, (and I swear this is true) on both of the occasions when I have been favored by this animal's presence, it has fallen overboard!

SERVICES

Dock charges are .45 cents/foot per night, and electricity/water hookups are supplied with the usual proviso that you will have to improvise your connections. If you have to anchor out within the dock area, then you will be charged some .15 cents/foot, but as you're likely to be moored less than a hundred feet from the dock it's not far to go in your dinghy. Conveniently, your boat may be left here if you need to leave the island for any reason, and in this case you might probably be able to bargain a better deal.

Fuel is available dockside at .55 cents/litre for diesel (.80 cents for gasoline) and there is a ship's store across the road (behind the excellent local bar) where, within reason, you can get any provisions you desire. In addition, there is also a smaller, fancier, and more expensive shop operated by the K. P. Winters boat-charter operation just off the eastern end of the docks.

Due to the lack of any established city or village life (all local workers have to be flown in for their stints) there are no Paladars on the island. To eat ashore you have to patronize the official restaurants, so be prepared for the prices to be higher than you may be accustomed to on the mainland. As well as the cafe-bar on the dock there is a surprisingly good restaurant just to the left, and if you wish to be serenaded all night over an excellent meal, by all means patronize it. The prices in the hotels are not cheap either, so once will probably be enough, and most cruisers seem to end up eating and drinking on each others boats.

In the immediate surrounds of the dock there are a number of buildings which serve in various capacities. On the right, past the usual tee-shirt/art shops, you may visit a turtle-farm, and just north of that there is a medical post and pharmacy which we have had occasion to use in the past (thank you, socialized medicine).

If you wait for the hourly ferry to return to the dock, free buses collect tourists from the dock and take them to any of the hotels five miles along the southern beaches.

The wilder of these tourists are entertained by twice-weekly discos at the marina, so along with a certain amount of friendly debauchery, be prepared for some loud music if you're close to the bar.

The bus runs east alongside the airport

(which comes complete with its own disco too) and if you wish to stop anywhere along the route just shout up to the driver. Likewise, when he delays too long after stopping.

At the hotels there are hard-currency shops where prices are surprisingly competitive and we have been able to purchase some beautiful books here. Just remember that the products on sale cater more to the land-based tourist than the sailor.

Tours to other parts of the country are advertised in the hotel lobbies, and if you fancy a ride in one of the huge radial-engine Russian biplanes which drone overhead then this is the place to get it. There is no reason to come all this way and not see as much of Cuba as possible, so for what in the greater scheme of things is really little additional cost (e.g. $25 to Havana), you might wish to fly on to parts of the mainland you would otherwise miss. You may rent bicycles outside the hotels, and even horsemen may encounter their favorite transport for hire. Just be on the lookout if riding your horse along the water's edge, as just past the main hotels (outside the last cabañas at the Villa Cappricio) there is a nude beach, and you don't want to startle the beast.

A dive boat departs the docks.

Home to the best water in Cuba, all varieties of watersports are available in Cayo Largo; and at the dock you're ideally placed to take advantage of scuba diving, jet-ski rentals, and boat-tours to various beaches for barbecues and booze.

Bonefish (macabí) and tarpon (sábalo) can be fished amongst the cays to the west, and if you want to use your dinghy then inform the resident Guarda Frontera at the dock. For the fly-fishermen among us, professional fishing guides can be arranged if you'd prefer to scare even more fish than you'd find on your own.

Close by your dock, around the corner and to the north, there is the aptly named Cayo Iguana, easily accessible by dinghy. Don't be afraid of the hundreds of friendly, prehistoric-looking creatures which make this cay their home, as they are really quite harmless. They, for their part, are totally unafraid of you.

You may also reach Cayo Rico, five miles away to the west, which is where those polynesian trimarans head for in the morning with their cargo of sunburned Italians. Going by yacht, be prepared to anchor well off the beach as it gets a bit too shallow close in, so if your tender has sufficient engine then it may be better to do the trip in that.

ARRANGE CLEARANCE IN ADVANCE

Clearing out should best be arranged in advance as the officials may have to come from the nearby airstrip, and there is the question of paying your bill.

If you are heading on for somewhere like Casilda to the east you will still need to clear with customs and immigration, and inexplicably you may once again be searched by a drug dog. I don't know who's bright idea it is that we all come to some remote part of Cuba to buy drugs, but nothing amazes me anymore.

OVERNIGHT STOPS ALONG THE WAY EAST

Travelling east to Casilda or Cienfuegos (both next chapter), is a long trip, so there are two options. If you wish to make it in one stop, then the best time to leave will be probably be around evening, allowing for a convenient daylight entry next morning. However, if you prefer, you may make the entire journey in daylight, stopping off at a handy group of smaller cays halfway along your route, along a course of more or less 85°M. Far away from any source of pollution, these cays come highly recommended.

A typical tourist "canoe".

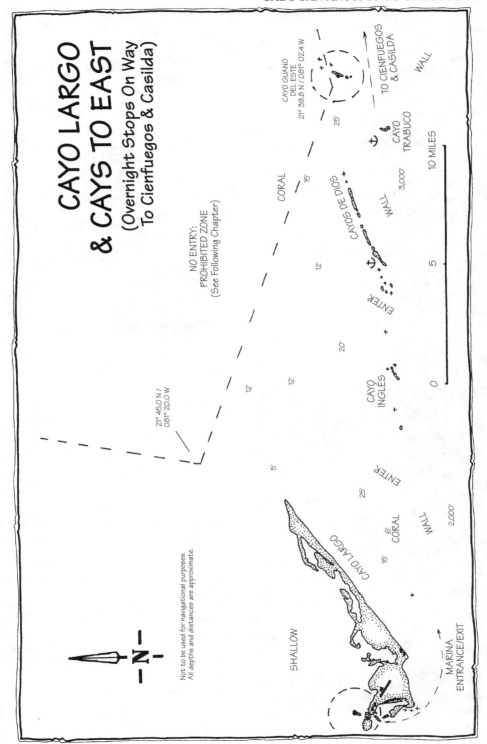

CAYO LARGO
& CAYS TO EAST
(Overnight Stops On Way
To Cienfuegos & Casilda)

NO ENTRY:
PROHIBITED ZONE
(See Following Chapter)

21° 45.0 N /
081° 20.0 W

Not to be used for navigational purposes.
All depths and distances are approximate.

-N-

SHALLOW

CAYO LARGO

CORAL 6'

WALL

2,000'

15'

MARINA
ENTRANCE/EXIT

ENTER

25'

5'

12'

12'

20'

CAYO
INGLÉS

ENTER

CAYOS DE DIOS

WALL

3,000'

12'

15'

CORAL

CAYO
TRABUCO

WALL

CAYO GUANO
DEL ESTE
21° 39.8 N / 081° 02.4 W

25'

TO CIENFUEGOS
& CASILDA

WALL

0   5   10 MILES

The first of these, Cayo Inglés is some 20 miles to the east of Cayo Largo at 21°37.2N /081°15.8W. It is only a couple of hundred yards long and is almost devoid of vegetation apart from a few bushes. There is a reef to the east and northeast with depths of some six feet but that's the side of the prevailing winds so shelter is best found close to the southwest end, where in any case there is an easy passage through from the outside.

The second cays worthy of note are the Cayos de Dios, a string of long, narrow islands, beginning at 21°37.6N /081°10.9W and stretching ENE for some four miles to 21°39.2N / 081°07.2W. Reefs extend from the most extreme ends of the group and roughly in line with the direction of the cays, so entry from outside can best be effected about 1.5 miles before the most westerly island or one mile past the most easterly. There is a small beach on the north coast of the most westerly and if the wind is from the east then there is also a shallow bay there which can offer some protection.

Following these cays, and some three

Preparing to clean glass-bottom boats viewing ports.

miles to the southeast is Cayo Trabuco which is set sideways on to the prevailing winds and therefore more capable of giving shelter. At 21°37.9N / 081°04.9W, it isn't very large but offers good snorkeling and is another convenient stop off along the way. It has a small reefy section to the southeast, so is best approached from the west where it is free of obstruction all the way.

Lastly we come to Cayo Guano del Este, which is really a group of four small cays clustered very closely to each other. Flat and rocky, it is home to a lighthouse, and also marks the extent of the *Zona Prohibida*. This is a large area to the north which is off limits to all foreign craft. For information on that, please see the beginning of the next chapter where it is covered; but suffice to say that you cannot legally travel *north* of the cay which is situated at 21°39.8N / 081°02.4W. There is, in any case, a reef extending out from the northeast of the cay; so to stop here you must approach from either the west, where there is good clear water all the way, or from the southeast.

Preparing to board an international arrival from Grand Cayman.

SOUTH CUBAN BONUS:
A SIDE TRIP TO THE CAYMAN ISLANDS!

Okay, okay, so you didn't know about this when you bought this book, but by now you're as close as you'll ever be to these islands. This could be the one and only opportunity you'll get as they're not on the way to, or from, anywhere else.

Clear immigration out from Cayo Largo, spend a week in the three small British-administered territories to the south, and return to Cuba (at Casilda or Cienfuegos) without having travelled much out of your way. Sounds good, eh?

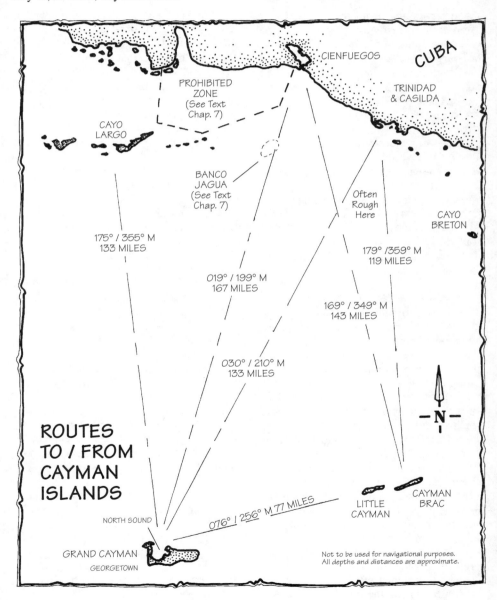

PROHIBITED ZONE
(See Text Chap. 7)

CIENFUEGOS

CUBA

TRINIDAD & CASILDA

CAYO LARGO

BANCO JAGUA
(See Text Chap. 7)

Often Rough Here

CAYO BRETON

175° / 355° M
133 MILES

019° / 199° M
167 MILES

179° /359° M
119 MILES

169° / 349° M
143 MILES

030° / 210° M
133 MILES

— N —

ROUTES
TO / FROM
CAYMAN
ISLANDS

NORTH SOUND

076° / 256° M 77 MILES

LITTLE CAYMAN

CAYMAN BRAC

GRAND CAYMAN
GEORGETOWN

Not to be used for navigational purposes.
All depths and distances are approximate.

If you have any mechanical work to be done then this is a good place too, as there is a boatyard which can handle all aspects of maintenance, parts are more far easily obtainable than in Cuba, and you just possibly already speak the language (English).

An excellent place to become properly certified, scuba diving is the main attraction in the Caymans.

GRAND CAYMAN
DMA CHART NO. 27241 (U.S.)
(Or even a good atlas will do)

A direct course from the exit at Cayo Largo to Georgetown Harbor along the west coast of Grand Cayman is 177°M, and the journey is 138 miles. You will be assisted greatly by the countercurrent, which, looping southwards here, can add up to two knots to your speed at times.

You may aim towards the middle of the island on 175°M if you prefer not to miss, but time your journey for a night-arrival, and you'll have the lights to aim at from well out to sea. Just be aware there is a reef all along the north coast, and what lights you see are well inshore from this; sometimes five-to -six miles inshore.

If you do come in by night, radio permission will be given for you to moor among the other craft in front of the city, thus allowing a good night's rest before clearing in.

All arrivals in Grand Cayman must be made at the Georgetown harbor (19°18.ON / 081°23.1) and the best times to arrive are Sundays and Mondays as cruise-liners visit most of the other days. You can contact the authorities at any time on channel 16 by calling *Georgetown Port Security*.

At night be careful to avoid the unlit dive-boats (and the yellow mini-submarines) which are moored up to 200 yards offshore. Use a flashlight to find a sandy patch for your anchor. The water is perfectly transparent, so you have no excuse for doing otherwise. This law is strictly enforced everywhere in the Cayman Islands, and to this end there are permanent dive-moorings (free on a first-come basis) situated along the wall offshore on all the islands.

Note that these moorings must also be carefully avoided when making an approach, so pass just off the wall at night. Passing by during the day, you must still beware the mooring balls along the wall as divers below will not be pleased if you pass closer than 100 yards away from any of them and the dive boat skippers above will give you the benefit of their wrath.

The coordinates given should put you 300 yards off the town's bakery and you'll usually be expected to clear in 1/2 mile to the southeast.

There are now two different sites utilized for visiting yachts:

The first is alongside a sloping concrete ramp on the northern side of the larger container wharf where ships moor for discharge. For this you will need long lines as there are only two (large) bollards available for your use.

Due to the maniac activities of the water-taxis serving the cruise-ships there can be a lot of violent swells present and the slope will make for a tricky mooring, so leave your lines slack, and have someone fending off all the time you are alongside. Better yet, avoid the days on which the cruise-ships visit.

In an unfortunate contrast to Cuba, only the idle or curious will help with your lines here.

Sometimes, if there are no cruise-ships in the bay, you may be allowed to dock in a small cove just a hundred yards south of the above dock, on the other side of the container wharf, and altogether far more convenient.

You will have to present your Cuban clearance papers, fill-in customs and immigration forms, and receive a perfunctory spraying down by the mosquito research official who charges you $25 for the privilege. This gentleman never has any change, so if you don't want to get stiffed have the exact money ready.

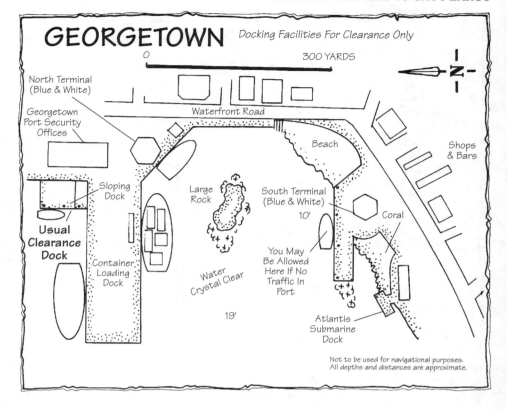

GEORGETOWN — Docking Facilities For Clearance Only

0   300 YARDS

North Terminal
(Blue & White)

Georgetown
Port Security
Offices

Waterfront Road

Beach

Shops
& Bars

Sloping
Dock

Large
Rock

South Terminal
(Blue & White)

10'

Coral

Usual
Clearance
Dock

Container
Loading
Dock

Water
Crystal Clear

You May
Be Allowed
Here If No
Traffic In
Port

19'

Atlantis
Submarine
Dock

Not to be used for navigational purposes.
All depths and distances are approximate.

Again, in stark relief to the friendly comfortable welcome you receive in Cuba, you may find that your reception here is *extremely* formal. I must stress that this has never happened to me personally, but there are reports, too frequent to be ignored, of customs being somewhat overenthusiastic, and indeed threatening. Be careful of the appearance you present, as they are apt to judge you by this.

Do not let this deter you however, for once past this hurdle, things will lighten up considerably, and ashore you will find that the island makes every attempt to accommodate the tourist.

MOORING

You may remain at anchor a bit further north in the bay for the duration, and oddly enough, this is probably the best place to be, as it gives you immediate access to the city of Georgetown and there are lots of docks (some belonging to bars) where you may moor your dinghy.

Alternatively, if you prefer, seek out a berth inside North Sound 12 miles away. In this case, go round the top of the island and enter the 1/2-mile marked channel at 19°22.8N / 081°19.6W. Don't assume you will see the indistinct lights from any distance in the dark, so do this in daylight hours.

This large sound is relatively shallow in places but largely navigable across its area. A large, completely enclosed anchorage is available in the wide expanse of Governors Creek, in the northwest corner. Within this too, there is a recent Japanese-funded development called the Cayman Islands Yacht Club, where you may moor alongside good floating docks. The entrance to both of these options is in the northwest portion of the bay.

To get there, pass through the main channel out at the reef, continue south into the sound for about 300 yards, then turn 250°M towards the small markers at the entrance to Goveners Creek at 19°21.5/081°22.1 The

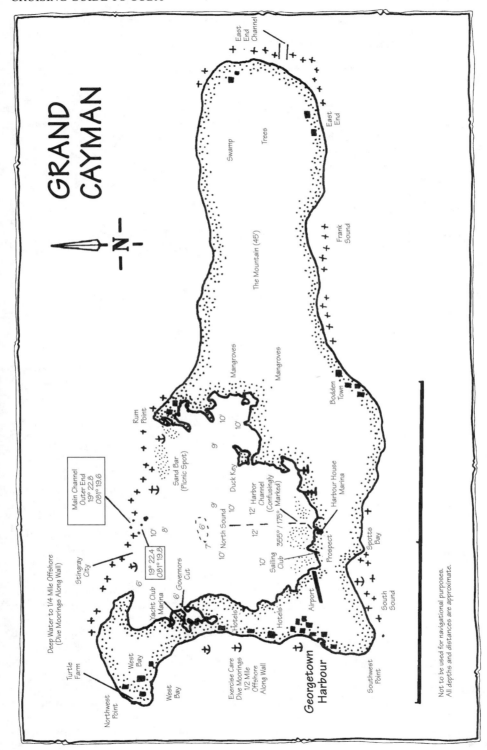

Not to be used for navigational purposees.
All depths and distances are approximate.

depths along this course can drop below 8 feet in places so be careful to go slowly.

Once inside, free anchorage is available immediately before you, or the the yacht club marina is to be found behind the fuel docks over to the northwest, accessible through a wide canal east of that. If staying here, you will have to get used to a less personal touch, and considerable inefficiency. The marina staff doesn't seem to show much interest in cruisers, preferring to deal with the dive and fishing boats which make up the majority of the occupants. As an ex-

The stern deck on passage to Grand Cayman.

ample, the live-aboards there have had to club together to buy a portable plastic outhouse to avoid fouling the water here.

Note that if you're going to show up at the marina, it's best to call them (telephone 947-4322, or channel 16) to ensure that there is space. However, sticking too exactly to the entrance directions given over the VHF will more likely put you in the Tipsy Turtle saloon bar (on the main road into town) than the marina.

To be truthful, the marina's a bit of a desert wasteland at the moment, with no shops, houses, or anything else within a mile of your dock; so you'll have to be prepared to arrange alternative transport.

To get into town by road (three-to-four miles), buses will stop if you flag them down, so just stand outside the entrance on the main road and hang about.

BOATYARD WORK

If you require any type of boat repairs or maintenance, a course of 175°M from the main reef opening will take you to *Harbour House Marina* (channel 16) on the extreme southern edge of the sound where all work can be carried out.

You will have to go through markers showing a dredged channel (6-foot max) just east of the marina as the sound is shallow along there, but don't be confused

by the earlier floating marks which merely denote the limits to the Marine Replishment Zones in the sound.

Unfortunately limited to about six-foot draft at the final entrance canal, Harbour House is in fact a proper boatyard equipped with two Travel-Lift hoists (75-ton max.) and facilities for hull, propeller, and engine work. There is also, on the premises, a 6,000 sq. ft. showroom containing all of the spares and equipment that the cruiser could possibly wish to find. Expensive to be sure, but at least available. Finally, there is a fuel dock at the marina. Diesel prices on the island are about $2.00/gallon (US), but if you're leaving then the fuel will be duty-free and thus cheaper. Fuel up the day before departure when you already have your papers to present.

Immediately past the marina, in the small canal along its eastern end, you may be lucky enough to find space alongside another dock for the duration of your stay. Ask around, just outside the gates to the marina, for Emile's house — Well, it's just next door. He offers monthly terms, and can handle up to four yachts at a time. Trouble is, anywhere out here is *way* out of town and you'll need your own road transport to get around.

Go berserk in the supermarkets. After so long in Cuba you deserve it. Everything you were accustomed to before is once again on the shelves, but be careful not to blow your budget as prices are generally much higher than elsewhere.

As befits an island which makes so much of its money from the marine environment, there are lots of good places for boaty stuff in Georgetown. Here you can get that recalcitrant outboard starting easily again (try Scotts Industries on Eastern Ave. or any of a dozen similarly large establishments nearby). You can replace the lures you lost to some unnamed grey monster on the trip across (Melody Marine on the way to Harbour House marina), or if you need navigation stuff like protractors and the like, then Cap't. Solomon (off Eastern Ave.) will find it for you somewhere among the confusion of his stock.

Get your scuba training done in Grand Cayman too. You'll never encounter a better place for it, and in any case you really *should* be properly trained (they even offer courses run in Japanese!).

Note: Rental cars are cheaper here, but cigarettes and booze are far cheaper in Cuba.

DEPARTURE PROCEDURES

If departing Grand Cayman for the sister islands (Little Cayman and Cayman Brac), it is considered that you are going international, so you will need clearance. It will probably be best to travel overnight, in which case arrange your papers the day before in the Port Authority offices downtown, just north of the cruise-ship terminal. Your clearance is valid for 24 hours and you may leave directly from North Sound if you wish, but be extremely careful about the exit channel through the reef at night.

Departing for Cuba or anywhere else, follow exactly the same procedure.

The *inner end* of the short channel is at 19°22.5N / 081°19.8W, but the course through the reef is 25°M and *not* north/south as might otherwise appear. The markers are indistinct at night and more than one yacht has been lost coming through on the wrong course, so it might be wisest to leave in the last light of the day.

RETURNING TO CUBA?

Note: If going back to Cuba from North Sound then the course to Cayo Largo is 355°M for 133 miles.

The course to Cienfuegos is 019°M for 167 miles (see later notes about the Jagua Bank), and if going to Casilda head 030°M for 157 miles.

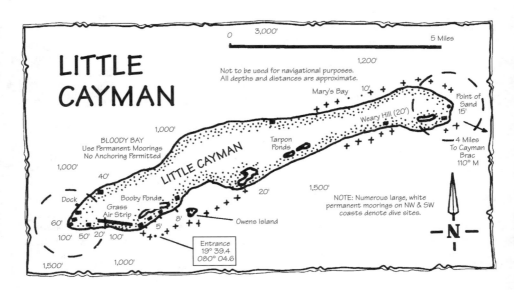

This can be a rough passage against both the prevailing winds and currents, so wait for settled weather (go to the airport for an up-to-the-minute forecast) and favorable winds before departing.

These twin islands both lie along the same course and due to their shape make a narrow target, but 076°M for 77 miles will take you from the reef exit in North Sound to the entrance at Owens Sound on the southwest coast of Little Cayman.

This is a narrow entrance, and due to its position relative to the prevailing swells should not be attempted in a southeast wind of any strength at all. Review the section on Reef Entrances if you have to do it under these conditions, and be careful. Many boats have been lost here to incautious skippers.

There are markers on the reef and also range-marks ashore that will guide you through (0°/180°M), but the sound is rather shallow, so turn right once inside and pick up the permanent mooring about 1/4-mile east near the reef. On no account attempt to approach the docks onshore as they require local knowledge and a draft of less than four-foot

Note: If there is any doubt, go round to the north side where you can tie up to any of the strong permanent dive-boat moorings along the wall in Bloody Bay. Except temporarily, don't trust the exposed concrete wharf there.

Even though you are coming in from Grand Cayman you will still require clearance here so you should contact Little Cayman Customs on channel 16 before arriving. Don't worry, here the process is friendly and extremely quick. The officer will come out to you in his boat if you're in the sound, and if you're in Bloody Bay you can skip it until you get ashore as long as he knows about you first.

In the sound, a convenient landing spot will be the customs dock where there are two or three small turtle-raising tanks under cover. Near the airstrip, and run by the local customs officer in his spare time, this admi-

rable project is designed to increase stocks in the waters off the coast.

It may appear on first glance that Little Cayman presents too many difficulties to be worth it, and to a visitor it may seem that all they do here is drink and dive, but the diving along the northwest coast in Bloody Bay really is superb.

If you visit any of the four small hotels ashore (those in the sound have docks even if too shallow for a sailboat) they will be pleased to include you in their regular organized dives. I'll admit to bias here, but if I wanted the absolute best I'd dive with Gaye at Pirates Point Resort (on Channel 16).

Little Cayman is also famous for its iguanas who have the run of the island and can often be seen mooching about near the small terminal at the eastern end of the grass airstrip. If you do rent a car from the island's one shop remember that both iguanas and aircraft have right-of-way on the road!

Excellent food is also to be had at Pirates Point Resort, while the eccentric proprietor, Gladys Howard, takes guests on nature-walks every Sunday morning.

CAYMAN BRAC & LEAVING FOR CUBA (AGAIN)

If you are leaving for Cuba you must clear out from the slightly larger and considerably more organized island of Cayman Brac, just east of Little Cayman. This can be done from the immigration offices in Stake Bay (19°43.ON / 079°50.OW) in front of the prominent radio tower 4 miles along the northwest coast.

There are permanent moorings just off the small concrete landing so you can dinghy ashore with the ship's papers to clear in or out. The offices are 200 yards along the road.

Clearance only takes 15 minutes, and there's a supermarket just opposite the government offices where you can stock up on ice, and whatever else you've managed to forget.

Equally supplied with dive sites (even if they're not quite as good as Little Cayman) the Brac also has a sound in the southwest corner of the island where most of the diveboats moor.

The entrance at 19°40.9N / 079°52.9W is marked, but this sound is also shallow, and there is a rock immediately inside the entrance, so you will have to pick your way carefully, and do not attempt this entrance in bad weather. Were I drawing more than four or five feet, I'd moor to one of the permanent buoys off Stake Bay, but if indeed I did come in here then I wouldn't be chivvied about by the Brac divemasters who seem to be a grumpy lot. As confirmed by the marine protection officers here, you have equal rights to mooring anywhere in the sound.

There are no surprises clearing back into Cuba from the Cayman Islands, especially if you have retained your previous Cruising Permit/Safety Inspection Certificate.

The course to Cienfuegos from Stake Bay is 349°M for 143 miles, and if you prefer to go direct to Casilda set 359°M (I use the north-star) for 119 miles. Both these courses will put you a safe mile or so west of the main entrance channels. (See Pg. 187 for sketch.)

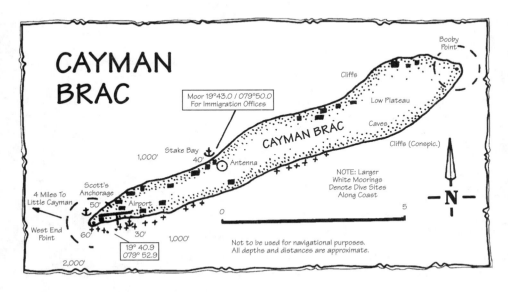

CAYMAN BRAC

Booby Point

Cliffs

Low Plateau

Moor 19°43.0 / 079°50.0
For Immigration Offices

Caves

Cliffs (Conspic.)

CAYMAN BRAC

Stake Bay
1,000'   40'
Antenna

NOTE: Larger
White Moorings
Denote Dive Sites
Along Coast

— N —

Scott's
Anchorage
4 Miles To
Little Cayman   50'   Airport

0   5

West End
Point   60'   30'
1,000'

19° 40.9
079° 52.9

Not to be used for navigational purposes.
All depths and distances are approximate.

2,000'

Cienfuegos

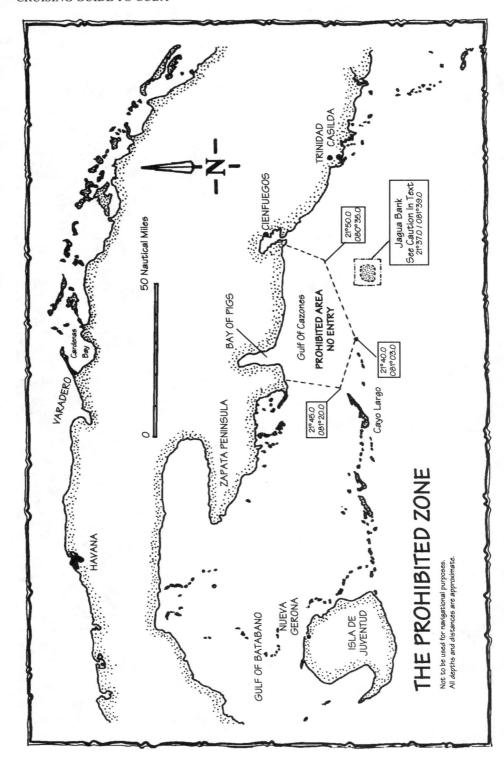

THE PROHIBITED ZONE

Not to be used for navigational purposes.
All depths and distances are approximate.

50 Nautical Miles

0

VARADERO

Cardenas Bay

HAVANA

ZAPATA PENINSULA

BAY OF PIGS

CIENFUEGOS

TRINIDAD

CASILDA

Gulf Of Cazones

PROHIBITED AREA
NO ENTRY

21°50.0
080°35.0

Jagua Bank
See Caution In Text
21°37.0 / 081°39.0

21°40.0
081°03.0

21°45.0
081°20.0

Cayo Largo

GULF OF BATABANO

NUEVA GERONA

ISLA DE JUVENTUD

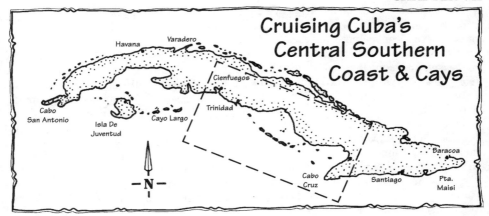

Cruising Cuba's
Central Southern
Coast & Cays

Havana Varadero

Cienfuegos

Cabo
San Antonio   Isla De   Cayo Largo   Trinidad
            Juventud

Baracoa

–N–

Cabo
Cruz   Santiago   Pta.
                  Maisi

CAYO LARGO TO CABO CRUZ
ROUTES

At the western extreme of this section there is a large area surrounding the Bay of Pigs in the east of the Gulf of Cazones. For various reasons, strategic, political, and historic, this area is a prohibited zone and is marked as such on all Cuban charts. If using any of the foreign chart issues, then it will probably not be shown. If so, draw it in.

As you can see, there's still room to go round if you're transiting the coast and wish to enter the Ensenada de Cazones (Chart No. ICH 1160), just on the northwestern edge of the territory, but do not pretend innocence if you're found inside the *Zona Prohibida*. The history of this area is too symbolic to the military for them to resist giving the unwary a rough ride.

Between Cienfuegos and Casilda there isn't much in the line of strategy to consider, but going eastwards over the next 150 -200 miles you may choose to take either the inside passage, along a low lying coast, or an outer route through the cays which angle progressively further offshore.

EAST ALONG THE INNER ROUTE

Beginning at the port of Casilda, the inner route is plied by commercial vessels delivering cargo up and down the coast, and

is thus extensively marked. You can do the entire route miles away from the outer reef, along major channels signposted by a familiar mixture of large concrete box-structures, floating buoys, and rust-streaked pylon affairs — all camouflaged by a fertile mixture of bird feathers, droppings, and dried fish heads.

This route will take you 180 miles east from Casilda, through the gulfs of Ana María and Guacanayabo (another name which requires practice) where the only townships deal more or less exclusively in the export of sugar. At the other end it runs up against the jutting peninsula of Granma province where the city of Manzanillo offers a better chance of resupply. From here it jinks down south past Niquero, to the tip of the mainland at Cabo Cruz.

THE OUTER ROUTE

The outer route will take you, as before, from Cienfuegos to Casilda and the inland city of Trinidad, but here it diverges south along the line of the cays, following them through the Gardens of the Queen and the Twelve League Labyrinth. At any stage of this route you may dodge north to link up again with the inner route.

Subject to my earlier remarks, the prevailing easterlies are much modified by the considerable land mass of the island, and there is also a convenient southeast countercurrent which can assist a cruise outside of the cays and along the wall. So it's more likely that you will have favorable winds for easting along this stretch than the more exposed Bahamas-side of Cuba.

The very nature of this almost totally deserted and untraveled multitude of islands, makes it almost impossible to give an extensive cay-by-cay guide except for a few selected anchorages along our route. Certainly you will discover others off to the side, and even find that some reported here are supplanted or made redundant by your own discoveries. That's only how it should be, and out of all the cruising areas in Cuba *this one offers the most opportunities for further experimentation.* After all, the area enclosed by the cays here is approximately 5,000 nautical square miles!

In addition, there are no inhabitants here, and while you may sometimes run across tourists in the various halts prior to the southern cays you most assuredly will not come across many here. Apart from the occasional fishing boat you will be as isolated from your fellow man as you've ever been.

PASSAGE PLANNING CONSIDERATIONS

Regarding passage planning, along the outer cays your courses should be set only after consulting adequate charts, and you should be prepared to abandon fixed courses when necessary. Along here there are numerous passes, occasionally calling for six or seven course changes in a relatively short distance and precisely detailed descriptions can be mind-numbingly complex.

You may prefer therefore, to lay out your own courses through the cays following only a general description of the route. For this you should be prepared to use both the experience you've already gained in reef-navigation, and proper charts.

If, on the other hand you're taking the inner route, then the main ship channels between the major ports along the coast are well-marked along their length and need little description.

Something to look out for along here is a peculiar weather pattern which sets in during the early months of the year and lasts until perhaps May. For months on end, you will find that the wind remains high during the morning hours, only dropping in the afternoon. These incessant gales can raise large waves all the way inside the gulf and

Picturesque towns are found on the mainland of the south coast.

will certainly affect your travel, so be aware of how you schedule your departures.

There are a variety of charts on the market dealing with this section of Cuba. When we first travelled here we had a disparate mixture, including a few older photocopies obtained from different sources, and it was only much later that we obtained a complete matched set of original Cuban charts.

Welcome sign at Cienfuegos.

While we still maintain that the best are the ICH series (black and white or colored), if they are difficult to come by then by all means use from among the others. Just be prepared to feel your way through the smaller passes, after all, everyone else does.

Note: The magnetic deviation which has been sneakily increasing as you've progressed from Cabo San Antonio in the west is now going to grow from two degrees at Cienfuegos to three or four degrees at the Cabo Cruz end, so don't forget to factor this into your courses.

CAUTION!

You may be planning to arrive in Trinidad from Cayo Largo, taking the direct route across the Gulf of Cazones. If so, consider carefully the shallow Jagua bank along your path. This isolated area of reef leaps vertically up from the depths to within a few feet of the surface and contains several wrecks perched atop a 36-square mile sub-

marine pedestal some 5,000 feet high. It would be best to avoid an area three-to-five miles in all directions from position 21°37.ON / 080°39.OW, unless passing by during the day and considering a dive along its undoubtedly promising walls. There are three others, similar but not so shallow, some way further over to the east and closer to the cays.

Perhaps due to these obstructions and the currents swirling through, the waters in the gulf can also be far, far rougher than expected. So have the boat well prepared for what is in any case an open offshore run.

We have moreover come across heavy squalls, making for such uncomfortable passages that the crew has had to be brought below for safety in the confused seas.

If encountering this phenomenon while coming north from the Cayman Islands to Casilda it is sometimes best to seek shelter in the lee of the cays over to the east, rather than slogging along the direct route.

CIENFUEGOS
CHART NOS. ICH 1142,1158, OR 1840 (CUBAN)

The city of Cienfuegos, one of the oldest in Cuba, is somewhat marred visually by large cement works, and work on the abandoned but imposing nuclear generating station (two or three miles west as you approach the entrance) is rumored to be recommencing soon. Nevertheless, for the cruiser there are splendid views along the

entry routes past the castle guarding the splendid harbor. And, whatever else you can say about the place, it does seem to be a city with a culture and a soul.

It is also one of the largest ports in Cuba and any marine repair work one might desire can be carried out within the usual confines of parts availability. A yacht ma-

199

rina is situated at the southern end (the Punta Gorda peninsula), and international arrivals are catered for. If this is your first port in Cuba, then you can get all your onward documentation arranged here too.

ENTRANCE

The narrow entrance to this enormous bay is deep (up to 180 feet), free of any outstanding dangers, and may be made visually from anywhere around the outer buoys at 22°03.0N/080°27.4W., with range marks inside if you need them. There is a Guarda Frontera post one mile in and some 600 yards before the old fortress high on the western shores of the entrance channel, so you must stop here for clearance before continuing onwards. Sometimes they flash a searchlight to indicate that you should approach, but in any case you'll recognize it from the large sign painted across its walls , "Welcome to Socialist Cuba".

From close alongside, shout across to indicate that you're going to the "Santiago Marina", and you may be signalled to continue on for later clearance at the docks, but don't always count on it.

Whatever, if a pilot is offered, resist this by saying you already know the way, and avoid paying a totally unnecessary $30 fee. As well as being perfectly obvious, it really is a rather beautiful passage through the canal here, so enjoy the view on either side all the way over to the marina.

Pass west of the small cay at the inner entrance to the bay (where the old wooden buildings resemble the Bates Motel in *Psycho*) and from the No.15 buoy aim across the bay just right of the chimneys, heading 024°M to pass west of the peninsula at Punta Gorda. The yellow and grey docks of the marina (22°07.5/080°27.2) will be on your starboard, north of the hotel Jagua, south of a fantastic old building which used to be the yacht club itself, and close to the public beach. My logbook notes that you'll find yourself surrounded by weird and wonderful structures here, like something out of Disneyland.

The moorings more or less radiate outwards from a central dock parallel to the shore, and it will be wisest to berth at one of the northernmost docks so as to be as far as possible from the beach. We know of at least one foreign yacht which lost its dinghy here, so secure yours properly. Admittedly this happened in the exodus of 1993, and no such thing has *ever* happened to us, but it is also as well to relate another tale here.

In 1996 while clearing in with a customs gentleman at the dock I brought up the subject of swim-aboards. "Never has such a thing happened here," he expansively assured me — which I knew for a fact to be untrue at the time, but diplomatically let pass except to look pleased for him. Not three minutes later, and now on dockside, we were approached by the sleepy French captain of a home built cruising catamaran. He'd just woken up to find that the escape hatch (underneath, on a cat) had been left open and now, just inside the opening, all his shaving stuff was gone!

The marina at Cienfuegos with the old yacht club in the background.

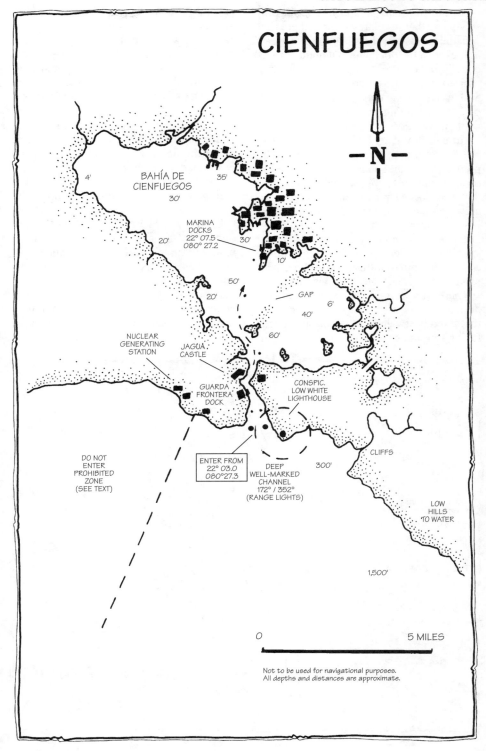

CIENFUEGOS

– N –

BAHÍA DE
CIENFUEGOS

4'

35'

30'

MARINA
DOCKS
22° 07.5
080° 27.2

20'

30'

10'

50'

20'

GAP

6'

40'

60'

NUCLEAR
GENERATING
STATION

JAGUA
CASTLE

CONSPIC.
LOW WHITE
LIGHTHOUSE

GUARDA
FRONTERA
DOCK

CLIFFS

DO NOT
ENTER
PROHIBITED
ZONE
(SEE TEXT)

ENTER FROM
22° 03.0
080°27.3

DEEP
WELL-MARKED
CHANNEL
172° / 352°
(RANGE LIGHTS)

300'

LOW
HILLS
TO WATER

1,500'

0   5 MILES

Not to be used for navigational purposes.
All depths and distances are approximate.

To put this into perspective, both ourselves and that same crew shortly thereafter became accustomed to leaving our boats unlocked at the dock without undue preoccupation, or ill result. In fact, we later cruised more or less in company for another 500 miles along the coasts without any problems, leaving our boats unaccompanied on countless occasions.

International arrivals: For those arriving from abroad, one thing you must be prepared for is the somewhat overpowering official reaction to your arrival. I once noted that a 32-foot Danish yacht with only two crewmembers was visited by a total of 12 customs/immigration inspectors and a dog. Later that afternoon, two more "state inspectors" showed up for their piece of the action. It's not that there's a problem, it's just that everyone wants to get in on the act.

There were several yachts damaged here during the storms of early 1993 and those that fared best were on the northern docks facing into the swells. This of course, will depend on conditions at the time, but remember that the bay is large, and winds can be strong when the fronts sweep down in winter; so moor with your vessel held slightly off the concrete edges. Put anti-chafe guards of some sort on the lines, and extend them across to the adjoining dock if possible.

Be careful of rusty reinforcing steel rods which protrude from within the concrete along the dock walls. They are perfectly positioned to puncture both hull and fenders of the unwary.

Regarding prices, at time of publication, the marina charged 25 cents per foot.

Electricity (110/220v) and water is supplied, but as usual in Cuba, the marina's man will have to finesse the connections, while diesel fuel is also available at .75cents per litre.

Interestingly, as Cienfuegos becomes better known, cruisers are beginning to leave their boats here on a long term basis.

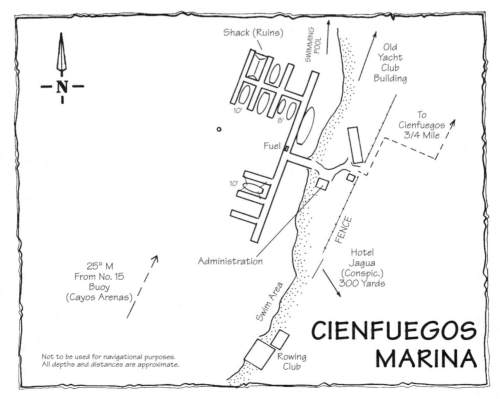

CIENFUEGOS MARINA

MARINA IS NEAR HOTEL

Once ashore, the city is a mile to the left, while the hotel Jagua is over towards the right at the tip of the peninsula. Being so close, the hotel can be utilized for phone calls, tour inquiries, car rental, taxis, casual supplies and so on, while there is a source of wholesale provisions (beer and booze) for the boat at the storeroom just inside the marina gates.

Ships Chandler: There is too, a "Proveedor de Buques" or a proper ship chandlers, west along on the main waterfront road in town. Called *Sumarpo* (as they all are now) and situated on Avenida 46, at the corner of Calle 33. This convenient and sometimes priceless service, features stacks of onions and other vegetables piled on the floor of a dim warehouse. It is reached by heading into town along the main road then turning left at 46, along the Malecon waterfront road. You can also contact them by VHF Channel 16 or by telephone (dial 3845).

When in search of the social scene, go north along the main road into town until past Av. 46 where the road changes into the Paseo del Prado. There are lots of picturesque horse-drawn buggies which cruise the route, so for a peso you can just flag them down and hop on. Don't be timid about this, as it's normal transport outside of Havana, and a great way to touch the soul of Cuba.

At night, when you're out cruising the streets yourself and looking for a private paladar-restaurant, just ask any of those same buggies parked on any street corner. They'll not only tell you where to go, but they'll take you there.

If you're looking for the older parts of town, then you're in luck. Pueblo Nuevo just west of the Paseo is where the most interesting places such as the José Martí Square, museums, and historic buildings are located.

For an idle day in the streets, turn left at Ave. 54, opposite the Ciné Prado and just before the Post Office. Several places are worthy of your visit, but my personal favorites are the Teatro Tomás Terry, the Palacio Valle, and the original City cemetery.

The old cemetary in Cienfuegos.

Situated in José Martí square, the Tomás Terry is an original 19th century theatre which you can tour for two dollars. In addition to those at floor level, banks of dark wooden seats line the galleries; while creaking stairs, velvet curtains, and rooftop views across the square, are among the other attractions. The ceiling above the dimly lit auditorium is exquisitely painted, with various ladies floating among the clouds and pointing at a clockface. The hands show the exact time the painting was completed, and to complete the display, an ornate marble statue of the founder graces the lobby,

This wonderful building is still in use, hosting everything from music-hall comedy to ballet and opera. If you prefer, then just show up for any of the evening performances (pay in pesos at the box office), and imagine yourself some sort of Edwardian taking his leisure.

The Valle Palace is not more than 500 yards to the right of the marina on the main road and next door to the Hotel Jagua. A blend of Moorish and Spanish architectural features, blended with a pinch of fantasy, this extraordinary building was built as a wedding present around the turn of the century. Having survived Batista's casino designs, the building is now a working restaurant which can be toured with an elderly guide giving you running commentaries on each and every room. The roof is

now an open-air bar, and a delightful place to spend half an hour with a frosted cocktail of some sort.

As for the Cementario Municipal de La Reina (the old graveyard from 1836), this is where the original inhabitants of the city lie in a tumult of marble graves and sepulchers. Here, a fantastic jumble of pious virgins and angels stand guard among crumbling monuments, twisted wrought iron railings, vines, and nooks in the cemetery walls. You may park your bike with the curator, who will also be only too delighted to point out the finer examples of immortal-

ity, but be certain to ask after the Sleeping Beauty, a lovely marble statue. If my memory serves me right, the curator told me that she too would one day be buried in her family's old plot.

To get to this one, you have to skirt the port area, passing the old railway sidings and go round to the western shores of the city, only 15 minutes by bike.

By the way, there are small ferries which connect the city with the entry channel. If you wish to tour the Castillo de Jagua (the ancient fort you passed on the way in), then take the midday ferry which leaves from the northern end of Calle 29. The journey across the bay only costs a couple of centavos, and takes about an hour.

While it's not everyone's cup of tea, I guess you can tell I like Cienfuegos. And as a matter of fact, in some weird way, it always strikes me as being a city that really should know better, but still...

CASILDA
CHART NOS. ICH 1141,1432 OR 1431 (CUBAN)

Despite the limited appeal and downright ugliness of this particular port, it does serve the city of Trinidad some six or seven miles inland (See Pg. 208). There is absolutely no excuse for visiting Cuba and neglecting *that* jewel of a city, even if you have to do it by land from somewhere else. So beautiful is it that UNESCO has placed it on the World Heritage list.

Casilda is the gateway to the southeastern cays and the Escambray mountains.

In many ways this is the most convenient entry point if you are coming up from the Cayman Islands and intending to cruise the southern cays. Complete entry formalities (international and local travel) are available here, and you may also arrange all further documentation.

There is usually a motley collection of small fishing boats out at the reef, so go slowly past them as they don't have a lot of freeboard. Usually powered by simple sails made of crudely-stitched canvas and sackcloth, these tiny affairs are solely balanced by the crewmembers' precarious seating-

position with little in the way of ballast to help. If they don't wave back it's probably because they're scared to let go.

Once at the tip of the peninsula, the main channel will open up along a properly marked and maintained passage west-north-west into the inner bay harbor and whether you're coming in from Cayo Largo, Cienfuegos, or the Cayman Islands you will still have to put up with approximately the same formalities when docking.

The port officials here, unusually enough, will sometimes answer repeated VHF calls to "Seguidád Marítima" on 16 and will offer instructions if you are unsure, but in any case you should proceed in as described below.

THE ROUTE INTO CASILDA

Whether approaching from the outer gulf of Cazones or from Cienfuegos, the way into the sheltered gulf of Ana María at Casilda is through the Pasa de las Mulatas, actually a few miles south of Casilda.

This pass through the reef is used by major vessels and is consequently marked

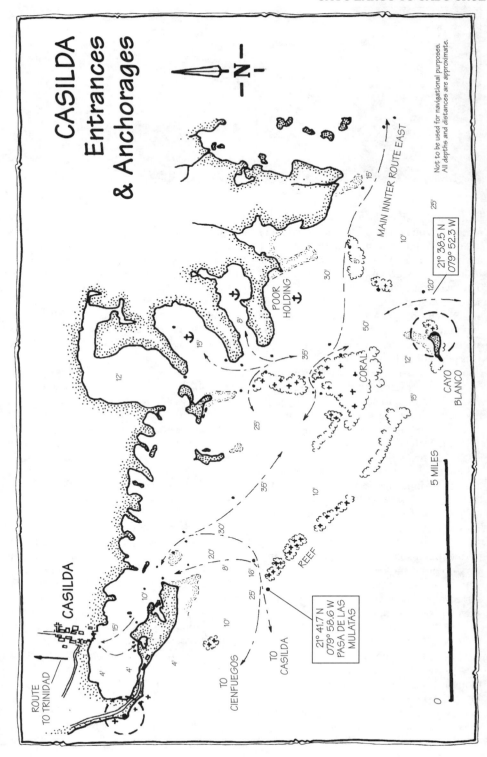

CASILDA
Entrances
& Anchorages

—N—

Not to be used for navigational purposes.
All depths and distances are approximate.

MAIN INNTER ROUTE EAST

POOR HOLDING

CORAL

CAYO BLANCO

21° 38.5 N
079° 52.3 W

REEF

21° 41.7 N
079° 58.6 W
PASA DE LAS
MULATAS

TO CIENFUEGOS

TO CASILDA

CASILDA

ROUTE TO TRINIDAD

5 MILES

0

Trinidad buildings.

by a light at position 21°41.7N/079°58.6W., although you could safely enter anywhere up to a mile north of this. Go through along a course of 65°M and turn north at the following green marker 2/3 of a mile in. This will take you over waters of about seven or eight feet to the channel light at the eastern end of the Ancón peninsula some two miles away, fine on the port bow. There are shallows either side of your course as you get within half a mile of the light so don't stray off-line. Luckily, the sandbank on your starboard is marked by a stake so you will be able to see whether you're on line. Once past the peninsula, follow the main channel through to the northwest.

If you prefer, there is a deeper route (20-30 feet all the way across) just a bit further to the east. To use this one, do not turn north at the green inner mark after entering through the reef, but rather continue east for another half-mile before making the turn north. This way you'll pass to the *right* of that same shallow sand bank off the eastern tip of the peninsula, passing through some very obvious markers there before making your turn northwest and picking up the same main channel into the harbor (see sketch previous page).

DOCKING

The large, well constructed wharf northwest across the basin to the right, inviting though it may be, is not your destination. Instead, you proceed towards a closer sagging wooden affair crowded by fishing vessels of all descriptions, and containing a small sentry-post/shack halfway along its

length. There are some dangerous pilings barely protruding from the surface directly off the end, so come in from a bit over to the right where there is eight-to-nine feet depth and find a gap into which you can maneuver. Be flexible in your attitude towards fenders here as the top of the wharf is irregular to say the least, and it may be better to have crewmembers permanently assigned to fending-off once secured at the dock.

For those who prefer, you may anchor just off the dock and they'll come over to you in a small boat.

Over the years, we have had contrasting fortunes with our reception here. Usually there are endless delays when checking in (officials have to come from the ship's terminal across the basin), and upon arrival they used to be somewhat picky. Now, they're absolutely relaxed about the whole thing, and it has recently been a real pleasure dealing with the crew on duty.

At one stage too, this was one of the only places on the coast of Cuba where you would be sniffed over by a dog (this is increasingly common now), so lock up the ship's cat if you see one approaching.

Things can be slower on a Sunday so avoid this day like the plague, and you won't have to pay extra dues for the privileged. Mind you, you can pass the time watching the small fishing dinghies being cleared too when they come in.

AFTER CLEARING CUSTOMS

Having cleared customs and immigration (both of these august bodies will require their pound of flesh), it will be suggested that you proceed to the Base Nautica across the bay south where you can see the top of the hotel over the mangroves. Translated literally into "Nautical Base", this is an airless, ugly, mooring between mosquito infested cays behind the Hotel Ancón complex. The various boats serving the tourist industry anchor there at night but the entrance is shallow and not shown on all charts, so I would advise care and a sharp eye on the depth-sounder. The bottom is soft mud, so no harm can come to you, but in any case the base is a charmless place to spend any time and it may be better to anchor off to the side of the main Casilda entrance channel.

You will, even moored inside the base, have to use your dinghy to come ashore so the additional inconvenience will be minimal.

The one advantage offered by the Base Nautica is that it does have a dirty concrete wharf alongside which you can draw if purchasing fuel, and there is a stand-pipe for water too.

Fuel is available, and we have also obtained ice here by requesting it well beforehand and including it in a deal for provisions.

To get to the Base Nautica, go west from the dock to pass north of the green mark close by. From this, head across the bay in seven-to-eight feet of water, in a curve as shown in the sketch. There is a red mark over there which should be passed to starboard, and you can now proceed directly towards the green mark right inside the mouth of the inlet. It is shallower at the mouth and you may prefer to wait for high tide before making the trip, but in any case the mud here is extremely soft so you can't really come to grief.

MOORING YOUR DINGHY

Your dinghy may be moored at the low concrete dock inside the Base Nautica, a short red-dust walk from the hotel fronting the beach on the other side of the peninsula. There are two other hotels a couple of miles along the beach, but too far off to be much use to a cruiser.

The Ancón seems marooned in the 1950's and 60's and although this ghastly object is crumbling at a goodly pace, unfortunately, it hasn't collapsed yet. Nevertheless, with luck, it may no longer blight the beachfront when you arrive. The dimly-lit lobby is crowded with package-tourists looking emptily at the dust covered walls and wondering what there is to do except hang out on the beach, or take even more package-tours to other parts of Cuba. They wear colored wristbands to denote their group (and rate), eating at prescribed times in prescribed refectories. Horseman, pass by.

Better spend your time in Trinidad, or if you wish to experience a more typically Cuban day out then spend Sunday afternoon on the sand at La Boca just down the coast road on the way to Trinidad. This beach, at the mouth of a narrow river is where the inhabitants of the area meet to relax in a lively congregation of music, flirting, and fist fights. They're far more interesting than the dowdy crowd of pale visitors from the north along the Ancón Peninsula, and you'll be made more welcome too.

As you're moored close at hand, the unfortunate hotel Ancón will have to be your base of operations for renting cars (in spite of the advertisements, there may not

Trinidad street.

be any available just when you want) or obtaining taxis into the city. A trip into the spectacular Escambray Mountains will be a welcome diversion after having been aboard for some days, so explore this possibility with regards to the rental car question, combining it with your visit to Trinidad. If driving, beware of the hordes of local cyclists wobbling two-up along the beach roads, and the additional hazard of incongruously helmeted foreigners on cycling tours!

If you have to take a taxi, there are few opportunities for getting a cheaper rate at the hotel as only official ones are allowed in the compound. For a privately operated taxi (*taxi particular*) you have to wait until you're in Trinidad where you can easily find one by asking around.

There are a couple of hard-currency shops on the premises too, and although the range of goods sold is limited you may be able to re-provision somewhat if you've used up your roasted peanuts and bottled olives. The liquor racks are always full though, and you may find cosmetics and skin-diving equipment at competitive prices.

As in other hotels in Cuba, there is always a cigar-maker rolling his products by hand in the lobby.

Medical Service: In a contrast to my usually jaundiced view of the Ancón, one of our crewmembers got ill on a passage once (I blame the demon drink) and received excellent attention at the well signposted medical post under the hotel, so don't forget this service.

TRINIDAD THE BEAUTIFUL

One of the original seven colonial villas (garrisons) in the era of the Conquistadores, this city once thrived on sugar. Thousands of slaves were imported to till the fields of the rich families who built their majestic dwellings around the cathedral of Santisima Trinidad off the main square. Interestingly, some of the streets have old cannons buried muzzle-down to protect the corner-houses from being damaged by wide-turning horse-drawn vehicles and the like.

The old mansions in the cobbled streets have largely been preserved and tourists are encouraged to visit these. For a dollar or

two you can stroll about opulent rooms filled with their original furniture, all the time followed by an informative middle-aged matron who precisely describes (or makes a wild guess at) any of the objects you might wish to pause over. One of the museums here, devoted to the years of CIA destabilization campaigns, even has a hands-on exhibit of a captured "pirate" vessel used to prey on official or unofficial Cuban boats and to land agents in the area. A fast cabin-cruiser, painted strangely matt-black and converted to fire heavy machine-guns from fixed mounts. Many's the time I've wished for one of my own.

Behind the Cathedral on the hill, there are a couple of cave systems which are worth a visit. One of these, was even the haunt of Carlos Ayala, an ancient brigand who would bring his victims here to meet their fate.

The city seems to have rediscovered itself over the last few years, and there is now a glut of private restaurants (paladars) available to the cruiser. You are quite likely to be intercepted by runners acting for these, who will advise on which door to knock on. For the first-time visitor to Cuba this may be a strange experience, but you soon get used to the way things are done.

The same person who advises you about local eateries will also know a friend with a car. This, to be truthful, is a far better deal than official taxis — or even renting your own. For example, at about half the price of a small rental auto, you can obtain the services of a car, driver with local knowledge, guide, and friend. This in turn (everything in Cuba leads in logical steps from one to another), will lead to an acquaintance of the driver knowing where you can obtain locally grown provisions outside of the market system.

Make sure your driver knows that you want to visit the mountains outside the city. It's a steep drive and you should allow a half-day or more, but you can soon find yourself in an environment which seems more like Switzerland than the Caribbean. The second highest peak in Cuba (el Tope de Collante) is in the Escambray mountains here, with a nearby waterfall which you can reach only by foot after an exquisite hike.

You might think that with the increase in tourism there would be a certain "West Indian" tension in the streets, but thankfully I have never noticed anything of the like. We have wandered all over the lesser travelled lanes on the edge of town, but have encountered only wonderful people who absolutely adore talking about life, their country, and their futures.

LEAVING

If planning to go far afield from Casilda you will have to return to the Guarda Frontera post on the dock and await clearances and your despacho. They'll even give you a Guía de Recala (list of stops) extending all the way to Santiago or Havana, so avail yourself of this facility, emphasizing that you're going by way of the cays and will be anchored out most of the way.

If you're only going out for a day or two among the cays here then the local Guárda Frontera officer at the Base Nautica itself will probably be able to issue you with the despacho.

THE INNER PASSAGE ALONG THE MAINLAND:
CHART NOS. ICH 1141, 1139, 1138, 1137,
&1431 *(A REALLY GOOD ONE FOR THE FIRST TRICKY BIT).*

There will be several points along the way where both the inner and outer routes converge, so in the interest of simplicity I shall first describe the inside route as far as the mid-gulf cays of Cuervos, Manuel Gomez, and Algodón Grande. Here the two passages come close together, and thereafter, you may swap between them as you see fit.

To be truthful, once past the first fifteen miles, if you don't have any detailed charts, all you have to do to get to the end of the island is to follow the coastline. Whenever you come to a line of cays extending out (sometimes up to ten miles) from the shoreline, then look for the markers showing the canals through.

There are a couple of notable passes to be negotiated, namely: The Canal de Balandras off Jucaro (this one can be avoided entirely by turning due south to the mid-gulf cays), the long Canal del Pingue, the passes north of the Canal de Cuatro Reales, and the pass through the banks at Chinchorro.

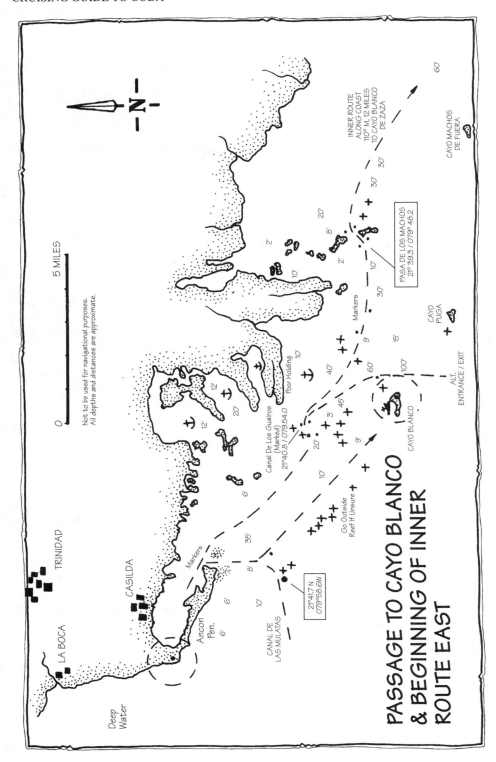

PASSAGE TO CAYO BLANCO & BEGINNING OF INNER ROUTE EAST

5 MILES

Not to be used for navigational purposes.
All depths and distances are approximate.

TRINIDAD

LA BOCA

CASILDA

Deep Water

Ancon Pen.

Markers

CANAL DE LAS MULATAS

21°41.7 N
079°58.6W

Go Outside Reef If Unsure

Canal De Los Guairos (Marked)
21°40.8 / 079°54.0

Poor Holding

Markers

CAYO BLANCO

CAYO PUGA

ALT. ENTRANCE / EXIT

PASA DE LOS MACHOS
21°39.3 / 079° 48.2

INNER ROUTE ALONG COAST
110° M, 12 MILES
TO CAYO BLANCO DE ZAZA

CAYO MACHOS DE FUERA

Escambray Mountains

Inner Route: To leave Casilda and the nearby passes, follow the large markers out, but do not turn south at the tip of the peninsula along your original entry route. Instead, continue on to the end of the markers, go southeast four miles along 137°M to pass Cayo Guayo well off to your port side, then onwards into a marked channel turning back northeast at 21°40.6N / 079°54.2W at the Canal de los Guairos. At the other end, go east-southeast following intermit-

tent marks to the Pasa de los Machos, another well signposted northeasterly channel at 21°39.1N / 079°48.3W.

Cayo Zaza de Blanco is 12 miles east of the above passes, and can be reached by merely heading east and remaining two or three miles offshore. This is the first of the planned rest stops described here.

Following that, remaining mostly five or six miles offshore will get you all the way southeast to Manzanillo.

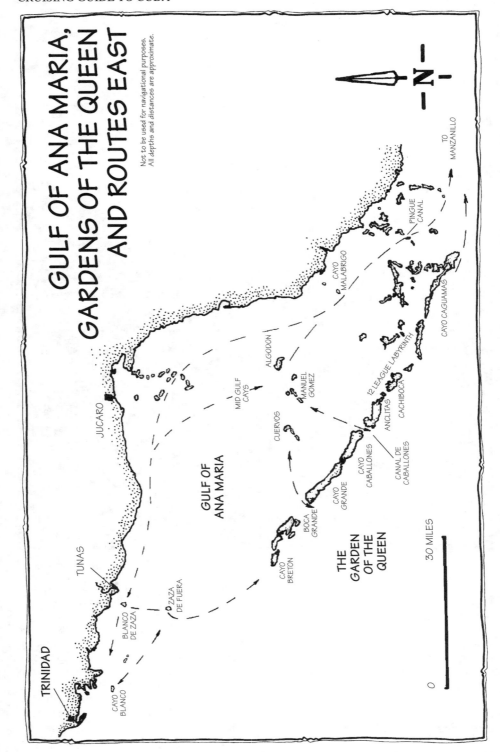

GULF OF ANA MARIA, GARDENS OF THE QUEEN AND ROUTES EAST

Not to be used for navigational purposes.
All depths and distances are approximate.

N

TO MANZANILLO

PINGUE CANAL

CAYO MALABRIGO

CAYO CAGUAMAS

ALGODON

12 LEAGUE LABYRINTH

MID GULF CAYS

MANUEL GOMEZ

CACHIBOCA

ANCLITAS

CUERVOS

CANAL DE CABALLONES

JUCARO

CAYO CABALLONES

GULF OF ANA MARIA

CAYO GRANDE

BOCA GRANDE

THE GARDEN OF THE QUEEN

CAYO BRETON

TUNAS

ZAZA DE FUERA

BLANCO DE ZAZA

TRINIDAD

CAYO BLANCO

30 MILES

0

CAYO BLANCO DE ZAZA

Just before the town of Tunas de Zaza, and not to be confused with Cayo Blanco or Zaza de Fuera (both on the outer reef), this is the first of the natural stopping points along the inner route. About 11 miles east of the Pasa de Los Machos, this pretty island offers better shelter than the bay just east of Tunas, and has some lovely sandy beaches on the west side. Over there on the mainland, the aforementioned bay is shallow, muddy and offers extremely poor holding, so don't even bother to look.

There is a light on the cay, and if you moor south-southwest of that (around 21°35.9/079°35.9) you'll be in 10-11 feet and sheltered from the northeast winds.

The last time we were here we were visited by a single Guarda Frontera later that night, but a quick flash of the paperwork seemed to work wonders.

Be careful of the corals extending from the northern and southern tips of the island and give them wide berths when leaving.

From here you can easily navigate eastward along the coast by remaining some two or three miles offshore until you come to a chain of cays just past the mainland town of Jucaro, itself about 45 miles east of Cayo Blanco de Zaza.

JUCARO AND ONWARDS

Situated in a large shallow bay, Jucaro is guarded to the east by a more or less continuous string of cays which stretch out nearly 15 miles south of the mainland. The town itself is quite small, and bases its economy on fishing and pilotage. There is a long wharf here which caters to the shipment of sugar in barges, and another one just east of that which is where the fishing boats moor.

Ice and fuel can be obtained here, and it is notable that the tenders which supply a new floating hotel down in the cays to the south (see Piedra Grande on Pg. 225) use this port as a base to collect both supplies and their European clientele arriving by road and rail from Havana.

Past Jucaro, the marked course goes through a short canal between the cays. This can be entered from the west at 21°26.2/ 078°47.4, but in any case the route swings south immediately after leaving, so rather than passing through these islands, it is best to turn due southeast before you reach them. Head 160°M from approximately 21°30.0/078°00.0. This will take you towards

Cayos Cuervos, Manuel Gomez, and Algodón Grande. These cays, which lie some 27 miles away, are only a couple of miles off the main commercial channel and offer excellent cruising and anchorage. They are also halfway between the outer reef and the mainland, so are equally accessible to both routes. We will deal with them in a short while (see Pgs. 221 and 222).

THE OUTER ROUTE ALONG THE CAYS:
CAYO BLANCO
CHART NOS.1141 & 1431

Along the outer cays near Casilda, this island is deserving of a visit even if you're going to take the inner route (see charts). You can snorkel for lobster close off the eastern tip in the elkhorn coral forests, and follow that up with a midnight barbecue on the beach. There is a light beacon situated on the eastern end.

To get to the cay, retrace your entry route, but instead of actually exiting the pass out through the reef at the Pasa de las Mulatas merely proceed from the inside marker along a course of 132° M to the remains of a wreck on the coast of Cayo Blanco some 5.5 miles away. You might alternately parallel the reef along the outside on a similar course.

Be careful when mooring near the wreck, as there is an underwater bank east and south of this point. This can cause problems if the Kabatic effect causes a wind shift (as it surely will around here) in the night.

We've found it best to remain a hundred yards north of the wreck and to make sure the anchor is well dug in especially in the spring as the early morning winds can be strong here. The aforesaid wind shifts once caused us to seek out shelter across the bay in the Fondeadero (anchorage) Jobabo close in to the mangroves. That's about three miles away on 30°M. Be careful of the

holding at Jobabo and if you can't get a grip then you can follow the marked channel round to the west and north where there are a couple of enclosed anchorages (sketches on Pgs. 205 and 210) which are better. We have also had to use these once, during a midnight storm while bypassing Casilda on our way east from Cienfuegos. In a southerly gale, it was just too rough to travel anywhere near the reef so we had to enter from outside, coming through just to the east of the light. We made our way over to the shelter of the mainland, but under those conditions the holding off Jobabo wasn't good enough so we had to search out better grip in the bays further in.

Cayo Blanco is the very occasional destination for boat tours from the hotel Ancón, and they like to moor to what's left of the wreck itself.

The tourists aboard stare at you in frank envy but don't stay long. You on the other hand can spend an entire day lobstering from the dinghy, or wandering along the beach and through the middle of the cay to the other shore.

On that southern side there is evidence of a long ago cataclysmic storm which has heaped up enormous mounds of dead coral, ripped from the depths to bleach in the sun.

Coral banks heaped up by the sea on Cayo Blanco.

CAYO ZAZA DE FUERA
(SEE SKETCHES ON PGS. 212 & 218)
CHART NO. ICH 1431 (CUBAN)

Travelling southeast along the outer cays we need places to rest up overnight and the first of these could well be Zaza de Fuera at 21°27.5N / 079°34.3W, easily attainable from either the inner or the outside routes. Fishermen use this and other cays along here as an overnight shelter too, so be prepared to bargain for all kinds of seafood and lobster.

If coming from Casilda along the inner route: Proceeding from the last pass at Los Machos, take up a course of 113°M some 10 miles towards the light on Cayo Blanco de Zaza with its odd structures nearby; then a further a mile along 168°M (or visual if you can see that far) to the tip of the island.

If coming here from an earlier halt at Cayo Blanco: The easiest route is outside the reef via the passes at either end of that cay, then back in past the lighted buoy at the Canal de Tunas (21°31.0/079°41.4) about 13 miles southeast of Cayo Blanco. From there it's visual (117°M), approximately seven miles to the anchorage.

At first we anchored here on the west side of the island among the shallows in five-to-seven feet, but later found a secluded inner lagoon with an entrance close to the north-west end of the island (21°27.9/079°34.4),

some way north of a wreck and a large stake.

From the west, the approach depths will not drop below nine feet and you can maneuver into this fascinating bayou to find yourself totally surrounded on all sides by a protecting wall of tall mangroves with deeper water inside.

Taking the dinghy south, you can break into other, larger lagoons within the island, with fish leaping, birds nesting, and passing through to the other northeast side of the island you can trail a hook or take your spear for even better luck over the coral there. And speaking of which, the bottom on the east side is a lot shallower and sharper, so when the time comes, leave the cay on the side you came in.

From Cayo Zaza de Fuera heading further along the inner routes, give the north-west tip of the cay a wide berth and proceed north to Tunas, or 98°M to pick up the channel markers north of Manatí Bank some 14 miles away.

On the other hand you may be continuing along the outer passages to the beautiful archipelago of cays and reefs called "The Gardens of the Queen" and the "Twelve-League Labyrinth".

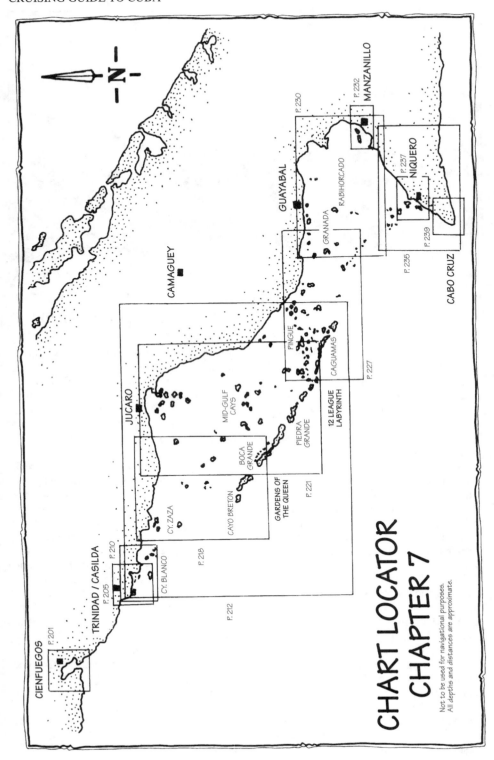

CHART LOCATOR
CHAPTER 7

Not to be used for navigational purposes.
All depths and distances are approximate.

ROUTE TO THE GARDENS OF THE QUEEN
CHART NOS. ICH 1141 & 1430 (CUBAN)

Apart from the obvious one of going outside the reef, there are two routes between Zaza and Cayo Breton. The direct line from the southwest tip is closely proscribed by the presence of a long bank on the starboard side of the boat, so you should aim to pass of either side of this bank.

The deeper route means taking your vessel round the shallows and northeast of Zaza. This enables a course of 170°M over the 27 miles to the lights at the inside of the Bretón reef entrance, at a position of 21°11.4N / 079°28.9W. Here you can visually steer in a gentle parabola into the lee of Cayo Bretón.

A shallower, but more convenient, 25 mile passage is made by leaving your overnight anchorage and heading more or less west-southwest towards the reef. As you approach, the bottom will become discolored by a broad band of coral (but still deeper than 12 feet), then quite unbeliev-ably, a broad white sandy path will suddenly show, leading towards the southeast. Sticking to this very obvious path down the length of the reef will take you south-southeast all the way to Cayo Bretón. It's just like following the Yellow Brick Road.

Along the entire length of the coral bank through which you are gently led, the depths will not drop below seven feet as long as you stick to the road; and if at any stage you get too nervous, then favor the western side of the path.

There are marks on the southeastern end of the reefy road, with the main channel marker further out at 21°08.5N / 079°30.5W showing commercial vessels the way in through the Canal De Bretón. Five miles across that canal lies the fittingly named Gardens of the Queen (*Los Jardines de la Reina*). Generally characterized by inner lagoons, this string of cays stretches for the next 70 miles.

CAYO BRETÓN

The most westerly cay in the Gardens of the Queen, Cayo Bretón is a heavily dissected island with a rewarding series of wide passages leading into an large shallow body of water up to a mile wide. The easiest way into that is to aim about 53°M just behind the tall light on the western tip. The depth upon approach will shelve to about seven feet, but immediately after it will drop once again to 20 feet. The passage has

"Hobbes", purposely beached for shore exploration.

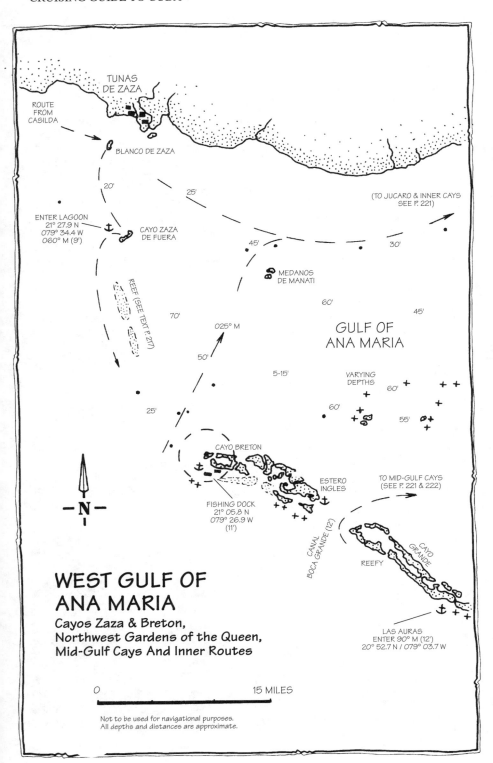

TUNAS
DE ZAZA

ROUTE
FROM
CASILDA

BLANCO DE ZAZA

20'

25'

(TO JUCARO & INNER CAYS
SEE P. 221)

ENTER LAGOON
21° 27.9 N
079° 34.4 W
060° M (9')

CAYO ZAZA
DE FUERA

45'

30'

MEDANOS
DE MANATI

60'

45'

REEF (SEE TEXT P. 217)

70'

025° M

GULF OF
ANA MARIA

50'

5-15'

VARYING
DEPTHS

60'

25'

60'

55'

CAYO BRETON

ESTERO
INGLES

TO MID-GULF CAYS
(SEE P. 221 & 222)

FISHING DOCK
21° 05.8 N
079° 26.9 W
(11')

BOCA CANAL GRANDE (12')

CAYO
GRANDE

REEFY

LAS AURAS
ENTER 90° M (12')
20° 52.7 N / 079° 03.7 W

-N-

WEST GULF OF
ANA MARIA
Cayos Zaza & Breton,
Northwest Gardens of the Queen,
Mid-Gulf Cays And Inner Routes

0   15 MILES

Not to be used for navigational purposes.
All depths and distances are approximate.

branches off to the east, with acres of totally enclosed waterways up to 200 yards wide, leading to the very shallow lagoon. If you are going to anchor overnight here, then I would advise that the current reverses and reaches speeds of 1.5 knots, so set yourself with this in mind. You may if you're just going for a walk, actually run your boat up onto the banks at the base of the light, strapping it loosely to the undergrowth for stability.

At the southwest tip of the cay, out towards the fringing reef, there are more of the Acopios or fishing-service docks as described in chapter five (see *Cayos de la Lena*). Here you can obtain ice or any other services you wish to beg, borrow, or buy; and this is a good place to put up for the night .

This is the most productive lobster fishing area in Cuba, and the largest of the acopios here handles over 400 tons per year. When there is room you will be made most welcome alongside in 11 feet, but be careful of the way you moor as the sharp edges on the dock can easily cut your lines. It is also a good idea to be ready for squalls and 180° wind shifts if you are there in winter.

It's quite interesting to notice that the hold which "Telenovelas" (Soap Operas) have on the Cuban population extends as far as the outer cays. The last time we were here, there were thirty gnarled fishermen sitting in the main room at the end of the dock lit only by the flickering blue tinge of a snowy television screen. Within, there was hushed, tense silence, interspersed only by whispers and the sound of a quarreling Raquel (bad) and Ruiz (good) as they played out their nightly drama. At ten o'clock, immediately following the novella, the entire group decamped to their fishing boats in a noisy rehash of the night's proceedings; and inside two minutes, every single boat had departed into the blackness, leaving only the three permanent inhabitants on the dock to look for company on board *Hobbes*.

Departing: In the morning, there are three options depending on the wind:

A) You may go round to the northern side

of the cay.   B) Follow the reef on the outside.   C) Proceed east along a channel between the reef and the cay — this last option will probably mean that you intend to pass over to the northern side at the end of Cayo Bretón as it gets a bit shallow near the canal at that end.

Northern side: If you have a shallow draft, going round to the north is probably easiest done by going through the channel just behind the light and following the deeper water east. On this side there is a reef which parallels the coast, but it is generally too deep to cause trouble at this end. Look out however, for an uncharted rock at 21°07.6/ 079°23.3 just after passing across from Bretón to Cayo Cinco Balas and near the shallow entrance to the lagoon at that end of the cay.

All the entrances on this side of that cay are shallow, but if you are willing to pick your way you may find (as we have) passages into the heart of the cay, rather like on Cayo Bretón. For example, if you take the left fork after the shallow (five feet) entrance at 079°20.7W it will take you into the central lagoon there, but the depths inside the lagoon are equally shallow. The right fork will take you through, back again to the south side, but here you can follow an inside route all the way east, just behind the outer cay there, until you come out the other side at Estero Inglés behind Alcatraz Grande. Depths varying between five-to-20-foot along this route will necessitate a sharp eye on the depthsounder, but it certainly is a fascinating route. If you've got the time, it's what you came for.

At this point you are at the Canal Boca Grande, a deep and wide channel between major groups of cays.

Trailing southwest after the Boca Grande canal as far as Caballones, there is a long mostly-submerged inner reef separated from the cays by a half a mile and in a northeasterly blow this might appear to offer some shelter from broadside waves if traveling on the northern side of the cays. Don't be tempted, as we've found that the reef is usually too deep to abate much of the seas. It also shallows between the reef and the cay, and you need to be constantly on the lookout for coral heads. Just travel instead on the southern side of the cays.

Southern side, *outside reef*: From Cayo Bretón, traveling on the outside of the reef south of the cay means going back out the way you came in, west of the cay, or looking for the deeper passes just east of the sandbank south of the acopio itself. Here you will find anything like 10-15 feet at a longitude of 79°26.6W. and you can proceed more or less as you please. Apart from the major entrances such as Boca Grande (Big-Mouth canal, at 079°15.6W) there are many lesser breaks in the reef (see text for suggestions).

You can come in through Boca Grande, or parallel the north shore off any breakers along the cays (Cayos Las Doce Leguas), but do not try to continue east between the reef and Las Doce Leguas. As mentioned above, it gets shallow in the sound there and although we have spent hours looking, we eventually found it best to go outside the reef.

It is of note that the outer route, all the way along these cays, is blessed with waters of a startling blue. You will be able to see 60-100 feet down at any point, so reading the bottom is not only easy, but a pleasure.

Southern side, *between cay and reef*: Leaving the Cayo Bretón dock, pass north of the smaller of the two acopios and head east in about 12 feet Apart from the reef over to the south, there are some drying banks to either side so pass between these, passing the whithies here to port. At the end of the island, there is another stake in the water which marks your turn north between the cays. The water will shallow to about seven-foot now, but immediately inside the passage between the cays it once again drops to 20 feet and you will have no trouble passing out to the northern side.

We have in the past picked our way in between the reef and Cayo Cinco Balas (Five Bullets Cay), endeavoring to find a way into the lagoon between Cinco Balas and Alcatraz Grande. But this is a tricky prospect, and although we got there we couldn't actually enter the lagoon in the end. We did find an entry through a gap in the reef 240°/160°M at position 21° 02.4N / 079°19.7W, which you might use if you wish to anchor overnight in this area as we have done peacefully at Alcatracito. Gosh, I just love the names of these cays.

All of the above routes offer a convenient route depending on your preference as to the wind, with the outer passage offering more beaches and the inner route more tempting if it's rough outside.

Do not imagine that the inner passage will always be calm, as within this large gulf stormy northeast winds will have quite enough time to reach a goodly velocity. We

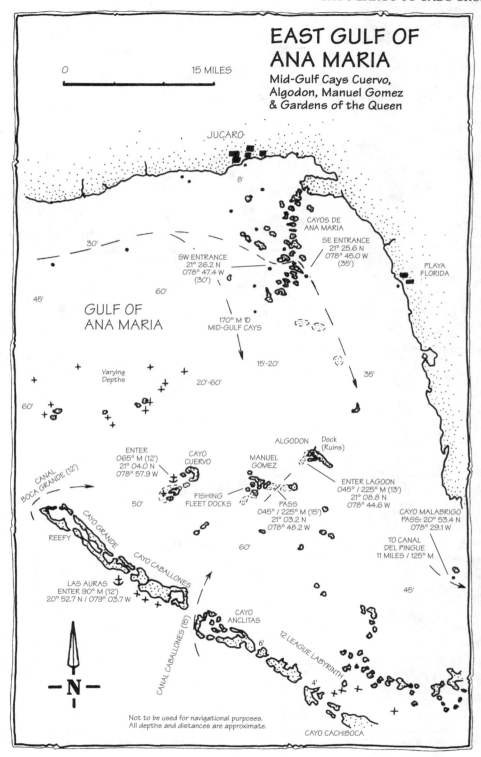

EAST GULF OF ANA MARIA

Mid-Gulf Cays Cuervo, Algodon, Manuel Gomez & Gardens of the Queen

0   15 MILES

JUCARO

8'

CAYOS DE ANA MARIA

SE ENTRANCE
21° 25.6 N
078° 45.0 W
(35')

PLAYA FLORIDA

30'

SW ENTRANCE
21° 26.2 N
078° 47.4 W
(30')

45' 60'

GULF OF ANA MARIA

170° M TO MID-GULF CAYS

15'-20'

35'

Varying Depths

20'-60'

60'

ALGODON   Dock (Ruins)

ENTER
065° M (12')
21° 04.0 N
078° 57.9 W

CAYO CUERVO

MANUEL GOMEZ

ENTER LAGOON
045° / 225° M (13')
21° 08.8 N
078° 44.6 W

CANAL BOCA GRANDE (12')

50'

FISHING FLEET DOCKS

PASS
045° / 225° M (15')
21° 03.2 N
078° 48.2 W

CAYO MALABRIGO
PASS: 20° 53.4 N
078° 29.1 W

CAYO GRANDE

REEFY

CAYO CABALLONES

60'

TO CANAL DEL PINGUE
11 MILES / 125° M

LAS AURAS
ENTER 90 M (12')
20° 52.7 N / 079° 03.7 W

45'

CAYO ANCLITAS

12 LEAGUE LABYRINTH

CANAL CABALLONES (15')

6'

4'

— N —

Not to be used for navigational purposes.
All depths and distances are approximate.

CAYO CACHIBOCA

have experienced endless days of high winds during the winter and spring which have blessed us with waves of up to 10 feet well inside the gulf where we might have expected much less. There have been times when it was so rough inside the gulf here that we were not even able to maintain the log. Please note that at this time of the year, this is a daily feature of the weather, and not a passing phase.

Luckily, it quiets down in the afternoons, but you may be assured that it will pipe up at night and early in the morning once again.

Note: To continue along the chain of outer cays, please see P. 224, where the text deals with the Twelve League Labyrinth.

THE MID GULF CAYS:
CUERVO, MANUEL GOMEZ, & ALGODÓN GRANDE
(SEE SKETCH ON PREVIOUS PAGE)
CHART NOS. ICH 1139 &1428 (CUBAN)

Equally accessible from the inner route east-west or from the outer cays, there is a group of islands worthy of note.

Some 13 miles to the east (80°M) of Boca Grande canal on the inside, or 12 miles north of Cayo Caballones, these wonderful cays offer good shelter and lots of room and opportunity for cruising at leisure. The fishing fleet hangs out around here with their Centros de Acopios for ice, water, stores etc., but in the main the place is pretty well deserted and this group of cays with their smaller cousins could well be deserving of a week or so.

These cays also make for a convenient jump-off point for the inner ship canal towards the southeast or if visiting the town of Jucaro further to the north.

Cayo Cuervo: The most westerly of these mid Gulf cays is Cayo Cuervo (Crow Cay), which may be entered along a course of 65°M into a crescent shaped anchorage which offers excellent protection. There is a sentry-box type mark on the west side (the light is generally not working) which must be passed about 100 yards to the south around 21°04.0/078°57.9 in anything up to 20 feet. There are some ruins of an old acopio over to the north side of the bay and one small shallow spot half a mile over to the southeast of that (21°04.3/078°57.3), but apart from that there is nothing to look out for.

Cayo Manuel Gomez: Only six miles to the east, the Cuban shrimping fleet moors around a freestanding dock on the east side of Manuel Gomez at 21°02.7/078°50.8

Well guarded by reefs, this cay is made up of a collection of smaller islets in a scattered group; some with beaches, and some with sandbanks blocking the passes between. To the southwest of the cay, a reef extends out for a mile of two, but if you are going east you may pass through a narrow pass at 21°02.2/078°51.0 with 50 ft. available along a course of 170°/350°M. Further east, some two miles away, there is a smaller cay called Algodoncito, with some beautiful beaches on the north side. There is a long submerged reef between this cay and Algodón Grande, so if intending to pass through, then make sure you do it at around 21°03.2/078°48.2 along a course heading of 045°/224°M.

Cayo Algodón Grande: Situated about five miles northeast of Algodoncito, the last of the major cays here is Algodón Grande, but it is definitely the nicest. Over to the north side, just off the beach a small dock protrudes into the blue-green waters. Unfortunately it is in ruins, as are the cabins ashore, but this is what is normally described as "under repair" in this part of the world. This is a real shame for someone, as it really is a lovely spot with a beautiful beach, which being on the north side would have a pleasant breeze. Nevertheless, over

on the southwest side of the cay there is a superb anchorage with an easy entrance carrying good water all the way.

A submerged reef extends wide out from the southwest tip, with a large stake marking the end of the shallows. Pass this stake about a quarter of a mile off to port (say 21°05.5/078°44.9), aiming 45°M, and you'll be in 12-18 feet, all the way into this beautiful bay complete with tiny beaches dotted all around. This lovely little spot, perfectly protected from all sides (including the west), is truly worth a couple of days of anyone's time.

Routes east: At this point, the mainland has begun to bulge downwards for a while, so from these cays you may once again return to the outer cays, or take up the main commercial inner route which runs southeast-northwest through the middle of the Gulf of Ana Maria.

If choosing this latter option, then merely head approximately 130°M for some 18 miles to the Pasa Malabrigo and the Canal del Pingue.

PASA MALABRIGO & CAYO GITANO
CHART NO. ICH 1139

Halfway along the route to the canal through the Cayos del Pingue, there are a couple of reefy spots just south of Cayo Malabrigo and lit by a marker at postion 20°53.4/078°29.1. In any case, provided you do not pass between the cay and the light, nothing else around here is shallow enough to cause any real problem. From this light at Pasa Malabrigo, the course to the next major pass (Canal del Pingue) is 125°/305°M for 11 miles.

Unfortunately, due to its size and shape, the cay doesn't provide much protection so it is not of any real benefit as an overnight anchorage, but four miles northeast of here, and only a mile off the mainland we find Cayo Gitano.

Approaching Gitano at about 70°M you can anchor just off the narrow beach to the southwest (20°57.1/078°26.6). The advantage this cay holds is its shape which offers good protection from the east winds, and fishing boats both large and small use this

area to rest up. If you do not wish to return to the Pasa Maladrigo, from Gitano the course to the next important pass at Pingue is 145°M for 12 miles.

THE CANAL DEL PINGUE
(SEE SKETCH ON PAGE 227) -- CHART NO. ICH 1138

Roughly north of the extreme eastern end of the Gardens of the Queen lies an extensive area of reef and small cays which obstruct the main inner channel running the length of the gulf. There is one major passage, some seven miles long, with depths of 25-50 feet along its length, at the Cayos del Pingue.

The northwest end of the channel is marked by a large black buoy (flashing green light) in 50 feet of water at position 20°47.0N / 078°19.2W with a red to follow a quarter of a mile onwards along a course of 140°M. After this, you may take up a general course of 175°M towards the next marks.

Although one should pass southwest of most of the red marks along this canal, and northeast of the greens; just to make things complicated, on occasion you will have to

use your discretion and ignore this rule.

To reinforce this, keep a sharp eye out for stakes and whithies marking the shallow patches either side of your route.

Along the bottom section of the channel, the course will tend more easterly (140°M) through the Canal Rancho Viejo, with a final red marker light in 50 feet situated at 20°41.2N / 078°16.1W.

From here, the inner route takes a course of 122°/302°M over the top of Cayo Granada and towards the Pasa Mate de Afuera some 10 miles away — see sections following Piedra Grande on page 226 .

If going to the outer cays then merely head due south to the end of the Twelve League Labyrinth at Cayo Caguama 10 miles down.

THE OUTER CAYS: CABALLONES, ANCLITAS & THE TWELVE LEAGUE LABYRINTH
(SEE SKETCH PAGE 221) – CHART NOS. ICH 1139 & 1428 (CUBAN)

If you haven't chosen to visit the mid-gulf cays or taken any of the inside routes from Cayo Breton, an interesting anchorage may be found inside Las Auras behind Punta Escondida on Cayo Caballones. In spite of it not being shown on chart No.1139 there is a reef entry from outside at 20°52.7N /078°03.9W along a heading of 90°M and carrying 12-15 feet below your keel. Within the sound, depths are seven-to-12 feet and

shelter can be found over to the cays wherever you wish to position yourself.

From the above position there is excellent scuba-diving all along the outer wall just where your depth-sounder suddenly drops off the scale.

The presence of the wall, even if a bit intimidating to the novice diver, does make for easy underwater navigation. Just head one way along the edge, and come back following the same route. You should do the deeper portion first, down the drop-off at your comfort/skill level and coming back along the shallower top edge where you will be able to pick up on the anchor, or the boat bobbing overhead.

Whatever, as usual, be aware of what you're up to, as I can well remember doing emergency first-aid repairs to a seriously wounded fisherman here, after he'd incautiously put his hand into a hole in which a moray eel had made his lair.

CANAL DE CABALLONES AND THE OUTER-REEF PASSES
(SEE SKETCH PAGE 221)

Between Cayos Caballones and Anclitas, we find the Canal De Caballones where lonely fishing boats occasionally raft together for company. Wide and deep at 20°49.2/078°58.0, this canal is another logical place to pass through the cays to the northern side or further into the gulf to get to the middle cays described previously. If a funny looking barge with a strange blue superstructure is moored somewhere in sight, then it may be the live-aboard hotel described shortly.

You may also enter the much shallower Piedra Grande or Piedra Chiquita passes to anchor in the flats there and to stock your freezer compartment, or alternatively continue on the outside for six more miles to Cayo Cachiboca where you can anchor in the western part of the pass.

PLEASE, ANYTHING BUT LOBSTER...

Be careful when attracted to the seafood on offer here, as my crew have complained bitterly about being served lobster for breakfast, supper, lunch etc., for a week and a half!

That trip, we even made lobster *soup* for a change.

Having left your overnight anchorages to continue along the coast you can again take a mid-morning break to scuba dive in beautifully clear waters over the coral reef and then continue your journey two hours later in the afternoon, cooled, refreshed and thrilled.

As before, lower the anchor near the wall for the best dives. Sometimes there are two distinct walls, say one at 20-30 feet and a further one at 70-80 feet going straight down. I've been repeatedly buzzed by inquisitive tarpon off the coast here at 60 feet, just above the second ledge. It's very startling!

PIEDRA GRANDE PASS, AND THE FLOATING HOTEL

There is an interesting experiment underway inside the Pasa Piedra Grande, consisting of a seven bedroom floating hotel which specializes in scuba and fishing holidays. This passage, through to the other side of the cays, is situated between Cayos Boca de Piedra Chiquita and Boca de la Piedra de Piloto. If contemplating its use to transit

Live aboard fishing and diving at Pasa Piedra Grande.

through the cays then be aware that it is only five-to-six feet deep at the bar on the northern end so it is limited to shallow draft vessels — apart from that, it is straightforward.

To get into the pass, enter from around 20°45.5/078°50.6 along a course of 20°M and into 12 feet depths until the far end which lies some half mile away to the north. **A warning:** The hotel does of course move about, visiting various sites depending on conditions at the time and may well be elsewhere when you arrive. In any case, if it *is* here, then only experienced skippers should attempt to get close as the side channel where it moors is shallow.

To get to the hotel, you will have to be prepared to deal with shallow waters in an eastern branch off to the side of the main pass, but if you can get alongside then you will most assuredly be made welcome. You may, of course, anchor in the deeper water available at the southern entrance and take the dinghy to the hotel.

As you progress deeper into the side channel the depths will get progressively shallower, so be careful to reduce your speed and look for the stake marking your path. Passing this stake closely to starboard, continue slowly in five-to-six feet of water into the eastern branch of the passage where it will deepen to 10 feet and you can approach the hotel which looks rather like a small Mississippi river boat. Depths alongside are around five-to-six-foot, but note that the hotel frequently moves its base, so this (and indeed all the above) may not hold

true when you get here.

Other sites: On occasion, the hotel is known to moor in the mouth of the Pasa Cachiboca, a bit further down the cays to the east at 20°42.0/078°45.2, and again it may be anchored on the eastern side of the Canal de Caballones which you passed seven miles to the west.

If it is in Caballones, then it will sometimes even be round the corner to the northeast of the canal, tucked in near Punta Nicola inside the northwest entrance to the lagoon there.

BEACH FRINGED CAYS

Proceeding along the coast in any wind north of east, the seas will make for relaxed cruising. The tiny cays are fringed with beautiful white beaches, and coming in over the wall it'll take a strong will or a tight schedule to resist pausing somewhere before Cayo Caguamas 20 miles on. There is evidence of hotel construction along the coast there just before the light tower halfway along, but this appears abandoned now, perhaps testimony to the difficulties of investment in Cuba.

Doubtless thoughts of retiring to a cay somewhere along the southern rim will have already come to mind, but take note of such signs. Many are the foreign investors in Cuba who have confessed disenchantment with local business practices, and broken promises.

Perhaps this is why the coast here will be so rewarding to cruise for so many years to come.

THE EASTERNMOST CAYS & INNER CHANNEL TO MANZANILLO
CHART NOS. ICH 1138 & 1426 (CUBAN)

As before, you will have noticed your courses needing still further adjustment to compensate for the growing magnetic deviation. Referring to my old charts, still pencil-marked with unerased courses, I see the notation. "Mag Dev seems to have grown to 3-4 deg".

Figure it in when deviating from those headings shown here.

The Gardens of the Queen come to an end at Cayo Caguamas, so the final stretch between the outer cays and the extreme eastern end of the gulf will best be done along the inside. From Caguamas, you may either go north to Cayo Granada, joining the inner route there, or continue eastwards along a less protected path to a small group of cays surrounding one of the main com-

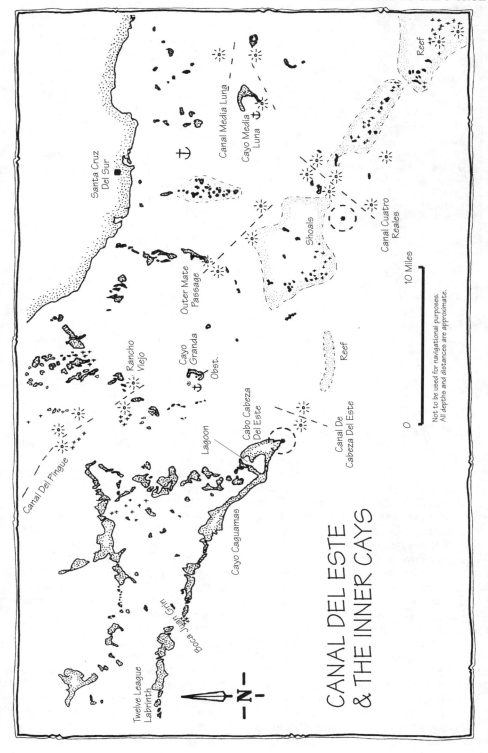

CANAL DEL ESTE
& THE INNER CAYS

Santa Cruz Del Sur

Canal Media Luna

Cayo Media Luna

Reef

Shoals

Canal Cuatro Reales

Outer Mate Passage

Rancho Viejo

Cayo Granda

Obst.

Cabo Cabeza Del Este

Reef

Canal De Cabeza Del Este

Canal Del Pingue

Lagoon

Cayo Caguamas

Twelve League Labrinth

Boca San Grin

0   10 Miles

Not to be used for navigational purposes.
All depths and distances are approximate.

N

227

Parking lot at Manzanillo.

CAYO GRANADA

From the outside passage you can come in through the buoyed channel at Cabeza del Este on the eastern tip of Cayo Caguamas where the fishing fleet has another small hideout. If the light still allows, there's a wonderful sheltered inlet located some eight miles away (30°M) at Cayo Granada and it's well worth making for here if you expect any trouble from the east or northeast.

This is a sickle-shaped cay positioned at (20°37.6N /078°14.8W), with good water anywhere inside its bay, and apart from an area of shoal waters on its northwest tip you may enter anywhere on the western side. There's a small and perfectly visible obstruction (a pile) in the bay just south of the middle, but apart from this you should have no problems here. We've used this cay to shelter from a violent cold front which swept in from the east, but in any case it makes an excellent jumping-off point for any of the the coastal towns like Santa Cruz or Guayabal along the route to Manzanillo.

mercial entries for international shipping, the Canal de Cuatro Reales (see description below). After Granada, the inner route passes near these cays, so either way you will be poised to join it without much trouble.

PASSES ALONG THE ROUTE EAST

From Granada, it's an easy eight-mile run 107°M to Pasa Mate de Afuera (Outer Mate Passage), a well-marked pass at 20°36.2/078°6.6 just off the southern tip of a string of cays reaching out from the mainland. A handy anchorage here is Cayo Guicho just to the north of the pass, on the western side of the cay, and I have used this very spot to pause for repairs to a broken engine on *Hobbes*. Tired fishermen also use this spot for resting up, and a lot of fun can be had in the clear waters here. Lobster, turtles, and anemones are all visible here and there's good snorkeling on the reef nearby to the south of the canal.

The route now bears 135°M along a string of marks to the next pass six miles on at Juan Suarez, whereupon it heads towards the ports on the peninsula of Granma Province. Just below Juan Suarez lies the Canal de Cuatro Reales with handy anchorages available for those who opt for going there direct from Cayo Caguamas rather than taking the Granada route.

Canal de Cuatro Reales: This canal is one of the most important entries for commercial shipping into the Gulf of Ana Maria. Best entered from 20°26.5/078°1.6, just east of the light on Cayo Carapacho the well marked channel will take you 230°/50°M through the reef into the gulf. There are various small buildings on the cays here, but you may anchor off quite happily. There are especially good places to moor, some two miles east of the passage, and south of Cayo Blanco. Lots of lobster traps can be found here, and snorkeling will be rewarded by supper, but once again do not molest the traps — catch your own.

The main inner route passes just a couple of miles to the north of the channel. If you wish to travel west, then a course of 300°M will join you up with it at Juan Suarez, while a course of 65°M will put you just south of Media Luna on the route east towards Manzanillo.

WORTHWHILE FOR SHELTER

Along the way to the Pasa Chinchorro (approximately. 90ºM — 30 miles) you'll pass closely by two other cays worthy of note. Media Luna, and Rabihorcada. (See chart on Pg. 230).

Media Luna: A large crescent shaped cay offering excellent shelter on its western side. There are only mangroves on offer and it is not very exciting, but with a bottom mixture of mud and sand, this is a good place in a blow. There is a dinghy channel in on the north side of the crescent, which goes in some 50-100 yards.

Cayo Rabihorcado: When using photocopies, or even original black and white charts, be careful not to misinterpret them and think that the reefs comprising the misnamed Esperanza Buena (Good Hope) bank to the southeast are really cays — they're not.

The first time we passed along here, using photocopies (of photocopies), we made the elementary mistake of bypassing Rabihorcado and heading for what we'd assumed was shelter 10 miles further east. Only when the expected cay failed to pop up over the horizon did we realize our error, and it was a bit of a scramble to get back to Rabihorcado before nightfall. Mind you, we did thereupon discover a strange inner-world inside the cay, entered through a narrow stick-marked channel on the western side.

This channel, not at all obvious and only 15 feet wide, lies in the *second* shallow bay from the northwest tip and progresses southeast from 20º31.2N / 077º38.1W into a series of secret lagoons splitting the cay. Lying on the *north* side of a tiny islet blocking the mouth into the lagoon, it is only 6-foot deep at the entrance and care should be taken to keep hard over to the right of the channel as you pass the islet.

If the entrance is a bit tricky, the deep and totally hidden anchorage is more than worth the trouble and really sums up what cruising the southern cays is all about. Clear, black, limpid waters, creepy with presence. Of what, we can only surmise.

At the other extreme of this large lagoon, there is an exit onto the eastern side of the cay. Unfortunately, it is shallow on that side so this is only for dinghy use.

Even if you don't want to enter the lagoon, there are a couple of nice bays on the western side, and the cay itself has a certain "body" to it, which makes it a good place to stop.

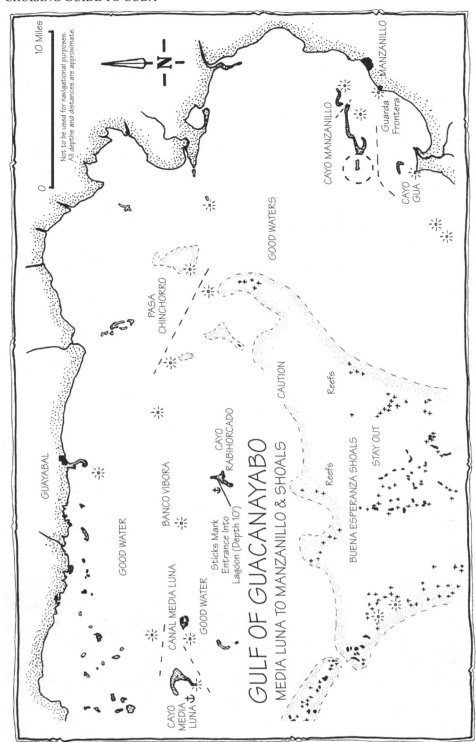

GULF OF GUACANAYABO
MEDIA LUNA TO MANZANILLO & SHOALS

230

FINAL ROUTE EAST

From the top of Rabihorcado, the route to Manzanillo takes us past a couple of shallow reefs, the most notable of which is just before the Pasa Chinchorro. This bank, difficult to see from a sailboat deck, is marked by a large stake at 20°31.4/077°27.7, and you would be wise to go around to the north of this. The pass now lies 3 miles east, at 20°30.0N / 077°23.6W, and itself is marked by two lights between which you proceed.

Passing through the canal at Chinchorro, it's a straight run (126°M for 17 miles) to Manzanillo on the mainland coast and guarded by three or four small cays right in front.

MANZANILLO
CHART NO. ICH 1138 (CUBAN)

This provincial city seems to have seen better days but still retains a certain charm with its malecon (sea-wall) edged with tiny public parks. The potholed main street runs parallel and at its northern end is lined with wide sidewalks sheltered by sagging, overhanging roofs. Supported by pillars, these roofs give it an intriguing if rundown colonial aspect. Further in, there are several older buildings around the main square where there is a museum, various bars, and a pretty good peso restaurant. In addition, there is an excellent *proveedor de buques* (ships' chandler), a market; and last, but not least, the most friendly people in Cuba.

Originally a smuggling port, but now dealing mainly with the more legitimate transport of sugar and general cargo, this is the best chance you will have for reprovisioning along the coast and for touring the mountains to the southeast.

If coming in from an extended cruise among the cays you're probably out of the habit of checking in, but this is one of the more major cities along the coast so they'll insist on proper documentation, and to speed this process up it is best to call the *Capitanía* (the port captain's office) before arrival.

We never used to get a reply from any of the harbor authorities here, but recently there has been an improvement, so if you call *"Portuaria Manzanillo"* they'll put the capitanía onto standby for your arrival. All official communications in Manzanillo seem to revolve around VHF Channel 03, but remember to use the *international* switch selector on your radio or you won't be able to transmit and receive. If there is no reply on 16, switch over. Using this frequency, you can even get a ships chandler to come out to your boat (see below) to deliver supplies, so leave the radio permanently on

A gazebo in the main square of Manzanillo.

231

Channel 03 while you are in port.

If you get no reply to either channel, then just show up as described below. Most people do.

Entry: Manzanillo is hidden behind a small group of cays. If you wish, you may go round them to the north or south (the main commercial routes) but there is a more convenient passage between the cays right in the middle at Pasa Honda, (enter from 20°22.4N / 077°10.5W) which is just as easy.

Pay no mind to the two dozen or so wrecked trawlers on the cay; they're just being disassembled.

Mooring: The Capitanía lies behind a wharf on the northern end of the town, near a cluster of small fishing boats, just past the end of the seawall (the malecon). You should moor a short distance off, in whatever depth makes you comfortable and wait for the authorities to come out from the wharf there. This can take some time, but once accomplished, the officials are some of the most friendly you're likely to meet.

International arrivals are catered to, and even if you've already been in Cuba for some time you'll still have to face a medical/agricultural inspection. One thing you will face is a strange regulation prohibiting your disposing of any waste ashore. Saying that this means you'll sooner or later have to dispose of it over the side should ensure a more reasonable attitude.

Some travellers have been told that someone should remain onboard at all times, but as this is so inconvenient nobody takes any notice of it. You're out in the country now, so reason seems to prevail more readily than in somewhere like Havana.

One feature of the harbour here is the strong surge which sets in every evening, especially in the winter and spring. This surge can be alarming at first, but the holding is so good that you learn to trust it. The nearby dock is in fact a beached steel pontoon, and you may tie the dinghy here when going ashore. Just be careful to remember the surge when mooring alongside, and make sure the sharp edges cause no damage

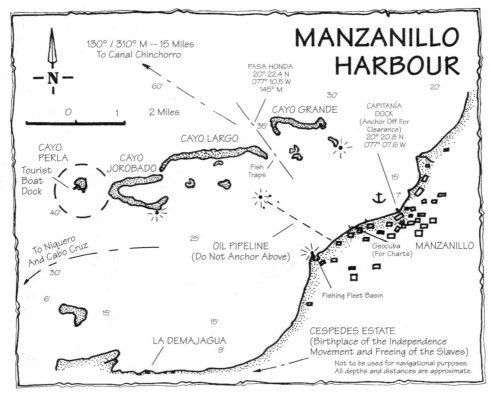

MANZANILLO HARBOUR

130° / 310° M -- 15 Miles
To Canal Chinchorro

-N-

60'

PASA HONDA
20° 22.4 N
077° 10.5 W
145° M

30'

20'

O   1   2 Miles

CAYO GRANDE

CAPITANÍA
DOCK
(Anchor Off For
Clearance)
20° 20.8 N
077° 07.6 W

CAYO LARGO

35

CAYO
PERLA

Tourist
Boat
Dock

CAYO
JOROBADO

Fish
Traps

15'

40'

7'

To Niquero
And Cabo Cruz

25'

OIL PIPELINE
(Do Not Anchor Above)

Geocuba
(For Charts)

MANZANILLO

30'

6'

15'

Fishing Fleet Basin

15'

LA DEMAJAGUA
9'

CESPEDES ESTATE
(Birthplace of the Independence
Movement and Freeing of the Slaves)

Not to be used for navigational purposes.
All depths and distances are approximate.

while you are away. Small brown boys and grey old men fish from the end of the dock, but I have never heard of any problems with dinghy security here. As a matter of fact, they'll look after it for you if you've screwed up.

Most evenings, on the seawall opposite your mooring, a few slow, rheumy eyed, townsmen hang around listening to boomboxes. But at weekends, hundreds of more lively inhabitants gather to dance in the square just a hundred yards up from the capitanía, while the people who operate the music, also sell little sweetmeats. The noise can be a bit intrusive at first, but it's wonderful to see all these people bogeying in a way the average cruiser can only dream of. If you've got the right attitude and want to join in, you'll be made most welcome, and some lithe soul will soon be showing how it's really done. But hey, this is another reason you're here — not just for the cruising.

Downtown, there are a couple of produce markets, and a couple of stores

(Panamericana) which sell foreign stuff at foreign prices. Better to obtain pesos from any of a dozen change artists in the street opposite, as this is one of the towns where it is actually easier to spend pesos than dollars. Around the Jose Martí square, an abundance of oddly Moorish architecture stands out, and more street peddlers offer snacks. Here you may buy an oyster cocktail under the arches, or a roast pork sandwich cut steaming from the joint, while if you prefer a proper restaurant, the *America* will sell you an reasonable meal; pork, rice, vegetables, and all the trimmings for 20 pesos. Bars, off to the side of the square offer rum (*Pinillo* is the local hootch) at a peso a shot, while beer comes more expensive at one and a half. I can live with that.

A tale: In 1996, at the same restaurant described above, I once attempted to purchase a meal, but on this occasion had no pesos. Dollars are not accepted here, so while the waitress hung onto our order we went in search of a money changer. Rapidly returning (nothing is easier in Cuba), we

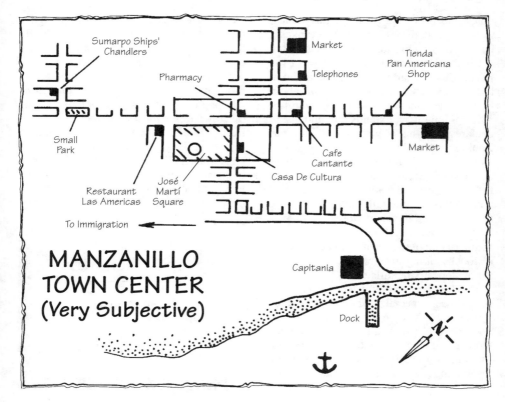

MANZANILLO
TOWN CENTER
(Very Subjective)

233

seated ourselves, only to be visited by a delegation of waitresses. They'd come to ask the rate we'd received, and to establish that we'd not been cheated by anyone!

If you wish to get about town, the quickest way is to flag down any of the horse-drawn carriages which ply for hire along the roadside. Room will be made for you, and you may alight wherever you wish. It costs a peso, as does the much more infrequent bus. Truly bliss, as you clip-clop, rattle and sway, along the seawall road.

Boatyard: On two occasions I have moored for long periods at a boatyard about a mile down towards the southwest. If you have to use the facilities here (haulout or machine work), then permission will have to be obtained from the management who will liaise with the capitania officers. Walk down the malecon, about a mile to the south, and you'll come to it. The yard itself consists of a slipway where large tugs and steel barges are repaired by arc-welders, or otherwise attended to by muscular men wielding large sledgehammers.

The wharf there is used mainly by tugboats and protected by large dirty black tires suspended by chains, but it makes a handy dock if you can wheedle permission.

Charts: You may purchase most of the ICH series of charts here in Manzanillo at the offices of Geocuba. Just walk about half a mile southwest of the boatyard, to where a long dock extends out, and a sign declares that this is now a Zona Militar. Looking more like an officers club, a collection of pink buildings surround an abandoned stage. Slogans and large paintings of the maximum leader adorn the podium and next to this are the buildings which house the offices and the chart stores.

Hotel Guacanayabo: Up the hill at the southern end of the town, it can be reached on foot by taking an extremely long, narrow set of steps up the hillside.

The hotel is a pretty depressing place sometimes, especially when it's darkened by electricity cuts in the off-season, but it does have a swimming pool which may tempt those who have had it up to here with saltwater for the time being. This pool is a fascinating place on the weekends when it

fills to overflowing with the townspeople, all seemingly intent on fun, but nobody fighting over it. Although I've met the most wonderful types here, ranging from hustlers and hustled, be careful about what you say to people in the bar and don't get involved with shady characters who may well be a lot more official than they pretend.

It was here that my good friend Brendan (a droll Irishman) offered the advice, "Don't ever trust a Cuban without biceps!". He may well be right.

Telephone: Although you may make international calls from the hotel, there is nowhere in town you may presently send an international fax from.

Supplies: The town does have a *proveedor de buques* (ships store) downtown, which supplies provisions direct to your boat at wholesale prices. Operated by Sumarpo now, this service is perhaps most conveniently contacted over the VHF on Channel 03 by calling "Sumarpo Manzanillo". For several years, the store has been staffed by the admirable Alberto Lorente, who speaks English and understands the needs of yachtsmen, so do not hesitate to call on the radio even if your Spanish is not up to snuff. Sometimes he even accompanies the officials out to your boat to welcome you to the port. They will also arrange fuel to be brought out to your boat at .60 cents/litre. Although at first glance unprepossessing, this town rapidly grows on one. To tell the truth, although I didn't think much of it at first, over the years, I have come to appreciate Manzanillo more and more. Stuck out in the backwaters of the country, it seems to have retained a sense of humor about itself, and an attitude that seems to say

---

Sumarpo — Ships' Chandlers

Loynaz #167
*(between Luz Caballero
and Martinez de Vietnam)*
Manzanillo. Tel. 55501

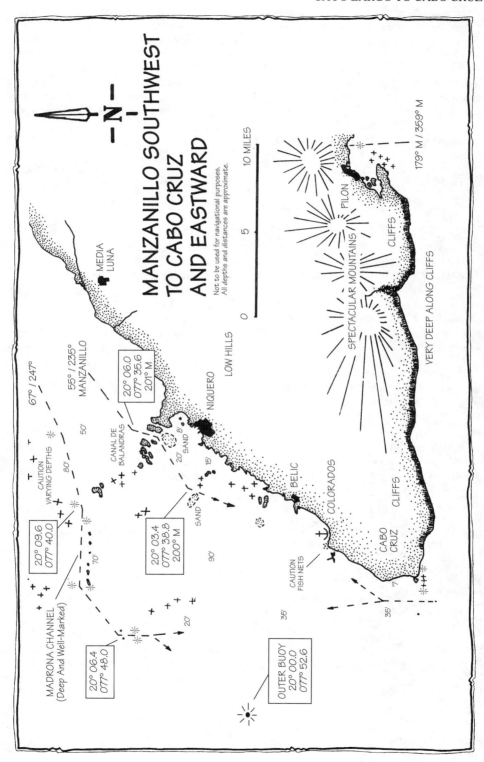

MANZANILLO SOUTHWEST
TO CABO CRUZ
AND EASTWARD

Not to be used for navigational purposes.
All depths and distances are approximate.

0   5   10 MILES

MEDIA
LUNA

67° / 247°
55° / 235°
MANZANILLO

50'

CAUTION
VARYING DEPTHS

80'

20° 09.6
077° 40.0

70'

MADRONA CHANNEL
(Deep And Well-Marked)

20° 06.4
077° 48.0

20'

CANAL DE
BALANDRAS

20° 06.0
077° 35.6
201 M

NIQUERO

SAND 8'

20'   15'

20° 03.4
077° 38.8
200 M

SAND

90'

35'

OUTER BUOY
20° 00.0
077° 52.6

LOW HILLS

BELIC

COLORADOS

CAUTION
FISH NETS

CABO
CRUZ

7'

35'

CLIFFS

SPECTACULAR MOUNTAINS

PILON

CLIFFS

179° M / 359° M

VERY DEEP ALONG CLIFFS

235

"Hello pardner..."

We are not the only ones who've stayed longer than planned.

In the event that you are planning to extend your stay in Cuba, then you will find that this can be accomplished here. It does require however, a visit to the Hotel Guacanayabo to pay $25, and a subsequent visit to the immigration offices. This last is about six blocks north of the capitanía along the waterfront road *1° Mayo*, and just past the shoe factory.

Leaving: Once again you have to arrange clearance and official visits before leaving the port. If you want an early departure, then this is best arranged the day before at the capitanía offices. You may obtain all necessary documentation for onwards travel here.

SOUTHWEST TO CABO CRUZ
CHART NOS. ICH 1138 & 1137 (CUBAN)

There are are two routes to Cabo Cruz in the southwest.

The inner passage takes you close to the coast and is visual all the way with a couple of tricky wriggles through more or less vaguely marked channels (See charts on Pgs. 235 and 237). This route takes you past the town of Niquero and the beautiful harbor at Cabo Cruz.

The outermost route, tending further away from land, is better marked, but unfortunately does not allow a convenient resting place for preparing for the trip round the cape. It is perhaps more suited to larger deep-drafted vessels which might not need or wish to rest up overnight.

Interestingly enough, the official south coast pilots (the service is called *"practicos"* if you should ever require it) receive their training in these waters.

THE OUTERMOST ROUTE

Taking the outermost route first, leave your mooring and approach the western tip of the cays fronting Manzanillo. There is a light on the end at Cayo Perla, and a 22-mile course from here along 247°M will run you into the light at position 20°1 1.2N / 077°35.6W about eight miles north of the town of Niquero, near the Madrona Channel.

Give the light a safe berth (pass it on your right, as it sits atop a coral head), and set a course of 260°M for four miles. This now takes you to the beginning of the 10-mile channel which will first tend west and then southwest at 20°9.5N / 077°45.0W. Finally, leaving the channel you can now set course 15 miles due south to Cabo Cruz, on the other side of which lie the cliffs of the southeast coast.

THE COASTAL ROUTE

If you prefer to take the more common inner route, close to the coast, then clear Cayo Gua southwest of Manzanillo by a couple of hundred yards to port and continue visually, southwest along the coast in comfortable water. A 25-mile run will bring you to the Balandras Keys jutting out just before you come to the town of Niquero. There is a narrow channel through the cays running 21°/201°M which, although marked, will require some care. You'll find the channel entrance near a position of

"Sumarpo", ships' chandler sign on door

20°06.0N / 077°35.6W.

This channel is bounded by white beaches on the southern side, but has none on the north. Look out for a rather conspicuous sandbank to your port immediately upon leaving and dodge round it to the north.

At the exit to the Balandras Channel the route continues past the town of Niquero (see description), continuing 240°M to the next pass some three and a half miles on at Azagua. This pass is marked only on its

northern side, by two stakes, but this may change with time or opportunity. Just be prepared with a sharp lookout for sand-banks on either side even though the channel itself is deep.

From here a course of 204°M will take you seven and a half miles to Punta Las Colorados where you may also find a sheltered bight with good water around 19°55.7N / 077°41.9W.

Note that some halfway along this final

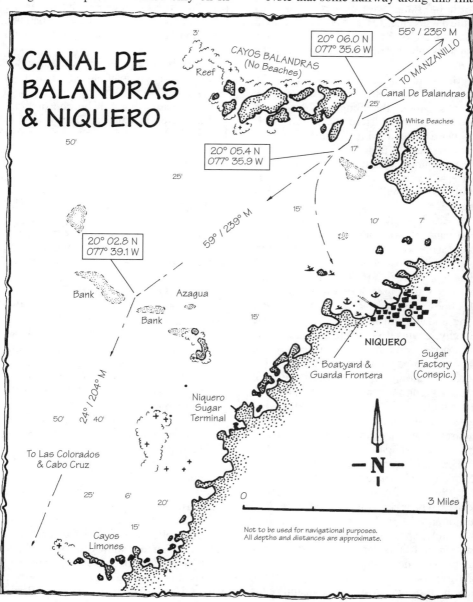

CANAL DE BALANDRAS & NIQUERO

3'

CAYOS BALANDRAS (No Beaches)

Reef

20° 06.0 N 077° 35.6 W

55° / 235° M

TO MANZANILLO

Canal De Balandras

/ 25'

White Beaches

50'

20° 05.4 N 077° 35.9 W

25'

17'

15'

59° / 239° M

10'

7'

20° 02.8 N 077° 39.1 W

Bank

Azagua

Bank

15'

NIQUERO

Sugar Factory (Conspic.)

Boatyard & Guarda Frontera

240° / 204° M

50'   40'

Niquero Sugar Terminal

To Las Colorados & Cabo Cruz

– N –

25'   6'   20'

O   3 Miles

Not to be used for navigational purposes. All depths and distances are approximate.

15'

Cayos Limones

237

route there is an obstruction off the cays near Limones a mile or two up from the village of Belic, so once again watch for the mark.

The rest of the way is best done visually, about a mile offshore until you come to the reef which extends southwest from the extreme tip at Cabo Cruz.

Along your journey between Manzanillo and Cabo Cruz, there are three places which I would recommend as rest stops before rounding the cape.

NIQUERO

Just south of the pass at Balandras, this port should not be approached from the north, but rather west or northwest. This route passes close to Cayo Niquero, a small island west of the town and avoids the shallows on the direct line between the town and the pass.

Although the fishing docks over to the north will tempt you, it is best anchoring on the other side of the pilings at the southern end of the town. Here there is a small boatyard with a white Guarda Frontera building next to that. This is, in any case, where your documentation will have to be done, so you might as well be here from the start; and you will also avoid the smell of the fish processing plant.

If you don't draw more than seven-foot you can get alongside one of the fishing boats at the boatyard to sort out your papers, but you'll probably have to anchor off for the night. Although the town is open to the west, the holding is good once you've set the hook. Formalities will not take very long, and you will be free to go ashore in the dinghy, leaving it alongside the docks there.

Ashore, Niquero is dominated by the picturesque sugar factory and associated wooden buildings, with fading filigree decorations along the main drag downtown. A 10-minute walk, left from the dockyard gate will take you there, past small wooden houses and along dirt roads until you get into the central part of town.

There are several small restaurant/bars in Niquero, and you can purchase shots (ask for Pinillo rum) for a peso at roadside kiosks whenever you feel the urge. The Communist Party HQ here, is housed in an old and rather quaint building, near the station with its splendid red fire engines, along with the 'phone service, the market, and a small park where you may relax for an idle hour or two. Just like Manzanillo, the people of Niquero are extremely friendly, making the most of strangers, so be prepared to visit someone's house to sample the local brew and meet the grandparents. Only don't expect to get back to the boat on time.

The girls have green eyes, the men are good drinking companions, and you'll not regret a stop-off in Niquero.

As an aside, this will be one of those places where you notice that the town comes to a complete and utter stop when the soaps come on. Apart from small clusters gathered outside any house which has a television, the streets are deserted at nine o'clock; whispering groups stand for an hour, peering in through the open doorways and windows of total strangers without anyone feeling at all embarrassed. Maybe this is why you have to get there early if you're going to patronize the peso restaurant downtown.

LAS COLORADOS BEACH

Southwest of Niquero, there is another overnight shelter in the bight off Colorados beach just north of Punta Colorados. There are no real dangers on the way in, but while it is still daylight, take note of any evidence of nets strung out from poles in the water. There are usually a few of these off the point at Colorados and you will likely be leaving in darkness for the trip round the Cape. Plot them on your charts for later avoidance.

This is an interesting spot, not merely for the abundance of life below the surface amongst the turtle-grass, but for more serious reasons.

You are now anchored off one of the more historic sites of the western hemisphere. No matter what your political persuasion, you cannot help but feel moved by the sight of the beach and the mangroves where Fidel Castro, his brother Raoul,

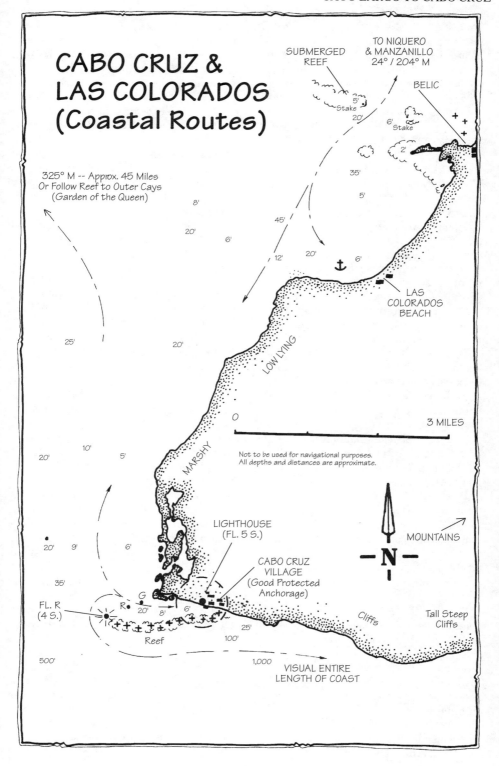

CABO CRUZ &
LAS COLORADOS
(Coastal Routes)

SUBMERGED
REEF

TO NIQUERO
& MANZANILLO
24° / 204° M

BELIC

5'
Stake

20'

6'
Stake

2'

35'

5'

325° M -- Approx. 45 Miles
Or Follow Reef to Outer Cays
(Garden of the Queen)

8'

20'

6'

45'

12'   20'

⚓   6'

LAS
COLORADOS
BEACH

25'

20'

LOW LYING

O

3 MILES

MARSHY

Not to be used for navigational purposes.
All depths and distances are approximate.

20'   10'   5'

LIGHTHOUSE
(FL. 5 S.)

MOUNTAINS

— N —

20'   9'   6'

CABO CRUZ
VILLAGE
(Good Protected
Anchorage)

35'

G

R   20'

FL. R
(4 S.)

8'   6'

25'

Cliffs

Tall Steep
Cliffs

Reef

100'

500'

1,000

VISUAL ENTIRE
LENGTH OF COAST

Ernesto "Che" Guevarra, and their compadres landed in the darkness of Dec. 2, 1956. By the time the smoke of ambush had cleared only 12 of the original 81 were still alive or not captured, and those survivors could only flee through swamp and bush to the nearby hills, starvation, and struggle.

From such inauspicious beginnings have enormous changes come and their worst enemies cannot but salute their bravery.

THE HARBOUR AT CABO CRUZ

The very last spot before rounding the cape, this offers a super little anchorage in clear waters at the foot of a marvellous lighthouse. Although at first glance open to the winds, it is also totally protected by a reef from the force of the seas, and moreover positions you perfectly for an early morning departure. From here, you may easily judge the conditions and make your travel plans accordingly; allowing you to arrive at any of the nearer south coast ports in only a couple of hours.

There is a Guarda Frontera station here, but the official presence is not large enough to handle international arrivals. For that you will have to use the port of Manzanillo within the gulf to the northeast. For internal cruising however, the officers here are friendly and efficient, and clearance only takes a couple of minutes — especially if your Gia de Recalas already shows this as one of your intended halts.

To enter the harbor, approach the extreme western end of the reef where it curls like the tail of a comet from the tip of mainland and come in a couple of hundred yards north of 19°50.2 N / 077°45.0 W. where there is a large sentry-box light (Fl.4s.) and the depths are over 20 feet. At this point you may go 100°M to the following R/G. lights, some 800 yards away, and well inside the sound itself. The reef outside here is quite jagged, and breaking all the way, so there is no problem with positioning yourself. Aim slightly to the right of the lighthouse and the depths

will slowly shelve to eight feet some 300 yards from the base. There are a few small yellow moorings just off the concrete docks there, so ask permission of any of the local fishermen (or the amiable gentleman from the Guarda Frontera who is peering at you from the dock) and moor to one of these.

This is a surprising little village, notable for the neatness of the tiny flower gardens in front of the fishing cottages which line the only road; and as is usual in the province of Granma, amazingly nice people (see comments about Manzanillo and Niquero for this too). In 1996, we passed a wonderful and totally unexpected afternoon in the company of some twenty local agricultural students on a tractor-powered jaunt from nearby Portillo. For hours it seems, we danced wildly, eating stewed mutton (a sheep had been sacrificed to the excursion) and drinking strong rum, in a small hut on the foreshore. Then, prowling the shoreline at the foot of the tall cliffs, we made our way to a wonderful cave and swam beneath the dripping stalactites within its dark interior.

But the star attraction of Cabo Cruz is undoubtedly the wonderful lighthouse, not a hundred yards from your mooring. Solidly constructed with creamish brickwork, and supported grandly by large columns, it makes a splendid sight at any time of day or night.

To leave before sunup, you will have to inform the Guarda Frontera the night before. But nevertheless, be prepared to walk to the compound (to the left on the hill leading out of town) and wake the duty officer if you wish to depart in darkness. They will probably prefer you to stay until daytime, but if you have a strong light on board (you should have) then it is a straightforward exit. Just remember to pass well to the west and south of the reef lights as you come round; but from here on you can hug the coast closely as you travel east along the massive cliffs which now line the rest of the extreme southeast coast.

Cabo Cruz lighthouse.

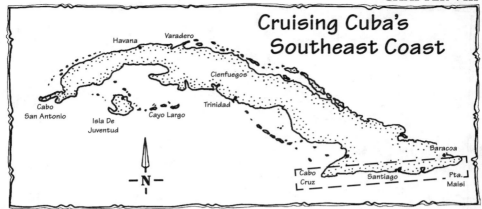

CHAPTER VIII

Cruising Cuba's
Southeast Coast

CABO CRUZ TO PUNTA MAISI

This chapter, albeit smaller than the rest, is nevertheless going to introduce you to what is without a doubt, the most spectacular coastline in Cuba.

Between the two acutely angled capes at either end, this sometimes arid coast is bordered for the next 220 miles by rocky cliffs and awesome scrub-covered mountains, one visible from as far away as Jamaica. Having coasted the Cuban cays, or perhaps come down from the U.S.A., this dramatic change will require a different technique, the key to which is merely avoiding travel in strong south winds.

TACTICS

The coast is evenly spaced along its length with secure harbors, each about a day-sail away from its neighbor. Once embarked on a passage however, there are few alternate shelters and passages can be long; so your preparations must be careful in this regard. Luckily the winds along the coast are usually quite predictable and can be calculated according to the time of day with some accuracy; thus leaving the question of passage planning to revolve around scheduling and mechanical efficiency, i.e., *leaving in good time*, and not breaking down along the way. As a matter of fact, the median wind velocities vary between seven-to-eleven knots in summer and five-to-seven knots in

winter, except for the eastern tip where the winds can sometimes be stronger. If you don't go berserk you'll more than likely have a nice gentle sail along what otherwise appears on the map to be a difficult stretch.

CURRENTS

Going west: The main current through the windward passage between Haiti and Cuba runs westwards, and this can be used to some advantage if you are going in that direction — just stay two or three miles offshore to gain its benefit.

Going east: In spite of the above-mentioned current, there's usually a goodly countercurrent near the shore running eastwards along your route, especially in early summer.

There isn't much in the way of outlying dangers off this coast, so to gain up to three knots sometimes, stick tightly to the coastline like glue; and I mean within *hailing* distance in many places.

Try it, and see your logged speeds going up.

As an aside, but still on the subject of cruising offshore, the channel between Haiti and Cuba is heavily patrolled by U.S. naval vessels. If you stray out over the 12 mile limit of Cuban territorial waters you are quite likely to be stopped and/or interrogated by radio. To avoid this hassle, don't

241

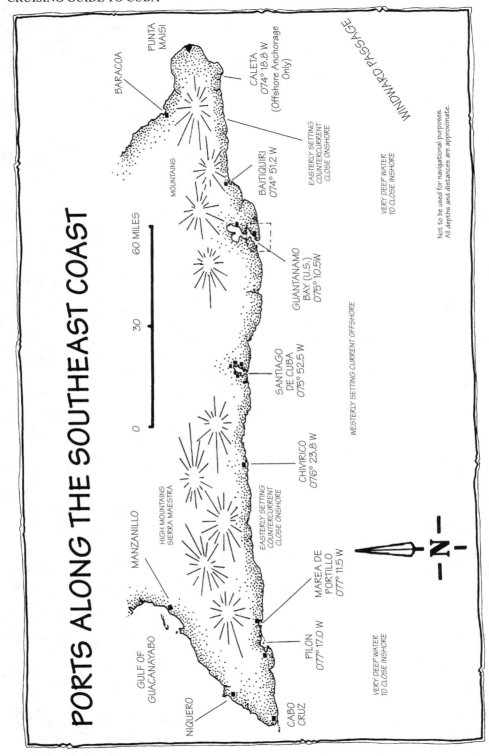

PORTS ALONG THE SOUTHEAST COAST

PUNTA MAISI

BARACOA

CALETA
074° 18.8 W
(Offshore Anchorage
Only)

MOUNTAINS

BAITIQUIRI
074° 51.2 W

EASTERLY SETTING
COUNTERCURRENT
CLOSE ONSHORE

WINDWARD PASSAGE

VERY DEEP WATER
TO CLOSE INSHORE

Not to be used for navigational purposes.
All depths and distances are approximate.

GUANTANAMO
BAY (U.S.)
075° 10.5 W

SANTIAGO
DE CUBA
075° 52.5 W

WESTERLY SETTING CURRENT OFFSHORE

60 MILES

30

0

CHIVIRICO
076° 23.8 W

EASTERLY SETTING
COUNTERCURRENT
CLOSE ONSHORE

HIGH MOUNTAINS
SIERRA MAESTRA

MANZANILLO

GULF OF
GUACANAYABO

NIQUERO

CABO
CRUZ

PILON
077° 17.0 W

MAREA DE
PORTILLO
077° 11.5 W

VERY DEEP WATER
TO CLOSE INSHORE

-N-

tack out that far . It isn't necessary.

For more on this subject, see the final paragraph in this chapter.

PLOTTING

Once again, we note that the magnetic deviation varies from about four degrees at Cabo Cruz to around seven degrees at Punta Maisí, but because it's visual all the way, this has little effect on courses, and plotting your position is fairly easy.

In general, chart work revolves around taking a quick look at the shoreline a couple of hundred yards away, then putting a nice neat cross on the chart just a little ahead of the last one. As the coastline runs almost dead east-west you can more or less forget about latitudes and navigate as close in as you feel comfortable.

STRATEGY

Regarding general passage-planning, the time of the day will determine your comfort level coming round the western corner; and early departures are called for to avoid an uncomfortable swell broadside on to your route. As a rule, we find that the daylight winds at the extreme west (Cabo Cruz) oscillate between northeast in the very early hours and southeast for the rest of the day; so it's best to round the cape before daylight and to anchor in Pilón or Portillo by midday after what can be an uncomfortable passage if the wind is strong. Happily, the view is best at this time of the day, and you've not yet been drugged by alcohol or the motion of your craft.

For the rest of the coast, the distances

between ports can be large (e.g., 60 miles between Santiago and Baitiquiri, going east), so departure times will be critical if you wish to arrive in daylight.

Be aware too, that for some obscure reason, there has been a recent sensitivity on the part of the officials in Santiago about visits made to Chivirico (See Pg. 252 for advice on this).

KABATIC EFFECT AND PREVAILING WINDS

Along the midsection (either side of Santiago) where the landmass is greater, the Kabatic effect is considerably more pronounced and winds usually start off anywhere around north northeast at daybreak, veering clockwise to south southwest by afternoon. The distances again call for early starts, but in general the wave motion is not going to cause any problems and you can coast as close as you dare. In any case, if you are motoring close-in under an onshore breeze you should have an anchor ready to deploy instantly in the unlikely event of engine failure.

Finally, at the extreme east (Punta Maisí) the prevailing winds overcome any local effect and are more or less constantly east northeast, veering or backing only as dictated by larger weather patterns.

Having said that, do not be worried by what might seem to be a difficult time ahead as severe weather is rare, and only a third (the weakest third) of the cold fronts reaching Cuba actually get down this far, and only the most determined of tropical systems will affect the coast.

CHIVIRICO HARBOR

ROUNDING CABO CRUZ FROM THE WEST
CHART NO. ICH 1137 (CUBAN)

The night before rounding the cape, after your swim and before the weather forecast, should be devoted to plotting and noting your courses. From any distance north of the inner reef harbor at Cabo Cruz you'll need to be leaving well before dawn and if on the way into your overnight anchorage you saw any nets or shoals they should be plotted onto the charts as you won't see them in the morning.

The engine and other inspections can also be done the night before, laying out your navigation instruments ready for use so nothing delays your departure once conditions are right. This passage can become rough if there is a south wind, and you might have to hang on, so prepare sandwiches in foil to avoid going below, set the alarm for two o'clock, take a stiff drink and get an early night. Wake, and leave while it's still dark.

A STRAIGHTFORWARD ROUTE

If coming from somewhere like Niquero or Las Colorados beach, this is likely to be the last time you use your compass for the next 200 miles. But just for now remember the three-degree variation, and it'll be a pretty straightforward route to the cape where the reef extends a mile or so west of the actual land mass. Note that unless you anchored at Cabo Cruz itself, there may seem to be a confusion of lights just off the cape, so give them a wide berth and head into the growing swells where the currents swirl off the point. Aim to be well south of the reef at the tip before making your westerly turn at about 19°49.0N to miss the anchored fishing-boat occasionally sheltering just off the point and the darkened headland. The swells along here will grow hugely during the morning as the winds usually shift round to the southwest by 10 o'clock, so you will probably be glad to make your first stop at Pilón or Portillo some 30 miles along an increasingly spectacular coast.

Cabo Cruz, inside the reef.

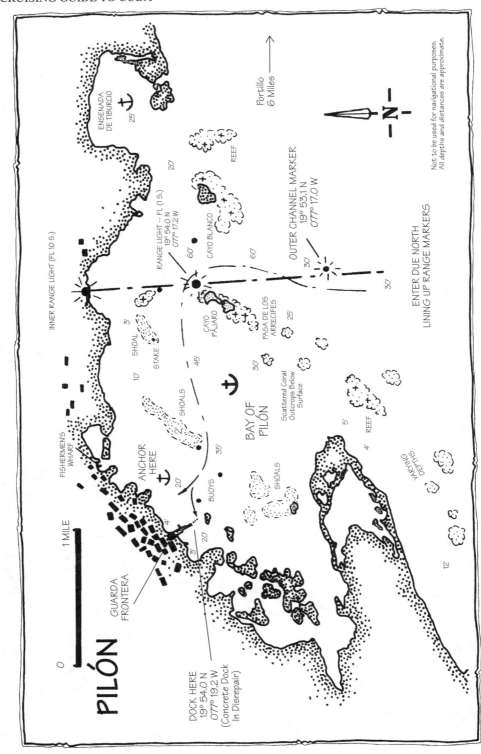

PILÓN

DOCK HERE
19° 54.0 N
077° 19.2 W
(Concrete Dock
In Disrepair)

GUARDA FRONTERA

0 1 MILE

FISHERMEN'S WHARF

INNER RANGE LIGHT (FL 10 S.)

ANCHOR HERE

4'

20'

3'

BUOYS

20'

SHOALS

35'

2'

SHOALS

10'

STAKE

3'

SHOAL

RANGE LIGHT -- FL (1 S.)
19° 54.0 N
077° 17.2 W

45'

BAY OF PILÓN

30'

SHOALS

Scattered Coral Outcrops Below Surface

CAYO PÁJARO

PASA DE LOS ARRECIFES

25'

60'

CAYO BLANCO

REEF

20'

25'

ENSENADA DE TIBURCIO

5'

REEF

4'

VARYING DEPTHS

12'

60'

OUTER CHANNEL MARKER
19° 53.1 N
077° 17.0 W

30'

30'

30'

ENTER DUE NORTH
LINING UP RANGE MARKERS

Portillo
6 Miles

N

Not to be used for navigational purposes.
All depths and distances are approximate.

246

Pilón, a sugar and fishing community of some 10,000 inhabitants is well guarded by reefs and numerous coral heads. The entrance however, is wide and well marked, and the reefs in fact offer good protection to the vessels within. In addition, the town itself, while not exactly Havana or Santiago, is sufficiently different from them, and interesting enough for you to pass an idle day or two.

If you have already been closely hugging the shoreline, note that this is the only place along the coast where there are major reefs, so you should hang at least a mile offshore as you come up to the bay of Pilón from the west.

At the mouth, there are range lights to bring you in due north from approximately 77°17.0W, taking you past the cay a mile inside. At this point, turn west, and further buoyage will direct you to the town of Pilón. Ahead, as you approach, there is a large Guarda Frontera building, with a large concrete wharf to the south of that. Although it is in bad repair at its extreme tip and little used, you can, in fact, temporarily moor along the left hand end of the main concrete dock in about 15 feet of water. Be careful of the large tires which hang here, and rig your own fenders up high, or your side rails may be caught if there is any swell entering.

You will be allowed to clear in with the officials from this spot, but they will generally ask you to anchor-off later, a bit to the east of the Guarda Frontera compound where there is a small dinghy dock and a cluster of tiny boats. Note that if you put out a lot of scope, an east wind can drift you back from an initial depth of 15 feet to a much shallower ledge only five feet deep close in. Drop the hook at least 200 yards west of the watchtower.

The majority of fishing boats use their own dock in a small cove north of your mooring, but this is shallowish and will probably be off limits to you.

We have found that the officials here are helpful, clearing in is not something that causes any great confusion, and there are no prohibitions on going ashore or wandering about at leisure. The health officer too may pay a visit, so be ready for your garbage to be taken away for incineration.

Pilón is a strange ramshackle place, seemingly held together by twisted lengths of old railway line, and based around a rusty sugar factory whose chimney still dominates. Hogs, sheep, and goats, wander among pieces of discarded rolling stock which poke out of the undergrowth, and in keeping with its agricultural traditions tractors careen along the byways. Nevertheless, the 10,000 inhabitants are a welcoming lot, offering a smile and a piece of cut sugar cane to the weary boater as he stretches his legs on the way out of town. If you wish a typical Cuban entertainment, then the local baseball team plays in the provincial leagues, and has a stadium in the town within easy walking distance.

There is a lively local bar just around the corner from the Guarda Frontera/Capitania building. Here, you can obtain sodas, beer, snacks, and rum for a peso or two, with lots of conversation thrown in for good measure. You will have noticed that the further you get from the major tourist cities (Havana, Santaigo, Varadero and the like) the easier it is to spend local pesos, and Pilón is no exception.

In the unwelcome event of needing it, you will find a medical post (*consultario*) along the way out of town northeast, while close by there is also a fishing station if you need anything to do with the boat.

From Pilón, it is only a short distance to Portillo, but Chivirico is some 50 miles or more so you may want to leave early if that is your destination. In any case, it will be wisest to inform the Captain of the Guarda Frontera the night before, before returning to the boat to retire. This way, you may be given permission to leave without having to go back to the dock for clearance in the morning.

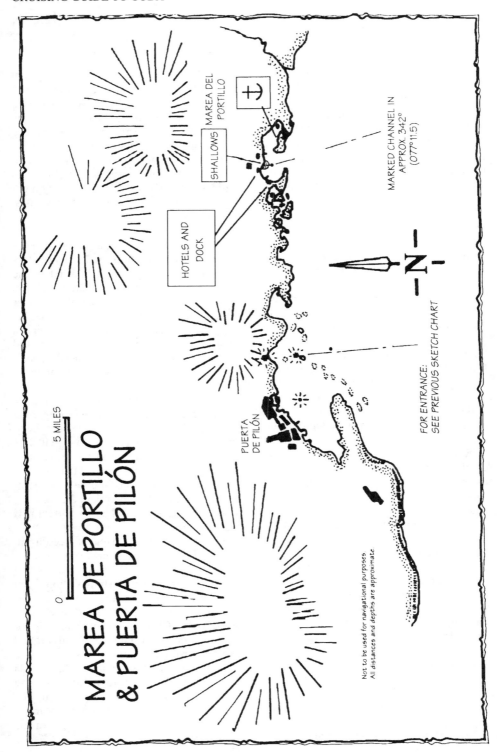

MAREA DE PORTILLO
& PUERTA DE PILÓN

0   5 MILES

MAREA DEL PORTILLO

SHALLOWS

HOTELS AND DOCK

PUERTA DE PILÓN

MARKED CHANNEL IN APPROX. 342° (077° 11.5)

N

FOR ENTRANCE: SEE PREVIOUS SKETCH CHART

Not to be used for navigational purposes
All distances and depths are approximate.

Easier to enter than Pilón, you will find Portillo only five miles further at around 077°11.5W. This tiny bay makes for the second of our three planned halts along the route east to Santiago.

The deep channel entrance, open to the sea and perfectly obvious, is visual directly through the R/G markers (342°M). Once inside, you are presented with a widening bay, with two largish hotels to the northwest and a flimsy dock reaching out between them. The bay itself is adequately deep for all keels (say nine-foot), but just be sure you don't approach too closely to the final (yellow) inner mark as it sits on a bank which suddenly alters the depth and heaps up the waves. As the beaches fronting the hotels are right in front of the entrance they are affected by surge, and you will probably be better off turning to starboard as soon as you pass the point inside. Over to the northeastern corner of the enclosed bay there is a tiny fishing village and you can find a beautifully calm, protected anchorage close to the mangroves opposite. You're not missing much by mooring over here as the hotel beaches are a fine mix of sand and silt, and unless you've come for some sort of weird cure I'd stay off them.

If you've made one of those early morning trips, exhaustion will have taken over, so you might as well get some sleep before going ashore later, but do not be surprised if a visitor in the form of a Guarda Frontera official is rowed out to you to inspect your documents in the afternoon. There isn't much in the way of official presence and it's likely that he's been dispatched from Pilón, so offer a soft drink and sympathy. He's probably hot and bothered, and the unfortunate fisherman who's just finished rowing him over will likely be similarly afflicted too.

DINGHY USE

There is a small, old and creaky dock over to the west which the scuba dive boat uses. You may be able to share it, but in any case the closer of the hotels has a scuba-shop just to its left where you can leave the dinghy. If the dock is undergoing repair at last (or has collapsed) you can practice making beach landings when you go ashore.

British, European, or Northern U.S. divers will already know the technique as they use it all the time with their inflatables. Take up a position outside the surfline and release the engine tilt-lock while (just like your big-boat entrances) waiting for your moment. Now go hard at the sand, trying to keep ahead of the surge, then just before driving onto the shore cut the motor and leap into the surf alongside. With any luck the engine really will have stopped and you won't lose a toe while grabbing the sides of the boat, and you can still physically drag it up as high as it'll go. They'll love you for the entertainment as you realize you've done it all in your dress-shorts (the ones with the crease), and your wallet's floating away alongside one of your flip-flops! So much so, that they'll even watch your dinghy for you.

Later on when you leave, you will have to wade the dinghy out into the waves and start the motor (in neutral) from alongside before leaping in one at a time.

THE HOTELS

Portillo's hotels take foreign visitors in winter and Cubans in summer, so what you get depends on when you arrive. Either

way, there are a couple of bars, a restaurant, telephone facilities and the usual stuff from the front desk (the *carpeta*). You can also obtain rental cars if you wish to tour the mountains where Fidel and the survivors of the landing at Los Colorados beach hid out during the first year of the revolution.

Remember, if you're going to eat or drink during the afternoon that it's going to be getting dark later and this may have a bearing on your trip back in the dinghy. Try not to drown just to entertain the curious. Believe me, a friendly throng of Cuban holiday-makers can cause a serious miscalculation at the bar.

If you are here during the foreign season, then you will have to put up with the growing practice of all-inclusive prices. What this means is that you have to pay a once and for all price which allows you to eat and drink without further charge. The staff will ask a budget-busting $50.00 for the privilege which allows a bedroom for the night. If you are staying on board then you'll have

to bargain them down more than somewhat.

Never mind, you may prefer instead, to spend your time in the small local village of Marea del Portillo closer to, and just north of, your mooring.

THE VILLAGE

Situated on the eastern side of the bay, the village is served by a small concrete wharf which you can also use. This dock is only for shallow draft vessels, but you may leave the dinghy alongside. From here you can walk up a neatly swept dirt road, alongside tidily trimmed cactus fences which border equally clean front yards. There is a local restaurant/bar in town and as is usual in this province, the people are among the most hospitable in Cuba.

There is no water on the dock, but a standpipe is available close by in the village, while if you ask around you will be able to purchase petrol and diesel. All liquids to be jerry-canned out to the boat.

ROUTE TO CHIVIRICO
CHART NO. ICH 1136 (CUBAN)

In pleasant sunny weather this passage can well be one of the highlights of the cruise. The distance involved means you'll have to get up early, leaving at or before first light, but you will be rewarded by the most amazing views and the best scenery of the whole trip. There may not be much in the way of shelter if the winds were to come strongly out of the south, but unless you've made a serious error in forecasting there's no reason to worry.

As usual the winds will be light early in

the morning. Later on as the sun gets high, you'll be well away from the influence of the cape, so although the swells offshore may be large, they'll be slow and easy. Inshore, the swells diminish, so provided the surge is not too great the absence of outlying dangers along the coastline means that you can cruise as close to the hard bits as you feel safe.

Along the way you will pass tall cliffs, rock-faces undercut by pounding surf, beaches, secluded valleys like oases filled with royal palms, and huge mountains sweeping right down to the waterside.

AN UNMISTAKABLE MOUNTAIN AND AN UNFORGETTABLE WRECK

Although it is by no means the only enormous landmark along this awesome coast, the tallest of these mountains (the Pico Turquino) at 6,500 feet is visible on a good day from as far away as Jamaica, 90 miles away. If you have time and the water

is calm you may even wish to make a rare dive on a perfectly preserved wartime wreck at the base of the mountain.

This seldom visited relic of the Spanish-American war is the cruiser *Colón,* sunk during a naval engagement in 1898. The wreck lies below the surface on a submarine ledge, with one half suspended at 50 feet and the rest hanging crazily down the slope as far as 150 feet.

To find it you need to pass the village of Ocujal and locate the Ensenada Turquino east of the peak, between the rocky point and the bridge over the river. Just east of the point and halfway up the slopes behind the shoreline there is a fence pointing directly at the wreck some 100 feet offshore at a position approximately 019°56.1N / 076°45.6W.

You will find that the visibility gets considerably better once below the first 10 feet but nevertheless it will pay to take along a good dive-light to explore this fascinating iron wreck, complete with engines, turrets, buckled steel plate and girders. A serious note of caution: If there is any danger of your boat being swept onto the shore by the surge then it will certainly be better to do a swim-out beach-dive, by road, from Chivirico 20 miles further on.

CHIVIRICO
CHART NO. ICH 1136 (CUBAN)

This wonderfully enclosed little cove 45 miles west of Santiago at 076°24.0W, makes for a convenient overnight stopover. Even were it not so, the harbor would be worth a stop just for the view only five minutes walk from your anchorage.

Immediately east of the protruding hill with the red-roofed hotel and two and a quarter miles west of Punta Tabacal the entrance is marked by two range-lights along a course of 340°M. The course along which you come in is closely guarded, both east and west by coral heads, so you should turn to come in from a fair distance out and be careful to keep on line. There are some outer banks of coral to be aware of too, and after a welcome break in the southeastern outer cays we are now going to be threatened once again with the "Curse of the Submerged Snorkeller". Keep your eyes open.

As you come in, you will see the coral banks submerged alongside the point to the west clearly visible in the midday sun and protected from the evening reflections by the hill, so approach the onshore range-marks closely and make a sharp turn to the west once the channel opens there. Here you'll find yourself inside a small cove enclosed on all sides by sheer rock walls and with depths of up to 10 feet. You can drop anchor wherever you see fit but it's best to set up near the small floating dock serving the scuba boat on the south side, not the abandoned old ore-facility on the northwest.

Sometime later, as you finally have everything put in its place, a perspiring soldier will cycle over from the Guarda Frontera post near the fishing boats and you can dinghy your documents over to him at the floating dock. Once again, clearance won't take any length of time, and you can take a walk along the track from the dock and up the steep road to the Hotel Los Galeones on the hill. If he doesn't show up before you leave for the hotel then he'll probably track you down at the bar later.

Take your camera and a good long lens to get some really nice shots of your own boat below, completely framed by trees, banks, and cliffs.

At the hotel you can rent cars, make phone calls, eat at the much improved restaurant, swim in the pool, and do a deal with the scuba divemaster to take you out to some hidden submerged banks or even back to the wreck of the *Colón.*

This beautiful spot is a really secure anchorage, and once I even came across a Canadian yacht which was moored in the basin while the owner returned home to tend to a sick parent. No one molested the boat which bobbed happily at anchor for

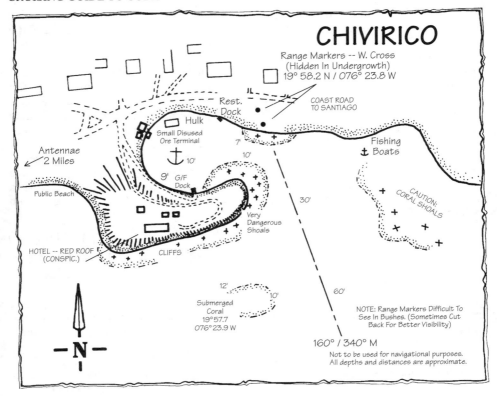

CHIVIRICO

Range Markers -- W. Cross
(Hidden In Undergrowth)
19° 58.2 N / 076° 23.8 W

Rest. Dock

COAST ROAD
TO SANTIAGO

Hulk

Small Disused
Ore Terminal

Antennae
2 Miles

7'

10'

10'

Fishing
Boats

9' G/F
Dock

Public Beach

30'

CAUTION:
CORAL SHOALS

Very
Dangerous
Shoals

HOTEL -- RED ROOF
(CONSPIC.)

CLIFFS

12'

10'

60'

Submerged
Coral
19°57.7
076°23.9 W

NOTE: Range Markers Difficult To
See In Bushes. (Sometimes Cut
Back For Better Visibility)

160° / 340° M

Not to be used for navigational purposes.
All depths and distances are approximate.

-N-

more than three months, and it's unlikely that anything short of a slap-bang head on full force direct hit by a hurricane could disturb you once inside. Mind you, there would be a press of small fishing-boats which more usually moor over to the northeastern side of the entrance to the bay where they have their own facilities.

I should also mention that the bar/restaurant just north of your mooring, is accessible by dinghy (the dock), and a good place to have a drink, and to party at weekends.

On the other side of the hill there is a long beach, thronged with inhabitants of Chivirico and the outlying areas who arrive by splendid horse-drawn buggies to enjoy the weekend. These buggies are a feature of the southeast coastline and make a wonderful sight, all gaily painted, crowded with people, and visible from your yacht cruising just offshore.

If you have made a road excursion to Chivirico from Santiago you will probably be glad to know that there's a gasoline station just a few hundred yards northwest of the onshore range-marks where you can exchange your coupons for fuel.

You'll be interested to see the firing-ranges alongside the road where the populace can shoot off their rounds at comic pictures of snarling Gringos in uniform. It's not personal, just that the revolution started here and they rather see themselves as still in the vanguard. Don't worry, everyone I've met has been almost overpoweringly friendly and would probably just die of embarrassment if it turned out you were a Norteamericano yourself.

CAUTION

Now, before leaving the subject of Chivirico, I have to say that lately (1996) there has been some strange reluctance on the part of the officials in Santiago and Havana to allow visitors there. I have even had "Not allowed to visit Chivirico" scribbled onto my *gia de recalas*, even when leaving Santiago in the *opposite* direction, and having arrived there from Chivirico in the first place! Unfortunately, if it continues, the effect of this prohibition is to make an already long journey (going west) into an even longer one.

If they have stricken that port from your itinerary, then this can mean a 75 mile journey between Santiago and the nearest other sheltered anchorage (Portillo) on the western half of this coast. Or even an 85 mile trip if you're going to jump from Baitiquiri on the east coast, direct to Chivirico and missing out Santiago instead.

If you obtain a local despacho in another port, then there doesn't seem to be any problem (especially if you are somewhat delicate about your intentions), and in fact the officials in Chivirico are absolutely delighted to see boaters.

Incidentally, I have never heard of anyone actually being turned away from Chivirico itself.

ROUTE TO SANTIAGO
CHART NO. ICH 1136 (CUBAN)

Be careful not to foul the coral heads to the southeast as you leave Chivirico for the east, but once you're on your way and past the grotesque beige hotel on the coast at Quiebra Seca (five miles) you'll have another great run. There is a promising looking entrance there but it's shrouded by fishnets strung across, and further along this stretch of the coast the few rivers that make it down to the sea have bars at their mouths.

It's another 45-mile run to Santiago, cruising alongside an equally splendid seashore, sometimes so close you can hear the kids whistling over at you, and the buggy passengers will point in fascination from the roads cut along the water's edge. Then suddenly, above the surface in the

Asseradero Harbour at 0760 08.5W is another Spanish-American war wreck. This time with the turret and cannon pointing skyward! This sad sight, the cruiser *Viscaya*, brings to mind the whole wretched history of a war touted by a newspaper publisher (Randolf Hearst) who wanted to drum up sales, and a president (William McKinley) who went along for the ride.

In 1898 the old Colonial empire was contracting and Spain was only too eager to save face while leaving Cuba, but the strange explosion which sank the American battleship *Maine* in Havana Harbour was the perfect excuse for low-risk slaughter, the making of reputations, and more importantly the long sought expansion of U.S.

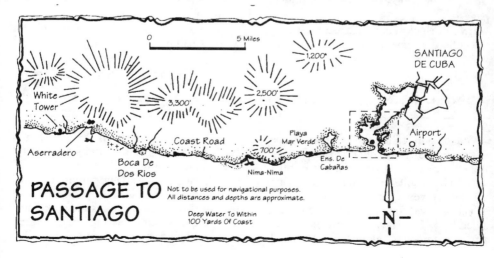

PASSAGE TO SANTIAGO

Not to be used for navigational purposes.
All distances and depths are approximate.

Deep Water To Within
100 Yards Of Coast

SANTIAGO DE CUBA

White Tower

3,300'

2,500'

1,200'

Airport

Aserradero

Boca De Dos Rios

Coast Road

Playa Mar Verde

700'

Nima-Nima

Ens. De Cabañas

-N-

influence in the Caribbean and the Pacific.

The modern American fleet totally outgunned the ancient Spanish cruisers holed up in Santiago Harbour and when they broke out on July 3rd they were butchered in four hours by the eager gunners. When it was over, the death toll along the coastline here was 474 Spanish sailors to two American casualties.

By the time history had played out that particular hand, huge areas of Cuba had become exclusively North American property, the seeds were sown for further strife, and now the whole cycle seems poised to renew itself once again.

Further along, closer to Santiago, there is more war-wreckage in the shallow bay of Nima-Nima, but soon you will have other things to occupy your mind. The enormous harbor of Santiago is only seven miles further and there may well be large commercial vessels proceeding through the narrow entrance, so in spite of the static prevalent on the VHF it is probably best to contact them with your intentions. In spite of my earlier advice, it is better in this instance to call the official harbor authorities direct.

Call *Morro Santiago* (the hill overlooking the entrance) on Channel 16, and they will sometimes reply. But on the other hand you may get no reply at all (I remember a flotilla of Jamaican sport fishing boats who came for a tournament in 1996 and got no response to any of a dozen calls), so just steam on in as described in the following pages.

If you're lucky enough to receive a reply, the radio station uses a working frequency of 10, and will liase with the marina at Punta Gorda inside the entrance so that by the time you've arrived all will be ready for your reception.

Just prior to Santiago, however, there is one other bay which may be of some interest to a cruiser.

Called the Ensenada de Cabañas, this small bay is situated about two and a half miles west of the entrance to Santiago Bay, and consists of a small pocket bay (similar, but smaller than those all along the northeast coast) with a narrow entrance channel.

Presently used as shelter for small Cuban fishing vessels, it may be suitable for a yacht as well, if the inner depths and height restrictions permit.

To help recognize the entrance, there is a white colored vertical rift in the slopes on the western part of the canal, while near the eastern side of the entrance there is a house along with other small constructions.

The channel is some 200-300 meters wide, with the navigable part approximately 50-60 meters. between the the shallows which extend from the eastern point of the entrance, and the reef which sticks out from the western point.

There are also two electricity pylons on each side of the entrance, and you should note that the height of the cable over the channel is reported to be only 10 meters.

Within the harbor, the land just along the water's edge is low and bordered by mangroves, but rises steeply, as is usual along this part of the coast.

Inside, north of the entrance canal, and on the eastern side, there is a small espigón where small boats can dock.

SANTIAGO DE CUBA
CHART NOS. ICH 1136,1137, OR HARBOR CHART NO.1805

Grandiosely called the "Ciudad Heroe" or the Hero City, it is regarded as second in importance only to Havana, but in many ways the inhabitants of Santiago de Cuba see themselves as first among equals.

The city was founded around 1514, considerably before Havana, and its first mayor was the famous conquistador Hernando Cortéz, before he went off to do his thing further afield in Central America. The city grew rapidly, drawing its wealth as it still does from mining and agricultural regions surrounding it, and in spite of disaster following disaster, from pirates and pestilence to earthquakes and uprisings, it nevertheless continued to grow until during the

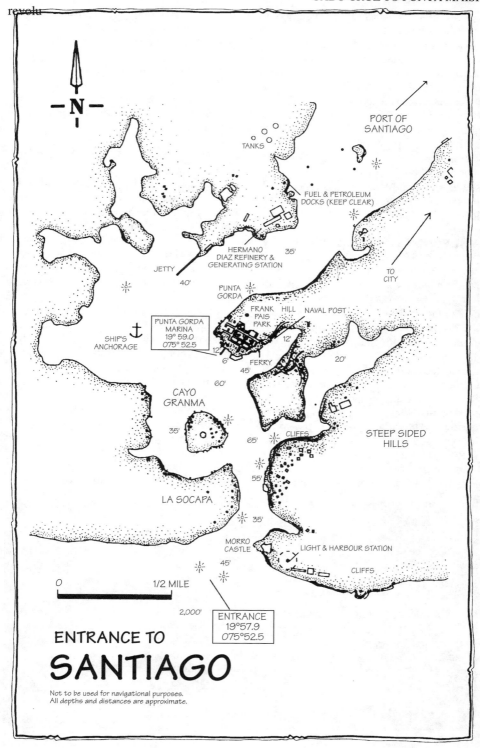

revolu

-N-

PORT OF
SANTIAGO

TANKS

FUEL & PETROLEUM
DOCKS (KEEP CLEAR)

HERMANO
DIAZ REFINERY &
GENERATING STATION

35'

JETTY

40'

TO
CITY

PUNTA
GORDA

FRANK HILL
PAIS
PARK

NAVAL POST

PUNTA GORDA
MARINA
19° 59.0
075° 52.5

12'

SHIP'S
ANCHORAGE

12'

6'

FERRY

45'

60'

CAYO
GRANMA

20'

35'

65'

CLIFFS

STEEP SIDED
HILLS

55'

LA SOCAPA

35'

MORRO
CASTLE

45'

LIGHT & HARBOUR STATION

CLIFFS

0   1/2 MILE

2,000'

ENTRANCE
19°57.9
075°52.5

ENTRANCE TO
SANTIAGO

Not to be used for navigational purposes.
All depths and distances are approximate.

revolution when it became more or less the focus of the struggle.

Here, downtown at the Moncada barracks (now a museum and schoolhouse), the opening shots were fired in the battles to come and to this day it still retains a special place in Cuban spiritual heritage. July 26th (the anniversary of the unsuccessful 1953 attack) is presently celebrated all over Cuba as the major festival of the year.

It may not be everyone's cup of tea, but there is a certain vibrance to the place which sets it apart, and I admit that it's certainly *my* favorite Cuban city, with a flavor all of its own.

A SUPERB CITY LOCATION

The city is superbly located, standing among the eastern foothills of the Seirra Maestra and looking out onto an amazing bay. It is also guarded by a narrow entrance and a magnificent fort dating right back to the original days of its founding when it could be said to control the Caribbean. There is a wonderful cosmopolitan feeling too, reflected both in the architecture and the people who have variously come from Spain, Africa and France. With a million inhabitants, the streets are consequently narrow and bustling; with old houses pressing for space along pavements interspersed with tiny plazas where hustlers and *jineteros* compete for your dollar.

If the harbor authorities on the Morro have not given entrance instructions, you may be intercepted outside by a grey military patrol boat, or inside by a small boat shaped incongruously like a wooden-shoe. This sometimes brings the immigration authorities out from the main offices.

In any case, you're most likely to be sent to the dock at Punta Gorda, the original site of the oldest yacht club in Cuba.

EASILY IDENTIFIED ENTRANCE

The entrance to Santiago de Cuba is easily identified by the castle and lighthouse installations atop the steep hill on the eastern side of the mouth. There are a couple of large buoys immediately outside the entrance at a position of approximately 19°57.9N / 075°52.5W. From here you can come in 34°M through the center of a deep channel some 200 yards wide, impressively guarded by the ancient castle and the more recent Spanish fortifications lower down.

Follow the line of buoys through the channel, pass the first inlet on your right and on your left you will see Cayo Granma. Although covered with houses, this cay is totally cut off from the mainland and accessible by the inhabitants only in small personal boats. A restaurant is situated here, its diners curiously looking on as you sail past, wrestling with your sails in the swirling entrance-vortex.

From here the marina is a couple of hundred yards north, a little to the left of the

Street carnival: Santiago

256

enclosed swimming area. It's easily identifiable by the low, light blue buildings with their red roofs, and the dock with its reception committee waiting under the canopy at the outer end.

DOCKING AT SANTIAGO MARINA

Following the increase in traffic over the last two or three years, a floating section has been added to the end of the marina dock. Med-mooring will be required if there are more than five or six boats alongside (as there will be) so have all ready before coming into port. It is significant that the holding off the end is not all that good, so put out lots of scope on your bow anchor or be prepared to have to reset it when the swells put an extra strain on things. On the other hand, you may be lucky to find space alongside on the left of the dock where the water at eight feet is adequate for most cruisers.

On the right, the southeastern side, you are likely to be battered about somewhat by the swells filtering into the harbor. If you do have to moor there you should dinghy-out an anchor some 20 feet off, and by means of a taut line to that, you can keep off the dock while still remaining alongside. Whichever you choose, don't disembark until the immigration officers arrive and clear you in.

Even on the western side you are still liable to be tossed about by the wake from the multitude of turbine-powered military patrol-boats going to their nearby docks and the large vessels proceeding through the channel. Hang lots of fenders over the side and look out for the antenna or the shrouds getting crunched against the roof overhead when the boat rocks. Move as far as possible along the platform to leave room for others who may well have to med-moor on that side too.

FORMALITIES AND WOES (Getting the negatives out of the way first)

Santiago is an international port, and understandably there is likely to be a more formal entry requirement than you've become accustomed to over the last few weeks. Unfortunately, in spite of the increasing numbers of arrivals (from within and with-

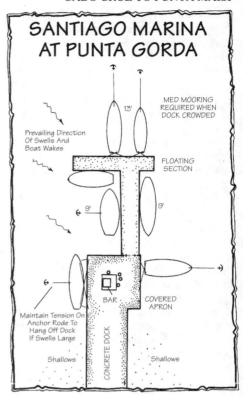

out Cuba), things seem to have gone downhill over the last couple of years. On one occasion recently I watched a small visiting yacht searched for over two hours before being allowed to *depart* for the coast, and they'd been in Cuba for a week already. A day later, eight officials swooped on us, but this time it took almost four hours, with the added precaution of divers being put into the water to inspect our bottom. The boat was examined inch by inch, our logbooks were read, all electrical equipment was checked, medicines sampled, and the engine probed.

At this stage we'd been three months in the country, and once again, we are left to ponder the incongruity of being suspected of coming to Cuba (Cuba?) to buy drugs, or indeed, to sell them... yeah.

There is too, the ever present guard not more than a couple of feet from your boat, and who always seems to be watching *you*.

In spite of the foregoing, it has to be said that the customs officers who inspected the vessel were scrupulously courteous, and so professional in their approach, that every single item which was disturbed was replaced *exactly* as it had been before. Even the clothing was properly refolded (La Fiona is normally very touchy about this sort of thing), and a formal document was given to us stating that we had offered "good cooperation".

Nevertheless, I have received various reports which suggest that more cruisers are becoming dissatisfied with the treatment being meted out here. Only time, or a change of attitude to cruisers, will cure this ill.

One unwelcome chore you're likely to be faced with is that of cleaning your boat every morning to remove the gritty deposits which rain out of the sky courtesy of the cement factory close by.

There is also the horrible black tarry deposit which washes out of the filthy harbor daily and quickly congeals along your waterline. This cleaning job may be postponed if you don't wish to take your chances

in the water alongside but it should be attended to as soon as you have the chance further along the coast.

Don't let any of your fenders or ropes trail into the water either, as they're even more likely to be permanently soiled.

An additional point is that at 90°F the water temperature in the harbor is some 10-15° more than the outside waters, and this encourages a heavy growth of barnacles or weeds. This stuff quickly fouls your log impeller and coats the hull/prop in a week or so. Clear it off as soon as you have the opportunity to go underneath in cleaner waters, and before it has time to harden.

Having said all that, and in spite of all I have said about the officials, this will be the best and most efficient place to sort out all further documentation — as far afield as Havana if that's where you're eventually going.

A "proroga" can also be arranged here if you need an extension on your entry visa.

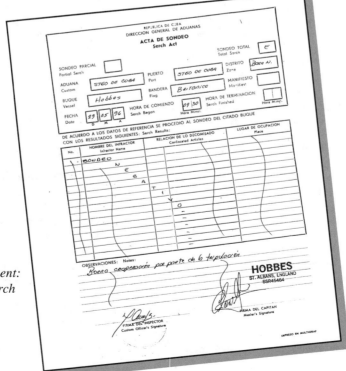

Search document: Results of search "negative."

MARINA OPERATIONS

The marina costs .45cents/foot daily. Power is available alongside even if you have to improvise somewhat with the electricity connections, and deal with leaky water connections. If there is no water available you will have to ask any of the workmen variously employed around the dock to turn on the pump (*la turbina*), as you will when requiring showers nominally available ashore. The marina offices are contained in the building at the foot of the dock. Here you may (occasionally) find the staff who, sad to say, are not amongst the most efficient or enthusiastic you will meet on your travels. More often than not, however, you will have to search them out somewhere at the rear of the premises surrounded by fruit trees and lounging watchmen. On the whole, the staff here are not particularly cooperative (they can be downright rude), and changes will have to be made if the marina is to regain it's former ambience.

Available here are the normal services like calling taxis or arranging for rentalcars, and as usual the marina will sort out your documentation with the authorities. Remember to ask about this well in advance, and keep bugging them about it.

The marina at Punta Gorda handles general boatyard duties for a variety of smaller local vessels, accommodating them both ashore and afloat in a couple of covered bays.

If you require fuel or oil you will either have to pull alongside one of the sagging wharves over to the left, (easily identifiable by the oil-blackened workshop and depot), or it will be delivered dockside to your boat in a barrel (at .50 cents/litre).

MEDICAL EMERGENCIES, CHARTS, AND SERVICES CLOSE BY

Just across the road from the gate to the marina, there is a small medical post (the *consultorio*) underneath an otherwise indistinguishable two-story house. The nurse there will sort out any minor repairs in a jiffy, and if further work is required, then she's the one to arrange it. When I took a junior cruiser there to have a splinter removed from his eye, his father was astounded by the speed and no-nonsense effi-

Santiago castle

ciency with which it was attended to. As usual in Cuba, treatment is free, but if you have any medical stuff aboard which is surplus to requirements then please remember them.

Laundry can also be done by a friendly Cuban lady who lives near the dock. Again, you will have to ask around to find her. Never mind, word of mouth is the normal way of obtaining information in Cuba, and you too will have to take part in the system if you wish the latest advice.

Charts are available close by in the offices of the excellent Geocuba organization. In fact, they may even send a representative down to the dock to canvas for sales occasionally. Although you are using this guide, I cannot stress how important it is to have good charts. The official Cuban ones are the best, and cost only $15 U.S. each, which is not a lot in the overall scheme of things.

Note: Even though the officials are intrusive, the harbor filthy, the marina a bit tacky, and the staff definitely need a fire lighting under them, *the city itself more than makes up for everything else.*

TRANSPORT

From the marina you're a couple of miles out of town, and it's a $20 ride to the center of the city; so rather than going broke or putting up with the prices of rental cars you will have to find a private taxi. Never mind, this is not at all difficult if you ask around near the dock, and will only set you back

about $5.

Do a deal for the whole day so that you can get about the countryside and visit the inland cities or the prehistoric parks and resort areas to the east.

If you balk at the idea of taxis and the like, then buses are a viable (if slow) alternative when getting into town. For this you'll have to walk a few blocks northeast to the main road. Asking anyone at the side of the road will get you instructions as to the place to wait, and it'll cost you less than a peso.

Railway services are available for transport to Havana ($35) and other cities along the backbone of the island. The station is next to the waterfront, a couple of blocks down from the Parque Céspedes.

You may even take a local ferry from the wharf near the marina all the way into town, and of course, the airport is just next to the Morro Castle at the entrance to the harbor.

OUT OF TOWN RIDES

East of the city, we find the Gran Piedra Park, with a huge stone which commands a wonderful view of the surrounding countryside. Further on, there is the Siboney farmhouse-museum where the first action of the revolution was planned. At the side of the road there are macabre monuments every few hundred yards with the names and professions of those who later died in the fighting (winning side only; thank you).

If you crave more naïve amusement you can visit the prehistoric park where large concrete dinosaurs cavort in front of bemused tourists. And a short ride out of town

along the same route east you can stop off at the hotel Buccanero to refill any scuba tanks you may have emptied along the way.

You may even find it rather fun to go back along the coast road in the direction you've just come from—towards Chivirico and the Sierras Maestra if you did not have the chance to visit previously.

Near to Santiago is one of the most religious sites in Cuba, with a lovely church and a virgin who (significantly for you) has several times appeared before imperilled sailors and guided them to safety. You may visit the church by taking the Avenue de Las Americas and going 11 miles northwest through the mountains to the valley of El Cobre. The church is open daily and the faithful meet inside to worship in front of the statue (wheeled about town in procession on feast days) and to bring a strange variety of offerings which are displayed behind the altar.

A MULTITUDE OF DELIGHTS

The city of Santiago itself has a multitude of delights, and it's unlikely that you could exhaust them in a week, so plan to stay some time. You might as well get it over with and start off at the Parque Céspedes, the spiritual center of the city, where the cathedral and town hall oppose each other in a neat if unconscious political statement. The first-floor restaurant balcony of the newly repaired Casa Granda hotel is a good place to sip a cocktail and look out over the crowds in the square. On weekends, little children promenade in their Sunday finest and even mount a train pulled by gaily-decorated goats; but at any time the plaza is a fascinating spectacle, with a variety of human interest stories laid out for the entertainment of all.

Hustlers, for which the city is justly famous, intercept vague bespectacled camera-toting tourists from the nearby tour-buses, and arm-in-arm parade them about like trophies. Meanwhile, the secret police (everybody knows who they are) look on to make sure it all doesn't get out of hand, and to check on who's talking to whom.

With a few delightful exceptions, the official guides in the hotel lobbies are usually not going to guide you anywhere except into the hands of the efficient money-extraction machine called the tourist industry; but sooner or later (despite your healthiest doses of cynicism), you are likely to be adopted by a Santiagero who "only wants to practice his English". Choose carefully, as the arrangement can be both to your benefit or detriment. On the one hand, you may be immediately tapped for the price of a meal or two, a pair of shoes, a night on the town, someone's sister, someone's brother; or you may with better judgement find a friend who will guide you to places and experiences you could never find or hear about on your own.

In any case, you are likely to encounter some of the most hospitable people anywhere, and a people who will unfailingly ask you back to share what little they have. I wish I could mention by name some of those who have shown me Cuban life as it is really lived. From whispered conversations in backrooms at four a.m. (whispered, to avoid listeners next door), to gatherings attended by mothers, grandfathers, the pharmacist on the corner, students home on holiday, watchmen, and lovers. They know who they are, and if perchance they ever see this, I thank you from the bottom of my heart.

PROVISIONS AND SUCH STUFF

Near the harbor there is a ships' chandler or proveedor, operated by *Sumarpo*, where you can get all manner of provisions at a much better price than any of the dollar-shops (less than half). Just ask the taxi driver to take you to Sumarpo at the Avenida San Bacilio No.106. If you are not worried about speaking Spanish, then you can call them up on the VHF on Channel 12 or by telephone at 25514.

There are also the usual hard-currency shops, aimed more at the diplomatic or business community. One, the Cubalse shop north of the ugly and futuristic Hotel Santiago stocks everything you might need to continue your cruise (including a fascinating selection of rather tacky dry-goods), and another sometimes more convenient if much less well-stocked *diplotienda* is near the airport up by the Morro castle. Although they are much more expensive than the chandlers, it must be said that these shops hold a much wider and less basic selection too.

Looking into Santiago's Bay from the castle.

For fresh vegetables, fruit, or meat, there is also a local produce market, just a couple of blocks downhill towards the harbor from the Parque Céspedes. As in all markets throughout the world, it is best to get here early.

The best rum in Cuba is sold in Santiago so stock up here, but take due note of the sign prominenty displayed above the road back to the marina, "Señor driver, drink is the enemy of the steering wheel."

And remember that the Spanish word for steering wheel (*timón*) is also the word for "rudder" too!

NOTES ON THE CITY

To avoid the danger of becoming a tour guide, I'm just going to end with a few quick notes about this marvelous city.

The supply of reasonable restaurants within Santiago is no longer as limited as before. To find a decent paladar or private restaurant, just ask any of your fellow cruisers at dockside. Failing this, ask your taxi driver, or just wait to be accosted. Mostly, they are downtown, and you will find several within a block or two of the (where else) Parque Céspedes.

There are also hotels, or expensive places like La Maisón downtown where you have to watch yet another dreadful fashion-show with your meal. Mind you, the models there will sometimes accompany you later to the wild discotheque across at the Las Americas hotel nearby. Curiously enough, although Cubans and foreigners can mingle inside to the right of the disco floor, on the left there is an enclosed area supposedly reserved for the higher party-functionaries.

Just east of your dock at Punta Gorda however there is a large Cuban restaurant where you can sometimes persuade the staff to serve you for pesos. Good food, great value, and the more of these we find, the more we'll be persuaded to send ashore, rather than being forced into eating on board to avoid the debtors prison.

Incidentally this is where the loud music

comes from.

THE CAY

Across the bay, at the same Granma Cay which you passed when you came in, there is an excellent seafood place, El Cayo. Well worth the price, there's an inexpensive boat service ($3 return, each) via a noisy Russian twin-cylindered dinghy from the marina to the dock in front of the restaurant. This fascinating cay is inaccessible by land and the only way onto the island is by personal boats which the inhabitants moor in small bays underneath the upper floors of the shorefront houses. There is a baseball team up the hill on the cay, and sometimes a helicopter can be seen using its playing field as a landing ground.

TELECOMMUNICATIONS

There is a telephone office underneath the cathedral on the Parque Céspedes where you can make all your calls back home. You may purchase prepaid telephone cards there too, but since the most recent tensions these are not valid for calls to the U.S.A. or the Caribbean (it's a U.S. area code, 809). If the operator has to make a U.S. call for you, she'll ask for I.D. which to be truthful we *never* carry. Just look astounded that anyone would want such a thing.

To send or receive faxes, then use the front desk facility at the Hotel Casa Granda opposite. "She Who Must Be Obeyed" always gets a bit weepy when receiving a fax here from her sister, but the plush armchairs nearby are a great comfort when reading them. And you can even take the elevator all the way up to the rooftop bar for the best view in the city and a reasonably priced cocktail to put it all into perspective again.

VISIT THE MUSEUMS AVAILABLE

Santiago has recently undergone an extensive facelift, and freshly repaired museums abound. Among them, I would recommend the Bacardí museum in the city center, and the old home of Diego Velasquez (the original govenor of Cuba), but whatever your state of mind there is one place you should not miss, and that's the amazing castle you cruised past at the entrance to the harbor.

This nearly four-hundred year old building is accessible just ten minutes by car from your dock, turning right instead of left as you reach the main Santiago road. Go early and sit in silent wonder above the spectacular harbor, or sight along the cannons still looking out to sea for the approaching pirates who coveted the wealth they once guarded. Fittingly, there is a museum devoted to those very pirates within the castle itself.

Again, take lots and lots of film. At least there's a half decent restaurant nearby at the summit and if you beat the Dutch and German tour buses to it you can get a splendid meal with a view that only a sailor can really appreciate.

An equally wonderful view, in a more secluded environment, is available near your dock from the Parque Frank Pais; so named after one of the original heroes of the guerilla war. The grounds are at the summit of the hill behind the marina, and a 20- minute climb will reward you with a welcome respite from the noise and bustle of the city.

A beautifully maintained park, this contemplative spot looks out onto the inner harbor of Santiago Bay, and is surveyed by a large statue of the revolutionary holding a U.S. M15 carbine at the ready.

OBTAIN AN EXTENSION TO STAY LONGER

Finally, if by now you have been seduced into staying longer than anticipated in Cuba you can get an extension (a *prorroga*) to your entry permit by taking your passports, pink slips, and $25 to the immigration offices at 412 Calle San Bacilio, between Carbarrio and Carniceria.

LEAVING SANTIAGO

No matter where you're going later, you should sort out all documentation here in Santiago.

Some of the ports further along the coast are not used to private foreign boats, so if you're continuing on along the coast and west to Havana it's best to have arranged all subsequent documentation in advance. When filling in your guia de recala (the list of ports), put in as many as you can find space for. You might not actually stop there, but it's as well to have the name down.

If you are leaving Cuba for foreign parts this is the only place along this stretch of coast that you can be legally cleared out, so you will likewise have to plan accordingly. The next international port is Baracoa, round the corner on the way back up the coast to the northwest.

It is important to repeatedly stress your departure time, and to insist that your documentation will be ready at that time. If your departure is delayed more than an hour, the distances involved can mean your losing a whole day, and I have witnessed this happening more than once.

FEW OPPORTUNITIES FOR SHELTER

Between Santiago and the eastern tip of Cuba there won't be many opportunities to find good shelter overnight, so you may choose to do it all in one go or to stop once along the way.

There is a Cuban port (Caimanera) situated inside the bay at Guantánamo behind the U.S. Naval Base, but entering can possibly involve you in unwelcome hassles

further down the line so I'd give it a miss.

The harbor of Puerto Escondido just east of the U.S. territory at Guantanamo is closed to civilian traffic, so that's out too. You might instead go to Baitiquirí 20 miles on, or merely seek shelter from the prevailing winds along the coast in a couple of shallow bays (Caleta is the most convenient) before rounding Punta Maisí.

The harbor officials will have to come to the dock in their boat to clear you, so make your arrangements in good time with the marina management and schedule their visit for *early* in the day. They are accustomed to handling foreign yachts, but this is still Latin America so don't fret too much when the whole process takes what seems to you to be an unnecessary length of time. Once the documentation is sorted out and the despacho and clearances handed over, you will not be allowed to go ashore, and in fact the immigration boat will sometimes accompany you to the mouth of the bay. Wave at them, toot your horn, and then turn left.

ROUTE TO PUNTA MAISI
CHART NOS. ICH 1135 & 1134 (CUBAN)

By now the wind is probably on-shore and the surge has gotten up, but as long as you feel up to it you may once again hug the coast as closely as you dare, passing steep cliffs deeply undercut by wave-action. The rock faces along here may be as high as 200 feet, but you will also come across little bays sprinkled with sand and set with tourist tables and umbrellas. If the wind is right and the surge is not too evident you may even pause by Siboney where there is normally a bit of shelter in front of the public beach. A mile or so further there's the tiny cove in front of the Hotel Bucanero, but it's a bit surgey.

As you may have noticed by road, this is the main holiday area (both national and foreign) around Santiago and there are many hotels and beaches along the shore. The mountains are still evident all around, but you get to see even more cliffs than along the western half of this coastline.

Along here, the deep bay opposite the substantial hotel complex at Baconao is worthy of consideration if you were in the mood to stop for the night and the winds were favorable. You'll find this at around 075°26.4W, and surrounded by tall mountains it offers protection from all but south winds.

At longitude 075°13.9W we come across the great divide between U.S. held territory and the rest of the country. This area at the mouth of the Guantánamo Bay was ceded by the U.S.A. to the U.S.A. at the beginning of the century and is still a bone of contention between the two governments. It does seem a bit odd to see the American positions and installations on either side of the entrance to the bay, with shiny well-appointed radar domes, tall pylons, and airstrips facing off against the rather more fundamental Cuban affairs you're now accustomed to.

If you do not intend to go in, then make sure you aim well outside the southern limit, passing beyond latitude 19°51.1N.

You may in fact, pass through the entrance *north* into Cuban territory again, so if you are going to the port of Caimanera then hoist a U.S. courtesy-flag, contact port control on 12, and proceed on through. You will be subject to interrogation and possibly searches by the U.S. authorities on the way, so have your documents ready. In any case you are not allowed to land at the naval base.

The entrance is well buoyed past the base as far as the southern section, where the bay widens and the small town of Caimanera is situated round the corner on the left. There is a small boatyard here, and there are road and rail links with the city of Guantánamo 20 miles away. On the right is the more major port of Boquerón where there is a large wharf set up for commercial vessels, and like its neighbor there are links with the inland. The bay offers good shelter in any weather, but there's not a lot to attract the cruiser and in light of potential problems it may be as well to give it a miss until the

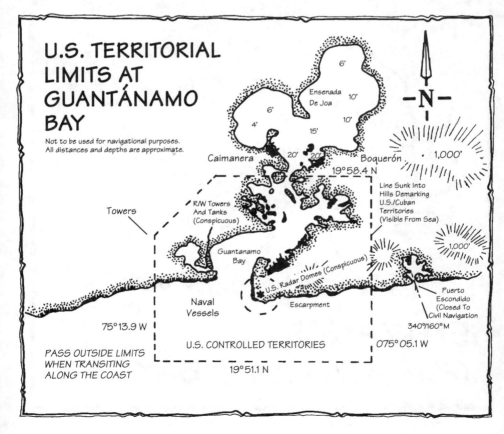

U.S. TERRITORIAL LIMITS AT GUANTÁNAMO BAY

Not to be used for navigational purposes.
All distances and depths are approximate.

Ensenada De Joa

6'
6'
4'
10'
10'
15'

Caimanera
20'
20'
Boquerón
1,000'
19°58.4 N

Line Sunk Into Hills Demarking U.S./Cuban Territories (Visible From Sea)

Towers

R/W Towers And Tanks (Conspicuous)

1,000'

Guantanamo Bay

U.S. Radar Domes (Conspicuous)

Puerto Escondido (Closed To Civil Navigation

Naval Vessels

Escarpment

340°/160° M

75°13.9 W

U.S. CONTROLLED TERRITORIES

075° 05.1 W

PASS OUTSIDE LIMITS WHEN TRANSITING ALONG THE COAST

19°51.1 N

-N-

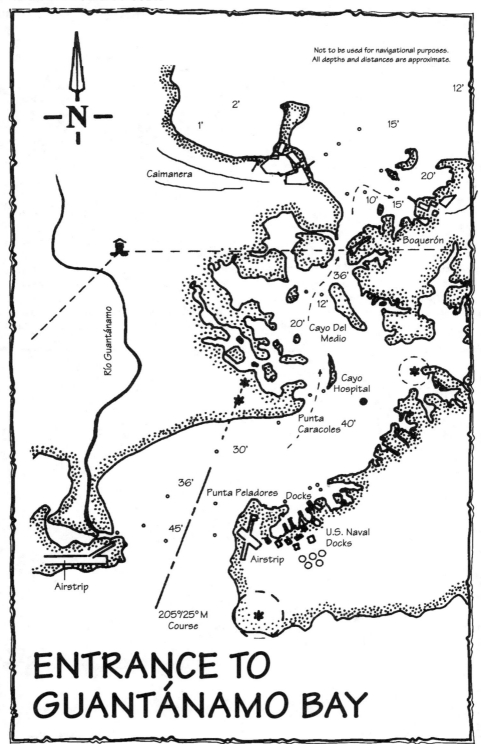

Not to be used for navigational purposes.
All depths and distances are approximate.

12'

2'

1'

15'

Caimanera

20'

10' 15'

Boquerón

36'

12'

20'

Cayo Del
Medio

Río Guantánamo

Cayo
Hospital

Punta
Caracoles 40'

30'

36'

Punta Peladores Docks

45'

U.S. Naval
Docks

Airstrip

Airstrip

205°/25° M
Course

ENTRANCE TO
GUANTÁNAMO BAY

present unpleasantness dies away.

From outside the scene is frankly fascinating, helicopters buzzing in and out, large coastguard or navy ships, and borders defended by watch-towers and fences. There is a system of trenches dug into the hillsides along the boundaries and these, clearly visible from offshore, are a good indication of just when you have passed the limits on the far side (075°05.1W) and can come back close inshore again.

PUERTO ESCONDIDO

There is a convenient habor just past the Guantánamo enclave but unfortunately it is off-limits to civil traffic so we'll just have to go on towards the east.

For the sake of those who may one day enter, I include a drawing of the bay.

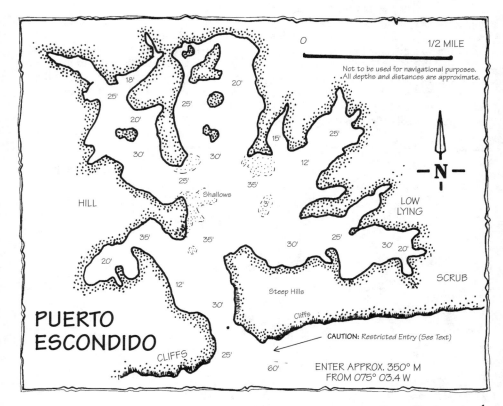

BAITIQUIRÍ

Just 20 miles past Guantánamo, we find this small so-called pocket-bay (a feature of the east and northeast coasts). It is situated some 3.5 miles west southwest of the point at Sabanalamar where a conical hill called Pan de Azucar rises 800 feet, and is marked by a large pylon light just 200 yards to the eastern side of the entrance.

This super little harbor, with a narrow, but easy entrance at 20°01.5N / 074°51.2W, and a sheltered anchorage within, is the only protected refuge presently available to a cruiser east of Santiago.

To the north, the land surrounding the bay is relatively low and edged with mangroves except where there are some salt pans, a small township of some 1,000 inhabitants, and a couple of small docks. Behind this, there is a wide valley containing expanses of sugar fields and some agricultural buildings.

On either side of the entrance, east and west, there are steep hills which protect the inner bay from anything the elements can throw at it.

Enter along a course roughly northwest and, avoiding the reefs awash on either side, keep to the darker, deep-water center of the channel which shelves gradually from about 25-to-10 feet at the end. The channel is clearly marked (R/G poles), but only some 50 feet wide at its narrowest point so exercise due care until within the wide bay and you can head across.

Over to the northwest there is a wooden dock some 50 feet long where fishing boats come alongside, and ashore a Guarda Frontera post near a white building which houses a freezing plant. Left of all this, there is a small boatyard surrounded by ferrocement wrecks. On the eastern side of

the bay is a sunken barge and a salt-works consisting of various yellow constructions and a large concrete dock. The northern side of the bay is taken up by rectangular salt pans.

Although you may come alongside in 10-foot., the northwest fishing dock is normally in use, so it may be better to anchor off. In any case, the captain of the port will row out to you. Although Baitiqirí is not visited by a lot of boats, the traffic *is* growing, so entering or leaving, formalities will not take long.

Behind and north of the small port, the village of Baitiquirí makes its living from fisheries, salt production, and agriculture. The terrain surrounding the town slopes gradually up into the mountains, and if you need it there is a road on the lower slopes connecting the town with the interior.

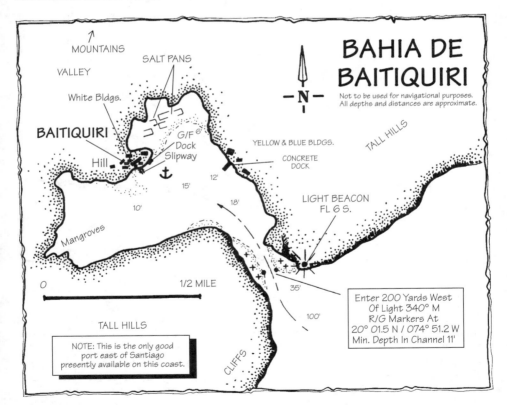

BAHIA DE BAITIQUIRI

Not to be used for navigational purposes.
All depths and distances are approximate.

MOUNTAINS

VALLEY

SALT PANS

White Bldgs.

BAITIQUIRI

Hill

G/F
Dock
Slipway

15'

12'

10'

18'

YELLOW & BLUE BLDGS.

CONCRETE DOCK

TALL HILLS

LIGHT BEACON
FL 6 S.

Mangroves

0   1/2 MILE

35'

100'

TALL HILLS

CLIFFS

Enter 200 Yards West
Of Light 340° M
R/G Markers At
20° 01.5 N / 074° 51.2 W
Min. Depth In Channel 11'

NOTE: This is the only good
port east of Santiago
presently available on this coast.

The remainder of this run to Punta Maisí should be no problem and is unremarkable except for the fact that there is no shelter available should you really need it. It is therefore wisest to wait up in Baitiquirí until the weather is settled. It is, after all, almost 80 miles to the port of Baracoa, round the corner and to the northwest.

About 10 miles southwest of Punta Maisí, an outcrop called Nelson's Bank rises a couple of thousand feet from the depths to within 300 feet of the surface. This can cause a rather disquieting change in the motion of your boat if you are not aware of the cause, but apart from that there isn't much to worry about.

FINAL MOORING ON SOUTHEAST COAST

Some 10 miles before Punta Maisí, there is a promotory which extends slightly southwards from the coastline. As well as providing anchorage in the shallow bay west of the light pylon at Punta Caleta, there is a permanent mooring consisting of a buoy near the mouth of the River Caleta. This is the last realistic spot to shelter before Pta. Maisí.

Look for a green can buoy close inshore at 20°04.8/074°18.8, some 200 yards west of the beach.

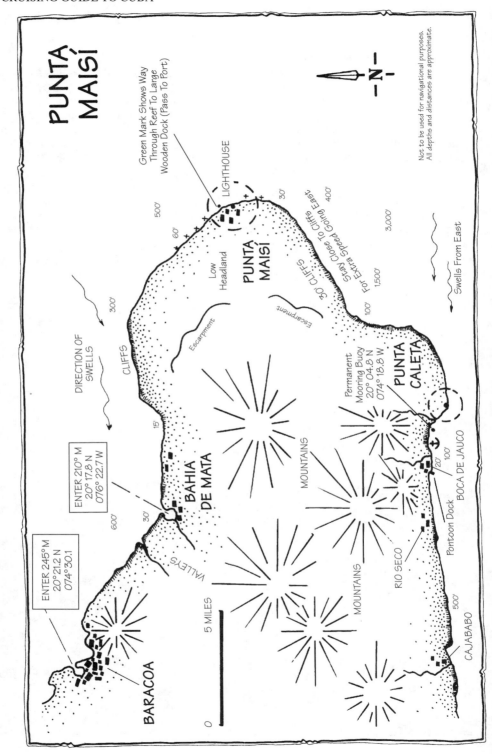

PUNTA MAISÍ

Not to be used for navigational purposes.
All depths and distances are approximate.

Green Mark Shows Way Through Reef To Large Wooden Dock (Pass To Port)

LIGHTHOUSE

Low Headland

PUNTA MAISÍ

Escarpment

Escarpment

30' CLIFFS

Stay Close To Cliffs Going East
For Extra Speed

500'

60'

300'

DIRECTION OF SWELLS

CLIFFS

15'

Swells From East

3,000'

1,500'

400'

100'

Permanent Mooring Buoy
20° 04.8 N
074° 18.8 W

PUNTA CALETA

BOCA DE JAUCO

MOUNTAINS

MOUNTAINS

MOUNTAINS

RIO SECO

Pontoon Dock

20'

100'

ENTER 210° M
20° 17.8 N
076° 22.7 W

BAHIA DE MATA

600'

30'

VALLEYS

ENTER 245° M
20° 21.2 N
074° 30.1

BARACOA

5 MILES

0

500'

CAJABABO

Just off the point, the currents can be influenced somewhat by the winds, and we can get a strong westerly flow in winter. When the occasional summer southerly persists the current can reputably flow east against the trend, while just to be different the currents flow south if the winds come out of the north! Nevertheless, the water here is among the clearest I've ever seen in my life, and the coral fingers extending out along the bottom sand are perfectly visible at anything up to 100 feet. There are no offshore dangers, so in good weather ignore all the above and remember to stick really close to the coast to gain whatever benefit you can from the counter current. Our log recorded a boost of some 2.5 knots once.

There is a large lighthouse on Punta Maisí, with a marker showing the way through the reef. Behind this is a large wooden dock and a considerable, if widely dispersed, settlement of habitations and works.

While all the above sounds somewhat complicated, you really shouldn't have any difficulties in anything but the most unwise circumstances, but it is as well to note that this area is called the "Pass of the Winds" in Spanish.

In spite of the above, the low coastline at this most extreme part of Cuba is usually subject to prevailing easterlies unaffected by any Kabatic effect, so once you're round the point you have the winds and current at your back. There is little to choose between making a daytime or night passage, so in the final analysis it's probably down to when you actually departed from your last halt as to when you actually arrive round the corner in Baracoa. Although on principle we always prefer to round such capes at night, we have also done it in calm, clear seas during the day, and the view makes for a much more pleasant experience.

Along the way you may sometimes have the dubious pleasure of listening on the VHF to the U.S. Coast Guard interrogating or even intercepting various vessels on the high seas. Whatever your position on the actual legality of this practice you should be aware of it, and outside the 12-mile limit you may well be asked questions regarding the boat's name, flag, last port, owner, captain, and even your date of birth! A foreign-flagged vessel in international waters may, in fact, justifiably refuse to either answer or to stop, but although unlikely to come to this, be aware of the fact that they have the Gatling gun and you in all likelihood have none.

271

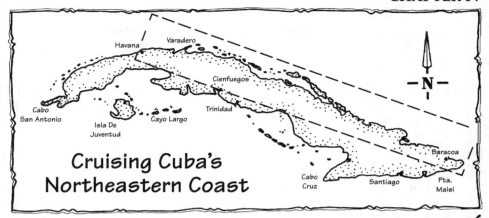

CHAPTER IV

Cruising Cuba's
Northeastern Coast

PUNTA MAISÍ
TO HAVANA

his gentle curve, stretching 520 miles northwest from the mountains near Punta Maisí to the lowlands of Havana is divided into two distinct sections. The first 220-mile stretch of coastline as far as Cayo Verde contains deepwater pocket-bays neatly spaced along its length, while the next section, almost as far as Varadero, offers more in the way of cays and islets.

More than any other section of Cuba, this coastline is also notable for the beautiful beaches it offers.

An odd feature of this coast, is the abundance of sometimes strangely designed but always beautiful lighthouses.

Along the route, you are likely to see far more in the line of holiday development than elsewhere in Cuba. Lest this worry anyone seeking solitude, this still only means that you will come across maybe three or four international hotel complexes in the 460 miles before Varadero.

By basing yourself in any of the inhabited stops along the way the cruiser can visit a multitude of inland towns and cities. But elsewhere, the cays are more or less deserted, and there are countless miles of brilliant white beaches for you to enjoy.

Finally, although infrequent, there are one or two excellently run marinas along this section. Most notably, those in Varadero

and the Bahia de Naranjo.

POCKET BAYS: HARBORS

These pocket-bays (characteristic of eastern Cuba), provide harbors for all types of vessels, from tiny fishing boats with room for one man and his dog, all the way up to large ocean-going commercial ships. They are usually entered through a narrow channel, whereupon the bay widens out considerably into a deep expanse of water protected on all sides.

As the inner bays are so large, we will in general confine our remarks to entering and clearing in, leaving the question of where you might wish to moor within up to the individual skipper.

CAYS: SHALLOW INNER SOUNDS

The cays are similar to those on the south and northwest coasts, with the proviso that waters within the inner sounds here are usually relatively shallow. You should check the depths carefully before venturing inside for a long run through.

STRATEGY

Having rounded Punta Maisí, the prevailing winds and currents are with you all the way, and the shelters are spread out along easy runs. With any good downwind rig, you should have an exhilarating run along the coast, surfing along at top speed if

273

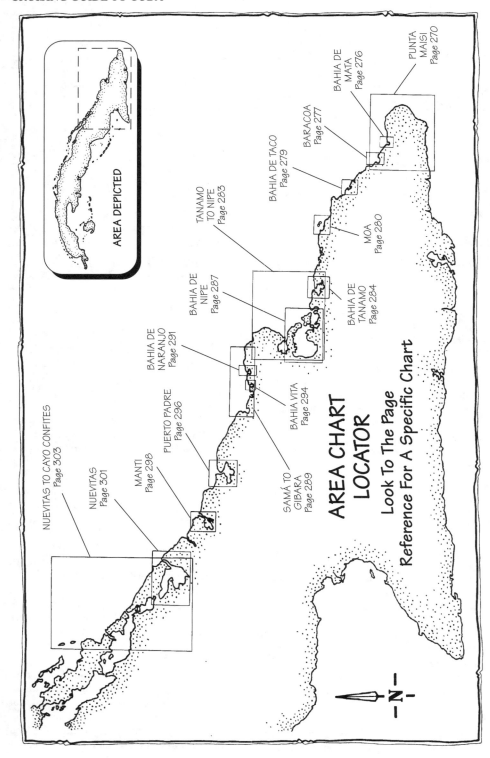

PUNTA
MAISI
Page 270

BAHIA DE
MATA
Page 276

BARACOA
Page 277

BAHIA DE TACO
Page 279

MOA
Page 280

TANAMO
TO NIPE
Page 283

BAHIA DE
NIPE
Page 287

BAHIA DE
TANAMO
Page 284

BAHIA DE
NARANJO
Page 291

BAHIA VITA
Page 294

PUERTO PADRE
Page 296

SAMÁ TO
GIBARA
Page 289

MANTI
Page 298

NUEVITAS
Page 301

NUEVITAS TO CAYO CONFITES
Page 303

AREA DEPICTED

AREA CHART
LOCATOR
Look To The Page
Reference For A Specific Chart

N

your vessel is fast enough. If the waves are small then you can pole-out the Genoa and gull-wing along, or even set a spinnaker if you have one. Exercise caution though if the wind is up and your boat is slow, as the swells can rise considerably and even swamp the vessel from behind. Under these conditions our lovely old trawler fishtails alarmingly as the swells overtake its seven-knot top speed and the autopilot clanks alarmingly trying to keep up with things. In this instance we find it best to hand-steer to ease the strain and to prevent any possible damage. A helmsman *anticipates, while* an autopilot merely *reacts* and thus needs huge steering-changes as the stern gets pushed round.

Once again you may come in over the wall if there is room and depth, but be careful about uncharted shoals, or even islands. We once did this stretch with old U.S. charts, and while they were more than adequate, there were a few notable errors calling for care just along the reef. If necessary, reread the early sections on navigating in coral.

Remember that a lot of the cays along here are quite shallow on the inside. There are lots of marked entrances and channels, but check your charts well to be sure about the depths. You may see the occasional medium to large fishing boat inside but most of these only draw about three-to-four feet, so the water may not be enough for a deep keel.

Despite this, the clarity of the water means that there really isn't much to worry the prudent mariner (as they're always called in the official warnings) and we always like to moor inside the reef whenever possible.

Watch out for those northerly stretches,

e.g., just west of the Bay of Nipe to Punta Lucrecia or around Cayo Romano where the current and prevailing winds strike more or less at right angles to the coast, and the swells can roll you unmercifully. If you have to tack out, then do it early in the day when the wind and waves are smaller.

GOING THE WRONG WAY

If you have been left with no choice but to make a west to east passage along this coast, all is not lost. Although nominally the winds and currents are in your face, there is a convenient counter-current close in. This is not always apparent, but when found, it can be a useful aid to what might otherwise be a painful beat into all the prevailing elements.

CHARTS

Again the best charts to have are the Cuban Government ICH series, but if coming up from the islands (as many are now doing) it is unlikely that these are available to you. Luckily there are a multitude of U.S. or Admiralty charts dealing with the heavily passaged Old Bahama Channel, the Florida Straits, and the areas between Crooked Island and Inagua in the Bahamas down to Haiti and Punta Maisí in Cuba.

Almost any of these will serve perfectly well as they cover the Cuban coastline along their bottom edges, and as the U.S. charts are easily available on order to anywhere in the West Indies, I shall give the requisite numbers for those too.

If you have none at all, then the reference chart opposite, dealing with the *eastern* half of this chapter shows where you may access my own sketches.

PUNTA MAISÍ TO BARACOA
CHART NOS. ICH 1134 OR 1133 (CUBAN) & DMA 26240 (U.S.)

Having rounded Punta Maisí the motion of the swells is likely to abate somewhat, your boat-speed will pick up a bit ,and it's an easy coastal passage west northwest for the remaining 20 miles.

Some five-to-six miles before reaching Baracoa however, there is one port you can

use. This is the port of Mata (see sketch on following page), the first of the smaller pocket-bays referred to above. Early morning views are pleasing, with mist pouring out of the valleys and it's worth a pause if you are not on any particular schedule, or if you just prefer to gunkhole awhile.

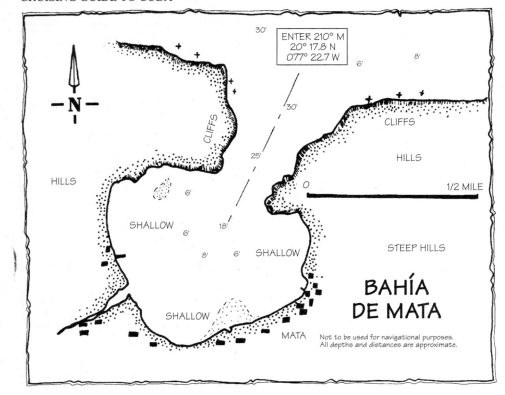

ENTER 210° M
20° 17.8 N
077° 22.7 W

BAHÍA
DE MATA

Not to be used for navigational purposes.
All depths and distances are approximate.

Westward from here you come to an escarpment covered with palms, and the bay of Miel (Honey Bay) opens up in front of you. The bay is large and open, with a good enclosed harbor serving the city which sprawls across the hillside behind. The port of Baracoa at the western end, is the best place to enter if you are passaging along the coast from the West Indies towards Havana.

BARACOA (OPPOSITE)

The city is recognizable from well out to sea by a peculiar flat-topped mountain further to the west. There is a modern stadium at the eastern end of the town, a long malecón (sea-wall), and a stately yellow ochre building looking out from the hillside near the harbor.

Coming from the east, aim more or less directly at El Yunque (the flat mountain visible) and this will take you to the harbor (20°21.2/074°30.1) at the west end of town. When you see everything all lined up, steer 245° M towards the inshore marker (a metal post) and remember to keep to port, closer to the large steel hulk moored on that side. The hulk in fact marks one side of the harbor mouth and to that end should have a light mounted on its stern. But, having said all that, the last time I entered this harbor, not one single light was actually functioning at night, so don't depend on them too much. This problem may be corrected soon, but if not, the general directions still hold good.

Passaging up the island chain from the West Indies, this may well be your first Cuban port so you will not be familiar with the procedure, but never mind, it's more or less the same for those coming round from Santiago and not so different from any other island.

Just inside the mouth, on the left, there is a concrete dock serving the needs of the port with a mix of fishing and tug boats, with

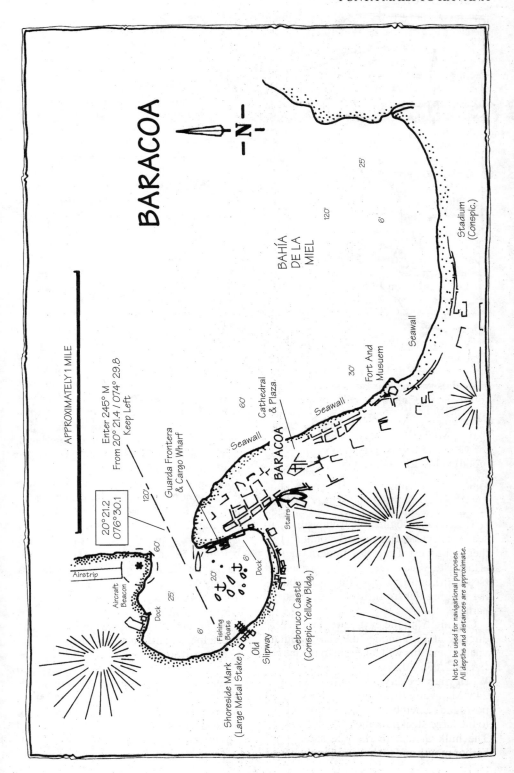

BARACOA

N

BAHÍA
DE LA
MIEL

APPROXIMATELY 1 MILE

Enter 245° M
From 20° 21.4 / 074° 29.8
Keep Left

20°21.2
076°30.1

Guarda Frontera
& Cargo Wharf

Seawall

Seawall

Seawall

Seawall

BARACOA

Cathedral
& Plaza

Fort And
Musuem

Stadium
(Conspic.)

25'

120'

6'

30'

60'

120'

Stairs

Dock

20'

6'

6'

Aircraft
Beacon

25'

60'

6'

Fishing
Boats

Old
Slipway

Seboruco Castle
(Conspic. Yellow Bldg.)

Shoreside Mark
(Large Metal Stake)

Airstrip

Dock

Not to be used for navigational purposes.
All depths and distances are approximate.

277

perhaps a patrol boat thrown in for good measure.

Approach slowly, stopping close outboard of the moored vessels, and make your intentions clear by shouting over to the curious spectators. At this point there is likely to be a comedy of uniformed characters pulling shirts on, pointing in different directions, and calling out contradictory instructions. Unless obvious indications to the contrary, they are probably telling you to anchor somewhere close off the wharf and to await boarding by customs and immigration officers who will be brought out by a press-ganged fisherman in a skiff.

This port can handle international arrivals, so it makes a convenient place to enter from the other Caribbean islands. Formalities are much as anywhere else in Cuba (see Havana sections on entry procedures), and as the port is well-used by foreign yachts there should be someone who has the requisite experience to keep things simple. As elsewhere, you should try to keep things light and stress that you are continuing onwards after a day or two in town.

For those who are already legally in Cuba, your existing Guia de Recala should show your itinerary so there won't be a huge delay before you are requested to moor amongst the other fishing boats some 80 yards off in 20 feet of water. As the port is used by many small fishing boats they sometimes like you to hang a line back from your stern to another more tightly moored vessel to prevent you swinging too much at anchor. In fact my recent experiences here even involve the officials themselves rowing out and setting our second anchor for us. This extremely helpful attitude bodes well for future relations with cruisers.

To go ashore later you may leave your dinghy over by the steps on the inner end of the dock where swimming children will pester you with questions until chased off by the fishermen.

Entry into the tiny port area is restricted so don't worry, your dinghy will be safe while you set off up the hill directly in front of the gate. Don't forget to politely notify the officials at the post just outside that you are visiting their town. It isn't strictly necessary, but it makes a good impression on everyone and they'll just smile delightedly and give you directions to all the sites of interest.

THE OLDEST COLONIAL TOWN IN CUBA

Baracoa was originally founded in 1510 by Diego Velasquez who established seven garrison towns to defend the coast of Cuba, but there is also some discussion that Columbus first landed here when he discovered Cuba in 1492. Whatever, it is still the oldest colonial town in the Americas and its relative isolation from the rest of the country has enabled it to retain a certain discreet charm and a style of its own.

The area surrounding the city specializes in the production of cocoa and coconuts. Although the town is supposedly famous for its chocolate you will sometimes be hard pressed to find any, even if some visitors report that this shortage is seasonal.

The main vantage point in the city is the castle you saw when coming in (the yellow-ochre building on the hillside), and called at various times Santa Barbara or Seboruco Castle. Well worth a visit, this building was originally constructed in the 1700's, was restored early this century with the help of American engineers, and following further restoration is now a splendidly situated hotel. The castle bar on the top floor is one of the most pleasant places in Cuba to spend a few hours, providing marvellous views of both the city and the mountains surrounding the bay. Over to the west you can see El Yunque, the flat-topped mountain which marks Baracoa. Also plainly visible is the exciting "Sleeping Beauty" or *La Bella Durmiente*, a remarkable formation of hills which look exactly like their description. Downstairs, alongside the pool, there is an excellent restaurant where I remember having grouper with an unlikely but delicious tomato and coconut sauce — the cost: a well-spent $5.00.

At night the local students gather near the main square in the lovely narrow streets to listen to music. Speakers are set up in windows and the sound reverberates off stone columns supporting the overhanging eaves. You'll have to help "practice my English" here too.

A walk east along the seafront/malecón will take you to the town museum and fort. Nearby there is a statue of Columbus looking remarkably like Klaus Kinski, who himself acted as a conquistador during his distinguished film career (shame on you if you aren't familiar with his work).

In a rather grisly claim to fame, Hatuey, the Indian chieftain from Hispanola, who spearheaded the resistance to Spanish occupation was burned at the stake in Baracoa. Legend has it that when offered the chance to repent his pagan ways and be baptized, he asked whether there were Christians in heaven. When told that there were, and that he could join them, he chose the flame as a pagan instead.

Later they made up for this indignity by naming the national beer after him.

Across from your anchorage to the north-western side of the harbor is the airstrip and a tourist hotel easily accessible by dinghy to the waterside bar. Here you may experience a rather undistinguished meal or the tepid delights of the disco. There is a hard-currency shop too, so if you need to reprovision you might be able to get a few of the more unnecessary items which have found their way down here.

DEPARTING FROM BARACOA

Departing Baracoa could not be more simple. If you have been suitably pleasant to all concerned at entry you will have received prior permission and it may not be necessary to do more than wave and set off. Otherwise it's probably simpler to row your documents over to the dock for inspection and to collect your despacho... What you get depends on who you get.

NORTHWESTWARD ROUTE
CHART NOS.ICH 1133 (CUBAN) & DMA 26240 (U.S.)

Between Baracoa and the nickel-mining port of Moa (30 miles) the course is purely visual and the coast is free of any dangers except where the reefs begin to extend offshore after Punta Guarica. Prior to that however there is a small cove at Maraví (enter 224° M from 20°26.3N / 074°32.9W) which could provide an idle shallow anchorage if you so desired.

Along this portion of the coast there are a multitude of little inlets generally accessible and accompanied by tiny beaches fringed with coconut trees and inviting slow passages. If you do enter, just be on the lookout for nets which are often strung across the entrances.

Another excellent bay is that of Taco: Enter obliquely along 255°M from position 20°31.7N / 074°39.SW to avoid the shallows then turn south southwest when just between the outer points of the entry channel.

Scuba dives along the coast here are interesting for the evidence they will provide of the rapid growth of barnacles acquired in Santiago harbor, and this is probably the first time you'll have the opportunity to clean them off the propeller or hull. If so, do it now, before they've grown accustomed to your place. My dive-logs also note persistent thermoclines, causing

Not to be used for navigational purposes.
All depths and distances are approximate.

279

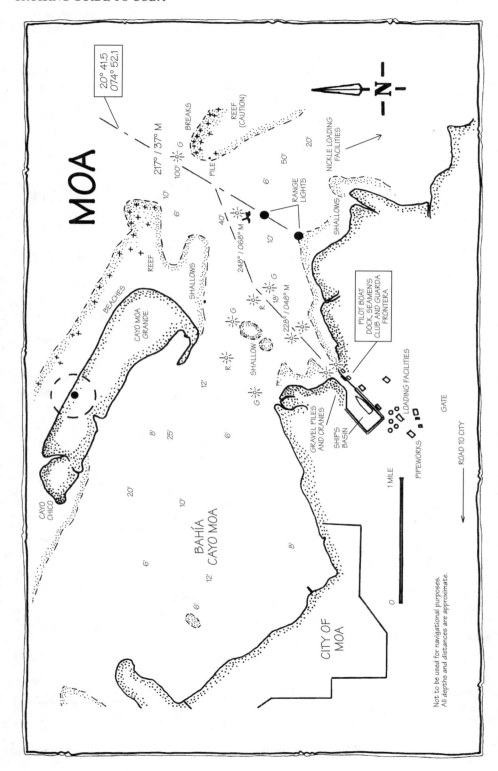

MOA

20° 41.5
074° 52.1

217° / 37° M

REEF (CAUTION)

BREAKS

PILE

100' G

NICKLE LOADING FACILITIES

20'

50'

6'

RANGE LIGHTS

248° / 068° M

40'

10'

SHALLOWS

10'

BEACHES

REEF

SHALLOWS

6'

10'

6'

G

18' G

228° / 048° M

R

SHALLOW

G

R

G

CAYO MOA GRANDE

12'

6'

PILOT BOAT DOCK, SEAMEN'S CLUB AND GUARDA FRONTERA

LOADING FACILITIES

GRAVEL PILES AND CRANES

SHIP'S BASIN

PIPEWORKS

GATE

ROAD TO CITY

CAYO CHICO

8'

25'

20'

10'

6'

BAHÍA CAYO MOA

12'

6'

8'

6'

1 MILE

0

CITY OF MOA

Not to be used for navigational purposes.
All depths and distances are approximate.

ripples in the visibility underwater as light is refracted by temperature changes at depth.

Another feature of the coastline here, is the amount of floating coconuts; while, in the spring, you see large tree trunks washed out from the rivers and floating just on the surface. A gentle tapping on the hull may be perfectly all right, but a solid thump may call for a closer inspection.

As you pass Punta Guarnica near the Bay of Moa, you'll begin to notice wrecks and associated bits of steel strewn about, so treat the reefs with caution and hang a bit further out. The lights along the coast are set back about a half-mile from the reef. At night keep away from them rather than being drawn to them like a moth to a flame. Large chimneys ashore on the other side of the reef will indicate the bay and nickel-processing facilities of Moa.

MOA

Note: Moa is a strange, oddly "sci-fi" place, quite unlike the more normal Cuban ports, and with few casual visitors. Entering here with a private boat can perplex some officials and the unfamiliar procedures may sometimes lead to a more intrusive search than you are accustomed to along the same coast.

Remember that it is a tricky entrance, with the harbor not obviously evident without some advice, a good local chart, and of course this guide. Once inside the bay, heading too far west towards the city itself is going to run you aground.

Do not approach the outer mark from due east as there is a reef (marked by a stake) close by on that side, but enter from a position approximately 20°41 .5N / 074°52.1W, well outside the green marker, and go in along a course of around 217° M along the line of the range marks.

Just under half a mile past the green outer mark, or around 20°40.8N / 074°52.5W, turn 248°M aiming between the two red/green marks marking the channel to the harbor, and a mile on from that take up a course of 228° M into the enclosed docking area. Along the way you will notice that the waters have changed from a clean transparent blue to a foreboding satanic red, stained by oil and the scummy overflow from the nickel plants southeast within the bay.

Inside the narrow docks you will be expected to come alongside a rickety wooden affair usually used by pilot boats and close at hand to a disused seaman's club. Here you will be boarded by the local officials.

It is a fair distance into town so you will have to request a call to the taxi dispatcher from any of the officials or pilots. While you wait you can look over at the mosquito-plagued firing-range close by the ruined Seaman's Club. Boldly displayed is a message from the President (El Comandante) who lists among the prerequisites to be a good soldier, "Learn to shoot, and shoot well."

If you have ever seen the classic film "Soylent Green" you will be familiar with the environment here. The city is based around the extraction of minerals, and the associated plumbing is a feature of the place. Huge leaking pipes along the roadsides hiss and bubble, oozing green slime and weird fumes from every joint all the way into town.

In the darkness around the gate, small groups of predatory girls await sailors from the ore-transports and the whole scene is one of unrelieved bleakness as the city itself looms ominously ahead, with dreary concrete apartment blocks and unlit streets. If tempted to the darkened hotel in town be careful about what you eat and stick to the

Ships entering Moa.

vegetables at all costs.

If all this suggests a certain jaundiced view of the place, apparently l am not alone. I have also heard tales suggesting that Cuban engineers have been known to sacrifice their careers rather than serve time there!

Finally, just to make it worse, the Je-Jenes (no-see-ums) around your dock are the worst in Cuba and are particularly active at dawn as you hurry to clean your boat of the gritty crud that has dropped from the sky overnight. Use the hosepipe ashore to clean off the decks, grab your papers, head 048°M dead center through the buoys (very important), and clear out of the dread place.

Of course, as a counterpoint, the pilots stationed there were extremely nice to us while we were there. They even went to the extent of establishing radio contact with us the first time we entered, preventing us from getting into trouble in the shallow bits after they noticed we had strayed too far westwards in the bay.

ROUTE TO BAHIA NIPE
CHART NOS ICH 1132 (CUBAN) & DMA 26240 (U.S.)

It's another 40 miles to the enormous bay of Nipe. You must remain well off land for the first 10 miles, but having cleared those reefs you can come in a little closer (about 3/4-mile offshore) along the edge of the reefs. This particular stretch of coastline seems to have claimed a fair share of wrecks, so don't let your guard drop. Fishermen in fact can sometimes be seen wading right out to the reefs where they cast their nets by hand.

You must also be aware of the nets which are usually strung along the shallow western gaps through the Moa reef (around 075°02.5W) or where the view changes to rolling countryside sometimes more reminiscent of England than Latin America.

The possibilities for diving along the wall here are endless and from the deck you can clearly see the bottom at 75 feet, so if you have time then take the opportunity. If you prefer to cruise uninterrupted you can remain about 100 yards off the reefs in about 30 feet while looking at the gorgeous beaches inside. It's a bit smoother too, as the larger swells are calmed by the presence of the wall below.

Before you reach the bay of Nipe there are a couple of other large bays worthy of note (see opposite and overleaf).

Northeast coast inlet.

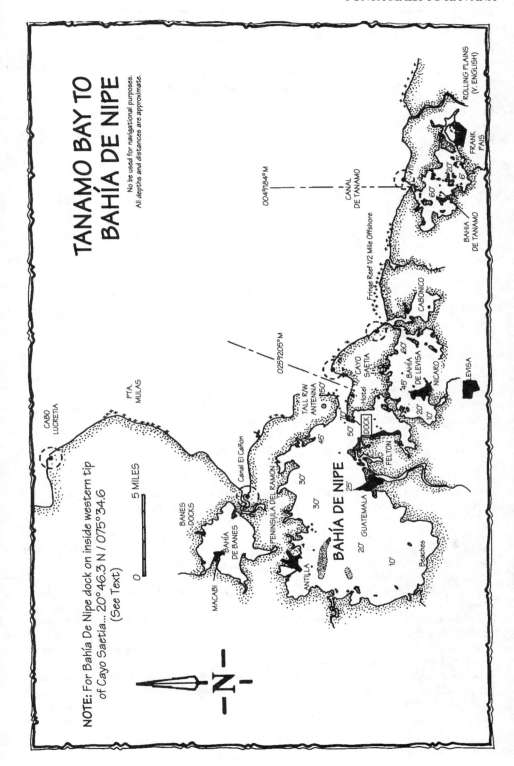

TANAMO BAY TO
BAHÍA DE NIPE

No be used for navigational purposes.
All depths and distances are approximate.

NOTE: For Bahía De Nipe dock on inside western tip
of Cayo Saetia... 20°46.3 N / 075°34.6
(See Text)

0 5 MILES

N

CABO
LUCRETIA

PTA.
MULAS

Canal El Cañon

BANES
DOCKS

BAHÍA
DE BANES

MACABI

ANTILLA

PENINSULA DEL RAMON

30'

30'

45'

50'

BAHÍA DE NIPE

20'

10'

Beaches

GUATEMALA

25'

FELTON

DOCK

Hotel

TALL R/W
ANTENNA

150'

70'

CAYO
SAETIA

45'

BAHÍA
DE LEVISA

NICARO

20'

10'

LEVISA

60'

CABONICO

0259/205° M

Fringe Reef 1/2 Mile Offshore

0049/184° M

CANAL
DE TANAMO

BAHÍA
DE TANAMO

60'

20'

6'

9'

FRANK
PAIS

ROLLING PLAINS
(V. ENGLISH)

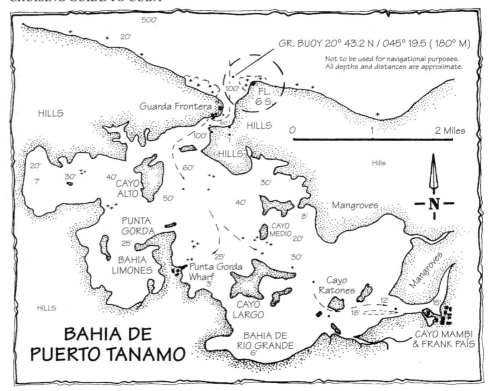

GR. BUOY 20° 43.2 N / 045° 19.5 (180° M)

Not to be used for navigational purposes.
All depths and distances are approximate.

BAHIA DE
PUERTO TANAMO

TANAMO

About 14 miles east of Nipe is the truly gorgeous bay of Tanamo, just as enclosed, and well-marked all the way inside. To enter, pass west of the green mark at (20º43.2N / 075º19.5W) avoiding the reef and its obligatory wreck. The deep channel here is about 300 yards wide, and the range marks can be followed past the high watchtower and through the steep-sided entrance into a large bay. There is a Guarda Frontera post just round the corner where you can either hook up to a permanent mooring, or if there's room, go directly alongside the small dock in 13 feet.

In my experience, formalities here are conducted with speed and efficiency, but if there is a delay it may be amusing to notice the variety of transports utilized by the Guarda Frontera to arrive at the dock. They may have to be called from their duties in the nearby vegetable gardens where corn, beans, goats and pigs coexist comfortably. The last time we parked here, the guard arrived on a splendidly saddled horse, smartly dressed in green uniform, polished boots and pistol.

Past the cay on the left (Juanillo) this beautiful bay is now open to you, with channels either side of the cay immediately in front. If you wish to go ashore at a dock then head 154°M towards a saddle-shaped cay one and a half miles away whereupon a file of markers will take you further east towards Cayo Mambi. This serves the small sugar town of Frank Pais in the southeast. The dock here is in a state of ill-repair, so if you prefer, you may turn off to the right as you near the markers and approach the dock on the southern side of the bay off Punta Gorda.

Outer Bays: A distance of nine miles past the entrance to Bahia Tanamo and only five miles before Nipe is the common entrance (at 075°28.3W) to the bays of Levisa and Cabonico.

Having come in through the entrance, the channel forks. The right branch takes you southwest into the bay of Levisa with the town of Nicaro, and the left passage goes east into Cabonico.

Nicaro is situated three miles southwest of the entrance and has a couple of wharfs, but unfortunately navigation within the large bay outside of the port limits is limited regarding civilian vessels and you might have to argue with the Guarda Frontera at the entrance to move about freely.

The eastern bay, Cabonico is somewhat encumbered by unmarked shallows and coral heads to within a couple of feet of the surface but excellent shelter is nevertheless to be had, especially at the entrance. The coasts inside this bay are steep and rocky with yellow cliffs scattered about and the main evidence of inhabitation is along the entrance canal.

BAHIA DE NIPE

This is a "must" stop along the way. Typical in its shape if not its sheer size, this is the biggest pocket-bay in Cuba, and containing at least 50 square miles is easily large enough to have its own weather-system. My ship's log records the remark that if you can get into trouble coming in here you shouldn't have left home!

The entrance, 1.5 miles wide, is marked by a large light-pylon on the eastern side and there are range marks taking you through 206°M from approximately 20°48.5N / 075°32.0W.

There is a dock and some tiki-huts forming a tourist complex along the beaches on the eastern side of the channel but you can visit these later.

First you have to clear in, so follow the marks round to the west, swing south past the patrol boats moored there, and come all the way round the corner to the dock at position (20°46.4N / 075°34.6W) on the southern (inner) side of the promontory at Cayo Saetía.

Clearing in will take place here and should be a relatively painless process, assisted by staff from the tourist complex. After the formalities have been completed you may well be coaxed into an old Chinese army jeep and transported at breakneck speed up the hill.

The road will take you past a camp where Cuba's Young Pioneers come to learn farming techniques (looks rather fun, what with clay ovens and so on) and up to the complex of cabanas and the hotel-bar at the top of the hill.

Peculiarly, Cayo Saetia is stocked with exotic animals from Africa (perhaps trophies from the Mozambique adventures of the eighties); and the holiday resort there follows the same theme, with stuffed animals (even a shark) in the lobby. The buildings are deliberately rustic in style and the menu is the most varied and best cooked we've experienced in Cuba. All on board our vessel regard it as one of the nicest places to stop in the whole island; and with luck, the curse of officially decreed staff-turnover has not yet affected the wonderful atmosphere.

TOUR THE BAY AT YOUR LEISURE

This beautiful bay is far too large for me to give a thorough guide to the cruising areas within its boundaries, so use the docks as your base and wander as you see fit. By land, tours to all parts of the area are available here and they even go to the extent of arranging trips for the hunting, shooting, fishing set if that sort of thing is your bag.

When mooring alongside the docks for any length of time remember that

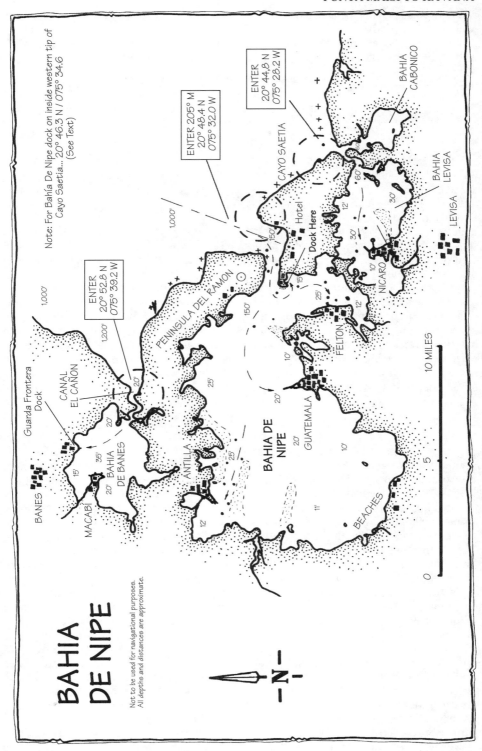

BAHIA
DE NIPE

Not to be used for navigational purposes.
All depths and distances are approximate.

-N-

Note: For Bahia De Nipe dock on inside western tip of
Cayo Saetia... 20° 46.3 N / 075° 34.6
(See Text)

ENTER 205° M
20° 48.4 N
075° 32.0 W

ENTER
20° 44.8 N
075° 28.2 W

ENTER
20° 52.8 N
075° 39.2 W

BAHIA
CABONICO

BAHIA
LEVISA

LEVISA

NICARO

CAYO SAETIA

Hotel

Dock Here

PENINSULA DEL RAMON

FELTON

GUATEMALA

BAHIA
DE NIPE

BEACHES

ANTILLA

MACABÍ

BAHIA
DE BANES

BANES

Guarda Frontera
Dock

CANAL
EL CAÑON

1,000'

1,200'

1,000'

150'

150'

60'

30'

30'

30'

15'

12'

12'

12'

10'

10'

10'

10'

11'

20'

20'

20'

20'

20'

20'

25'

25'

25'

25'

15'

15'

35'

0   5   10 MILES

287

the tour-boats serving the area use them as well, so make arrangements accordingly.

I have read somewhere that sharks abound in the bay, but repeated questioning elicited only puzzled looks. Certainly apart from the dusty and rather unhappy-looking inhabitant of the lobby we've seen none while swimming in the crystal waters here.

ROUTE TO BOCA DE SAMÁ AND NARANJO (35 MILES)
CHART NOS. ICH 1132 (CUBAN) OR DMA 27040 (U.S.)

Leave early to lessen the effects of the winds which are going to be broadside to your northerly course for the first 20 miles. At Mulas point there is a large observation station rather like an airport control tower, and a large iron wreck ashore, but the

waves do tend to calm a bit as you come round Cabo Lucretia. There is a beautiful lighthouse on the point here comprising a tall white brick tower. Below stands a white building dressed up with pink columns and what appear to be minarets on the corners. It's a lovely sight.

You can pass close to the picturesque lighthouse if the waves are calmed sufficiently, but take note of yet another wreck northwest of the light. A desperately sad sight this is, bolt upright sitting on the reef and pointing out to sea as if giving one last dying effort to get back home.

You can coast along some 200 yards offshore now in 300 feet of water, passing uninhabited wooded countryside, low green hills, and the delightful entrance to the Samá Bay with its high escarpments to both sides.

BOCA DE SAMÁ

This excellent harbor can be recognized by the massive granite outcrops on either side of the entrance (175°M and 21°07.3N / 075°46.3W). On the western side, there is a Guarda Frontera post, comprising of a few white concrete buildings, a watchtower, and of course, the ubiquitous searchlight. Next to these is the large pylon light erroneously marked on some charts as being on the eastern side — it is not.

Just inside the mouth, on the same western bank, there is a collection of buildings with a floating dock extending out at right angles to the wind and waves, and another smaller, more rudimentary, wooden landing a few yards further on. With inexorable logic, the ramp which hinges the floating affair has been damaged by the elements and the dock was unserviceable in 1996. Perhaps it will have been repaired (or better still, repositioned) when you are visiting. There is, in any case, some 10-12 feet of water at the end.

Whatever, if it has not been repaired, there is about eight feet of water at the nearby wooden dock where you may want to stop temporarily. There is always a lot of (rather aimless) activity onshore close by, which means that someone will soon call the officials down to your boat. The dock is somewhat rickety, and sometimes a Cuban tourist boat uses it as a base, so after your paperwork has been completed, there are a half-dozen permanent moorings which might be more attractive. These moorings, some 50 yards off, will also allow you to swing with the currents rather than remaining broadside to them. On the opposite side of the bay, there is a small sandy beach, where local tourists and pleasure seekers swim and play, but there are few if any buildings.

The community here is a neat collection of yellow and white houses halfway up the

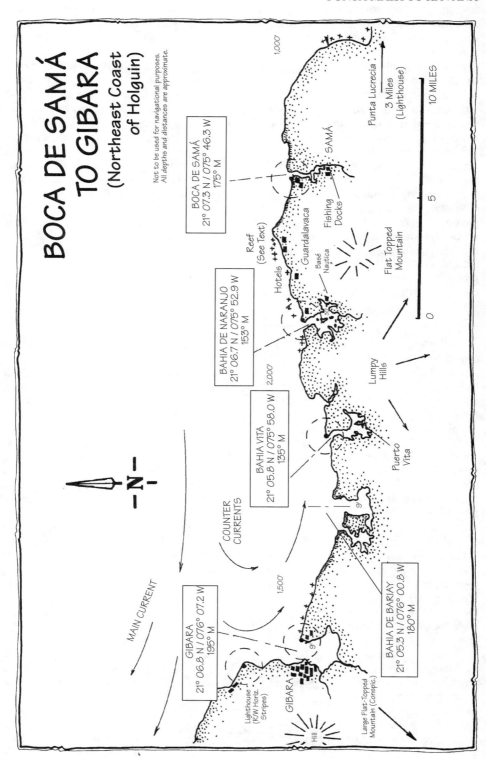

BOCA DE SAMÁ TO GIBARA
(Northeast Coast of Holguin)

Not to be used for navigational purposes.
All depths and distances are approximate.

BOCA DE SAMÁ
21° 07.3 N / 075° 46.3 W
175° M

BAHIA DE NARANJO
21° 06.7 N / 075° 52.9 W
153° M

BAHIA VITA
21° 05.8 N / 075° 58.0 W
135° M

GIBARA
21° 06.8 N / 076° 07.2 W
195° M

BAHIA DE BARIAY
21° 05.3 N / 076° 00.8 W
180° M

-N-

Reef
(See Text)

Hotels

Guadalavaca

Basé
Nautica

Fishing
Docks

SAMÁ

Punta Lucrecia
3 Miles
(Lighthouse)

Flat Topped
Mountain

10 MILES

5

0

1,000'

2,000'

Lumpy
Hills

Puerto
Vita

9'

COUNTER
CURRENTS

MAIN CURRENT

1,500'

9'

Lighthouse
(R/W Horiz.
Stripes)

GIBARA

Hill

Large Flat-Topped
Mountain (Conspic.)

289

incline on the western side of the bay. Close to the dock, just past the gatehouse, there is a small stone floor with a modest kiosk/ shop alongside. You can buy freshly squeezed lime juice for some 50 centavos; or flat, dried casava bread with perhaps a tomato, for 80 centavos. It was here, when indulging in some light discussion about the nature of things, that the proprietor — a gentle ex-geography teacher — offered this fascinating viewpoint. "We are at the same time," he said, " both spectators and victims".

And he's right, you know.

Walking up the hill, past the turnoff to the Guarda Frontera buildings, will take you to a roadway which leads down from the summit, and runs alongside the bay to the inner extreme. This is a pleasant walk, with some pretty views, and a half hours exercise will take you to the "combinado" where the

local fishing fleet moors to unload its catch. This end of the bay is really well protected from any weather conditions, and is certainly useful in a storm.

As usual in Cuba, it is best to arrange for clearance well in advance (the day before is always a good bet). If the appointed time comes and there is no official to clear you out, then it means a trip back up the hill to the post . This is not perhaps the best way to start a days journey.

Nevertheless, I once met the official coming the other way and we did all the paperwork seated comfortably on a park-bench off to the side of the road. So civilized was this that I forgave all in a heartbeat, and even felt a bit ashamed about my ill-natured impatience. We were after all, in a beautiful bay on a beautiful morning, and it really wasn't far (six miles) to the next stop at the Bahia de Naranjo.

NARANJO

You'll know you're coming up on the bay of Naranjo when you see the Mediterranean-style white and terra-cotta hotel buildings along the beaches at 075°50.5W, and the conspicuous flat-topped hill behind them.

The beaches here are totally protected from the surf by a reef, which along with a couple of yellow dive-moorings, has one or two shallow breaks directly in front of the hotels.

Just to the west of these hotels however, there is an entry at 075°50.2W, and you can get behind it to visit the beaches by dinghy or shallow-draft vessel.

Further along, very close to the bay itself, and past a line of cliffs which separate them, there is another, larger, group of hotel buildings at 075°52.2W. With an entry from the northwest, this offers a more convenient dinghy entry to the beaches.

Of all the marinas and basé nauticas in Cuba, this one seems to have undergone the most improvement over the last couple of years. While the facilities are not perhaps as sophisti-

cated as those in Havana, Varadero and the like, it is certainly right up there with regards to the attitude of the excellent staff whom I cannot praise enough. Compared with the poor service evident in some places (see Hotel Colony/Siguanea and Santiago for recent examples) this pleasant stop-off will be a welcome breath of fresh air. The marina is run by Gaviota, in contrast to the usual Puerto Sol operations elsewhere.

Also on offer here is an good harbor, easily entered and well protected from all angles; plus some of the best views and beaches on the northeast coast. Transport to interior cities such as Holguin (capital of the province) can also be arranged quickly and conveniently at any of the four or five well run and maintained hotels nearby. If you are a diver, the waters offshore are

crystal clear over the reef, and indigo-blue over the wall.

Make a wide arc outside the silver pylon-light on the point and (allowing for a strong current which may sometimes push you off to the right) come in 153°M past the lighted outer R/G

BAHÍA DE NARANJO

153° / 333°M

21° 06.7
075° 52.9

NOTE: Watch For
Dive Moorings

Reef

Dinghy Route
To Beaches & Hotels

Hotels

G

R

25'

Punta
Sotaventa

40'

Rock Face

Low
Headlands

R

G

Aquarium
Wharf

40'

Shallow

BAHÍA
DE NARANJO

20'

Anchorage

Nets

25'

30'

26'

Marina
Dock

12'

Oyster Beds
And Nets

Route
To
Hotels

Bridge

O   1 MILE

Not to be used for navigational purposes.
All depths and distances are approximate.

- N -

291

marks at 21°06.7N /075°52.9W. The channel is some 150 yards wide, and there are further (unlit) markers inside.

The channel passes east of the restaurant/aquarium complex in the center of the channel. There are rumored plans for this complex (*el Acuario*) to become the marina, but so far they have not come to fruition and they do not take yachts at time of writing. Doubtless times will change, but for the present, unless otherwise indicated, you should proceed past the complex to starboard and continue on into the widening bay.

The channel is wide, and is marked all the way to the end of the southeast branch at 21°05.7N / 075°52.0W (see sketch).

You will be required to clear in at the Basé Nautica there, a colorful concrete wharf with corrugated iron roofs. If there is space, you may be allowed to dock alongside, in which case be careful as the dock is used by a variety of local fishing and scuba boats. Whatever, there will be plenty of willing hands to assist and there is about 12 feet of water at dockside. Sailboats should note however, that only the outer end is available for their use as the roof (some 30 feet high) extends over the side berths. Usually however, the dock is heavily occupied, and if there is no room at the inn you will need to move to the unobstructed area northwest of the wharf where you can anchor in 25 feet. The holding is good, so once the anchor is set you shouldn't have any trouble from the multidirectional squalls which sometimes affect the area in the springtime.

In the event that you are anchored, a small boat will come out to you for documentation. Owing to the increasing popularity of the bay, you will find that formalities are quickly dealt with, but the port is not really set up to handle international arrivals, as officials may well have to come from far afield.

The local representative will sort you out with a visit from the Provedor if you need any stores. Fuel (55 cents/litre), good water, and ice are also available here, so ask about these as soon as possible so that arrangements can be made. Fuel is delivered to dockside by a small truck and siphoned into your tanks if needed.

An interesting excursion can be made to the entrance to the bay where the Acuario plays host to various marine shows. Here, you may attend the dolphin display, watch an aged sea-lion work for his living, or dine at a restaurant. This freestanding structure, is connected to the mainland by a series of bridges, but you may find it more convenient to visit by dinghy.

If you have a fast dinghy, then it might well be more fun (or more convenient) to go round to the hotel beaches by passing outside of the bay and cutting back inside the reef at the most westerly of the entrances described in the opening paragraphs of this section.

If however, you wish to visit the resorts

by road, it's a five-minute ($4) journey in a taxi called for you by the official on the dock. There you will be startled by the first truly international quality facilities since Santiago, with restaurants, bars and satellite televisions. Of course, if you have become accustomed to patronizing local (peso) restaurant-bars be prepared for the shock of international prices.

The hotels, frequented by tanned Germans and Italians who lounge (startlingly, to a visiting North American) topless on the beach, have phones, faxes, post offices, water sports, scuba diving, rental scooters and transport. Just don't assume that the DHL or other special delivery signs on the post office wall have any real significance.

Interestingly enough, alongside the first hotel complex is a landing ground from which, large Russian helicopters will take you into the heart of the county on excursions to places like Santiago, Holguin and the like. Tours on these droopy-rotored monsters cost about $100, but there are equivalent road trips for about half. Meals and refreshments are included.

Information about these and other tours can always be found pinned up in the hotel lobbies, alongside the advertisements for the nightly discos and of course the "animation".

Finally, upon your return to the dock, you will find a friendly welcome at a clean cabaña bar nearby. Answering a call of nature behind the booth, I remember seeing the the local alarm system hanging from a short trestle.

Painted bright red, this apparatus consists of, in order, an old fire extinguisher, a short length of railway line, an automobile wheel-rim, and a dangling iron rod on a rope.

An attached notice gives the instructions: In case of Vandalism, bang on the extinguisher "discontinuously". In case of Terrestial attack, bang on it continuously. The rail is to be beaten continuously in case of Fire, and finally if you are aware of a Chemical Attack, then ring the *wheel rim* continuously.

Yeah, like I'm going to stand there beating endlessly on a wheel rim, while the yellow cloud descends on me?

Not!

ROUTE WEST, TO PUERTO PADRE
CHART NOS. ICH 1131 (CUBAN) & DMA 27040 (U.S.)

This is a 40-mile run and if you don't think you can make the bay at Puerta Padre then there are alternative shelters along the route at Bahía Vita (sketch overleaf), Bahía Bariay, and the ancient city of Gibara (see earlier chart for all positions). Apart from the silty water issuing from the rivers, the waters along this coast are a clean, dark blue.

Along the way you will see evidence of an officially encouraged paranoia (it encourages patriotism apparently) in the form of clusters of concrete machine-gun emplacements on the beaches. This inevitably leads one to wonder about what these crumbling pillboxes were meant to repel. Modern warfare has long rendered them obsolete, and the threat of invasion may be less serious; but they remind us of a time the threat was very real.

**PREPARE FOR
STRONGER SWELLS**

The Old Bahama Channel narrows here, squeezing the flow of water unmercifully, and speeding it up with an accompanying strong wave-action. Consequently, there are always the chances of higher swells

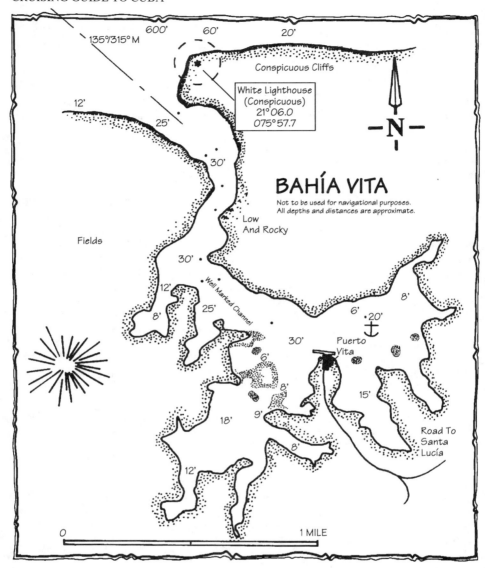

135°/315° M

600'   60'   20'

Conspicuous Cliffs

White Lighthouse
(Conspicuous)
21° 06.0
075° 57.7

12'

25'

30'

-N-

BAHÍA VITA

Not to be used for navigational purposes.
All depths and distances are approximate.

Low
And Rocky

Fields

30'

12'

Well Marked Channel

25'

8'

8'

6'

20'

8'

30'

Puerto
Vita

6'

8'

15'

18'   9'

8'

Road To
Santa
Lucía

12'

0   1 MILE

coming in to Gibara on the west of the one mile wide bay. The officials want you to dock on the west side, near the Guarda Frontera dock, but this exposes you to incessant swells. If you wish to stay any length of time then you really should argue for docking on the more sheltered east side. Nevertheless, as this now isolates you somewhat it may be better to do your exploring by land from a halt either side of this historic city.

Far behind the impressive seafront buildings and church cupolas marking the town you can see a flat-topped mountain. This , looking like a snapped off Grecian column, was probably the hill noted by Columbus when he first landed in Cuba, an honor later confused with (or high-jacked by) El Yunque at Baracoa (perhaps), and a point endlessly argued since then by the two cities. Mind you, there's one at Naranjo too, isn't there?

Once past Gibara, the terrain is dull and flat with little to note except lighthouses, and nothing in the way of refuge for the next 30 miles.

Another large pocket-bay with an entrance well marked and free of any significant obstruction until well inside. Enter along a course of 200°M between the outer red and green buoys aiming towards a sandy area fringed with palms then follow the marked channel through the neck and into the bay (See chart overleaf).

A point to be noted here, is that (along with the Nuevitas), this is a large port. We have been made welcome here certainly, but the facilities are not really set up to handle much in the way of yacht traffic. You'll have to be prepared to jostle for your own space if you play with the big boys.

If you do not intend to enter the bay, but rather merely need to shelter for the night, then clear in with the Guarda Frontera at the small community on the right as you come into the channel.

I have never had the slightest problem here, but recent reports suggest that on occasion the officials do not like you to anchor temporarily at the mouth. Nevertheless, if you stress that you don't want to go into the bay, then all should be well.

THE SUGAR TERMINAL

Official clearance procedures within the bay itself are done at the sugar terminal, so if heading there the Guarda Frontera might come out in a boat from their dock to put one of their number aboard. He will accompany you the rest of the way into Carupano where you must officially clear in no matter what your final destination is.

The Carupano sugar terminal is situated on Cayo Juan Claro some two miles south through the narrow channel and three quarters of a mile southwest as you come out into the bay itself.

As with the other major international ports along the northeast the harbor authorities monitor Channel 16 on the VHF.

In the absence of contrary instructions, go round to the western side of the island and proceed a little further south to the enormous concrete wharf-docking alongside where space allows.

The sugar loading facility is well maintained with several huge mobile cranes set along a wharf some 250 yards long and 10 feet high. The large black rubber fenders hanging down are set a bit high for the average yacht, so be careful to make suitable arrangements to avoid damage to your superstructure.

FACILITIES FOR
OCEAN-GOING VESSELS

The facilities here are really intended for large ocean going vessels so you may feel

dwarfed by the praying mantis cranes looming overhead and the 150-foot deep concrete apron. Nevertheless the officials will have had enough experience with foreign ships to deal with your needs perfectly adequately, and any further cruising inside the bay can be cleared with them. The port of Puerto Padre (population 23,000) lies about three and a half miles southwest of Carupano and counts on a couple of docks to handle the needs of passenger and fishing traffic. Note that there is always a stiff east northeast wind within the bay.

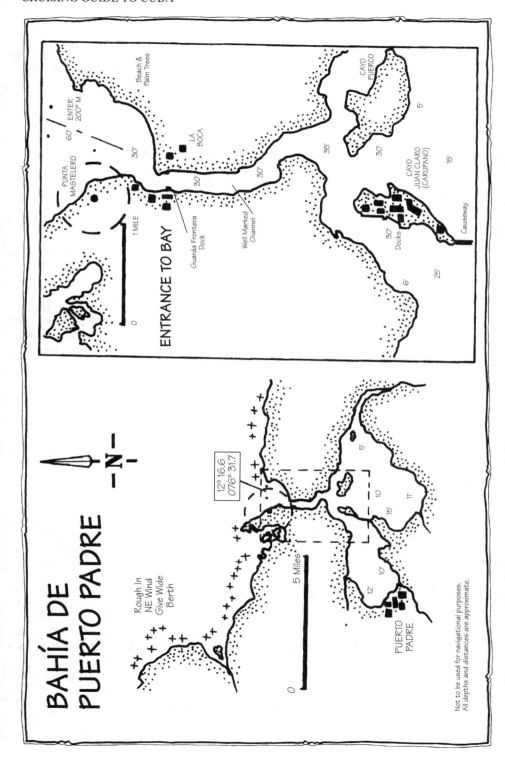

BAHÍA DE
PUERTO PADRE

-N-

Rough In
NE Wind
Give Wide
Berth

12° 16.6
076° 31.7

5 Miles

0

PUERTO
PADRE

12'

10'

15'

10'

11'

5'

Not to be used for navigational purposes.
All depths and distances are approximate.

ENTRANCE TO BAY

1 MILE

0

PUNTA
MASTELERO

ENTER
200° M

60'

30'

30'

Beach &
Palm Trees

LA
BOCA

Guarda Frontera
Dock

Well Marked
Channel

30'

30'

30'

35'

CAYO
PUERCO

5'

30'

CAYO
JUAN CLARO
(CARUPANO)

15'

Docks

30'

Causeway

6'

25'

REMAIN AT DOCKSIDE

The terminal is connected with the mainland and the town of Puerto Padre via a causeway so you may find it convenient to remain at the dockside and communicate by road. If so, be careful to keep your windows and doors closed against the constant sandstorm blowing off the apron and over your boat. Note that the oily fenders will foul your topsides too.

There is a seamans' club 200 yards away from the dockyard gates so it might fall to you to finally sample the dubious pleasures therein.

It consists of a small building with a bar, a small tacky hard-currency shop, and as is usual in such places, a few young ladies hanging out. They politely make their position quite clear from the start, but in fact are quite friendly even outside of their normal business relationships.

After the bar begins to pall, if you are especially interesting you may even get a lift across the causeway and into town; three to a motorbike! There you can continue carousing in local restaurant-bars until the dawn comes up.

A final point to note here is that the port is really geared towards ships rather than boats, so when leaving request your clearance papers well in advance and don't fret if they are late.

ROUTE TO MANATÍ & NUEVITAS (40 MILES)
CHART NOS. ICH 1131, 1130 (CUBAN) & DMA 27040 (U.S.)

If you are going direct to Nuevitas, then this is another long run, but it can be made possible in daylight by the prevailing winds and the currents which are being thoroughly squeezed into a venturi by the Great Bahama Bank just to the north. The swells, however, heap up uncomfortably at times, so relax in port if there is a depression in the offing.

There is an offshore reef just six miles west of the entrance to Puerto Padre bay, so give it a suitable berth by staying well out.

An additional advantage to going wide early is that it enables you to approach the entrance to Nuevitas from a more easterly direction rather than having to make a coastal passage broadside to the waves when they are at their height later on in the day.

If you favor a more relaxed approach to cruising, then the port of Manatí, some 16 miles west of Puerto Padre, makes a pleasant and convenient stopover along the route.

MANATÍ

There is a conical white lighthouse (FL12s.) on the western point at the half-mile wide entrance and a lighted buoy at the head of the channel. This large green outer mark is at position 21°23.5N/076°48.6W., and a course of 210°M will take you through to further R/G marks. Low cliffs line the entrance, with lots of abandoned buildings scattered untidily on the banks. At this point, depths will not drop below 25-50 feet.

Once into the channel and past the second green mark, there is a large sandbank on the western side to be avoided, so veer slightly to port (190°M) to the following red marks and do not head directly at the very large L-shaped dock plainly visible almost two miles in. Neither should you attempt to anchor north of the dock (La Gloria) on that side, but rather go past it and moor on the south side. This cargo dock, a substantial concrete structure with railway lines running along it, is simply too large to be of any use to a yacht. The protruding upper surfaces would be about level with your spreaders, it does however, provide shelter.

There is a small Combinado (fishing station and dry-dock) just south of the wharf, but it is also shallow nearby, so you will probably be better to drop the hook some 100 - 200 yards outboard of that in about nine feet.

The port serves the town of Puerto Manatí some eight-to-10 miles away and although it nomimally handles sugar and molasses,

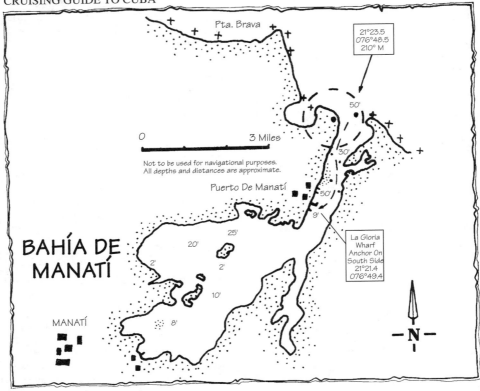

it is not a very busy place.

There are customs and immigration facilities here as well as the usual communications by road and telephone. In my experience, the formalities here are completed quickly, and you are allowed to wander around at will.

There is too, a dollar-shop, a bar, and a convenient train station at the foot of the large dock. This rather sweet little two-carriage affair makes the run to the nearby town of Manatí at 6 a.m., noon, and 6 p.m., belching smoke, tooting its horn, and clanking away madly.

NUEVITAS BAY

This is another large bay with the usual feature of a long narrow neck and a wide bay. There is an extensive hotel complex along the beautiful beach of Santa Lucía just east of the entrance, so if this is your fancy then stay at the mouth.

If you intend to enter the bay be prepared for a five-mile journey through the sheltered entrance channel before the enormous expanse of water opens before you, and there's another seven miles after that.

You should note that this is a large port, designed for ocean going ships, with few if any facilities for private yachts. You will be expected to moor alongside large wharves,

and may have to move if any cargo vessels are due. Conditions inside the large bay can also be blustery, causing a nasty chop from the east.

Nevertheless, I have moored there, and you may be interested in doing the same.

BEWARE OF AN OFFSHORE REEF

If the multitude of protruding wreckage hasn't already tipped you off, be advised that there is an offshore reef extending some 10-15 miles east from the entrance. A stake (077°04.2 W) near the western end might tempt you through, but the entrance it marks is a bit shallow. If you are coming

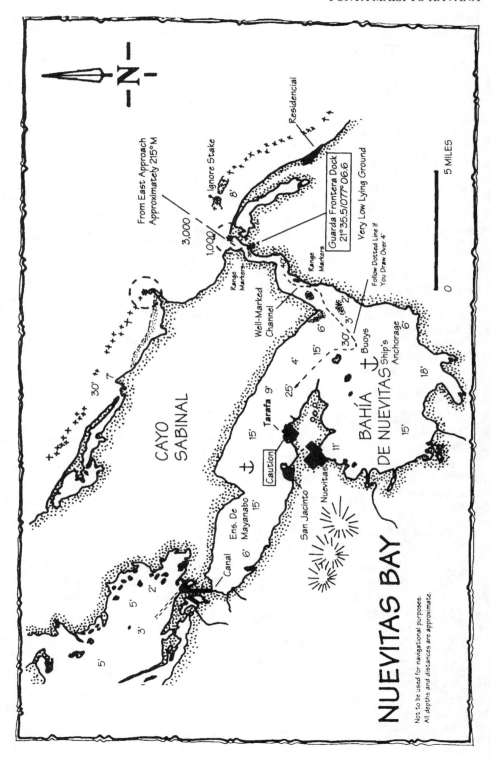

From East Approach
Approximately 215° M

Residencial

Ignore Stake

Guarda Frontera Dock
21°35.5/077° 06.6

3,000

1,000

8'

Very Low Lying Ground

Range
Markers

Range
Markers

Follow Dotted Line if
You Draw Over 4'

4'

Well-Marked
Channel

30'

3' 3'
6'

6'

30'

Buoys

2'

15'

4'

Ship's
Anchorage

6'

CAYO
SABINAL

7

30'

Tarafa 9'

25'

15'

18'

BAHÍA
DE NUEVITAS

15'

Caution

11'

Ens. De
Mayanabo

15'

15'

San Jacinto

Nuevitas

Canal

6'

5'

5'

3'

2'

5'

NUEVITAS BAY

Not to be used for navigational purposes.
All depths and distances are approximate.

0   5 MILES

299

from the east, continue on northwest about one-and-a-half miles and come in 215°M from anywhere around 21°37.2N / 077°05.7W towards the mark in the center of the channel. There are range-marks inside to guide you through, but you should remember to turn off to port (21°35.5N) where the Guarda Frontera have their dock. They will radio the port authorities inside Nuevitas if you are continuing in, and while awaiting permission to enter you can inspect one of the "Batmobiles" — fast Russian patrol-boats more reminiscent of a '57 Chevrolet, what with fins and things!

If you're going to be spending any time at the beaches, then it's probably better to stay at the mouth.

MOORING NEAR THE ENTRANCE

Moor about 200 yards downstream (south) of the Guarda Frontera post and well out of the way of any ships leaving at night. There are some rocky bits close inshore but you can easily find good anchorage in 12-14 feet. The tremendous flow through the channel at rise and fall of the tides will cause your propeller to rotate all night so don't be alarmed if you hear a

strange whirring sound from below, but despite this there is excellent snorkeling in the immediate area. As the floor is criss-crossed with old cables and other stuff you might also want to have a look at just where the anchor has come to rest if you want a quick getaway in the morning.

Charter boats which serve the tourist trade also use this area, so with luck there may even be the offer of a permanent mooring.

About four miles east of the mouth, some of the finest beaches in Cuba are to be found at Playa de Santa Lucía. There has been extensive hotel construction over the last few years, and these have become popular destinations for package tourists. Conditions here are much as described in the section on Naranjo.

You will need a fast dinghy to get to the hotel beaches (see sketch), inside the reef, but there are also some nice places just to the west of the mouth. The Guarda Frontera will have to be notified in advance.

CONTINUING INWARDS
TO TARAFA

You will be continuing to the port of Tarafa on the promontory splitting the bay, so proceed through the serpentine channel following a combination of range-marks and standard red/green buoys for at least four more miles. Large sugar-transporters use this port, so give them a wide berth.

Once into the bay, unless you have an exceedingly shallow draft, do not be tempted to cut directly over to the west where the port lies. Rather, follow the marks roughly southwest towards the ship's anchorage before making your cut, then come round north of the storage tanks and the jetty and continue two miles north northwest to the port itself.

At the northern end there are a series of quays pointing roughly north-northeast, with enough space between them to dock large ships. These wharfs can be rather crowded and if there is a large swell entering then they can become dangerous for a small boat, so give thought to your lines while awaiting the port authorities.

As with Puerto Padre, the officials here

Patrol boat: Nuevitas

will deal with your papers quickly even though they don't get many (if any) private boats. Once you are cleared-in, ask if you can move to more sheltered conditions and go round to the far side of the dockyard or to a position of your own choosing elsewhere in the bay.

Note: Be careful of the shallows close in to the rear of the wharf on the northwestern side of the dock complex. You may be advised to go round there, and it is more sheltered, but do not approach the extreme southwestern end of the dock.

We once had the experience of a so-called harbor pilot leaping aboard with an offer to show us the way to a convenient mooring. True, he may have been a pilot but he certainly didn't know much about that side, and because he was aboard I must have shamefully lowered my guard. Before we knew it we were hard aground, being pushed sideways by the swells further into the rubble below the surface there.

Luckily some Cuban divers with whom we'd been chatting while awaiting our inward clearance saw our predicament and came to our assistance. With everyone cursing and swearing in the water, we waded anchors far outboard with lines attached, and when tension on these didn't work we moved *all* equipment and baggage forward.

Lightening the stern had the desired effect, and reversing hard while hauling on the lines finally got us off, but it was a close run thing.

As you may well imagine, everyone involved partied late into the night, to the accompaniment of loud music and it was with serious hangovers that the next day was spent checking the hull below for damage.

As captain, needless to say, the fault was really mine for relaxing when someone supposedly "knew the way", and to this day I have been especially aware of the potential for this sort of thing happening again.

Guarda Frontera dock.

LOCATING THE HARBOR AUTHORITIES

Ashore, you can find the harbor authorities by leaving the port through the gate and heading up the hill directly in front of you. In a most impressive columned building at the summit you will find customs, immigration, and all other functionaries whom you might need. As this is a major port all the normal dockyard facilities and services are available.

There is another less Bacchanalian seaman's club to the east near the harbor offices if you need to purchase any stocks for the boat.

Interestingly enough, apparently Soviet missiles and technicians came ashore here in 1962 and in the park at the foot of the hill there is a plaque dedicated to the missile crisis.

This bay is the last of the pocket bays along the coast and continuing west will now take you immediately into the cays. There is a channel cut through the western side of the bay into the sound on that side, but the waters inside are rather shallow for general cruising so it may be better to take the outside route northwest.

At 50 miles, the next leg (to Cayo Confites) will require an early start if we are to have any chance of achieving our goal of a daylight run. To that end it is probably best to make arrangements with the harbor authorities to collect your despacho and clearance during the afternoon of the day before travelling. This way you can make the long journey out to the very entrance to the channel, rest up there, and depart at first light (or earlier) next day.

The need for this will be apparent when you realize that the authorities will probably be late in arriving with your papers, and the journey back across the bay is always into the teeth of a stiff east wind.

It is best to wait for winds less than 10-15 knots as the first stretch can be rough. The waves are not violent, but they heap up to alarming proportions as they

302

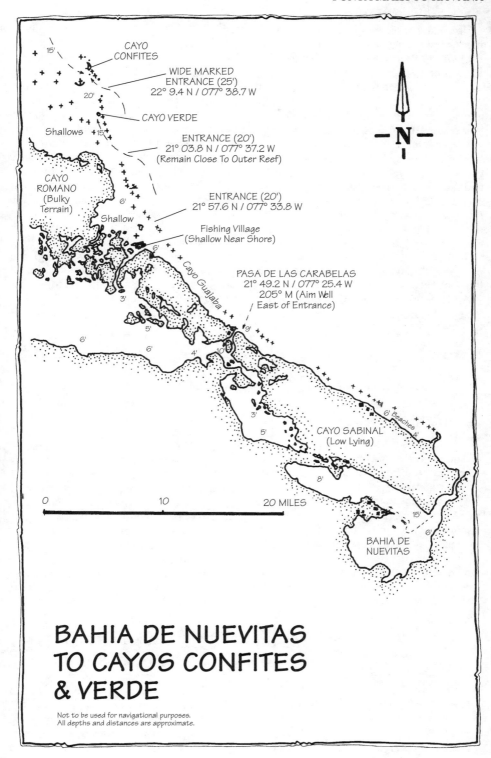

CAYO CONFITES

WIDE MARKED ENTRANCE (25')
22° 9.4 N / 077° 38.7 W

CAYO VERDE

15'

20'

Shallows

ENTRANCE (20')
21° 03.8 N / 077° 37.2 W
(Remain Close To Outer Reef)

CAYO ROMANO
(Bulky Terrain)

6'

Shallow

ENTRANCE (20')
21° 57.6 N / 077° 33.8 W

Fishing Village
(Shallow Near Shore)

Cayo Guajaba

PASA DE LAS CARABELAS
21° 49.2 N / 077° 25.4 W
205° M (Aim Well
/ East of Entrance)

3'

5'

6'

6'

4'

10'

9'

3'

5'

8'

CAYO SABINAL
(Low Lying)

6' Beaches

4'

0   10   20 MILES

15'

6'

BAHIA DE NUEVITAS

BAHIA DE NUEVITAS TO CAYOS CONFITES & VERDE

Not to be used for navigational purposes.
All depths and distances are approximate.

sweep along and lift the stern in a sickening corkscrew motion. Never mind, further on there will once again be protection and the neck of the Bahama Channel will eventually widen to decrease the flow speed.

There is some danger of being pushed inside of your desired course too, so keep alert against the possibility, and as before, if you're going to go out wide, then do it early.

West of Nuevitas Bay, the cays begin, so from here on we will have to adopt a different philosophy regarding the reef, the wall, and the weather. The water here is usually crystal clear, so where possible, a smoother passage can safely be found either inside the reef, or at least just above the wall (see Chapter 3 for this feature).

Shelter too, can be found overnight, by passing in through the reef into the sound or the gaps between cays.

An early example of this would be the Pasa de Carabelas, 22 miles west of Nuevitas, and where you can come in from 21°49.2 N / 077°25.4W along approx. 205°M. Once inside, aim at the eastern bank, missing the sand shallows off the western tip, then turn west in the darker water when closer to shore. You will have to clear with the Guarda Frontera on the western bank where there is a long dock, a tower, and a few red and white buildings, but use the left fork to pass through.

Another superficially tempting entrance will take you through the reef at the Pasa Guajaba. There are entrances earlier, but the best one is a mile past the ramshackle buildings ashore. You can come in at 21°57.6N/077°33.8W. Unfortunately, there is no way to get really close to the fishing community ashore or to pass through the inviting gap in the cays (shallows and nets), so this merely offers a calm overnight anchorage on the inside of the reef.

ROUTE NORTH

An interesting sidelight on Cayo Confites...
In 1947 an unknown young man called Fidel Castro joined an expedition based here, with the intention of overthrowing President Trujillo of the Dominican Republic. That time, the attempt was successfully broken up by the Cuban government.

This is really not much more than an overnight stop, but it's handy enough while making the passage to Cayo Coco where better facilities exist. Unlike the coastline to the east, along this section the reef sits on a shelf which extends a bit further out from the inner cays, in this case about a mile off.

From the east, there are two entrances which we can use. The first of these is some seven miles southeast of Cayo Confites, coming through the reef around a position of 22°04.0 / 077°37.2W, and passing inside behind the much smaller Cayo Verde. This will afford you a much smoother passage if conditions outside are a bit rough, and also it'll get you out of any countercurrent which may exist. The reef breaks in a continuous line either side of this two-mile wide entrance, so it's a pretty easy entrance, and once inside, there's usually about 15 - 20 feet of transparent water below. Just remain about 200 yards inside of the reef and head approximately 340°M towards the small outer cays ahead.

CAYOS VERDE AND CONFITES
(See sketch on Page 303)

Cayo Verde: A dainty little spot (no more than 1.5 acres) at 22°06.9N / 077°39.0W. With a lovely beach on its southwest tip, some coconut trees, and a ruined light, it does provide a certain amount of shelter, and certainly a bit of privacy (no officials); but there is a permanent mooring just ahead at Cayo Confites which you may prefer. If so, then merely proceed onwards, about four miles north-northwest to that cay.

Cayo Confites: The second entrance mentioned above, leaves out the passage behind Cayo Verde, instead remaining outside of the reef all the way until just southeast of Cayo Confites.

The entrance is deep, and about two miles wide, so you can come in due west between the stakes marking gap between the reef. Enter anywhere between 22°08.2N and 22°10.1N, then turn due north when well inside. There is a small permanent mooring on the south side of the cay at position 22°10.7N / 077°39.8W, to which you may moor. Here you will be in 16 feet. and have a comfortable shelter just 400 yards inside the reef.

You will not be protected in any way from the winds, but the waves are thoroughly broken-up and the motion of the boat at rest will assure you of a good night's sleep.

Note: Do not fall for any misplaced advice from the officials ashore about anchoring on the western side of the cay. The bottom there is merely a skin of sand over a hard sheet of smooth rock. In anything over a puff of breeze, you will drag — unless you manage to swim your anchor into a hole of some sort.

This is the eastern control station for the Cuban traffic-control scheme which monitors hazardous cargos through the narrows of the Old Bahama Channel. Ashore there is a complex of military/coast guard buildings, with a small dock on the west for the large patrol boat stationed there. They will not be too happy about your going ashore, but will certainly be helpful in giving you entrance instructions if you need them. They answer to "CLG 60" (or in bad phonetics... "Estassion, seh-elleh-heh sessenta") on VHF Channel 16 and will speak halting English if you so desire. We have only good things to say about the officials here, and as far as these things can be, we found it a pleasure to deal with them regarding paperwork and the like.

From the west, except for the very northern tip of the island (where it's marked), there is little or no reef to worry about. So you can come in over the wall at your pleasure, and merely keep a sharp eye out for occasional coral heads breaking the water or otherwise discoloring the surface.

LEAVING FOR THE NORTHWEST
CHART NOS. ICH 1129 (CUBAN) & DMA 27060 (USA)

When leaving for the northwest you can pass outside of the reef on the southeast side of Cayo Confites, or merely pass inside the cay and remain above the shelf all the way to Cayo Paredon Grande. As mentioned above, there is no barrier reef to worry about, and the only thing you have to watch out for will be the occasional scattered outcrop. If you stay about a mile in from the wall, then the depths along this section will only rarely drop as shallow as 15 feet., and will more usually remain at about 25 - 30 feet. Although there is no reef to protect you, the wall and shelf will still provide a lessening of the incessant swells, but as the current is at its maximum you should still gain about a knot in the easterly direction.

You will now be passing some of the largest cays in Cuba, with seemingly endless beaches along the coast of Cayo Cruz. There are plans afoot to develop this area, with a pedraplén (stone causeway) already under construction; but meanwhile, in the interval between the intention and the action, you can enjoy these gleaming white sands and crystal waters in absolute solitude.

Despite the warnings on

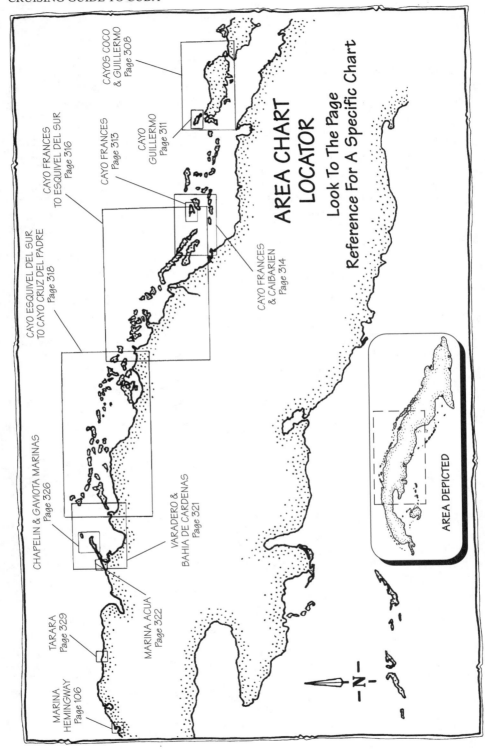

AREA CHART
LOCATOR

Look To The Page
Reference For A Specific Chart

CAYOS COCO
& GUILLERMO
Page 308

CAYO FRANCES
TO ESQUIVEL DEL SUR
Page 316

CAYO FRANCES
Page 313

CAYO
GUILLERMO
Page 311

CAYO ESQUIVEL DEL SUR
TO CAYO CRUZ DEL PADRE
Page 318

CAYO FRANCES
& CAIBARIEN
Page 314

CHAPELIN & GAVIOTA MARINAS
Page 326

VARADERO &
BAHIA DE CARDENAS
Page 321

TARARA
Page 329

MARINA ACUA
Page 322

MARINA
HEMINGWAY
Page 106

AREA DEPICTED

-N-

the U.S. charts the lighthouses seem to be in excellent repair and it's fun to be hailed by the stations along the coast here who inform each other of your progress. They inquire whether you are having a good time and wish you luck for the rest of your journey.

CAYO PAREDÓN

Be careful when coming up to the splendid yellow-and-black lighthouse on Cayo Paredón as there are some uncharted reef outcrops just off to the east which could surprise you if you have begun to relax in the smoother water. In any case, by now you should be well accustomed to reading the waters ahead and can steer round these or just go out wide. Be careful however, of the snorkelers who occasionally are to be found here, and keep a lookout for signs.

If you need to stop for the night, a good shelter is to be found at approximately 22°28.8N / 078°10.4W in the bight formed behind the small adjoining cay just west of the light. Sometimes local boats use this spot, and depths are perfectly adequate as long as you don't approach too closely to the light itself. In many ways, this can be a good alternative to going on to Cayo Coco.

Heading west from Paredón, there are occasional outcrops and the shelf shallows somewhat, so it's probably better if you go over the wall and continue on the outside until you arrive at Cayo Coco, or if you are discouraged by the following, Cayo Guillermo.

CAYO COCO

This is one of the larger cays in Cuba and is being developed along the lines of a tourist complex and nature reserve. It is important to realize that vessels which draw more than six feet should not attempt to approach the stone dock on the eastern side, but rather should continue on west to the more obvious harbor past the hotels and the beaches.

A potentially pleasant spot, there are unfortunately some drawbacks which must be mentioned.

Among the points to be made are, that although there are docking facilities for local tourist craft, foreign sailboats will have to anchor off the crowded breakwater. Also, the otherwise excellent hotels (some seven miles from the eastern dock) do not cater for any but package tourists, and a visitor may have trouble obtaining service.

Finally, a negative attitude to cruisers seems to have recently developed among the officials on the dock here. If you are not prepared to put up with rudeness and an almost insulting rummage through your possessions, then I cannot recommend this as a stopover.

Approaching from the east, one should take up a position outside the reef line, turning 180°M when exactly due north of the dock at around 078°18.6W. This dock is sometimes difficult to see, but there are some pinkish buildings clustered around it (not the larger buildings over to your right on the tip of the island). Along this course, the water will shallow from around 30 feet down to about seven feet when due east of the sand spit which extends out from the northeast promontory.

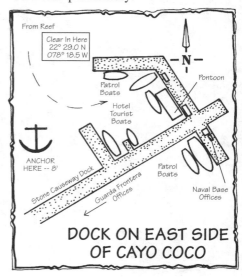

DOCK ON EAST SIDE OF CAYO COCO

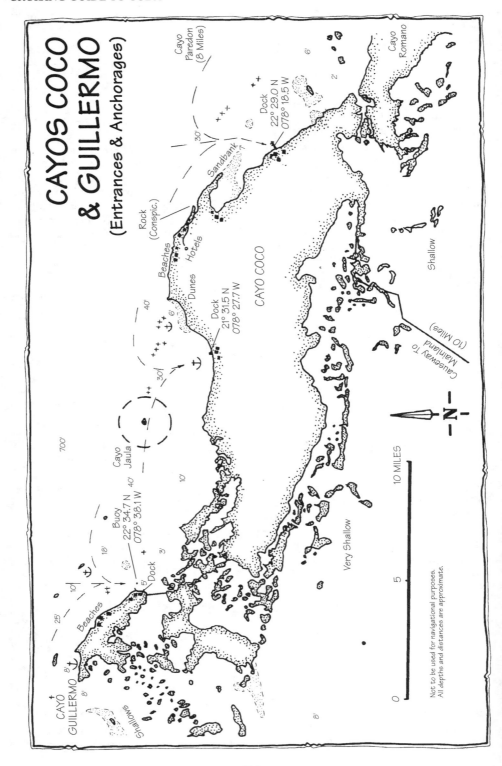

CAYOS COCO & GUILLERMO
(Entrances & Anchorages)

Cayo Paredon
(8 Miles)

Dock
22° 29.0 N
078° 18.5 W

Cayo Romano

Sandbank

Rock
(Conspic.)

Beaches

Hotels

Dunes

CAYO COCO

Shallow

Dock
21° 31.5 N
078° 27.7 W

Causeway To
Mainland
(10 Miles)

Cayo
Jaula

Buoy
22° 34.7 N
078° 38.1 W

Dock

Very Shallow

Beaches

CAYO
GUILLERMO

Shallow

N

10 MILES

Not to be used for navigational purposes.
All depths and distances are approximate.

There is a red mark on the end of the sandbank which in any case is easily seen through the water, and if desired, you could even give it an additional berth if the tide is low. Once past it, the water will again begin to deepen slightly as you head towards the long breakwater-wharf which points at you from land.

Approaching from the west is similar to the above, except that you can adopt a gentle curve towards the spit of sand, curving round it as shown on the sketch.

The rude stone wharf (almost a breakwater) is a massive affair, which in addition to the local tourist boats (picnic, dive, and snorkel) now seems to be host to a small naval squadron of patrol boats. It is thus, quite crowded at the end, and you will only be allowed to moor alongside temporarily while you clear in.

In an unhappy contrast to former days, the reception afforded a cruiser here seems to be one of deep suspicion. When we were last here, an unhappy looking soldier was made to pry into every nook and cranny, while (until I put a stop to it) his Capitan put his feet up and idly read through all our magazines. Emergency flares were temporarily confiscated (a most unusual occurrence), and glib comments made. All this was justified in the vaguest terms by mentioning the demon drug, and what appear to be "delinquents" aboard ghost ships which threatened the coast regularly. In addition, they made it clear that they would not be clearing us out at dawn, but rather, when it was more convenient. Lest you think that this was an isolated incident, similar tales have been reported to me by others.

Having survived this (hopefully things will have returned to the relaxed days I remember from before) you will have to anchor a little way to the southwest of the breakwater tip. Holding is good, but the dock is unfortunately designed so as to point into the prevailing winds, and you will have to tuck in tightly to achieve as much shelter as possible.

If you require fuel, water, or stores for the boat, then you will have to arrange it on the dock, but fresh vegetables may be harder to obtain. On the other hand, mosquitos are *not* harder to find, being most aggressive anywhere on the cay, and especially around the foot of the dock where the Guarda Frontera maintain a large post. Maybe this is responsible for the negative aspects mentioned.

DEEPER DRAFTS

For those vessels drawing more than six feet, then the bay just west of the hotel beaches is far more convenient. The easiest way in, is past the first small reef entrance after the point, and coming in through the wider gap around 22°34.0N / 078°28.8W. Or if you were actually coming from that direction, then anywhere west of the pylon light on Cayo Jaula at approximately position 22° 34.1N / 078°31.0W.

Having entered, there are depths of 15 feet over the shelf until you arrive at the small settlement and dock in the Ensenada de Coco. You can anchor in 10 feet at 22°31.7/078°27.7 some 150 yards off the dock there. The local official will row out to your boat, and thankfully things are unlikely to be quite as difficult as on the other side.

TRAVELING TO THE
BEACHES OR HOTELS

There should be someone on the breakwater who can call taxis if you wish to travel to the hotels or beaches spread along the northern edge of the cay, but if you can wangle it, then hitch a ride with any of the buses which transport the foreign tourists to and from the day boats.

The dusty stone dock is a fair distance to the hotel complex so plan your day accordingly, but there is a lot to do while in the area. The cay's natural resources are being managed by the Cuban conservation group "Flor y Fauna," so there are many distinct varieties of wildlife to be seen and tours may be had from the hotel lobbies.

The hotels are large, but not at all like the usually impersonal government managed affairs sometimes encountered. The staff is entirely Cuban but management functions are being controlled by foreign experts and the increased level of efficiency shows. They are clean and offer services the equivalent of anything on offer elsewhere in the world.

For the first time since leaving Santiago you will be able to change your travellers-cheques. But there is a problem of actually getting served in the hotels here as seemingly, they only cater to all-inclusive travellers from abroad. If you wish service at the bars you will have to arrange it at the front desk. For this, you may have to pay firstly an "entrance fee", and then put down a deposit.

When leaving for the west, remember that once again, some of the obstructions following Cayo Coco do not show up on the charts. Luckily, they're easy enough to see, and to steer round, on a general course of 290 - 300° M from just off the northern tip of Coco.

CAYO GUILLERMO

This short 20-mile run over to the next cay can be accomplished most easily by visual courses along the outer reef. There is another hotel complex on the north shore, with the associated boats moored on a dock just to the east. A long skinny walkway leads out from the hotels, which is as well, because nothing over five feet can get into the main dock. Others will have to anchor and dinghy in. Nevertheless, the aggravation factor on Cayo Guillermo seems much reduced from that of its sister cay, and I have always enjoyed staying here.

There are two outer islets abreast of the eastern tip of Cayo Guillermo (itself recognizable by the large thatched hut, the wharf, an enormous overhead tank, and the recent causeway linking the two cays). Once between them, take up a course of approximately 195°M to pass a large white buoy at 22°34.7N / 078°38.1W. Depths along this course, will slowly drop from 20 feet down

to seven feet close alongside the buoy, which you should pass to port. You can see the boats moored only a short distance away, over to the southwest, so carefully proceed across the bar heading 210°M along a visible dredged channel to the narrow wooden dock. Be careful to pass 50-60 feet east of the end and only dock on the deeper southern side. When making your turn, do not actually go past the dock, as it gets even shallower there, and it is not unknown for a yacht to lose a prop that way.

Note: At low tide you've only got 5 feet of water at the bar so be careful to look at the bottom colors for signs of the channel (light green).

Occasionally, if you exhibit signs of uncertainty, one of the boats stationed at the dock, will come out to show the way but I'd not always gamble on this happening.

At the dock you'll have to be cleared in by the captain of the port. They have always shown an admirable efficiency and the whole process doesn't take more than ten minutes. Administration will also show up to let you know what you can expect here and despite it being somewhat out-of-the-way they will make a determined effort to assist in anything you require. We once rather optimistically requested propane gas of Sr. Manolito (the then head of administration), and within 2 days our small bottle

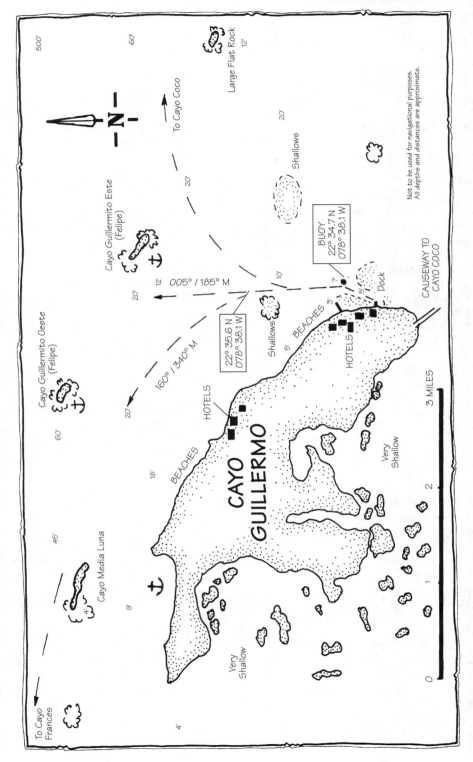

had been transported to a nearby town and (via a soldered connection) refilled from a larger one! Subsequent managers have continued the policy of good relations with yachtsmen, and even if you have to wait on the tide to enter, I would still recommend it. Fuel, ice, and water is also available.

There are plans to dredge the channel and to move the Basé Nautica to another site, closer to the causeway. So far these have not come to fruition, but given the present crowding at the dock, it seems only a matter of time.

For those who have to anchor out, there is good shelter behind either of the two cays offshore, but it is a long way in (nearly two miles) to the beaches, so you may find it better to moor round the corner just west of the cay. Here a handy point reaches out northwest, creating a small bight, and if that's not deep enough, then just past that you'll find more shelter. From here the dinghy is the best way in to the beaches and the hotel/dock facilities.

Once again this is another foreign managed hotel complex and being guided by the principal of "No profit, no job," thus achieves a much better standard of service. It is perfectly amazing just how much better sometimes.

The staff here are personable Cubans who have been thoroughly trained (some waiters even have to take dancing lessons!) and there is a constant effort to entertain the guests rather than to merely endure them.

The guests here tend to be Italians, and a stylishly dressed lot they are, dancing wildly at night in the dockside disco-hut... pleasantly undressed too, along the beaches.

Much like the hotels on Cayo Coco, it is difficult to use cash at the bars in the hotel. However, at the front desk you may obtain a voucher for the sum of $25.00 which allows you to eat a really excellent meal at the buffet, and to drink anything you please until you pass out or the bars shut (at 2 a.m.) Whether or not you see this as a bargain may depend on just how long you've been on the hook, but it's certainly a pleasant task trying to get your money's worth. Do not schedule any important appointments for that day.

ROUTE TO VARADERO
CHART NOS. ICH 11428, 11427, 11426 (CUBAN) & DMA 27060, 27080 (U.S.)

It's still a long way to Varadero so you should plan on stopping two or three times along the route. Shelter is available at a variety of places, and we'll be discussing Cayo Francés outside the channel to the port of Caibarien, the port of La Isabela itself, Cayo Esquivel del Sur, and the Bahía de Cadiz.

Along the way the Santa Maria lighthouse at Cayo Caiman Grande (a beautiful compound looking like a set from Beau Geste) may call you up to wish you a happy trip and as the Bahamas Channel widens, so too will the current flow diminish.

The cays along the route, show endless

sparkling white beaches lapped with clean, clear waters, and offering almost unlimited opportunities for increased tourist development. To that end, the cays here are slowly being linked to the mainland at Caibarien by a long causeway. Who knows just how long it will take, or who will be the eventual participants, but there is still plenty of room; and so far, you will have noticed that what resorts do exist, are isolated from each other by miles and miles of virgin territory. Small fishing boats too, dart in and out of the cays, some with large stiff mesh baskets on long poles. The boatman looks down through the water with a

glass-bottomed biscuit tin, and having identified his prey, merely leans over and scoops
a wriggling lobster up to the surface. This,
of course, is the easy way.

Too, there is a strange increase in the

seabird population. Ospreys begin to be
show themselves, while roseate terns, laugh-
ing and boneparts' gulls, trail your vessel
for miles before plunging into the clear
waters in search of afternoon tea.

CAYO FRANCÉS (40 MILES)

This cay is notable both for its shape and
for the old hulk moored in the bight on the
western side. The shape is rather like a
Salvador Dali painting, while the ship is
still in use as a depot for molasses (and a
Guarda Frontera post).

There are two good anchorages here, one
near the northwest tip, and the other in the
bight further down near the ship.

If you come round the northwest tip, give
the shallows a wide berth and moor in good
water south of the traffic control station
there. The tides along the coast now are
slowly (but definitely) becoming more of a
factor again, so leave yourself a couple of
feet below if necessary.

There are a couple of large buildings with
a good-sized watchtower and a couple of

antennae, but despite all this, and the spectators along the roofs, you may well feel
you have to swim ashore to clear in if they
don't reply to transmissions. Of course,
having done that, they'll say they don't
need to see your papers and you can continue on without a despacho.

Little fishing boats will wander in and out
of the inlet leading into the cay, and further
over to the south there is the large white
(OK, dingy grey) ferro-cement hull which
has been there since World War II. There is
an excellent anchorage to the east of this
ship too, so if you prefer, then by all means
go over there. The Guarda Frontera maintain a patrol boat alongside the ship, and I
know one yacht which was offered the
option of mooring there too. It stays rela-

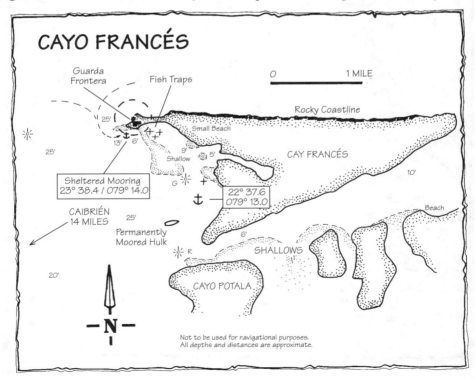

CAYO FRANCÉS

Guarda
Frontera   Fish Traps   0   1 MILE

Rocky Coastline

25'
Small Beach
13' 6'
9'
25'   Shallow   5'   CAY FRANCÉS
10'
Sheltered Mooring
23° 38.4 / 079° 14.0   G
22° 37.6
079° 13.0
CAIBRIÉN   Beach
14 MILES   25'
Permanently   6'
Moored Hulk   SHALLOWS
R
20'
CAYO POTALA

– N –

Not to be used for navigational purposes.
All depths and distances are approximate.

313

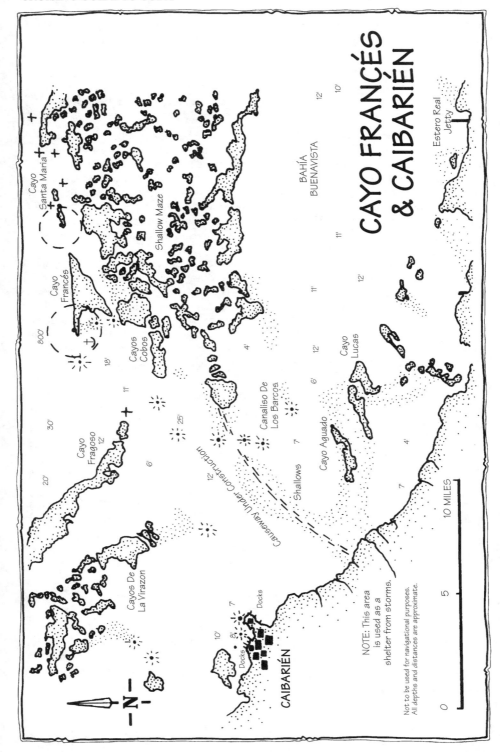

CAYO FRANCÉS & CAIBARIÉN

NOTE: This area is used as a shelter from storms.

Not to be used for navigational purposes.
All depths and distances are approximate.

10 MILES

0   5

BAHÍA BUENAVISTA

Estero Real Jetty

Cayo Santa Maria

Cayo Francés

Shallow Maze

Cayos Cobos

Cayo Lucas

Cayo Aguado

Canaliso De Los Barcos

Shallows

Causeway Under Construction

Cayo Fragoso

Cayos De La Virazon

CAIBARIÉN

Docks

N

tively deep until 200 yards offshore, and the holding is good (better than on the north-west tip), so don't worry too much about what nature may throw at you. You may also find it amusing to snorkel or to fish in the inlet. Although I've never *caught* anything while fishing, I have seen large tarpon here, and whatever bit at me also carried away all my lures.

The port of Caibarien lies to the south-west at the end of a well-marked channel. If you go there, you'll have to clear at the Guarda Frontera post to the northwest of Caibarien point where it's too shallow to go alongside. They'll ask you to remain in view, and to hoist your dinghy aboard at night.

ROUTES WEST

It's a long way to the next stop, but there are alternate shelters along the way in any of the cays lining the latter stages of the route. Were you to come in through the wide Pasa Marcos (22°50.2N / 079°37.4W) you'd find a large sheltered bay with plenty of room and depth.

There is a Guarda Frontera post on the western side of the channel.

Further still lies the port of La Isabella, down a long, time-consuming canal (anything up to two hours), while if you prefer not to deal with ports at this stage, then Cayo Esquivel del Sur is only seven miles past that.

LA ISABELA

About 22 miles past the Pasa Marcos, the Boca de Maravíllas canal will take you through, all the way to the large bay of Sagua La Grande and the city of La Isabela on the mainland. This city has seen better days, being the railway port which served the inland city of Sagua La Grande, but it has fallen on hard times since the reduction in trade. Nevertheless you may be interested in passing a night in

what is obviously a relic of more revolutionary times.

The channel is well marked along its length and can be entered southwards from the outer buoys at 23°02.0N / 079°58.0W. Further R/G marks mark the six-mile channel which curves south-southwest through the pass between two cays and into a large murky bay. The depths in the channel are around 30 feet but there is a strong riptide at times. You must be careful not to be swept off line by this east-west current so look back at your wake frequently to check.

La Isabela lies on a narrow promontory across the bay, and unless advised, you

should approach the western side. Call the capitanía (Channel 16) for instructions and you will be directed to any one of a dozen ancient wharfs on that side. Apart from those at the extreme southwest end to the town (good, but large and busy), the rest of the docks are all more or less collapsing. For safety, you may have to come alongside one of the pontoons which are decaying there. The depths here are about 20 feet.

The port was closed some time ago in '93, and has only just been reopened. Once again, we hear tales of this port being redeveloped, but...

There is a fishing dock (Basé Nautica) and a military naval station on the eastern side of the port, so you may be allowed to go there. If so, then go back northeast of the city and take a very wide route round to the east.

To approach this side, an easterly loop must be made from halfway between the original entrance-channel marks 20 and 18 (or the last cay you pass on your way in).

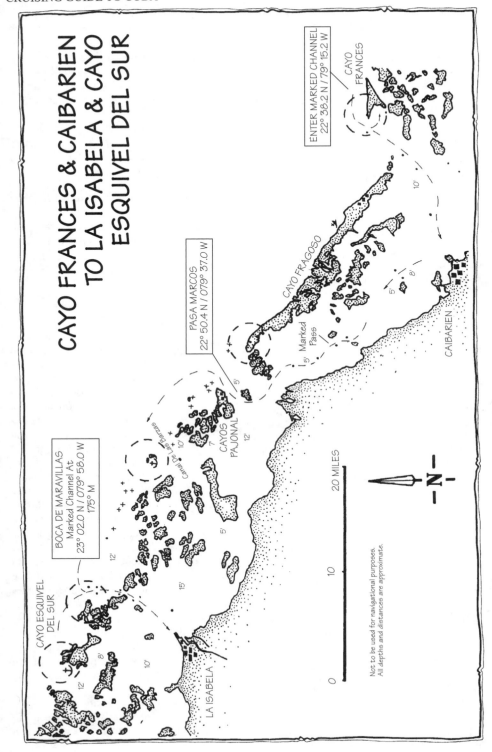

CAYO FRANCES & CAIBARIEN
TO LA ISABELA & CAYO
ESQUIVEL DEL SUR

ENTER MARKED CHANNEL
22° 38.2 N / 79° 15.2 W

CAYO
FRANCES

10'

CAYO FRAGOSO

8'

5'

PASA MARCOS
22° 50.4 N / 079° 37.0 W

Marked
Pass

5'

5'

CAIBARIEN

5'

BOCA DE MARAVILLAS
Marked Channel At
23° 02.0 N / 079° 58.0 W
175° M

Cañar De La Barza

10'

7

CAYOS
PAJONAL

12'

12'

5'

15'

CAYO ESQUIVEL
DEL SUR

12'

8'

10'

12'

LA ISABELA

N

Not to be used for navigational purposes.
All depths and distances are approximate.

20 MILES   10   0

316

Out in the bay, and south of your position now, there is a large mark (22°56.8N / 080°00.0W) which should be passed to port before approaching the docks on that side, half a mile away along a course of 235°fM. Although with care, you can find eight feet all the way, be extremely careful, as the water is murky and it can be shallow here. The charts do not, in fact, show clear water (and we too have grounded on the way in once), so pay attention to what lies ahead and go slow. On this side you may be allowed to moor to the capitanía dock, or the fishing wharf. In contrast to the western side of the peninsula, on this side you will be able to get water, electricity and ice, even if they are on separate docks.

Formalities, in my experience, are conducted quickly, except for the occasion when the screwdriver-wielding dog-handler decides to show his stuff. Nevertheless, it must be said that everyone we've ever encountered here was unfailingly cheerful and pleasant.

While you wait, you may watch the wizened fishermen in their tiny lateen rigged boats getting *their* despachos even if they're only going a couple of hundred yards out to cast a net!

Ah, well, every one of those is another nail in the final coffin.

THE TOWN

La Isabela is a strange place, anchored in the past, almost as if time has forgotten it.

It was once a thriving railway terminus for the sugar factories in Sagua La Grande, five miles inland to the south, and relics of that past are everywhere. Bits of track line the streets, some submerged in swampy gutters, some submerged under sand and asphalt, and some just ripped up and left there. Rolling stock has been abandoned to the sun, the rain and the weeds, while in the compound near the northern end of town, fertilizer bags wait in the open for someone to take them away.

Seemingly built over wetland, it once had a neat little malecón (seawall promenade), a bandstand, and a tiny waterfront park. Now, everything seems to be decaying, and in some perverse fashion, the town fathers have responded by covering the place with slogans and tired exhortations. A selection of the more fascinating would remind you that, "He who knows Cuba's history and still remains neutral is a coward". And that, "He who rises with Cuba today, will rise with the world tomorrow". We are also advised that "In case of war, you may contact the local CDR representative at ..."

In spite of all the above, the town must have been quite pretty in its heyday, and the wooden houses, although dilapidated, have some quaint touches. Raised a foot or so above the level of the water, they're generally built on short piles; and inside, they boast quaint vaulted doors, high ceilings, and internal windows between the rooms. Within the same street, houses often share a large common patio or courtyard, which more often than not contains a trapdoor in the center.

Regarding amenities on the western side of the peninsula, the sound of a vibrating boom-box may lure you to La Casona, a wooden disco bar built over the water. Within its dim interior you can drink seven-cent shots of rum, while watching a mirrored ball on the low ceiling and waiting for the floor to give way. Most of the other bars can be found along the main drag which is called Bartolomé Masso, and runs the length of the town.

Horse drawn carriages ply for trade along Masso, and on the northeast point a large hexagonal thatch-roofed restaurant can be found. Here you can get a perfectly acceptable three-course meal consisting of seafood, soup, desert, and maybe a beer or two; all at about a dollar-fifty for two. Service is slow as there may only be one copy of the menu to be shared by all, and diners are served strictly in order, but the scene inside is fascinating. Like anywhere else, Cubans like to dress well when eating out, with little girls pirouetting in ruffled skirts and lace

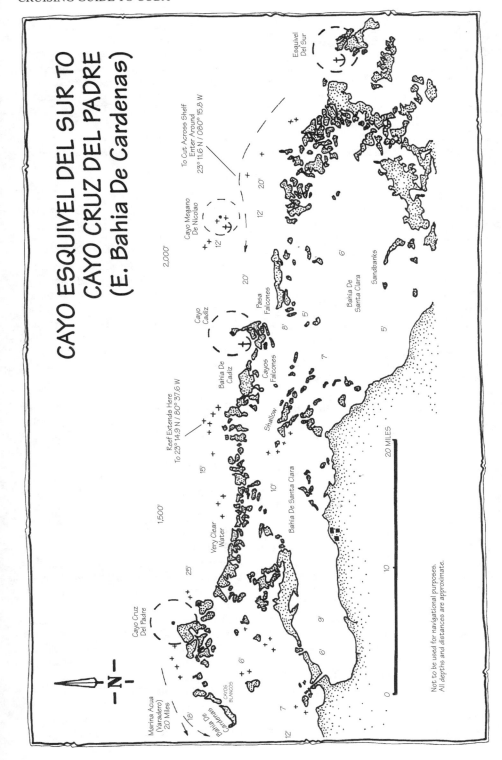

CAYO ESQUIVEL DEL SUR TO
CAYO CRUZ DEL PADRE
(E. Bahia De Cardenas)

Esquivel Del Sur

To Cut Across Shelf
Enter Around
23° 11.6 N / 080° 15.8 W

2,000'

Cayo Megano
De Nicolao

12'

20'

12'

Cayo
Cadiz

Pasa
Falcones

20'

6'

Sandbanks

Bahia De
Cadiz

8'

5'

Bahia De
Santa Clara

Cayos
Falcones

7'

5'

Reef Extends Here
To 23° 14.9 N / 80° 37.6 W

Shallow

15'

1,500'

10'

Very Clear
Water

Bahia De Santa Clara

20 MILES

25'

9'

6'

10

Cayo Cruz
Del Padre

6'

CAYOS
BLANCOS

7'

0

-N-

Marina Acua
(Varadero)
20 Miles

18'

6'

12'

Not to be used for navigational purposes.
All depths and distances are approximate.

318

while small boys grimace in the cleanest of shirts. The noise level is high, and outrageous flirting seems to be the order of the day, so no one takes much notice of you.

On a Sunday night, during the telenovelas (TV soap operas) the streets empty, televisions blare from open windows, and one can walk the length of the town without missing a single word of the drama surrounding *Women of Sand*. If you wish to watch, then just stand in any doorway. Everyone else does.

Although my description of La Isabela may be off-putting to some, this is not really a bad place. It may be somewhat rundown, but unaccustomed to visitors, it gives an honest picture of life in many coastal towns away from the tourist paintbrush.

CAYO ESQUIVEL DEL SUR

If the long canal into La Isabela has deterred you from entering, then simply bypass the entrance and continue onwards about 7.5 miles. There is a light on the western end of the cay, with a lovely little bay just in front of that. The bay is better protected than it seems on the chart, because the reef just off the northeast end curves round slightly. If you prefer, then go round the point to anchor 300 yards south of the light in 10 feet of water (approximately 23°04.1N / 080°05.3 W) where you will be well protected from all likely winds. The area is deeper than shown on the charts and the anchor can be dropped into deep gullies in the turtle-grass for extra security.

Apart from the obvious solitude, there is a ruined hotel complex on the island, and some beautiful beaches which you may explore at your leisure. Around here, on two occasions, we have been blessed to see pink flamingos lurching slowly by on great rhythmic wings, their legs stretched out behind; and in front, long, kinked necks, each with a noble Roman beak. It's a thrilling sight.

When leaving, be aware that there are some uncharted reefy spots breaking the surface just past Cayo Arbolito to the west of Esquivel del Sur. If you are leaving before first light, then go out over the wall, and set a safe course (315°M.) until it's light enough to steer visually (or a heading of 303°M).

THE ROUTE WEST

The water between this overnight halt and Varadero is startlingly clear. You might even be able to actually see individual fish on the bottom at 35-40 feet if going slowly enough. Not a bad thing, as there are increasing signs of drift-nets suspended beneath the surface from a haphazard mixture of polystyrene and cork floats. Among the cays too, there are lots of small one and two-man sailboats fishing away busily. Lateen rigged, and without any form of ballast, they adopt high angles of lean while buzzing about haphazardly, and changing direction like a flock of butterflies.

From Esquivel del Sur, the passage to Varadero is around 65 miles, so you probably don't want to make it all in one go. The safest way is, as always, following the wall; but nevertheless, to save a couple of miles, you can cut across the flats where the shelf bulges out in front of the Pasa Falcones east of the Cayo Cadiz light.

If you're going to follow the wall, you will find a nice anchorage nine miles before Cadiz at Cayo Mégano de Nicolao (23°13.3N / 080°19.4W). There is a light here, and the holding, in the sandy spots, is good. There is a reef about a quarter of a mile further out from the light, and between this and the cay you may dive a small blue hole! The diver will be rewarded here, by some lovely fish in the depression, while there is also a wreck under water on the northeast side of the reef.

BAHIA DE CADIZ

For another snug anchorage, you can duck into the bay behind the lighthouse on Cayo Cadiz which is really the northwestern end of the larger Cayo Falcones. Drop anchor at an approximate position of 23°11.6N / 080°29.2W in about eight feet Here you will be protected from all angles except the west and northwest, while at night, the light revolves torpidly, casting shadows across your boat. Lobster fishermen ply their trade within the bay, and sometimes, having come right through the center of the island from the other side, medium sized fishing boats will suddenly appear out of nowhere to anchor nearby.

There are various inlets in the cay, and one can spend hours in a dinghy pleasantly trolling for fish or getting lost within the

Cayo Cruz Del Padre light.

labyrinth. The lagoons to the north of your anchorage go nowhere, petering out after a hundred yards or so, but in the southwest of the bay (on Cayo Falcones) the passages are anything up to 100 yards wide in places. If I had to recommend one, then I'd say the one at approx. 23°11.2N / 080°31.5W is the most enjoyable, but there are several entrances and exits.

ON TO VARADERO

From here, it is a straightforward run, 40 miles to the main resort area in Cuba. Apart from the clarity of the water, there are only two things of note.

One is the reef in front of Cayo Juan Clarito which, at 23°14.9N / 080°37.6W, extends out somewhat further than shown on the charts.

The other is the picturesque freestanding lighthouse at Cayo Cruz del Padre. This extraordinary structure is surrounded by a shallow reef and set atop a rock some way from land. With none of the original rock visible, ancient stone walls support a squat white building. Above, an outer spiral stairway leads the keeper to the lantern in the open tower.

Finally, progressing west along the route to Varadero, you will note an increase in the amount of charter and day boats serving the huge tourist trade. At present, most of these are sportfishing and snorkel boats, but there are growing numbers of sailboats being chartered here.

VARADERO AND THE BAY OF CARDENAS
CHART NO. ICH 1512 (CUBAN)

Sometimes not shown on charts as Varadero (strictly speaking that's merely the name of the beach area), this largest of the Cuban vacation areas is situated on the outer northwest corner of the Bay of Cardenas. Along a long, skinny peninsula, you will find a large city, teeming with (and catering to) foreign tourists.

The important thing to remember when coming in, is that the Marina Acua where

you will be expected to dock is entered from the *outside* and is situated at the *western* end of the peninsula of Hicacos. Controlling depths into the marina are 15 feet at the entrance and dockside.

There is another marina which you may wish to use later (Marina Chapelin), but due to the present unavailability of customs and internal clearance facilities it is better to clear in at this end.

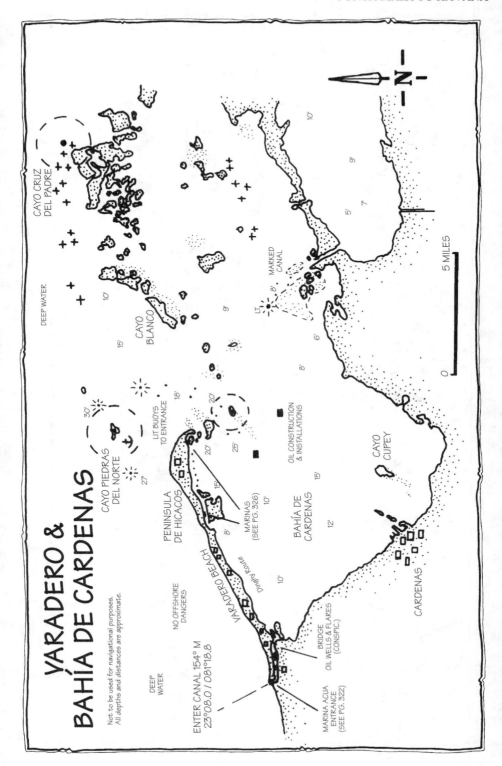

VARADERO & BAHÍA DE CARDENAS

Not to be used for navigational purposes.
All depths and distances are approximate.

DEEP WATER

ENTER CANAL 154° M
23°08.0 / 081°18.8

CAYO PIEDRAS DEL NORTE

LIT BUOYS TO ENTRANCE

PENINSULA DE HICACOS

NO OFFSHORE DANGERS

MARINAS (SEE PG. 326)

VARADERO BEACH

Dinghy Route

MARINA ACUA ENTRANCE (SEE PG. 322)

BRIDGE
OIL WELLS & FLARES (CONSPIC.)

BAHÍA DE CARDENAS

OIL CONSTRUCTION & INSTALLATIONS

CAYO CUPEY

CARDENAS

CAYO CRUZ DEL PADRE

DEEP WATER

CAYO BLANCO

MARKED CANAL

LIT.

5 MILES

0

N

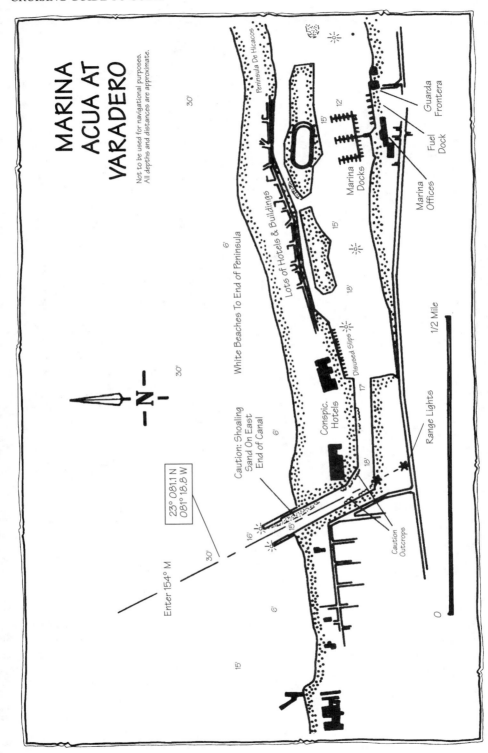

MARINA
ACUA AT
VARADERO

Not to be used for navigational purposes.
All depths and distances are approximate.

N

30'

Enter 154° M

23° 08.1 N
081° 18.8 W

Caution: Shoaling
Sand On East
End of Canal

White Beaches To End of Peninsula

Peninsula De Hicacos

Lots of Hotels & Buildings

Conspic.
Hotels

Disused Slips

Caution
Outcrops

Range Lights

1/2 Mile

0

Marina
Docks

Marina
Offices

Fuel
Dock

Guarda
Frontera

12'

15'

15'

18'

17

18'

18'

16'

15'

6'

6'

6'

6'

30'

30'

15'

DESTINATION MARINA ACUA

Your first destination will be the Marina Acua with which you should communicate in advance of arrival if possible. They monitor Channels 16 and 68 on the VHF and will make all arrangements with the customs, immigration, and Guarda Frontera. Telephone numbers are 66 8060 and 66 8066, while they can be faxed on 66 7456.

This is one of the best run marinas in Cuba. Even if they do not have such things as bath houses and the like, the docking facilities themselves are superior to those in Havana and anywhere else. In addition, the staff are efficient, and all onward documentation is available here.

Coming from the east, do not enter at the wonderful lighthouse in the middle of the wide entrance to the bay. Situated on Cayo Piedras del Norte, it marks the channel for the large commercial vessels which use the port of Cardenas in the southwest corner.

Instead, continue outside, parallel to the enormous resort developments and the crowded beaches, until you see the two large monolithic hotels at the base of the peninsula. Just past the most westerly hotel there are lights at 23°08.0N / 081°18.8W marking the outer ends of the canal into Paso Malo and the Marina Acua.

At night there are range-lights to guide you to the entrance, but in any case you should enter along a course of 154°M. Due to persistent shoaling of the channel right at the mouth, make absolutely sure you favor the western (starboard) half of the canal as the other side is much shallower.

Minimum depths in the entrance channel are 15 feet, but it is not advisable to enter in adverse conditions as the canal is narrow and the waves can easily sweep you off course. If you are faced with this sort of decision, then the best alternative is to enter the large bay itself some 12 miles northeast and to come round the peninsula into shelter.

Follow the canal round to the left and through the large markers on either side of the channel until you arrive off the marina where you should dock as you see fit.

The marina counts on some 30-40 spaces so there is always going to be room, but in general it will be better to dock in one of the berths along the central spine as local vessels use the outer branches.

Avoid the extreme tip of the eastern dock too. That's where a naval patrol boat occasionally docks.

HAVE YOUR DOCUMENTS READY

This is the closest port to Marathon in the Florida Keys, and in fact is the closest Cuban port to anywhere in the U.S.A. so it is perfectly feasible to enter the country here. In this case, then you should read the appropriate section (Havana, Chapter 5) dealing with the subject and have your documents ready for customs and immigration.

Even if coming in from somewhere else in Cuba clearance will still be required, but we've never experienced any hassles. Looking back at our logbook, I note that clearing in from along the coast once took us all of five minutes while the Canadian couple who had arrived just that morning from Havana took over four hours!

As mentioned before, it's all a question of having the right bits ready at the right time.

You are likely to be welcomed by a representative of the marina who will even offer you a contract to sign. This, written in English and Spanish, explains what you may expect from the marina, and what they will expect from you. Charges were 45 cents/foot in 1996, and fuel is also available at the dockside pump. Water is available at your dock, and this is also the only place in Cuba where I have found that your electricity cable will fit right into the connection without the use of twisted wire and tape.

For the rest, the old dockside disco is now gone. And as usual, no visitors are allowed on the boats.

To find the marina offices, go through the passage leading out of the main building and turn to your right. Along the outer wall, some way down, there are several offices. The one marked "*Direccion*" is the main office, while there are laundry facilities (*Lavandera*) on offer, and even a small shop which will sell you bread. For laundry, you just leave a bagful of clothes and pick it up later. It's not strictly necessary, but as such things are invariably in short supply, do everyone a favor and offer your own detergent.

Don Quixote approaches a whimsical water tower.

There is a surprisingly good ship's store to the left as you leave the main building. In here, you can get anything ranging from U.S.-made 6v golf cart batteries and fishing lures, to microwave ovens and tacky lamp shades.

If you need customs facilities for arranging your Guia de Recala (your schedule for further travel), then their offices are down a corridor in the same building. Ask anyone for guidance.

They will have to be notified of your departure plans in advance.

To contact the Guarda Frontera (you will after all need a despacho for travel along the beaches or to the lighthouse in your boat) then their offices are along the water just to the left of the main building.

There is one extremely annoying feature you will possibly have to put up with. The broadcast of the news over crackling loud-speakers seemingly aimed directly at your boat.

There are few things less appealing than the heroic socialist achievements of the Youth Brigade or Cambodian current affairs, at 6:30 a.m. In spite of everything else that is good about the place, the radio in Cuba lacks a certain something.

Luckily, if you need a break from the daily dose of exhortations, slogans, denunciations, and proclamations, you can pick up U.S. stations on AM (e.g. 940 WINZ). You can also sometimes pick up the odd stray FM signal from the Florida Keys. They may be equally biased, but at least you control the volume.

For the local attractions of Varadero I would advise acquiring a suitable guidebook as there are countless diversions on offer. This is Cuba's premiere holiday resort and despite the general non-participation of U.S. citizens, thousands of European tourists arrive here to spend their time on the beaches and to use it as a base for further travel.

Any normal tourist facilities which you may have felt denied while coasting offshore are now most certainly available by inquiring at the marina offices or in any of the hotel lobbies. On the other hand, the port of Cardenas is also nearby with shipyard facilities there for any more specialized needs (within the constraints of parts-availability).

TOURISM ORIENTED BAY

The bay plays host to countless boat-trips, with tourists of all descriptions crowding the decks of both foreign and local charters. If you have a large enough vessel and time to spare, then this is the one place in Cuba where there is the possibility of coming to some strange agreement with the government.

If you desire to visit the lighthouse at the entrance to the bay of Cardenas, then there is a lovely little cove, just on the northeast side of the cay. This little bay seems to offer something for everyone, and various yachts now make it their destination for day-cruises. There is a ruined dock on the south side of the cay, but you can anchor more or less anywhere off the coast.

There is also good snorkeling to be had along the outer cays east of the bay.

ALTERNATE MARINAS IN VARADERO

Cardenas Bay can be easily entered by any deep-keeled yacht. Pass either side of the lighthouse to link with the well-marked channel leading in. Follow it southwest past the tip of Cayo Buba and once through the channel you may make a wide turn to the north.

The most convenient bases for day cruising the bay itself are the Gaviota marina on the inside tip of the peninsula, and the Marina Chapelín halfway up along and also on the inside.

This is where most of the tour-boats are based.

You may also anchor in the bay here, and for good shelter you'll be able to snuggle in close to the tip.

GAVIOTA MARINA

Half a mile due north of the stake marking the western extent of the Cayo Buba shallows, you will find the entrance to the marina at 23°11.4N/081°07.8W. Pass closer to the red mark there and you will find 15 feet. There is a slipway visible from outside near the cay if you require a visual reference to find the entrance. The canal leads past the slipway to the east and the marina is right in front of you, with boats moored along the docks to port.

We have entered this marina direct from the cays, but although there is a Guarda Frontera official, there is no permanent customs post here. For entry from outside Varadero, you will need this clearance, and the officer has to come from the Marina Acua all the way into town. This can sometimes (usually) involve a long delay, plus a demand for transport fees which is seriously annoying. It's better to clear in at Acua and subsequently move here.

While perhaps a bit far from the amenities of the city, it does however, offer you easy access to the bay of Cardenas and the cays close by. Excellent boatyard facilities are also available here, with the potential to leave your vessel in storage ashore. In fact, this marina is making a strenuous attempt to attract the servicing trade, and more foreign boats are showing up for attention. If you're going to take advantage of this, then bring what you need from abroad. As always, supervise the blocking of your vessel.

Afloat, the marina charges 45 cents/foot, and fuel is also available. Diesel costs 45 cents/litre and petrol is 95 cents/litre. There is the usual tangle of wire gaining access to electricity, and water is also supplied. If cruising the cays has not put you off this forever, the restaurant maintains live lobster in cages at waterside.

Various scuba boats use this marina, so get your air-fills at the compressor station behind the restaurant.

MARINA CHAPELÍN

Just a bit further in to the west, and just as convenient for deep keels, this may be entered via the marked channel which runs parallel to the shoreline. Follow the general instructions for the Gaviota Marina, but turn to the northwest after Cayo Buba. The final channel is best entered around the No.1 marker.

Although the Chapelín marina only occasionally has room for casual foreign yachts it may be worthwhile calling (Channels 16 and 72) to see if there is any possibility of overnight space.

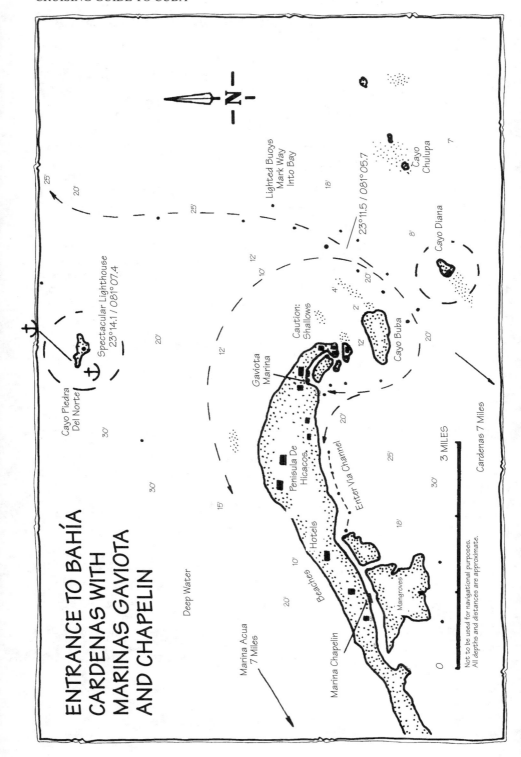

ENTRANCE TO BAHÍA
CARDENAS WITH
MARINAS GAVIOTA
AND CHAPELIN

Cayo Piedra
Del Norte

Spectacular Lighthouse
23°14.1 / 081°07.4

Lighted Buoys
Mark Way
Into Bay

23°11.5 / 081°05.7

Cayo
Chulupa

Cayo Diana

Cayo Buba

Caution:
Shallows

Gaviota
Marina

Penísula De
Hicacos

Enter Via Channel

Hotels

Beaches

Deep Water

Mangroves

Marina Acua
7 Miles

Marina Chapelin

Cardenas 7 Miles

3 MILES

Not to be used for navigational purposes.
All depths and distances are approximate.

There is an excellent restaurant alongside the docks at Chapelín too, and even though you may be based in Paso Malo (Kawama) at the Marina Acua it is worthwhile taking the dinghy further east through the canal and northeast along the peninsula to visit it. Be prepared for a long trip if your dinghy can't plane, and look out for the current going under the bridge, but it's a fun trip.

To get there from the marina Acua, you will need to inform the Guarda Frontera over in the guardhouse on your left ashore (just past the fuel dock), but a permit (a sort of mini-despacho) will be issued whenever you wish to take your dinghy out of the immediate area.

THE CITY AND PENINSULA

A lot of petroleum extraction takes place within the bay of Cardenas, and the dire need for fuel supplies outweighs all other considerations. There is even a small oil-field just behind Marina Acua, and the sulfuric fumes emitted at night from the flaring-off are deposited with the dew in the form of a weak acid all over your decks. It also dulls your fiberglass and will blacken and pit your stainless fittings in short order. The only way round this is to clean your boat scrupulously every morning while it is still damp, and to otherwise put up with the fumes.

Taxis are available through the marina offices to get you into town, but if you prefer you can walk or cycle as it is only a couple of miles.

The road into town leads east from the marina Acua, incongruously past a field of nodding donkey oil-wells, and opposite a beautiful tree-lined pathway. Crossing the bridge, you may proceed along the main road which tend northeast to the main hotel area. The beaches around here are crowded with bodies in every stage of delightful (and sometimes not so delightful) undress, with vendors selling everything from necklaces to ice-cream. *Xanadu*, the beautiful old Du Pont mansion and estate, is to be found along the beach here. This building now houses a very posh restaurant, but you may tour the premises at your leisure if that is the limit of your desire.

If you prefer the less obviously tourist part of the beach, then branch off to the north before the main highway takes control and pass along the Avenida Primera. This will give you the option of choosing your own beach, and also a more Cuban scene.

Along here, there are a multitude of restaurants of varying prices and styles, while you may even rent motor-scooters at roadside too.

On the bridge there is an extremely loud nightclub which offers nightly cabaret. Just over the bridge and down to your left, there are a couple of floating restaurants. Along the same road too, there are one or two pizza-style restaurant-bars where you can also watch U.S. television with your meal. For a quick meal out, then any of these will do, even if during the season, there is a greater choice by combing the side roads.

If you're interested in scuba, there are various scuba boats based at the marina. Ask around for these, and it's only the work of a moment to board one for a trip along the coast with a proper dive-guide.

FLIGHTS OUT OF TOWN

Before I leave the subject of Varadero there is one final feature of the resort which may be of interest. There are cheap, direct flights to Nassau from Matanzas just a

327

couple of miles away.

The flight on an old Russian aircraft lasts only 40 minutes or less and can be a god-send if you have to acquire spares quickly.

LEAVING VARADERO

When leaving Varadero, request early clearance from customs, and pay your bill at the marina offices. Be careful, if you are already legally in the country, not to be made to pay an extra fee for any customs documents. If necessary, then show your existing Guia de Recala, which already shows your authorized route.

If it's before sunup, the Guarda Frontera may have to be rousted out of their office, but the papers can be quickly prepared aboard. Coffee and cigarettes will help if the dreadful oil-well odor is too much.

Going west, the port of Matanzas is the first available port along the way, but it is somewhat open to the northeast, and might be off-limits except in an emergency. Instead, apart from a couple of smaller and seldom visited ports, there is a new marina at Tarara. To enter there, you will need to draw less than five feet. But failing this, then Havana is your destination.

As dealt with previously (Chapter 5), note that your destination is not in fact the harbor of Havana, but rather the Darsena de Barlovento seven miles on from there. Being a major commercial harbor, Havana is off-limits to casual cruising yachts, so schedule things accordingly for the extra distance involved. It is, in fact, a full 70 miles from Varadero.

ROUTE WEST TO HAVANA
CHART NOS. ICH 11425, 11424, OR 1106 (CUBAN)
& DMA 27080 (U.S.)

You can cruise as close in as you care, but be on the lookout for the snorkelers who may be found up to a mile offshore. Sometimes you can even come across two small rubber-tire rafts lashed together and being used as a platform on which these snorkeling expeditions are based.

In general the coastal character changes from high wooded escarpments to a softer, chalkier terrain. Ashore we find an uneasy mix of holiday resorts, oil fields, electricity generating stations and rusting iron constructions; ending more or less in ugly conglomerations of apartment blocks be-

fore Cojimar.

There is a small protected inlet at the river Bacunayagua (081°41.6W) where the ravine is spanned by a large bridge, but this is one of the few protected spots worthy of note.

About 15 miles west of Matanzas, there is an inlet at Santa Cruz del Norte, which can be entered along 168°M at 081°55.3W. There is a small but substantial dock about 100 yards in on the western bank, but the town is somewhat grimy, with only marshalling yards and industrial plants on offer.

MARINA TARARA

This is a small lesser-known marina which, halfway between those of Varadero and Havana, has plans to rival them. The cove is situated at 082°12.8W and can be approached south, aiming at the *western* side of the bay; but although there are plans to blast and dredge the entrance, it is presently restricted to drafts of about five feet There are no international clearance facilities at the marina.

To be truthful, Tarara is somewhat far from Havana, which (along with the ex-

pense of getting into the city) means that presently it is more or less restricted to those actually on passage. On the other hand, it does have much nicer beaches than anything on offer nearer to the capital such as the Marina Hemingway, and the friendly staff are making strenuous attempts to attract more cruisers.

Immediately following the hotel resort area and beaches surrounding the town of Guanabo, the entrance to Tarara can be recognized as a small cove and beach with

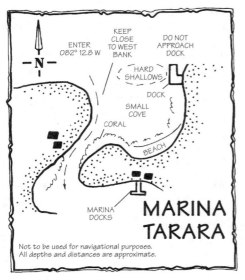

KEEP CLOSE TO WEST BANK

DO NOT APPROACH DOCK

ENTER 082° 12.8 W

-N-

HARD SHALLOWS

DOCK

SMALL COVE

CORAL

BEACH

MARINA DOCKS

MARINA TARARA

Not to be used for navigational purposes.
All depths and distances are approximate.

Do not approach the dock, as it is shallow (and hard) on that side, but instead stick tightly to the western side of the cove which is rather impermanently marked by a series of small buoys. There are a couple of rocks in the river, so remain no more than 10 feet from the starboard bank until past them. Just inside the river, on your starboard, is a Guarda Frontera post.

Med-mooring is the order of the day here, but there are the usual facilities such as electricity and intermittent water supplies. There are no showers, but dockage (45 cents/foot, with a small discount for longer term stays) is cheaper than either Havana or Varadero. Finally, there is a scuba diving organization based at the marina.

The marina can be contacted on VHF Channels 77 and 16, or by telephone on 33 5510 and 33 5501. They can also be faxed on 33 5499.

Ashore, the marina offices are part of a restaurant/bar, and there is also a large disco not 200 yards away. The establishment is part of a large dusty complex of rental houses, so there are other bars and restaurants available within walking distance of the dock, but Havana itself (12 miles to the city) is out of the question unless you use a bicycle, rental car, or taxi

a dock on the east side. On the western side, there is a small river which curves back round behind the cove to the marina; and from outside, one can see the masts of sailboats at the moorings inside. Behind all that, the brightly colored plastic whirly-gig rides of a fun-fair can be seen, and there is also a large viaduct in the background, with a busy roadway on top.

Marina Tarara

329

($20). Another drawback is the lack of genuine paladars (private restaurants), or private taxis which are far, far cheaper than the official ones.

Along the beach to the east, there is a large hotel complex alongside some beautiful beaches. In fact, referring to my logbook of 1996, I noted that the waters here are the nicest we saw in Cuba that time. "Blue, blue, blue", goes the notation.

Just to round this off; if you have come across any of the publicity materials for the international fishing tourneys which the marina runs in the summer and autumn months, then do not believe the lat/longs which are supplied. They will put you somewhere in the middle of the Yucatan Channel near Mexico.

THE REST OF THE WAY

There is only one coastal city between Tarara and Havana. A long time ago, when it was just a small town, Cojimar was the favorite haunt of Ernest Hemingway who based his most famous novel *The Old Man And The Sea* there. Just five miles west of Tarara, there is an impressive stadium overlooking the city while the old castle handles the defense along the western side of the seawall. But apart from that, the scene is now one of the most depressing in all of Cuba. In contrast to the beauty of so many Cuban cities, we are now treated to miles and miles of unrelieved bleakness, consisting of dull, miserable apartment buildings, without a hint of joy in their creator. Each can be recognized by its occupants only by varying shades of obscene brown or a different stairway.

To top it all off, there are a host of crumbling pillboxes strewn along the rust-strewn beaches, which leads you to wonder — who would *want* to take this place?

Maybe it should just be razed, and have salt sown over the ground. It's that bad.

HAVANA'S SKYLINE

Havana makes for a wonderful sight as you come up on it at last, with ugly buildings, impressive facades, and domed churches, all vying for your attention over to the far side; while the great castle at the entrance (El Morro) looks out across the river from the east.

Along the famous seawall, the decaying but still gaily colored facades only hint at their former glory, but it's nevertheless a wonderful sight as you come across the mouth of the harbor and parallel the city.

At this point it's a good idea to contact the Marina Hemingway on Channels 16 or 72, with details of your arrival. They will contact the customs and immigration officials in advance, and by the time you arrive at the Guarda Frontera post at the entrance, those officials should hopefully have had enough time to make their way out there.

The Marina Hemingway is covered in chapter five, and entry is the same whether arriving in Cuba for the first time or coming in from Varadero or Tarara.

You will be able to make visual contact with the entrance buoy at 23°05.4N / 082°30.6W from some way off, and from there on it's 140°M through the reef, and just a matter of following the procedures you are already perfectly familiar with.

A note from the author: As you might well imagine, a cruising guide is a transient thing. Ports and passages change with new administrations and with the passing of time. Many of the features mentioned in this book may have changed by the time you pass by. Indeed, you may have discovered newer and better paths to tread. Nevertheless, if you have any comments about this guide I would be grateful to hear from you. I may be contacted through Cruising Guide Publications, and would welcome your suggestions or advice for inclusion in future editions.

Sincerely,
Simon Charles

APPENDIX AND GLOSSARY

This is a short, or not so short, list of useful words you might come across in dealing with the various aspects of your cruise. There are a couple of different headings, so if you vaguely know which subject you should be interested in then flick to it and search for what you need.

It is deliberately led-off by the Spanish term to encourage you to read the whole paragraph while searching, and hopefully something you don't need just right now will sink in. Maybe it will miraculously pop into your mind one day when you might need it in a hurry.

Incidentally, I've not bothered with the more obvious words everybody already knows.

GEOGRAPHIC AND HYDROGRAPHIC
(Terms you might see on a chart)

Acantilado	Cliff, steep
Alga	Kelp or turtle-grass
Altura	Height
Angosta	Narrow
Arcilla	Clay
Arena	Sand
Arroyo	Creek, brook
Bahia	Bay
Bajo	Shoal (or low)
Bajo fondo	Shallow water
Balneario	Seaside resort
Banco	Bank
Barra	Bar
Barro	Mud
Boca	Mouth
Bosque	Wood
Brazo	Arm, branch
Buque	
hundido	Sunken ship
Cabecería	Group of reefs
Cabeza	Head (of coral)
Cabezo	Outcrop (of rock)
Cabo	Cape, headland
Caleta	Inlet
Canal	Canal, channel
Canalizo	Narrow channel
Cascajo	Shingle
Cayo (Cy)	Key, cay
Cima	Top
Corriente	Current
Costa	Coast
Cuenca	Basin
Cueva	Cave
Curva	
de nivel	Contour line

Darsena (Dars)	Dock, harbour
Destello (Dest)	Flash (eg. bouys)
Duna	Dune
Ensenada (Ens)	Cove, anchorage
Entrada	Entrance
Escarpe	Escarpment
Estero	Creek
Estrecho	Strait
Estuario	Estuary
Fango	Mud
Faro	Lighthouse
Farallón	Cliff, high rock
Fondo	Bottom
Fondeadero	Anchorage
Golfo	Gulf
Isla	Island
Islote	Islet
Isobata	Depth contour
Laberinto	Labyrinth
Laguna	Lagoon
Lengua	Tongue (of sand)
Loma	Hill
Mangle	Mangrove
Medano	Sandbank
Morro	Headland
Orilla	Shore
Paredón	Wall
Pasa	Pass
Paso	Passage

Pena	Rock		Restinga	Ledge
Pico	Peak		Rio	River
Piedra	Stone		Roca	Rock
Pilote	Pile		Rompeolas	Breakwater
Placer	Large sandbank		Rompiente	Rough
Playa	Beach			
Poco profunda	Shallow		Salina	Salt pan
Profunda	Deep		Sargazo	Sagasso
Profundidad	Depth		Sierra	Mountain range
Promontorio	Promontory		Silla	Saddle
Punta (Pta)	Point		Surgidero	Ancorage (shelterless)
Quebrado	Break (in reef)		Valle	Valley

WEATHER AND SEA CONDITIONS
(Sorry about most of these, the fault lies in the pessimism of human nature)

Aire	Air		Inundacíon	Flood
Aire frío	Cold air			
Aire húmedo	Moist air		Lluvia	Rain
Aire seco	Dry air			
Altura	Height		Marea	Tide
Aviso	Warning			
			Neblina	Mist
Baja	Low		Niebla	Fog
Barlovento	Windward		Nivel del mar	Sea level
Borrascoso	Stormy		Nube	Cloud
Bravo	Rough, angry		Nubosidad	Cloudiness
Brisa	Breeze		Núcleo	Core
Brisa marina	Sea breeze			
Buen tiempo	Good weather		Ola	Wave
			Onda	Wave
Calma	Calm			
Ciclon	Cyclone		Pendiente	Coming
Cielo	Sky (or heaven)		Picada (mar)	Rough
Clima	Climate		Pronóstico	Forecast
Chubasco	Shower			
Crepusculo	Twilight		Relámpago	Lightning
Disperso	Dispersed		Severa	Severe
Disturbio	Disturbance			
			Tempeste	Storm
Frente	Front		Terral	Land breeze
			Turbido	Turbulent, rough
Galerna	Gale		Viento	Wind
			Visibilidad	Visibility
Hondonada	Trough			
Humedad	Humidity		Zona	Zone
Huracán	Hurricane			

NAVIGATION AND MANEUVERS
(Terms you might hear)

A bordar	Board	Embalizado	Marked
A la deriva!	Adrift!	Embarcar	Embark
A popa	Astern	Embarcadero	Wharf
A proa	Ahead	Encallar	Run aground
A babor	Go to port	Enfilacion	Leading line,
A estribor	Go to starboard		range marks
Acerase	Approach (request)	Enfilar	Aim
Aguas	Waters	Escala	Scale
Alcance	Range, reach	Estima	Estimate
Altura	Height	Estribor	Starboard
Amarrar	Moor, tie up		
Anclar	Anchor (verb)	Faro	Lighthouse
Autonomía	Range, self-sufficiency	Fondear	Anchor (verb)
Approximarse	Close-in (verb)		
Arribar	Arrive	Jalar (halar)	Haul
Atracar	Come alongside		
Aviso	Warning or notice	Luces	Lights
Babor	Port, left	Marcación	Bearing
Baliza ciega	Unlit beacon	Metro	Metre
Baliza luminosa	Lighted beacon		
Boya	Bouy	Naufragio	Wreck
Braza	Fathom (armspan)	Nudo	Knot (both types)
Buque	Ship		
		Remolcar	Tow (verb)
Cable	Cable (1/10th mile)	Rumbo	Course
Carta nautica	Chart	Ruta	Route
Cuaderno	Notebook		
		Tendero	Holding (anchor)
Deriva	Drift	Tirar	Pull
Destino	Destination	Tome	Take
Diario de		Toda máquina	Full speed
navigacion	Logbook		

DIRECTIONS
(Just where am I...?)

Norte	North	Babor	Port
Sur	South	Tribor	Starboard
Este	East		
Oeste	West	En frente	In front
		Por atras	Behind
Septentrional	Northern	Al lado	To the side
Meridional	Southern		
Oriental	Eastern		
Occidental	Western		

PORT TERMS, OFFICIALS, PAPERS ETC.

(You'll need these ashore)

Acopio	Storage facility		Inmigración	Immigration
Administrador	Administrator			
Aduanas	Customs		Lancha	Launch
Agente	Agent		Leyes	Laws
Amarradero	Mooring berth			
Astillero	Shipyard		Malecón	Waterfront road
			Muelle	Wharf, mole
Bodega	Storeroom			
Buque	Ship		Nave	Vessel
Calado	Draft		Pasarela	Small pier
Capitán del			Patana	Barge
puerto	Port Captain		Pedraplén	Stone causeway
Capitanía	Harbour master's office		Práctico	Pilotage
Consignatario	Ship's agent		Ponton	Pontoon, hulk
Cuarentena	Quarentine			
			Remolcador	Tugboat
Darsena	Dock, harbour		Revisar	Search
Despacho	Clearance, dispatch			
Destino	Destination		Salvamento	Rescue
Dragado	Dredged, dredging		Senalizacion	Signals
			Sondeo	Search
Embarcadero	Wharf, landing			
Entrada	Entrance		Tuberia	Pipework
Espigón	Jetty, pier			
Fecha	Date		Varadero	Slipway
Fondeadero	Anchorage		Viaje	Voyage
Grua	Crane		Zarpe	Foreign clearance
Grada	Slipway			

YOU AND YOUR BOAT

(Simple words you may need to describe your boat over the radio
are grouped together first)

Achay Pay	HP		Procedencia de	Coming from
Ancho	Width		Tonnelada	Tonnage
Bandera	Flag, nationality		Tripulantes	Crew
Barco turistico	Tourist vessel (yours)		Velero	Sailboat
Caballos	Horses (horsepower)		Yate	Yacht
Calado	Draft			
Casco	Hull		Aleta	Fin, centerboard
Eslora	LOA		Ancla	Anchor
Fibra	Fibreglass		Alternador	Alternator
Lancha	Motorboat		Arboladura	Rigging
Nombre	Name		Arrancador	Starter motor

Balsa	Raft, dinghy	Helice	Propellor
Bandera	Flag		
Bay Achay		Lastres	Stores
Effe	VHF (radio)		
Bita	Bollard	Manga	Width, beam, hose
Bodega	Hold	Manguera	Hose, pipe
Bomba	Pump	Mareado	Seasick
Bote	Boat	Mastelero	Topmast
Brujula	Compass	Mástil	Mast
		Motonave	Motor vessel
Cabo	Line, rope		
Cadena	Chain	Petroleo	Diesel fuel
Caja	Gearbox	Popa	Poop, stern
Cambios	Gears	Proa	Prow, bow
Combustible	Fuel	Puente	Bridge
Contenedor	Container		
Cornamusa	Cleat	Roto	Broken
Cubierta	Deck		
Cuerda	Cord	Quilla	Keel
Defensa	Fender	Salvavida	Lifejacket
Ecosonda	Echo-sounder	Tanque	Tank (fuel, water, air)
Embarcación	Vessel	Toma	Supply hose, tube
Escala	Stair, ladder		
Escape	Exhaust	Timón	Helm, rudder
		Tripulación	Crew
Francobordo	Freeboard	Tripulante	Crewmember
Gasolina	Gasoline, petrol	Vela	Sail
Guia	Keel		
Guinche	Winch		
Gaz	Gas		

SCUBA TERMS

Aletas	Fins
Atmósferas	Atmospheres (14.7 lbs/in)
Buceo	Scuba
Careta	Mask
Chaleca	Jacket
Licencia	Dive card
Plomos	Weights
Presion	Pressure
Profundimetro	Depth guage
Regulador	Regulator
Superficia	Surface
Tanque	Cylinder

INCIDENTALS
(Add your own as you go)

Carpeta	Front desk (hotel)
Congrís	Rice and beans
Divisa	Foreign currency
Je Jene	No-see-um
Jinetero	Neer-do-well, hustler (literally cowboy/jockey)
Jutia	Delicious rodent
Mojito	Rum, spearmint, sugar, soda and ice.
Mosca	Fly
Mosquito	Mosquito
Pesca	Fish
Turbina	Pump (landside)

INDEX

CRUISING GUIDE PUBLICATIONS

ORDER FORM

To order, please fill out the coupon on back and send check or money order to:
Cruising Guide Publications, 1130-B Pinehurst Road, Dunedin, Florida 34698
For credit card orders only, call 800-330-9542
Fax: (813) 734-8179 • E-mail: cgp@earthlink.net

❑ $19.95   CRUISING GUIDE TO THE VIRGIN ISLANDS
(8th Edition) by Simon and Nancy Scott. New color charts and photos.

❑ $24.95   CRUISING GUIDE TO THE LEEWARD ISLANDS
(5th Edition) by Chris Doyle. Now with GPS coordinates and color charts.

❑ $19.95   SAILOR'S GUIDE TO THE WINDWARD ISLANDS
(8th Edition) by Chris Doyle. Color charts and GPS coordinates.

❑ $24.95   VIRGIN ANCHORAGES (Color aerial photos of the Virgin Islands with
sailing directions)

❑ $24.95   GENTLEMAN'S GUIDE TO PASSAGES SOUTH
The "Thornless Path to Windward," by Bruce Van Sant.

❑ $15.95   CRUISING GUIDE TO THE SPANISH VIRGIN ISLANDS AND
PUERTO RICO -- by Bruce Van Sant -- An all new guide.

❑ $15.95   CRUISING GUIDE TO THE SEA OF CORTEZ (From Mulege to La Paz)

❑ $14.95   CRUISING GUIDE TO TRINIDAD & TOBAGO -- A new guide from
Chris Doyle. Includes GPS coordinates, color sketch charts and color photos.

❑ $26.95   CRUISING GUIDE TO VENEZUELA & BONAIRE -- Another all new
cruising guide by Chris Doyle. Provides anchorage information, GPS and
full-color sketch charts.

❑ $24.95   CRUISING GUIDE TO CUBA -- 2nd Edition by Simon Charles -- New
sketch charts and important updates for anyone visiting this island.

❑ $19.95   CRUISING GUIDE TO THE FLORIDA KEYS with Florida West Coast
Supplement by Capt. Frank Papy.

❑ $12.00   CRUISING MANUAL TO THE KINGDOM OF TONGA IN THE VAVA'U
GROUP (Chart included) The Moorings.

❑ $9.95   GUIDE TO ABACO BAHAMAS -- By Steve Dodge. The popular Baha-
mian islands of the Abacos are covered in this guide.

❑ $29.95   YACHTSMAN'S GUIDE TO JAMAICA -- By John Lethridge -- 1st Edition.

❑ $99.00   CARIBBEAN YACHTING CHARTS -- 1) Virgin Islands, 2) Upper
Leeward Islands, 3) Lower Leewards and 4) Windward Islands -- 4 separate
sets. These color charts are coordinated with our guides. Six charts per set.
(Price per set.)

❑ $29.95   VIDEOS FROM CHRIS DOYLE -- CRUISING THE NORTHERN
LEEWARDS -- SAILING THE WINDWARD ISLANDS -- ISLAND
PORTRAITS: ST. VINCENT & THE GRENADINES -- TRINIDAD &
TOBAGO -- Four separate videos featuring these popular cruising spots.
(Price per video.)

❑ $14.95   THE NATURE OF THE ISLANDS: PLANTS & ANIMALS OF THE
EASTERN CARIBBEAN by Chris Doyle and Virginia Barlow.

❑ $22.50   AT ANY COST: LOVE, LIFE & DEATH AT SEA (Hardcover)
By Peter Tangvald; thrilling autobiography of a cruising sailor.

❑ $14.95 RESTUARANT AND RECIPE BOOKS -- Four separate books to the Leewards, the Virgin Islands, Puerto Rico and Chesapeake Bay. Color photography and easy to follow recipes. (Price per book.)

❑ $12.95 BAHAMA MAMA' COOKBOOK. Authentic Bahamian recipes.

❑ $14.95 SHIP TO SHORE I (A collection of 680 recipes & cooking tips from Caribbean charter yacht chefs) compiled by Capt. Jan Robinson..

❑ $14.95 SEA TO SHORE (280 seafood recipes and cooking hints— Robinson).

❑ $14.95 SWEET TO SHORE (Robinson's ultimate dessert collection).

❑ $10.95 SIP TO SHORE (Robinson's cocktails and hors d'oeuvres collection).

❑ $11.95 CARIBBEAN ADVENTURES -- Classic Cajun cooking and tales from the reign of pirates. More than a 100 Cajun-style recipes.

❑ $12.00 CALENDAR: THE BRITISH VIRGIN ISLANDS. Photography by Dougal Thornton (New year available in October of preceding year).

❑ $ 4.50 CLEAR, WATERPROOF, HEAVY-DUTY PLASTIC ZIPLOCK CRUISING GUIDE COVER holds Cruising Guide open and dry, leaving hands free for sailing. Grease pencil included, 10⅞" x 14½".

WATERPROOF CHARTS (INQUIRE ABOUT OTHER CHARTS AVAILABLE)

❑ $18.95 CARIBBEAN SEA AND THE GULF OF MEXICO

❑ $18.95 U.S. & BRITISH VIRGIN ISLANDS

❑ $18.95 BRITISH VIRGIN ISLANDS

❑ $18.95 UPPER FLORIDA KEYS

❑ $18.95 LOWER FLORIDA KEYS

❑ $ 8.50 CLEAR, WATERPROOF, REUSABLE PLASTIC STORAGE TUBE

ORDER FORM VISA MasterCard DISCOVER *(For orders only, call 1-800-330-9542).*

To order, check the appropriate box(es), fill out coupon and send check or money order to: Cruising Guide Publications, P.O. Box 1017, Dunedin, FL 34697-1017. Florida residents add 7% sales tax. See schedule for shipping charges. All books are shipped via UPS within 10 days of receipt of order.

Shipping & Handling			
	U.S./Terr.	Canada	Other
Up to $15.00	$3.50	$5.50	$7.00
$15.01-30.00	4.95	6.95	9.90
30.01-40.00	6.75	8.75	13.50
40.01-50.00	7.75	9.75	15.50
50.01-75.00	8.75	10.75	17.50
Over 75.00	9.75	11.75	19.50
Additional Address Add $3.25			

$ _____ Total Merchandise

$ _____ Sales Tax 7%
(Florida residents only)

$ _____ Shipping & Handling

$ _____ Total Enclosed

Name _____

Address _____

City_____ State _____ Zip _____

Daytime telephone (_____) _____

(Prices subject to change without notice)

340

Finally... Caribbean Cruising Charts That Take The Guesswork Out Of Caribbean Cruising

A series of full-color navigational charts with recent surveys and featuring fine contours with easy to distinguish color graduations of depth lines are now available through Cruising Guide Publications.

The GPS coordinated chart packages cover the Virgin Islands (Caribbean 1), the Northern Leeward Islands (Caribbean 2), the Southern Leeward Islands (Caribbean 3) and the Windward Islands (Caribbean 4). The charts are presented in a user friendly size (23 1/2" x 16 1/2") and are packaged in a thick, see-through plastic envelope which protects them and provides for easy storage.

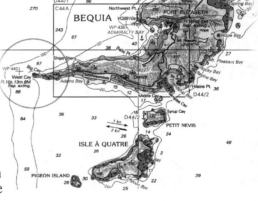

Red numbered waypoints with coordinates based on WGS 84 enable yachtsmen to navigate accurately with GPS. The chart sets are coordinated with Chris Doyle's guides to the Windwards and Leewards and *The Cruising Guide to the Virgin Islands*. Harbors and anchorages are cross-referenced with these three guides. Additionally, large scale approaches and land contour markings simplify the entrance into these anchorages. These charts will be issued with an amendment system for updates, which will be available through Cruising Guide Publications, the exclusive U.S. distributor.

Each chart package includes one passage chart and six coastal charts, including approaches and harbors. *Price per set is $99.00.*

CRUISING GUIDE PUBLICATIONS

1130-B Pinehurst Road • Dunedin, FL 34698 • Tel. 813-733-5322 • 1-800-330-9542
Fax: 813-734-8179 • E-mail: cgp@earthlink.net

Note: The above illustration depicts a portions of a chart from the Caribbean 4 series. All charts are in full-color. The Virgin Islands and southern Leeward Islands chart series will be introduced in the fall of 1997.

341

CRUISING NOTES

While cruising Cuba, if you have discovered anything that might be valuable to readers of future editions, comments or suggestions, please contact: Cruising Guide Publications, 1130-B Pinehurst Road, Dunedin, FL 34698; Phone: 813-733-5322; Fax: 813-733-8179; E-mail: cgp@earthlink.net.